Cotton Mather and Benjamin Franklin

T0381608

Cambridge Studies in American Literature and Culture

Other books in the series
Robert Zaller: *The Cliffs of Solitude*
Peter Conn: *The Divided Mind*
Patricia Caldwell: *The Puritan Conversion Narrative*
Stephen Fredman: *Poet's Prose*
Charles Altieri: *Self and Sensibility in Contemporary American Poetry*
John McWilliams: *Hawthorne, Melville, and the American Character*
Barton St. Armand: *Emily Dickinson and Her Culture*

Cotton Mather and Benjamin Franklin

The price of representative personality

MITCHELL ROBERT BREITWIESER
University of California, Berkeley

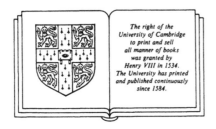

The right of the
University of Cambridge
to print and sell
all manner of books
was granted by
Henry VIII in 1534.
The University has printed
and published continuously
since 1584.

CAMBRIDGE UNIVERSITY PRESS

CAMBRIDGE

LONDON NEW YORK NEW ROCHELLE

MELBOURNE SYDNEY

CAMBRIDGE UNIVERSITY PRESS
Cambridge, New York, Melbourne, Madrid, Cape Town, Singapore, São Paulo, Delhi

Cambridge University Press
The Edinburgh Building, Cambridge CB2 8RU, UK

Published in the United States of America by Cambridge University Press, New York

www.cambridge.org
Information on this title: www.cambridge.org/9780521107877

First published 1984
This digitally printed version 2009

A catalogue record for this publication is available from the British Library

Library of Congress Cataloguing in Publication data
Breitwieser, Mitchell Robert, 1953–
Cotton Mather and Benjamin Franklin.
(Cambridge studies in American literature and culture)
Includes bibliographical references and index.
1. Mather, Cotton, 1663–1728. 2. Franklin,
Benjamin, 1706–1790. 3. United States – Civilization –
To 1783. 4. National characteristics, American.
I. Title. II. Series.
F67.M43B74   1985   973.2′092′2   84–9630

ISBN 978-0-521-26768-7 hardback
ISBN 978-0-521-10787-7 paperback

*To the graduate students and faculty
of the Department of English,
State University of New York at Buffalo,
1975–1979*

CONTENTS

ACKNOWLEDGMENTS

I have received a great deal of help with this book, and there are many people to thank. The following people read sections of the book and gave helpful advice: Janet Adelman, Paul Alpers, John Bishop, James Breslin, Richard Bridgman, Carol Christ, Frederick Crews, Jay Fliegelman, Ron Loewinsohn, Walter Michaels, D. A. Miller, Carolyn Porter, Thomas Schaub, Neil Schmitz, George Starr, Eric Sundquist, Henry Sussman, Nancy Ungar, and Alex Zwerdling. The following people were generous enough to have read the whole of the book in one of its several drafts: Sacvan Bercovitch, Albert Gelpi, Richard Hutson, Gregory Jay, David Levin, Robert Middlekauff, Michael Rogin, and Ernest Tuveson. The following people provided the unremitting and close personal sustenance that kept me going: James Breslin, Jay Fliegelman, Richard Hutson, Gregory Jay, D. A. Miller, Carolyn Porter, Neil Schmitz, and Nancy Ungar.

ABBREVIATIONS

Quotations from frequently cited works are followed in the body of the text by a parenthesis that contains one of the abbreviations below, volume number where applicable, and page number(s).

A Benjamin Franklin, *Autobiography*, ed. Leonard W. Labaree, Ralph L. Ketcham, Helen C. Boatfield, and Helen H. Fineman (New Haven, Conn.: Yale University Press, 1964).

B Cotton Mather, *Bonifacius, An Essay Upon the Good, that is to be Devised and Designed, By Those Who Desire to Answer the Great End of Life, and to Do Good While they Live*, ed. David Levin (Cambridge, Mass.: Harvard University Press, 1966).

CP Cotton Mather, *The Christian Philosopher* (London: Eman. Matthews, 1721).

D Cotton Mather, *Diary*, ed. Worthington Chauncey Ford, *Collections of the Massachusetts Historical Society*, 7th Ser., VII–VIII (1912).

MCA Cotton Mather, *Magnalia Christi Americana* (New York: Russell and Russell, 1967).

P Benjamin Franklin, *The Papers of Benjamin Franklin*, ed. Leonard W. Labaree, et al. (New Haven, Conn.: Yale University Press, 1959–).

W Benjamin Franklin, *The Works of Benjamin Franklin*, ed. Jared Sparks (London: B. F. Stevens, 1882). (The Yale Franklin Papers are not yet complete; I have used Sparks's edition for writings not available in the Yale edition.)

INTRODUCTION: THE ASPIRATION TO REPRESENTATIVE PERSONALITY

A reasonably well-read American living during the second quarter of the nineteenth century would have been familiar with the thesis that the spirit or genius of a historical period can condense itself, spontaneously, in the person of a single spokesman. Insofar as this typical American was dismayed by the class and regional divisions that were plaguing his nation, he might be attracted to the possibility of such charismatic unification, and support a politician such as Daniel Webster, who advertised himself as a digest of the people's gist, rather than simply as one who would be its advocate on specific issues. Should he be looking for an extra- or suprapolitical representative man, he might turn to literature, to statements quarried from Goethe, Fichte, Hegel, Cousin, or Michelet, and transferred to an American idiom by Emerson, Thoreau, or Whitman. A single thread of abstract assertion runs through the thought of these disparate figures: personification (*prosopopeia*) is a real item in the itinerary of history, not just a handy illustrative trope. The *vox populi* can emerge into the reflective clarity and coherence of a single voice. The American version of this thesis frequently has an additional twist: since the present age is the *telos* or destination of human historical experience, the modern American representative man is a digest of human nature itself, purified of time's localizing inflections.

As the title of this book reveals, I believe that the nineteenth century's idea of representative personality is as much a product of previous American thought as it is of contemporary European thought, dating as far back, perhaps, as the first American Puritans' enthusiasm for applying hagiography to their experience.[1] Like Emerson, Whitman, and Webster,

---

[1] Sacvan Bercovitch, *The Puritan Origins of the American Self* (New Haven: Conn. Yale University Press, 1975). For an interesting exploration of the Christian background to the idea of representative personality, see Peter Brown, "The Saint as Exemplar in Late Antiquity," *Representations* 2 (Spring 1983), pp. 1–25,

Cotton Mather and Benjamin Franklin sought to provide their divided, fractious, litigious societies with a sense of group meaning and coherence through personal exemplification of an underlying commonalty. Though the divisions they sought to cure, the conceptions of human nature they proposed, and the cultural legacies they drew on were significantly different from those of their nineteenth-century heirs, the central ambition was, in the abstract, the same.

The thesis that history emits such representatives still has currency: it can be found, for example, in the works of writers as different as Erik Erikson and Norman Mailer, and a more one-dimensional version is a regular part of electoral rhetoric. For my purposes in this book, however, it does matter whether this thesis is held to be valid or not. My personal feeling is that it has, in the main, diverted attention from questions that should have been confronted more directly. Be that as it may, what interests me here is that, during a period when this thesis seems credible, some men decide to make themselves into such a personification, devoting their energy and intelligence to the task. In the cases of Mather and Franklin, the incentive for this decision seems to me to be twofold: first, a sense of social obligation, to body forth a satisfying standard of legitimacy that will inspire a vital, general consensus;[2] and second, perhaps

---

especially p. 9: "Charisma, therefore, is seen less in terms of the extraordinary, set aside from society, so much as the convincing concentration in an event, in an institution, in a discipline or in a person of lingering senses of order and higher purpose. Rather than inevitably marking a moment of breakdown and of new departure, 'Concentrated and intense charismatic authority transfigures the half life into incandescence' . . . Hence the crucial importance of the holy man as 'Christ-carrying' exemplar. In almost all the regions of the Mediterranean, from the third century onwards, he was far more than an exemplar of a previously well-organised and culturally coherent Christianity: very often, he quite simply *was* Christianity."

[2] The questions of division and consensus are inescapable topics in cultural histories of the period. I have been most persuaded by: Sacvan Bercovitch, *The American Jeremiad* (Madison: University of Wisconsin Press, 1978); Jay Fliegelman, *Prodigals and Pilgrims: The American Revolution against Patriarchal Authority, 1750–1800* (Cambridge: Cambridge University Press, 1982); Perry Miller, *Orthodoxy in Massachusetts, 1630–1650* (Cambridge, Mass.: Harvard University Press, 1933); J.G.A. Pocock, *The Machiavellian Moment: Florentine Political Thought and the Atlantic Republican Tradition* (Princeton, N.J.: Princeton University Press, 1975); Richard Hofstadter, *The Idea of a Party System: The Rise of Legitimate Opposition in the United States, 1780–1840* (Berkeley: University of California Press, 1969); George B. Forgie, *Patricide in the House Divided: A Psychological Interpretation of Lincoln and His Age* (New York: Norton, 1979); and Michael Kammen, *People of Paradox: An Inquiry Concerning the Origins of American Civilization* (New York: Random House, 1972).

more elemental, an anxious suspicion that one's only life is spoiled or
wasted if it fails to rise to the universally human – a certain shame upon
discovering oneself as less than whole, as having mistaken a periphery of
humanity for its capital.

The technique is also twofold. First, the aspirant diagnoses what he
considers the nature of human nature with a great deal of specificity and
with an attention to abstract coherence, because he is designing a life,
rather than writing a treatise. His life is to *be* a speculative treatise with
extensive and meticulous application, so he has to ensure that his particular stances and opinions emanate from a single, explicit core. This diagnosis may provide him with a sharper than usual sense of the other
definitions of man implicit in the common sense of his time as adversaries with which he must compete, rather than as miscellaneous or indifferent options to be picked up or laid aside at convenience. As his diagnosis of human nature grows more explicit, reflective, and coherent, that
is, his perception of aggregate or variety may be replaced by a polarity
of purity and contamination. As Georg Lukács argues, mining for the
gist of human experience may in this way distinguish the potentially representative man from the merely typical man:

> The only essential difference between one life and another is the ques-
> tion whether a life is absolute or merely relative; whether the mutually
> exclusive opposites within the life are separated from one another sharply
> or definitively or not. The difference is whether the life-problems of a
> particular life arise in the form of an either/or, or whether "as well as"
> is the proper formula when the split appears.[3]

Determined self-design is the second aspect of technique. Once the
diagnosis is sufficiently developed, as it was for Mather and Franklin by
the beginnings of their third decades, the aspirant commits himself to a
course of vigilant self-surveillance and self-discipline. He attempts to enhance thoughts, feelings, scruples, and drives that are consonant with
human nature as he has diagnosed it, and to discourage or expunge all
that seems discordant, including any attraction he may feel toward adversary definitions of human nature. The aspiration becomes involved in
an interior strife, which may reproduce in miniature, as Lukács suggests,
the tensions of the aspirant's society.

Studying Mather and Franklin in terms of their shared aspiration has
two advantages. First, it identifies their lives as conscious projects, and
therefore does not rely on general models such as Marxism and Freudi-
anism to describe the tensions, exhilarations, assertions, and rhetorical
strategies that compose their particular life dramas. (Such general meth-

---

[3] Georg Lukács, *Soul and Form,* trans. Anna Bostock (Cambridge, Mass.: MIT
Press, 1974), p. 31.

ods, however, remain useful for inquiring into why the projects were first conceived.) By concentrating on their aspirations, we can identify Cotton Mather and Franklin as diligent reflections on, rather than reflections of, human life in their period. Second, the specificity and reflective coherence of the project may, if sufficiently acute, furnish a relatively pure and clear articulation of one of the notions of humanity implicit in the common sense of the period. This articulation is not a necessary result of any aspiration to representativeness, since eccentric or private notions of man are always possible. But if, as in the lives of Cotton Mather and Benjamin Franklin, brilliance and determination combine with a wide experience of contemporary society, a true representativeness may arise: not because history is spontaneously self-personifying, but because the aspirant has intended to embody an idea of man. And his representativeness would not be what he had aimed for: rather than a definitive exemplification of man, or even of the single genius of the age, that could command a general imitation, his representativeness would be a lucid emotional index of what was at stake in his society. In such a case, the labor of extrapolating the underlying significance of the talk of the time, the obligation of historical scholarship, is done on the spot. Describing the particularity of Mather's and Franklin's aspirations, therefore, may also demonstrate that they were representative. This statement is not a paradox if we remember Lukács's distinction between the representative and the typical: those who probe successfully for the central assumptions beneath contemporary commonplaces are rare in any age. An uncritical individualism has attempted to convince us that only dissenters stand out from the mass, but this is not so: though we may prefer thinkers who disputed the ideologies promoted by Mather and Franklin, we may not therefore assume that Mather and Franklin blur back into simple identity with those portions of society whose views they labored to render lucid.

I assume that Mather and Franklin were exemplars, in Lukács's sense, of Puritanism and Enlightenment in their American forms. This is no innovation. Even somewhat skeptical contemporaries of Mather and Franklin, such as Benjamin Colman and John Adams, were suspicious of them as representative spokesmen rather than as independent individuals. With few exceptions, popular and academic thought to the present has accepted Colman's and Adams's judgments: the vicissitudes of Mather's and Franklin's reputations have reflected the vicissitudes of opinion concerning Puritanism and Enlightenment. The only major exception was Perry Miller's rather vehement critique of Mather in *The New England Mind*, which was a result of his desire to detach Mather's life and writings from what he admired as the marrow of Puritan divinity. In fact, Miller did not wish to sever Mather from Puritanism as much as he wanted to divide what he admired in Puritanism from some of Puritanism's more painful intrinsic consequences. Whatever Miller's motives were, however, subsequent criticism has restored to Mather what he never lost in popular thought, his exemplariness.[4] I do not wish to challenge the

[4] Colman's eulogy for Mather is reprinted in part as an epigraph to David Levin's *Cotton Mather: The Young Life of the Lord's Remembrancer* (Cambridge, Mass.: Harvard University Press, 1978), which I consider the most measured and meticulous appraisal of Mather's life and work. Regrettably, it only follows Mather's life through 1700. Kenneth Silverman's *The Life and Times of Cotton Mather* (New York: Harper & Row, 1984) appeared while this book was in press. The biography to 1700 complements Levin's nicely, and the second half is extremely useful. My only criticism is that Silverman stresses Mather's reactions to momentary political and social exigencies more heavily than his internalization of Massachusetts Calvinism. Consequently, what I take to be Mather's dialectical complexities Silverman sees as indecision, nonintended contradiction, or even "ambidexter" opportunism. Adams's remarks on Franklin, written for the Boston *Patriot* in 1811, are included in *Works*, ed. C. F. Adams (Boston, 1856), p. 660. Among the many roads on which to follow the variations in Mather's and Franklin's reputations, the reader may investigate *Harper's Monthly*, Parson Weems, Washington Irving, Samuel Taylor Coleridge, Nathaniel Hawthorne, Herman Melville, Walt Whitman, Ralph Waldo Emerson, John Bach McMaster, Barrett Wendell, D. H. Lawrence, William Carlos Williams, and Vernon Parrington. These are highlights, rather than an exhaustive list. Richard Lovelace has included an excellent essay summarizing the career of Mather's reputation as an appendix to his *The American Pietism of Cotton Mather: Origins of American Evangelicalism* (Grand Rapids, Mich.: Christian University Press, 1979), which is the best treatment of Mather as a coherent intelligence. I know of no adequate summary of Franklin's reputation that would do what Lovelace has done for Mather's, Merrill Peterson has done for Jefferson's, or Donald Weber has done for Edwards's. It would be a fascinating project. The best overall treatments of Franklin are Carl Becker's biography in the *Dictionary of American Biography* and Carl Van Doren's still-supreme *Benjamin Franklin*. The best books on Mather, in addition to Levin's and Lovelace's, are Bercovitch's *Puritan Origins*, and Robert Middlekauff's *The Mathers: Three Generations of Puritan Intellectuals* (New York: Oxford University Press, 1971). On the issue of Mather's and Franklin's representativeness, I appeal to the authority of Peter Gay and Dumas Malone: "[Mather's] stature, and his oddities, make him remarkable, but he was neither unique nor eccentric among the Puritans; what gives him significance is precisely that he was characteristic of his time and of his tribe . . . It is Mather's representative quality that makes his *Magnalia* such an informative witness to the Puritan mind in America" (*A Loss of Mastery: Puritan Historians in Colonial America* [Berkeley: University of California Press, 1966], p. 59); "After Benjamin Franklin, [Jefferson] may be regarded as the fullest American embodiment of the ideals of the Enlightenment . . . Jefferson did not introduce the Enlightenment into the colonies but he

general conclusion, but to add that Mather's and Franklin's exemplariness originates in their conscious aspirations, that they epitomize the tensions as well as the credos of their worldviews, and that they do so in a way that is reflective, coherent, and extensive beyond what is found in the lives and writings of their contemporaries.

The study of their conscious aspirations, in other words, can tell us why Mather and Franklin have been selected as epitomes. Henry May has argued that Puritanism and Enlightenment were the major intellectual and emotional options available to eighteenth-century Americans, and that the contest between them shapes American thought well past 1800. However, according to May, the majority of eighteenth-century American intellectuals are "moderate," which means that their writings display an ad hoc, unsorted mixture of the two worldviews, a noncognizance of the disparity that May, from his historical distance, believes to be crucial. Similar contentions appear in Joseph Ellis's account of the intellectual life of Samuel Johnson of Connecticut, and in Alan Heimert's recognition that the arguments over the Great Awakening cannot be said to reflect point for point the difference between Puritan fideism and Enlightenment rationalism.[5] Confronted with such mixed stances, the student of the period may be tempted to decide that models such as Puritanism versus Enlightenment are factitious abstractions. But writers such as Mather and Franklin, discovering their society's either/or, demonstrate that this is not the case. There is no need for scholarship to prostrate itself before the typical discourse of the period, because to do so is to accept vagueness conditioned by incompetence at speculative abstraction, a concern for harmony, opportunism, or personal and political alliances, and thus to blur tensions that are quite real.

I do not, however, stop with the observation that the relationship between Mather and Franklin epitomizes a disparity. I also argue that the fact that they share formally similar aspirations reveals that the tension between them occurs within the framework of a meaningful continuity. Their life projects are based on important common assumptions: that there is a distinct and practically definable human nature; that this nature dwells within consciousness in an at least latently antagonistic relation-

---

became its almost perfect embodiment and, after Franklin, its most conspicuous apostle on his side of the Atlantic." (*Jefferson the Virginian*, vol. 1 of *Jefferson and his Time* [Boston: Little, Brown, 1948], pp. xv, 101).

[5] Henry May, *The Enlightenment in America* (New York: Oxford University Press, 1976), introduction and pp. 1–101; Joseph Ellis, *The New England Mind in Transition: Samuel Johnson of Connecticut* (New Haven, Conn.: Yale University Press, 1973), pp. 1–54; Alan Heimert, *Religion and the American Mind: From the Great Awakening to the Revolution* (Cambridge, Mass.: Harvard University Press, 1966), pp. 1–27.

ship with the rest of consciousness; that the will can sever its affection for these obstructive elements, and identify itself entirely with the cause of nature; that this purified will can then adequately appraise and govern the antinatural components of consciousness, the residue, from which it has divorced itself; and that those individuals who have accomplished this feat can then join together in a society whose harmony draws on the common discipline. The aspiration to representative personality is not simply a formal device, but instead an activity based on postulates that link philosophy, psychology, and politics in a theory of human order. For Mather and Franklin, the external authority of the political sovereign can be declared an abusive anachronism in a fraternal society where each of the members has erected an inner sovereignty of resolve: the monarch and the prelate become immigrant principles of consciousness. Thus Mather's and Franklin's common aspiration reveals agreement as well as difference: the distinction between them is a distinction between modes of interior sovereignty, between ways of replacing external politics with psychology. Franklin's argument with Mather is therefore a revision, or a modernization, not a clean break.

Because the issue of the interior sovereign is a practical issue for Mather and Franklin, a matter of life-planning, the numerous differences between them are organized around a single practical question: what is the proper relationship between the human nature enthroned at the center of the whole consciousness on the one hand, and the secular, innovative, and resourceful inclinations that Mather and Franklin associated with the word *self* on the other? This question of the self (and the word *self*) dominates their most important writings. And, when the topic at hand is something else, such as literary manner or empirical inquiry, the question of the self is in the background, as the incessantly pertinent consideration.

For Mather, personal legitimacy came only from a pious remembrance of divinity as it had embodied itself in the words and acts of those ancestors and predecessors he collectively labeled the fathers. Though these were exterior persons, their instauration as the voice of memory converted them into an interior principle of consciousness. Such vital memory requires a subjugation of self, which, if not subdued, would raise itself to anarchy and sedition in its determination to chip away at the continuity of the sacred. Self is what is governed by the aspiration to representative personality. The word *self,* then, in Mather's writings, does not conform to modern usage, which tends to apply the word to the whole of consciousness. In Mather's psychology *self* is the name of the group of impulses and thoughts that tend to assert themselves against government by memorial rectitude. *Self* is the governed insurgency of antinatural man.

For Franklin, however, self is the governor, the specimen of valid human nature that has legitimate title to design and direct the course of life. The past is only a mixed heap of resources and inanities, and memory is a servant to untrammeled ingenuity: to make memory into submissive fideistic remembrance is to adulterate nature. Franklin's conception of *self,* therefore, also diverges from the modern usage, because he takes it to signify the combination of rational calculation, ingenuity, and resolute industriousness.

For Mather, then, the self is that which is to be governed, whereas for Franklin the self is that which is to govern. But this neat formula obscures a mismatch or slippage between their uses of the single word *self.* According to Mather, calculation, ingenuity, and industry, if not subdued to piety, would be *among* the many faces of self: but for Franklin they *are* self, and all of self. The Franklinian self is therefore a portion of the Matherian self, but not all of it. Like Mather's superselfish piety, Franklin's self stands in detached constraining opposition to erotic and aesthetic feeling, to intensities of interest, to unreflective devotion, and to political sentiments that seem to go contrary to what has been deemed the universal interest. Franklin extracts calculation, ingenuity, and industry from the array that Mather called self, asserts their regulatory capacity, puts them in the place piety had occupied in Mather's scheme, calls them the whole self, and opposes them to the residue of consciousness (which has one new member, the usurped piety).

However, rather than clarifying his redefinition of the word *self,* Franklin allows the two definitions to be confused, because the confusion provides a rhetorical opportunity. It enables a felicitous conundrum: self-discipline is not onerous because it is self-fulfillment. Translated: the government of what Mather called self (minus what Franklin calls self) by what Franklin calls self is not a harsh discipline, because both parties are the same thing – *self.* The miracle decomposes when the semantic imprecision upon which the assertion is based is pointed out. But to a society that was both impatient with the Protestant psychomachy *and* wary of the anarchy that lurks within, the semantic imprecision of the conundrum was less important than the encouragement it could provide. Personal orderliness, and from it social orderliness, could be had without the severity of inner antithesis: the commodity could be had without the price Puritanism had put on it. Therefore, Franklin does not simply change self from governed to governor: he adds the promise that the new regime is a clean break from the punishing rigor of the old because now the governor and the governed are identical. Both are *self:* the self-determining, self-made man, the man who helps himself, is free of the faultline that ran through the Puritan consciousness; he is not therefore a disturber of the peace, but instead the agent of the peace. Accentuating the difference between his own and Mather's models of proper self-design, Franklin disguises the deeper continuity.

Consequently, the most frequent theme in Franklin's remarks concerning Mather, especially those from the period of his youth and early manhood, is the complete difference between their conceptions of the proper life. These comments represent an important moment in the formation of Franklin's worldview because Franklin's first authoritarian adversary was the Puritanism of early eighteenth-century Boston as it was embodied in Increase and Cotton Mather. When Franklin's father, Josiah, decided to "devote [Benjamin] as the Tithe of his Sons to the Service of the Church" (A:52), he may have been designing him as a sequel to Cotton Mather, because he had been taking the family to hear Mather's sermons at the North Church, which was some six blocks from their home at the corner of Union and Hanover streets. As Paul W. Conner suggests, Mather "represented what Franklin might have become had he been born a few decades earlier, stayed in Boston, and followed his father's wish that he serve the church."[6] But he did not follow his father's vocational instructions even after the question of the ministry had been retired, and he did not remain at the site of American Puritanism's definitive institutionalization. His self was to devise its own nature, rather than to be a pious remembrance of the authority that God the Father had conferred on godly fathers; and this rejection of the world and the will of his father was also a rejection of the patriarchal dogmas that permeated Mather's sermons and treatises.

His objections to Mather, however, were not left implicit and unspoken. Before going to Philadelphia, Franklin assisted in the writing and printing of his brother James's feisty and satiric *New England Courant*, which interspersed international news with sharp (some said libelous) commentary on the Mathers and their Calvinism, thus unfavorably contrasting piety with a secular and cosmopolitan interest in the world joined to Boston by commerce. The seventy-sixth issue contained an essay on specious religiosity that Perry Miller calls "a recognizable portrait of Cotton Mather,"[7] and, though James is the probable author, there is no reason to suppose that the younger Benjamin objected, because the essays he later contributed differed only in being more subtle:

> The World abounds with Knaves and Villains, but of all Knaves the *Religious* Knave is the worst; and Villainies acted under the Cloak of Religion are the most Execrable . . . If we observe them in their Con-

---

[6] Paul W. Conner, *Poor Richard's Politicks: Benjamin Franklin and His New American Order* (New York: Oxford University Press, 1965), pp. 197–8.

[7] Perry Miller, introduction to *The New England Courant: A Selection of Certain Issues Containing Writings of Benjamin Franklin* (Boston: American Academy of Arts and Sciences, 1956), p. 7.

versation with Men, we shall ever find them *seemingly Religious,* full of
pious Expressions, and more than ordinary prone to fall into serious Discourse, without any regard to the Time, Place or Company they are in:
Wheras, (everything being beautiful in its season) it must be acknow-
ledg'd, that such Discourse is not expedient at all Times. Or if we view
them in their Families, we shall find them nothing but Devotion and
Religion there. So if we observe them on the *Sabbath,* they are wonderful strict and zealous in the Sanctification of that; and it may be are exact
Observers of the Evening before and after it; or trace them to the sol-
emn Assemblies, and who is there so devout and Attentive as they?
Nay, sometimes they discover such distorted Faces, and awkward Gestures, as render them quite ridiculous. But yet these very men are often
found to be the grandest Cheats imaginable; they will *dissemble* and *lie,*
shuffle and *whiffle;* and if it be possible, they will overreach and defraud
all who deal with them.[8]

The attack is two-pronged. One tine is the accusation that men such as
Mather use a surface zeal to hide self-serving motives. This is not an anti-
Protestant argument, as the abundant literature on hypocrisy from Tyndale to Tennant demonstrates, and so it would not offend a Puritan audience on the ground of their convictions.

But the other accusation is anti-Puritan as well as anti-Mather. The
author criticizes Mather's extremity and rigidity, his determination to
impose piety on all the moments of life. The claim itself is certainly true:
Mather's diary contains repeated resolutions to make a pious improvement of every conceivable opportunity. But the author's claim that this
is reprehensible is based on an anti-Puritan assumption: piety is only one
among the seasons of man, rather than the master view, and to give it
dominion over the various activities of the self is to abuse life. This argument appears repeatedly in the *New England Courant,* for example in
the contention that the Mathers should stay out of the controversy over
smallpox inoculation because ministry and medicine are unrelated activities. This contention would have nettled Mather particularly, because
throughout his life he tried to compensate for his having chosen ministry
over medicine as a career by claiming that they were analogous activities,
and generally, because he believed that a minister's piety was the universal mode of consciousness: the minister attained to a representative frame
of consciousness that allowed him to comprehend and address men in all
their conditions, teaching them the place of their particular activities in
the overall coherent nature. Piety was a necessary, if difficult, addition to
all lives. Mather conceded that this piety would be a harsh subjugation
for those who were resolved on obeying the obstinate self. But resentment of piety was a sure sign of apostasy, of a self resigning from the

[8] *The New England Courant: A Selection,* n.p. after introduction.

universal order so that it might chase phantoms and ruin nature. For the author of the satirical essay, however, piety is just one of the many modes of sentiment, rather than the regulator of all of them, so to give it preeminence is to inaugurate an inner despotism. Notice, though, that the author claims for himself a universal familiarity with the seasons of man: the securing of social unanimity through the imposition of piety onto life is being contrasted with what is made to seem an easy unanimity which is indigenous to the secular life of the self. Franklin will appeal to this secular harmony abused by piety in the contributions he writes for subsequent issues, where he uses a number of personae not simply to protect himself from censorious prosecution, but also to demonstrate an ingenuity that can range across the spectrum of life without being domineering. This appeal is not a critique of the idea of representative personality per se, but a critique of such personality secured through the victory of a transcendental pattern over the self, in the interest of a representative personality that can appear to be the spontaneous and homogeneous product of common life.

Well before the seventy-sixth issue had appeared, Cotton Mather had already stopped James Franklin on the street and complained about his young parishioner's iconoclasm, and James had transcribed the complaint for the eighteenth issue, ostensibly for the purpose of giving both sides a forum. Mather begins by reminding James of a Hebrew patriarchal curse: "*Smite thro' the Loins of them that rise against him, and of them that hate him.*" He proceeds to apply the text to contemporary events:

> The Practice of supporting, and publishing every Week, a Libel, on the purpose to lessen and Blacken, and Burlesque the Vertuous, and the Principal Ministers of Religion in a Country, and render all the Services of their Ministry Despicable, and even Detestable to the People, *is a Wickedness that was never known before,* in any Country, Christian, Turkish, or Pagan, on the face of the Earth, and some Good men are afraid it may provoke Heaven, to deal with this Place, in some regards as never any place has yet been dealt withal, and a Charity to this Young Man, and his Accomplices might render such a Warning proper for them.[9]

But the heavenly wrath was preempted: in June 1722, James Franklin was arrested for contempt of the authorities, and, though his imprisonment was short, he was barred from continuing with the *New England Courant.* The mantle was passed to one of the "Accomplices," the sixteen-year-old Benjamin Franklin, who, having learned "the way of tact" and "the necessity for the oblique assault,"[10] continued the satire of Mather's dogma in a less abusive and, in the long run, more effective way. By 1723, the

[9] Ibid.
[10] Perry Miller, introduction to *The New England Courant: A Selection,* p. 8.

line of division between Cotton Mather and Benjamin Franklin had been clearly drawn: Mather was accused of an abusive and despotic religious excruciation which was irrationally inimical to human nature; and Franklin was accused of having joined the rhetorically suave "generations of the dragon" who invented easy *pseudodoxia* in order to disrupt the persistence of the good work.

After a long absence, Mather reappears in the writings of the aging Franklin, and the satiric rancor is replaced with cautious homage. This revision may be the calm of a balanced maturity, or it may be a politic judgment that nonpiety can be confused with impiety, and so reduce one's influence. But it might also be that Franklin, having established both the difference between his and Mather's ways and the orderliness of his way, could concede the continuity. In 1771, in Part One of his *Autobiography,* Franklin wrote that his father's copy of Mather's *Bonifacius: An Essay upon the Good* had been a major influence on his thinking – though he must have had to overlook Mather's strenuous contention, in the first chapter, that the man who does good works is a good man only if he has subjugated himself to an aloof and inscrutable god, that the aim of all good work is the glorification of *that* god, and that the works can do no more than evidence interior goodness with likely approximation. In July 1773, writing to Mather's son Samuel (who had himself denounced the *New England Courant* in January 1722), Franklin expressed a desire to see Boston again, its oppressiveness apparently having worn off, and he remembered Cotton Mather "in the vigor of his preaching and usefulness," though he recalled Increase Mather only as a feeble old man quietly sitting in an easy chair (*W,* VIII:68). Cotton Mather's usefulness came up again, in another letter to Samuel Mather, written in May 1784. Franklin repeated his homage to *Bonifacius,* but added that some few pages had been torn out of his father's copy, perhaps that first chapter. He remembered that relations between himself and Cotton Mather were sufficiently cordial that, in April 1724, the young Franklin, returned from Philadelphia to patch things up with his father and to solicit capital for his foray into printing, also paid a call on his former minister, and received some advice on Christian humility that was of the sort that had proved susceptible to conversion into practical advice on how to maintain an effective and inoffensive manner (*W,* X:82–5). In these later praising remarks, the adult Franklin judiciously passed over what he had rejected in Mather's way, in order to commemorate what had proved useful. This is revisionary acclaim, since for Mather the uses Franklin celebrated had to be subdued by the piety that Franklin does not mention. However, no discussion of Matherian piety was necessary at this late point in Franklin's life: he had, in the conduct of his long and diverse life, established the difference with patent clarity, so only the underlying consonance needed to be acknowledged.

The combination of contest and agreement in the relationship between Mather and Franklin has divided critical discussion, which has tended to assume that the relationship must be one of either antithesis or substantial identity. The vast majority of critics, of whom Vernon Parrington was perhaps the most eloquent, has subscribed to the idea of the clean break developed in Franklin's early satires, though they have not all shared Parrington's preference for Franklin's "critical realism." In the 1960s, however, David Levin and Phyllis Franklin uncovered a tendency to humane reason and civic commitment in Mather that anticipates Franklin.[11] However, replying to Levin and Phyllis Franklin, Campbell Tatham pointed to the first chapter of *Bonifacius* in order to suggest that they had unduly homogenized Mather and Franklin by overlooking Mather's deeply Calvinistic suspicion of independent reason and action.[12] In his introductory essay to the Harvard edition of *Bonifacius,* written before Phyllis Franklin and Tatham had entered the controversy, Levin had anticipated Tatham's objection, and he had attempted to synthesize the proto-Franklinian Mather with the anti-Franklinian Mather by referring to the Protestant dictum that good works were a means of glorifying God even if they did not cause or prove the doer's election.[13] This position seems to me to be the most satisfying since it shows that the relationship between Mather and Franklin is a combination of antithesis and continuity. Levin demonstrates how Mather rationalized a kind of communal role that objectively resembles Franklin's. However, he does not synthesize Mather's and Franklin's vastly different attitudes toward the meaning of such work: for Mather, the ability to do good was a talent given by God that would be abused if directed by the vigorous self, and the aim of such work was to glorify God and promote the glorification of God by others, rather than to advance secular comfort; for Franklin, however, the self was the admirable locus of a free talent whose works were good if they advanced the general social and physical happiness of himself and of his countrymen, and so attracted acclaim that glorified his ingenuity. As Richard F. Lovelace contends, when

[11] David Levin, "The Autobiography of Benjamin Franklin: The Puritan Experimenter in Life and Art," *Yale Review* 53 (1963), pp. 258–75; Phyllis Franklin, *Show Thyself a Man: A Comparison of Benjamin Franklin and Cotton Mather* (The Hague: Mouton, 1969).

[12] Campbell Tatham, "Benjamin Franklin, Cotton Mather and the Outward State," *Early American Literature* 6 (1971), p. 226.

[13] David Levin, introduction to *Bonifacius: An Essay upon the GOOD* (Cambridge, Mass.: Harvard University Press, 1966), pp. xxii, xix.

we take into account the entire body of Mather's writing, . . . it becomes apparent that what Franklin and others did was break down a
rather delicate synthesis of rational, orthodox piety which Mather and
other Puritans had put together in a state of balance and tension. Rationalistic moralism can be distilled out of Mather, but the product is
something entirely distinct from Mather's own position.[14]

The "distillation," that is, frees the ingenious self from the piety by
which it had been opposed: the young Franklin's satires challenge Matherian piety in order to free the self, but the elderly Franklin's praise reveals the continuity. I think, however, that Lovelace errs in accepting
Franklin's implication that the government of unruly affect by self is not
a tension akin to the government of self by piety in Mather's scheme.
The deepest similarity between the two men lies not in the objective
resemblances between some of their schemes, such as between Mather's
Society for the Suppression of Disorders and Franklin's Junto, but in the
common dedication of life to the unwavering project. In both cases, resolve is the conscious essence of the aspiration to representative personality, rather than merely a habit or an ingrained bias. Through self-
surveillance and self-government, resolve could curb the ever-present
danger of sinking into the confining limitation of particular interest, custom, occupation, or affection, thereby preserving the life as a purified
specimen of nature. Resolve maintained universal consciousness: by re-
stricting their susceptibility to the demands and enchantments of local
commitment, Mather and Franklin hoped to purge thought of everything that was not at least implicitly a common element in all men's
thought.

If the aspiration's price seems high, we must balance it against what
Mather and Franklin believed would be the three rewards – liberty, universality of interest and capability, and universality of social influence. It
might be objected that these are distinct or even unrelated traits, and it
may even be the case that Mather's and Franklin's disappointments ram-
ify from their failure to distinguish among them. Nevertheless, they did
not falter in binding the three into a practical unity of purpose: exclusivistic local attachment is a kind of captivity, in Mather's case sin, in
Franklin's waste, that traps one's humanity in one of its variants; rising
from this captive torpor, consciousness finds itself capable of surveying
all the variant seasons of man; and it is therefore capable of appealing to
men in all of their conditions.

Though the process of gratifying the aspiration required an iron discipline, liberty lay at the end, but not because the rule of life was plastic
or adaptive: Mather and Franklin, again, had defined the proper organi-

[14] Lovelace, *The American Pietism of Cotton Mather,* p. 41.

zation of life when they were quite young, and they adhered to the courses they had set for themselves. There is none of Emerson's sense that a life's trajectory is mysterious, given to reversals, revealing itself in brief luminous moments, and that an explicit and meticulous consistency is therefore misguided. Instead, the liberty that Mather and Franklin envisioned lay at the end of discipline, in its success at reducing consciousness to the essentially human. At this point, consciousness is free with respect to the higher law governing human affairs in the sense that, purged of all impulses to veer from that law, it is no longer subjugated to an exterior standard: it is at one with what it has adopted as its central principle. If such a consciousness were subjected to particular social laws that veered from the higher law of man, it would be constrained, but unjustly constrained; and Mather's and Franklin's political courage grows from their irritation with social power that lagged behind their own aspirations to conformity with a universally viable standard.

Reaching this pinnacle, the disciplined consciousness would have shed the parochialism or bias that had sought to restrain it, and attained to an eclectic cosmopolitanism. Thomas Schlereth, Peter Gay, and Henry Steele Commager have shown the importance of such eclecticism to the self-esteem of thinkers such as Jefferson, Hume, Holbach, Voltaire, and Franklin.[15] But this ambition also dominates Mather's pious Calvinism, in his conception of the minister as the unifying focus of Christian society, as the man capable of addressing men in all of their nationalities, conditions, and particular callings. It is difficult to see Mather's conception of the minister as a predecessor to Enlightenment eclecticism because we associate that eclecticism with the free self and with secular inquiry: but our difficulty only testifies to the success of thinkers such as Franklin, who severed eclecticism from its service to piety.

Unlike many of the philosophes, however, Mather and Franklin did not consider their able eclecticism to be a mark of distinction set between themselves and the mass of their contemporaries. Instead, they considered it a premonition of the human nature that was still, for the moment, in many of their contemporaries, obstructed and encumbered by factious particular commitments of the sort they had shed, but that could be actualized on a large scale by the activities of exemplary personalities such as themselves. This view is why Mather's and Franklin's frustrations more

---

[15] Thomas J. Schlereth, *The Cosmopolitan Ideal in Enlightenment Thought: Its Form and Function in the Ideas of Franklin, Hume, and Voltaire, 1694–1790* (Notre Dame: Notre Dame University Press, 1977); Peter Gay, *The Enlightenment: The Rise of Modern Paganism* (New York: Knopf, 1966), pp. 164–71, 267–8; Henry Steele Commager, *The Empire of Reason* (New York: Oxford University Press, 1977), pp. 2–3, 19–21, 41, 72, 163–4.

frequently took the form of irritation, tending to anger, rather than despair: they considered themselves frustrated by obstinacy, rather than impossibility. They were extraordinarily attentive to the progress of their reputations, and this attention is more than simple vanity: recognition by contemporaries was a reciprocal event, at once signifying the success of their self-discipline and instigating social consensus among those who had discovered their humanity in the moment of admiring the exemplar. Insofar as those contemporaries could let go of the provincial commitments that divided them in order to admire the capacious universality of a Mather or a Franklin, they learned that their provincial commitments were mere ornaments decorating a fundamental solidarity upon which a nation could be built. Admiring Mather or admiring Franklin would be tantamount to admiring human nature, and so to signifying the possibility of a nation conforming to human nature.

The differences, to repeat, lie within the common aspiration: freedom from self, or freedom of self? self as distraction from eclectic capacity, or self as center of eclectic capacity? self as the anarchic root of social fragmentation, or self as the one sure ground of social unity? And there is the added difference sought in Franklin's clever rhetoric: the freed, eclectic self that offers itself for the admiration of its contemporaries is not "contradictious," it will not be a harsh regime for either the exemplar or his admirers: the goods – freedom, eclecticism, solidarity, order – are available at a vastly reduced price, the inflationary rhetoric of the predecessor having been exposed. Thus though Mather and Franklin share the aspiration, they present different faces. For Mather, the resistance of self, or of the selves of those contemporaries who stalled before joining him in piety, was dark, rich, potent, coherent, monstrous, and damnably vital. But for Franklin the self was enforcer rather than the object of enforcement, and its activity of enforcement was to seem easy and spontaneous, so the resistance to self would be only a quirky obtuseness without any coherence at all. This difference is manifest in their literary manners: whereas Mather's writing at its best is vibrant with polarity and tension, Franklin's ordinarily maintains a limpid, mildly ironic serenity that is only occasionally aggravated into impatience. This difference is also manifest in their different perceptions of the rhetorical means to social consolidation. For Mather, the call to consensus was a call to emulate his own explicitly severe piety, and it took the form of a jeremiad denouncing men's declension from the example of their group past. For Franklin, the call to consensus could abjure such stridency in favor of mild irony and calm incentive, since he was asking men not to annihilate self but to indulge it – to indulge, that is, the self as he has defined it.

It may seem that I believe that there is no important difference between Mather and Franklin or even that I prefer Mather. Consequently, I should note that I do think that Mather's piety frequently assumed a contorted and punishing form; and I do think that Franklin's desire to release secular life from Puritan strictures resulted in inventions, a dedication to mediation, an opposition to special interest, and a congenial pedagogy that are all steps toward a more equable conception of society. These I consider foregone conclusions that have been abundantly chronicled in the available literature. But I take issue with Franklin's rhetorical assertion of his clean break from piety, from obscurantism to clarity and from domination to freedom: to admire Franklin's innovations is one thing, to accept them as proof of a move into the light is another. Such an acceptance reduces the dialectical complexity of Mather's thought to an obtuse and domineering crankiness; and it supports two of Franklin's most questionable claims, that there can be a self that purely embodies human nature and so needs no higher critique, and that there can be a lifelong personal project that is an adequate, spontaneous, and purely harmonious representation of the complexity of interest, motive, and emotion. For all that is baleful in his thought, Mather never assumed that there could be simple identity between human obligation and self or between discipline and the continuum of consciousness. The balefulness of Mather's thought, therefore, is always on display: he insisted on contradiction. Franklin understood this Puritan insistence, and the consequent stresses; more importantly, he knew that his American audience felt the stresses, and he realized that a demonstration that a valid and reputable life could be led without contradiction would be welcome. This is the Franklinian promise, and it is undoubtedly more alluring than the example of Cotton Mather. But if there is a continuity between Matherian and Franklinian discipline, then the promise will turn out to have been enabled by a systematic self-masking: it will be difficult to articulate (and to criticize) the new discipline *as such;* and the assertion that there must be a contradiction between obligation and inclination, even if it is added that each side must amend the other in a continual procedure, will be resented. Rather than a clear opposition between obscurity and light, the difference between Cotton Mather and Benjamin Franklin is a revisionary one, between a way of life that displays its rigidified contradictoriness and one that disguises the contradictions it nevertheless requires.

There is, finally, a literary difference between Mather and Franklin, in addition to the theoretical difference (self as governed versus self as governor) and the rhetorical difference (discipline as contradiction versus discipline as harmony). Though Mather always concedes that the relation between piety and self is one of strife, this battle is, for the most part, as I contend in my first two chapters, narrated from the point of view of piety, which tells of its victories, defeats, and horrors. Self is mute: it is talked about. However, as I argue in my third, fourth, and fifth chapters,

Mather's writing has moments where the rich recalcitrance of self seeks some provisional legitimacy, some chance to speak for itself, though in closely circumscribed ways. At such points, rather than a monologue recounting the battle spoken by one participant, a dialogue continues the strife onto the page. This is important, because it means that the resentment of undue piety with which most readers react to Mather's writing – the resentment upon which Franklin capitalizes in his assertion of the freed self – was anticipated by Mather himself, and suffered in advance. The modern reader is apt to notice what seems to be an absence of protest, and to conclude that Mather was a somewhat incredible pedant devoid of normal reactions to an intolerable conception of life. But he did not thrive in discipline, at least not in the simple way implied in the many stereotyped portraits. Protest can be detected at several points in Mather's writing, but it is guarded and elusive, and piety always reasserted its voice in triumph.

In Franklin's writings, on the other hand, the rhetorical implication that there is no contradiction between self and the whole of consciousness is accompanied by a virtually complete absence of even indirect protest against the rigor that the aspiration demands. Though at several points he is perhaps more vulgar, more magnanimous, or more jocular than the aspiration would seem to mandate, such points of slight straying do not coalesce as an objection to disciplined determination, and the writing is consequently monological. In the last chapter, which is speculative, I attempt to suggest a contrary murmur in Franklin's writings concerning the period of return to America after his first trip to England. But it is not significant enough to count as an objection, and as a resultant dialogism.

I aim to present, therefore, a Cotton Mather who has a normal reaction to an unrelenting discipline, who expresses the resentment upon which Franklin's rhetoric operates, and who is therefore a credible personality even though he did not go so far as to make that protest into a rebellion. On the other hand, if, as I contend, Franklin's rebellion against Puritan piety was itself a domination of full consciousness that was as rigorous and incessant as Mather's, I hope my reader will conclude with me that the absence of protest makes Franklin's serene and equanimous univocity seem like a kind of depersonalized and somewhat chilling blankness that is quite separate from the universal affability he sought to project.

I would like to conclude this introduction with two notes on my procedure. For the most part, I consider writings by Mather and Franklin where the self and its place are the topics at hand. At several points, however, I take up writings where the topic is something else – the lives of plants, smallpox inoculation, electricity, or money – as analogical discussions of the self. The inclination of thought toward analogy is much more confined now than it was in Mather's and Franklin's New England, where the exploration of nature and experience for subtle signs of the self's obligation and its progress was a popular and nearly constant activity – so much so that it can be called a general habit of mind. Therefore, Mather's comments on analogy's central place in the structure of the creation, for example, are a reflective codification of a common assumption, not a theoretical invention. Franklin was also familiar with this popular activity: during the years in which Franklin was being taken to the North Church, Mather used frozen rivers, midwinter thaws, the shade of trees, fruit, purged floors, floods in the Netherlands and Germany, famine, riches, and the sun as analogical emblems of the individual's spiritual estate. Franklin's later ideological and polemical commitment to Newtonian causality replaced analogy as his preferred mode for explaining the world, but it seems to me that the rhetorical and imaginative tendency to discover through figures survived his realism, in his aphorisms, for example.

Second, I wish to point out that this is an interior excavation of Mather's and Franklin's determining projects, and of the relation between their projects, rather than a venture at an objective historical description or a complete appraisal of their acts and works. Self-design is of course an important influence on writing and conduct, so I will invoke texts and biographical episodes in which the aspiration to representative personality unfolds: but this invocation is not the same as a complete appraisal based on more or less objective scientific paradigms. I do not reject such a design; I merely note that my reader will not find it here, but in the critical works I note as I go along. My intention is to inhabit Mather's and Franklin's thought by reconstructing their peculiar coherences, and to explicate those writings where the issue of self-design seems to me to be literally, figurally, or intriguingly present.

I have used masculine pronouns generally for such ambiguous beings as "the reader" and "the Puritan" because I am male. Women readers should mentally substitute "she" as they go along.

1

COTTON MATHER'S SELF

AB AMICO SATIS ADULATORE
ON COTTON MATHER

For *Grace* and *Art* and an Illustrious *Fame*
Who would not look from such an Ominous Name?
Where *Two Great Names* their Sanctuary take,
And in a *Third* combined, a *Greater* make.

> Too gross flattery for me to transcribe;
> (tho' the poetry be good).
>> Cotton Mather, transcribed and crossed out, in *Diary* (I:475)

And thou, Solomon my son, know thou the God of thy father, and serve him with a perfect heart and with a willing mind: For the LORD searcheth all hearts, and understandeth all the imaginations of the thoughts: if thou seek him, he will be found of thee; but if thou forsake him, he will cast thee off for ever.
> I Chronicles 28:9, quoted in Cotton Mather, *A Family Well-Ordered*

Walter Pater attributed the Renaissance to "the desire for a more liberal and comely way of conceiving life."[1] His adjectives are causally related: "the breaking down of those limits which the religious system of the middle ages imposed on the heart and on the imagination" permitted a liberality – a true plurality of possible lives – that encouraged some citizens of the age to set about choosing and designing identities suited to their own notions of comeliness.[2] Jacob Burckhardt agrees:

> In the Middle Ages both sides of human consciousness – that which was turned within as well as that which was turned without – lay dreaming or half awake beneath a common veil. This veil was woven of faith, illusion, and childish prepossession, through which the world

---

[1] Walter Pater, *The Renaissance* (New York: Random House, The Modern Library), p. 2.
[2] Ibid., p. xxix.

20

and history were seen clad in strange hues. Man was conscious of himself only as a member of a race, people, party, family or corporation – only through some general category.[3]

But, with the Renaissance, "the ban laid upon human personality was dissolved; and a thousand figures meet us each in its own special shape and dress."[4] Modern historians such as Michel Foucault would dispute the opposition between constraint and freedom that guides Pater's and Burckhardt's arguments. Foucault would argue instead for a substitution of one *episteme* for another, rather than a chapter in the liberty of the race.[5] But Pater's and Burckhardt's arguments are valid summaries of how Renaissance men saw themselves: the abatement of unquestioned prescriptions for generic identity comes in tandem with an open recognition of the individual as individual and as man, and with an explicit celebration of what Stephen Greenblatt calls "Renaissance self-fashioning." If self-fashioning did develop from certain unacknowledged cultural codes that were as completely binding on thought as those of the medieval period, these codes did not press themselves into an individual's awareness of his personal, self-determined excellence. The individual, to borrow Pater's verb, could think of himself as *conceiving* his own life, and to extend Pater's verb, he could think of himself as his own father, not biologically, but in the setting of his own occupation and life-contour. The result, according to Pater, is "special and prominent personalities," contributing to "an age productive in personalities, many-sided, centralised, complete."[6] Again Burckhardt agrees, finding "complete men . . . with a powerful and varied nature which had mastered all the elements of the culture of the age."[7] The individual could be an embodied digest of his cultural environment if he conceived himself properly. As Greenblatt asserts, concerning the Renaissance in England, "in the sixteenth century there appears to be an increased self-consciousness about the fashioning of human identity as a manipulable, artful process."[8] The act of self-fashioning, in other words, is not simply a description of what human beings did: it was a part of their consciousness of themselves.

We should take note of Pater's and Burckhardt's emphasis on the va-

---

[3] Jacob Burckhardt, *The Civilization of the Renaissance in Italy* (New York: Oxford University Press, 1944), p. 81.

[4] Ibid.

[5] Michel Foucault, *The Order of Things* (New York: Random House, 1970); *The Archaeology of Knowledge*, trans., A. M. Sheridan Smith (New York: Random House, 1972).

[6] Pater, *The Renaissance*, p. xxx.

[7] Burckhardt, *The Civilization of the Renaissance in Italy*, p. 84.

[8] Stephen Greenblatt, *Renaissance Self-Fashioning: From More to Shakespeare* (Chicago: University of Chicago Press, 1980), p. 2.

riety and many-sidedness of the great Renaissance personalities. Though the rise of mercantile and venture capital made this a period in which men began to substitute another vocation or home for the ones into which they were born, men such as Raleigh and Leonardo are remembered not because they substituted a vocation of their own choosing for the one to which they were born, but because their talent was abstract and versatile and not confined to a particular form. Their eclectic plasticity kept them from occupying a single place in a hierarchy of talent. Instead, they appropriated to themselves the universality that had been attributed to the god of Aquinas and of Nicholas of Cusa, who compared the divine person to an "omnivoyant face." In modern usage, the prefix in *omniscient* and *omnipotent* tends to be treated as a quantitative intensifier: there is no resistance or secret that the power of divinity cannot penetrate. In the rhetoric of Renaissance excellence, however, the emphasis would be on the multifacetedness signfied in the prefix *omni-*: man could now claim for himself the universality – the freedom from determination as a specific, limited particularity – that he had previously beheld in his god from the far place of his station in a cosmic hierarchy. As Pico della Mirandola wrote in his *Dignity of Man*,

> At last the best of artisans ordained that the creature to whom He had been able to give nothing proper to himself should have joint possession of whatever had been peculiar to each of the different kinds of being. He therefore took man as a creature of indeterminate nature and, assigning him a place in the middle of the world, addressed him thus: "Neither a fixed abode nor a form that is thine alone nor any function peculiar to thyself have we given thee, Adam, to the end that according to thy longing and according to thy judgement thou mayest have and possess what abode, what form, and what functions thou thyself shalt desire. The nature of all other beings is limited and constrained within the bounds of laws prescribed by Us. Thou, constrained by no limits, in accordance with thine own free will, in whose hand We have placed thee, shalt ordain for thyself the limits of thy nature. We have set thee at the world's center that thou mayest from thence observe whatever is in the world. We have made thee neither of heaven nor of earth, neither mortal nor immortal, so that with freedom of choice and with honor, as though the maker and molder of thyself, thou mayest fashion thyself in whatever shape thou shalt prefer."[9]

Himself nothing particular, man is a pure versatile potentiality, able to assume form according to his own judgment of comeliness; his freedom

---

[9] Pico della Mirandola, *The Dignity of Man*, in Ernst Cassirer, Paul Oskar Kristeller, John Herman Randall, Jr., eds., *The Renaissance Philosophy of Man*, pp. 224–5.

from indigenous, defining attachment to any part of the whole gives him a purview of the whole. And most importantly, he is self-fathering in an ongoing process, rather than self-fathered once and then committed. The forms he accepts he accepts freely, and he steps forth freely again, to embody the blankness of pure potentiality in particular abodes that do not mar its purity: the universality of his thought is not sullied by prejudices, customs, desires, affections, or habits peculiar to the abodes in which he sojourns.

But such an assertion of the validity of self was intolerable to Puritan ideology. Reacting to anxieties generated during a period in which the authority of church and (eventually) state had come to seem cynical, opportunistic, and devoid of credible principle, the Puritan theorists sought to restore the clarity provided by medieval polity, but in such a way that it would be immune to a repetition of the current degeneration. Their solution was minimalism: the social body would be contracted from the society at large to the individual congregation, where a vital unanimity could be ensured; and human mediation between the patriarchal sovereignty of divinity and men would be contracted from the ceremonial and sacerdotal hierarchy of the Anglican Church to the solitary minister. In this way, vigilance could maintain a close approximation of the medieval cosmos, but in a form never recognized by medieval theory, except perhaps in the persecution of heresies such as Catharism and Donatism. Puritan anti-authoritarianism is therefore not a critique of the concept of absolute patriarchal sovereignty, but an attempt to expose and refuse spurious claims to draw human authority from the divine sovereign; and the Puritan concept of the congregational organism, though it is a de facto innovation within the context of Anglican England, nevertheless resulted in a vigorous stigmatization of assertions of the free glory of the self.

Consequently, a century after the self-fashioners Greenblatt describes, Milton found Piconian man an apostasy, and he put self-fathering among the motives leading to Satan's damnation:

> That we were formed then saist thou? and the work
> Of secondarie hands, by task transferd
> From Father to his Son? Strange point and new!
> Doctrin which we would know whence learnt: who saw
> When this creation was? rememberst thou
> Thy making, while the Maker gave thee being?
> We know no time when we were not as now;
> Know none before us, self-begot, self-rais'd
> By our own quick'ning power, when fatal course
> Had circl'd his full Orbe, the birth mature
> Of this our native Heav'n, Ethereal Sons.

Our puissance is our own, our own right hands
Shall teach us highest deeds . . .[10]

Satan's vain refusal to believe that he was fashioned to a particular place
in the vast order, and that he is not "many-sided, centralised, complete,"
is for Milton abominable, and an expression of his Puritanism. Though
the Puritans recognized the excellence and variety of human individuality, they felt that the self – unconstrained by any determining law and
aspiring to a godlike universality – was vile and aberrant, rather than
resplendent, and best traumatically humiliated to make way for the infusion of a godhood completely alien to it: the self's center is outside of
it. The Puritan reaction against Anglican practice focused on the assertion (most powerfully voiced by Archbishop John Whitgift and Richard
Hooker) that explicit scriptural law pertained to a relatively small portion of human activity, and that the rest of human conduct, as long as it
observed general ethical precepts, was a "thing Indifferent."[11] This argument, used to defend surplices and the sacerdotal order of the church,
would also exonerate self-fashioning, since it restricted the field in which
creative innovation was interdicted. The Puritan recoil from such liberality would therefore encompass self-fashioning as well as doctrine and
liturgy, thereby expressing a deep anxiety about the potential anarchy
that would follow from unconcerned "new-modeling."

To the Puritan, the glory of self-fashioning was an empty and sterile
elaboration of godless invention. The Puritan preference for restraint in
dress, worship, and literary style was a deliberate reduction of the glory
of innovative individuality meant to submit it to ancient models of
Christian contrition. It would be wrong to see the Puritans as Malvolios
immune to the allure of the Renaissance: we should see rather than immunity to that allure an attraction mixed with a strong apprehension of
incoherence. This mixture resulted in tension in those eminent Puritans
who were not Malvolios. In Nathaniel Ward's *The Simple Cobler of Aggawam in America*, for example, written in 1647 to castigate the encroachments of toleration among the English brethren, the exuberant expressiveness of style is often in sharp contrast with the austerity of the topic:

> It is greatly to be lamented, to observe the wanton fearlessnesse of this
> Age, especially of younger professors, to greet new pinions and Opin-
> ionists: as if former truths were growne superannuate, and saplesse, if
> not altogether antiquate. *Non senescet veritas.* No man ever saw a gray

[10] John Milton, *Complete Poetry*, ed. John T. Shawcross (Garden City, N.Y.:
Doubleday, 1971), p. 363. (*Paradise Lost*, V, 853–71.)

[11] Perry Miller, *Orthodoxy in Massachusetts, 1630–1650* (Cambridge, Mass.: Harvard University Press, 1933), pp. 26–7; John S. Coolidge, *The Pauline Renaissance in England: Puritanism and the Bible* (New York: Oxford University Press,
1970), pp. 1–55.

haire on the head or beard of any Truthe, wrinkle or morphew on its face: the bed of Truth is green all year long. Hee that cannot solace himselfe with any saving truth, as affectionately as at the first acquaintance with it, hath not only a fastidious, but an adulterous heart.[12]

Innovative individuality is not a law to itself but an erosive lawlessness that dissimulates its intentions: it is a fornicator that sneaks away from Christ the bridegroom. Before the evergreen truth that Ward describes, the self is, to quote Norman Grabo's compilation of terms from Edward Taylor, "a crumb of dust" at best, and, at worst,

> a dirt ball, a muddy sewer, a tumbrel of dung, a dung-hill, a dot of dung, a varnished pot of putrid excrements, drops in a closestool pan, guts, garbage and rottenness. He wears a crown of filth, his cheeks are covered with spider's vomit, and he is candied over with leprosy. He is also a pouch of passion, a lump of loathsomeness, a bag of botches, a lump of lewdness; and he gives off a nauseous stink. He is wrapped in slime; pickled in gall; a sink of nastiness; and a dirty, smelly dish cloth; he is, in short, "all blot."[13]

Such ferocity must arise from a strong sense of the appeal of what is opposed, and, as Greenblatt argues in his chapter on Tyndale, rebellion against what was called a chaotic and deluded chase after splendor can itself be a form of self-fashioning. According to Michael Walzer, "(c)onscience freed the saints from medieval passivity and feudal loyalty, but it did not encourage the individualist, Italianate politics of faction and intrigue. Puritan ministers campaigned against the personal extravagance of the great Renaissance courtiers and deplored the role of 'private interest' in politics." Even so, "(t)he saint's personality was his own most radical innovation." David Hume rather sarcastically remarked on this ambivalence in his *History of England*: "[the Puritans in the House of Commons] were disgusted by the prevalence of the principles of civil liberty essential to their party, and on account of the restraint under which they were held by the established hierarchy."[14] Though the reformers announced their submission of self to ancient and evergreen truth, in practice they used this theoretical allegiance to justify severing their allegiance to the circumstances of their birth, parish, and parentage in order to fashion a life in accord with their rather austere notions of come-

---

[12] Nathaniel Ward, *The Simple Cobler of Aggawam in America* (Lincoln: University of Nebraska Press, 1969), p. 23.

[13] Norman Grabo, *Edward Taylor* (New Haven, Conn.: College and University Press, 1961), p. 53.

[14] Michael Walzer, *The Revolution of the Saints: A Study in the Origins of Radical Politics* (New York: Atheneum, 1973), pp. 12–13, 3; David Hume, *The History of England from the Invasion of Julius Caesar to the Abdication of James the Second, 1688* (Boston: Phillips, Sampson & Co., 1850), V, p. 4.

liness. They followed William Tyndale's advice: "And when they cry, 'Fathers, fathers,' remember that it were fathers that blinded and robbed the whole world, and brought us unto this captivity, wherein these enforce to keep us still." [15] The theoretical submission of self to the models of primitive Christianity disguised their radically self-shaping rebellion against the life into which they were born.

But if Puritanism was a kind of self-fathering opposed to self-fathering in its inception, it did not remain so in its transmission. When Puritanism changed from holy opposition to official ideology in Massachusetts, the repudiation of self-fashioning ceased being a kind of de facto self-fashioning and became dogma: whereas allegiance to ancient models had justified objection to contemporary models in England, in New England contemporary models were thought to have been constructed in accord with the divine will, and to have become a sufficient objectification of it. Consequently, exact and nontransformative accord was required. According to Perry Miller, "(w)hen the discipline was carried to America, it was immediately put to uses exactly opposite to those it had served in England. Instead of being the shield of an attacking party, it suddenly became the platform of a ruling oligarchy; instead of being invoked to delimit the sway of kings and prelates, it was now employed to rule a populace." Miller contends that "the task of dominating a new environment called upon the system to subordinate the radical insistencies of its youth to the responsibilities of a vested interest. The duty of the Church was no longer to hold aloft a barely attainable ideal of Christian virtue, but rather to train up law-abiding members." [16] Rather than devoting themselves to a superior law that carried them away from their circumstances of origin, the second- and third-generation heirs of the first plantation were obliged to acquiesce in a higher law that was sufficiently and specifically embodied in the all-embracing extant social order. If in its inception Puritanism indulged the spirit of self-design to which it strenuously objected, such indulgence ended when it was transmitted to heirs. These heirs, in obeying the explicit formulations of their predecessors' beliefs, were obligated to extirpate all traces of the predecessors' unacknowledged individualist vigor. Ward declares that it "is a most toylsome taske to run the wild-goose chase after a well-breath'd Opinionist," [17] but that is what the heirs were compelled to do, within the wilderness of self.

The quandary of the Puritan heir is nowhere more imaginatively and meticulously chronicled than in the actions and writings of Cotton Mather.

[15] William Tyndale, *The Obedience of a Christian Man,* in *The Works of William Tyndale,* ed. G. E. Duffield (Appleford, Eng.: Sutton Courtenay Press), p. 360.
[16] Miller, *Orthodoxy in Massachusetts,* pp. 176, 195.
[17] Ward, *The Simple Cobler,* p. 17.

He was the grandson of Richard Mather and John Cotton (whose names take refuge in his), and the son of Increase Mather, all three of whom were prominent in the spiritual and political life of Massachusetts. Increase Mather was a domineering presence in his son's emotional formation, but he never seemed to his son to be simply a strong individual will. Rather, Increase's vigor lay not in personal inclination but in his successful submission to the mandate of John Cotton and Richard Mather. The father's authority did not arise from his prestige as an individual, but from his pious maintenance of *his* predecessors' example. Though Cotton Mather undoubtedly felt the allure of self-fashioning, therefore, he successfully castigated this temptation in the interest of a rigid and literal sense of obligation to his dynastic predecessors. The consequent tension was of such emotional magnitude and intensity that it came to pervade the whole of his thought, infiltrating his speculations on a wide diversity of topics. As writer and as minister to Boston's North Church (which his father also served), Mather's lifelong task was to demonstrate his successful subjugation of self to his father's example of successful submission to the holy dynasty.

As a result, *self* is a key word in Mather's writings. It signifies both the individual integration of memory, desire, thought, and will that designates itself as "I," and an erosive force that goes against the sacred order of things: in Mather's thought *self* and *sin* are practically synonymous. This statement is not to contend that he did not recognize variety among men. As in the creation at large, the human community had been made diverse, each member having a specific function in the vast, whole body. *Self* was the apostate desire to be more than or other than this ordained part. Nor is this to contend that Cotton Mather was not a distinct individual, but instead that the articulation of the impact of the hostility to the self on Mather's thought is the hallmark of what is distinct about him.

Mather's writings are an unparalleled development of what Phillip Greven calls the "evangelical personality":

> The temperaments of evangelicals were dominated by a persistent and virtually inescapable hostility to the self and all of its manifestations. Thus evangelicals were preoccupied with ways to abase, to deny, and to annihilate their own enduring sense of self-worth and selfhood, convinced that only by destroying the self could they conform absolutely and unquestioningly to the will of God.[18]

Greven repeatedly chooses Mather to illustrate the evangelical personality, and it is an inevitable choice, since Mather represents the most lucid

[18] Phillip Greven, *The Protestant Temperament: Patterns of Child-Rearing, Religious Experience, and the Self in Early America* (New York: Knopf, 1977), pp. 12–13.

and imaginative example of it among the American Puritans. Mather believed that God had prescribed not just general rules of conduct, but an entire form of personal being to which the individual was to submit.

> My Mind, with all the Dispositions, and all the Operations of it, is continually under the Eye of the omnipresent God. Not only my Wayes, and my Words, but also the Thoughts and Frames of my Mind, come under the Observation of the glorious One. He takes Notice of all that passes in my Mind, and is intimately acquainted with it all. This is a Consideration, that often visits my Mind, and chases away from it such Things as ought not to be lodged in it. (*D*, II:155)

Self is the most prominent of these unwelcome tenants, and in fact self might be called the collective name for the things that must be chased out. Self was the name of the part of consciousness that resisted God's intentions for the man, that gloried not only in the error of base desires but also in the error of vanity – the enjoyment of personal independence and self-design. Its creative innovations were apostasies if they were more than superfluous ornaments. At best, self dispersed in the sunlight of divinity; at worst, it was an area of darkness and delirium.

The annihilation of self, or conversion, was the focal and inevitable concept in American Puritan thought. Not simply a condition of church membership, it also informed Puritan psychology, cosmogony, and social theory. As the first founders of Massachusetts felt compelled to explain and defend their ecclesiastical polity, they debated the nature of conversion and of preparation for conversion at length, and they developed scholastic, even etiolated, sequences of nicely discriminated phases. In Mather's writings, however, the list of steps tends to be reduced to humiliation, submission, and union. Some might call such reduction popularizing, but that conclusion is too condescending. Mather was after the intrinsic affective kernel inside precisian stipulations, the gist idea that informed an entire view of man.[19]

The process begins in a crisis that shocks the individual consciousness out of complacent self-satisfaction. The self that had considered itself sufficient because it survived and flourished in its daily life learned that it persisted only by the arbitrary kindness of God. This recognition was a severe trauma, and Mather repeatedly calls it a kind of dying. The es-

[19] The most inclusive analyses of the controversies over conversion are Edmund Morgan, *Visible Saints: The History of a Puritan Idea* (Ithaca, N.Y.: Cornell University Press, 1965) and Norman Pettit, *The Heart Prepared: Grace and Conversion in Puritan Spiritual Life* (New Haven, Conn.: Yale University Press, 1966). See also Patricia Caldwell, *The Puritan Conversion Narrative: The Beginnings of American Expression* (Cambridge: Cambridge University Press, 1984) and George Selement, "The Meeting of Elite and Popular Minds at Cambridge, New England, 1630–1645," *William and Mary Quarterly* 41, no. I (January 1984), pp. 32–48.

sence of "practical piety," he wrote in his diary, was to "Die Daily" (*D*, II:264). The function of trauma was to instigate reflection: instead of persisting in old thoughts, the fledgling was to ponder them. A part of thought would step out of self and look upon it. It would see two things: sin, that is, the baseness and vanity of self; and its inability to correct error.[20]

At this point, the rising soul would realize the utter vacuity of the life that had seemed full and of the self that had occupied the former life's center. And it would feel the agony of its estrangement from divinity: "(Christ) has made me weary of my *Distances* from God: So that I behold a *Vanitie* in all other Objects, and I abhor every *Lust* that carries mee after them, and I cannot bear to think with being putt off with any Enjoyments of this World for my *Portion*" (*D*, I:77). Weariness was a mild reaction to such estrangement: terror was more frequent. The cultivated self was no more than dust; the soul, or bit of divinity, was atrophied. This terror was what Thomas Hooker had called "a true sight of sin": rather than looking at specific acts, the converting soul saw and suffered in its profound distance from sustaining hope and love, and in its complete inability to repair the breach. As Mather wrote in his diary, sin is its own punishment (*D*, II:18). The man who has enjoyed self finds that self is not a prosperous capital, but instead a twilight to which it has banished itself. Chastisements were for Mather a part of the instigating crisis: the more severe agony in conversion is the horrible solitude of "A Troubled Mind which Apprehends the Face of a Gracious God Hidden From it": "You may now make light of it: But there will a Time come, that the Punishment will be found Intollerable; Your Groan will be, *I cannot bear it, I cannot bear it.*"[21] Such solitude is not the preview of damnation, it is damnation. The deserted soul wanders from anxiety to fright to despair.

There is still too much self, however, since anxiety, fright, and despair

---

[20] The issue of conversion pervades all of Mather's writing. My summary here is derived from his *Unum Necessarium: Awakenings for the Unregenerate* (Boston: B. Harris, 1693), unless noted otherwise. Richard F. Lovelace adds a step between reflecting on sin and the inability to correct it: "specific confession of areas of sin in the life – according to the decalogue – and of original sin." However this seems to me to be a further articulation of humiliation, rather than a separate step, except on the level of procedure. Lovelace's summary is quite good, though I think he fails to explain that the union at the end of the process has intellectual as well as emotional consequences. Richard F. Lovelace, *The American Pietism of Cotton Mather: Origins of American Evangelicalism* (Grand Rapids, Mich.: Christian University Press, 1979), pp. 73–110, esp. p. 81.

[21] Cotton Mather, *The Case of a Troubled Mind. A Brief Essay upon the Troubles of a Mind; Which Apprehends the Face of a Gracious God Hidden from It* (Boston, 1717), p. 19.

are self-centered emotions, though not confident ones. Only when it has wholly and truly conceded its impotence has soul emigrated from self: this terminates its plight. The self that had resisted and sought its own end is gone, and the law can be seen clearly. Now comes "melting" and "assurance," and acceptance of divinity as delight: "Tis by Regeneration that a Man who look'd up on Exercises of *Piety* and *Charity* as Intolerable, Insuperable, Impracticable, now comes to say, *Lord, thy Commandments are not grievous!* . . . Now he says, *Oh, how I love thy Law!*" [22] Such a soul is free not because, like Pico's man, it is without constraining limits, but because it has purged the self which was opposed to higher law: "Regeneration *is a Real and Thorough Change, wrought by the Holy Spirit, in a Fallen Man, Through the Infusion of a Gracious Principle into him, which Restores in him, the Lost image of God, and therewithal inclines him to comply with the Calls of the Gospel.*" [23] The law simply describes the contrite man whose pleasure it is. The man is now what God designed him to be, without any symptom of the "immorigerous" self's rebellion.

But in Mather's morphology of conversion the process does not conclude with this docility. The law gives each person a life to accept fervently. This individuality is a part in a vast plan, an order of the whole. Once acceptance is complete, the heart is infused with submission to divine will, and the mind can follow to a similar union, though this flight of reason will remain vulnerable to the heart's variations: "*Gospel Mysteries, cannot be discerned by an Unregenerate Man. He is, Born Blind, as so he continues, till the New-Birth has once Enlightened him.*" [24] When man acquiesces in holy pattern, he advances into enlightenment, a comprehension of the pattern in which he participates. As Mather wrote in *The Wonderful Works of God Commemorated,* "In our Lower Little World, no Creatures can be found capable of Conceiving and Expressing those Acknowledgements of God, which are, *The Glory due unto his Name,* besides MAN; who is therefore not unjustly called, *The High-priest of the Creation.*" [25] Once self is vanquished and God's particular intentions are accepted without a mite of resentment, the mind can rise to survey the whole of the pattern in which it has accepted its part. It is at once a dependent part and the reason that surveys with wonder the creation that owns it. It can participate in the universality of the divine omniscience:

> Methinks the Children of Men too much Imitate the Spider, when they look after nothing but building a little *House* for themselves, and concern themselves with nothing but the petty Affairs thereof. We should

[22] Mather, *Unum Necessarium,* pp. 11, 13.   [23] Ibid., p. 7.   [24] Ibid., p. 28.
[25] Cotton Mather, *The Wonderful Works of God Commemorated* (Boston, 1690), p. 6. The major premises of this early pamphlet are developed at greater length in *The Christian Philosopher.*

remember that we are Citizens of the WORLD, and as far as we can, we should visit every Corner of it, with our *Praises* to Him, *of whom and for whom is all!* I make no question but that we do in a blessed manner *Antedate* Heaven by doing so. The *Praises* of God are Exhibited in every part of the World, and we forfeit the Privilege of *Reason* if we do not put as many of them as we can into our *Acknowledgements*.[26]

God assigns the man a "little House," a specific and particular function in the creation: but, through a complete subjugation of self to that function, the mind follows the soul to a view of the whole. Mather's terminology – enlightenment, citizen of the world – plainly anticipates the philosophes and recalls the glamor of the great self-fashioners. But for him consciousness attains to this pinnacle through a traumatic devastation and a thorough acceptance of limitation in personal conduct and self-estimation. At the end, it is free and wide ranging, but only after the perception of the error-ridden vacuity of the "I," and after the self's extinction.

Mather had completed a formally satisfying conversion before he was sixteen. But, as David Levin suggests, conversion was less a specific event in his life than a recurring drama:[27] the experience of humiliation and subsequent assurance dominated his emotions for the rest of his life. As Edmund Morgan contends, the American Puritans considered a smug assurance that one had been saved or that one's reason comprehended the nature of things to be a likely sign that one had not been saved.[28] The result was a continuous anxiety that projected the trauma across the entire life of the most acute practitioners, to the deathbed. All enjoyment was tempered with the thought that crisis was imminent, and that competence would be brought low again. Cotton Mather was among the most acute: in his diary, he records humiliations in all years. His favorite place for humiliation was the dust of his study floor; he never raised himself from it once and for all, but always returned. In 1681, during the period of his conversion, he wrote, "Alas, I have the Seed of all Corruption in mee. My Heart naturally departs from God; it is not any Vertue of my own, that keeps mee from the most Enormous Villanies. Oh! *the Plague of my own Heart!*" (*D*, I:30–1). In 1686 he wrote, "I concluded the Day, with considering, *What shall I render to the Lord?* I then gave my *Self,* my whole *Self,* all my powers, Members, Interests, and Capacities, which I owned, was the least that I owned, unto the Lord" (*D*, I:112). In 1696 he wrote:

---

[26] Mather, *The Wonderful Works of God Commemorated*, p. 24.
[27] David Levin, *Cotton Mather: The Young Life of the Lord's Remembrancer* (Cambridge, Mass.: Harvard University Press, 1978), pp. 58–61.
[28] Morgan, *Visible Saints*, pp. 70–1.

> On the Tuesday, I therefore abased myself before the Lord, and that I
> might keep myself under a lasting Abasement, I composed, what I have
> entituled, *The true Picture of Cotton Mather*, wherein I have, with *black*,
> but yett with *true*, Characters, described my own vileness at such a
> Rate, that it cannot bee look'd upon without Horror of Soul; but I
> resolve often to look upon it. (*D*, I:195)

In 1711 he wrote:

> There is nothing of more Consequence to my Safety and Welfare, than
> a constant Strain, of the most self abasing Humility. Wherefore, I would
> constantly chase all vain Thoughts, and Vainglorious Ones out of my
> Mind, with the greatest Abhorrence of them. And if at any Time I
> begin to look upon any of my Circumstances which may carry in them
> any Temptation to Pride, I will presently ballance them with some other
> of my Circumstances (and alas, I have enough of these!) that have suf-
> ficient Humiliations in them. (*D*, II:77)

And in 1718 he wrote:

> And that I might be rendred the more meet for it, I came with the Acts
> of a consenting Soul into the Covenant of God, wherein He becoming
> mine, His ANGELS will be so too. I annihilated myself before the Lord;
> resolving that GOD alone shall be owned, as the Doer of all the Good,
> that is done for me, or by me, and whatever his ANGELS do, about me,
> He alone shall have the Glory of it all. I passed on to the sacrificing
> Stroke, and with the Exercises of the royal Priesthood, I made Sacri-
> fices of all, even my dearest Enjoyments: hoping that the ANGELS
> drawing near to me, would now do wondrously. (*D*, II:522)

In Mather's life, the damnable vigor of the self's free enjoyments and of
its enjoyment of itself was constant and hence required ever-renewed
psychomartial humiliation. Consequently, conversion was for him less a
temporally bounded event than a devastation that should have been always present.

This psychology was also a cosmogony. Divine grace, as Mather argued in his commentary on Genesis in the unpublished *Biblia Americana*,
was the structuring force in the universe, assigning the planets to their
paths and selves to their particular callings. With the exception of man,
each component of the creation observed its proper function automatically. Man, however, has a self, a principle of resistance that provokes
him to swerve from law: self and entropy are synonymous. There is only
one law: but, to borrow a distinction from Kant, the law is *constitutive*
with respect to the other creatures, it merely describes them, as the law
of gravity merely describes the fall of the apple; whereas, with respect to
unconverted men, it is *regulative*, it intends to curb the action and thought
of a being in tense opposition to its intentions.

According to Eusebius, whom Mather admired, this condition characterized the Jews with respect to the Mosaic law. The Mosaic law restrained them, but it did not permeate them: it kept them from murdering, but it did not reform them into men in whom the inclination to murder would never occur. Self, though balked, was still vital, and lurking. For Eusebius, the Christian advance was the rectification of the heart as well as of conduct: Christ made possible the soul's union with the divinity that was the spirit of the law. Rather than being governed by a regulative law, the Christian could aspire to identification with it, to a fusion that would render the law once again constitutive with respect to man, as it had been before Eden, as it always had been with respect to the other creatures. Christ was the fulfiller, not the transgressor, of the law.[29]

This line of argument allowed Eusebius to contend that Christianity perpetuated Judaism but in such a way as to surpass it. Consequently, it was appealing to the English reformers, who challenged not the spirit but the literal formalism of the English Church and who believed that their own situation resembled that of the primitive Christians. Confronting what they considered the punctilious but empty formality of Anglican practice, they conceived the idea of conversion to map the soul's emigration from meticulous rote exercise to quick emotive union. "'Tis only *Self,* that Clay Idol, *Self,*" Mather contended, "which puts this Pharisee upon Shows of *Piety* or *Charity;* and God is not before him."[30] Whereas the converted soul, according to Tyndale,

> shall do of his own inclination all that is required of the law, though
> never law had been given: as all mothers do of them selves without law
> unto their children, all that can be required by any law, love overcom
> ing all pain, grief, tediousness or loathsomeness: and even so no doubt
> if we had continued in our first state of innocency, we should ever have
> fulfilled the law, without compulsion of the law.[31]

According to Milton, "for that the Gospell is the end and fulfilling of the Law, our liberty also from the bondage of the Law I plainly read."[32] The gospel is liberty not because it releases the Christian from the law, but because it permits him to remove the obstinate part of self completely,

---

[29] Eusebius, *The Proof of the Gospel,* ed. and trans. W. J. Ferrar (New York: Macmillan, 1920), pp. 1–62. Similar arguments may be found in his *Evangelical Preparation.*

[30] Mather, *Unum Necessarium,* p. 30.

[31] William Tyndale, "Prologue upon the Gospel of St. Matthew," in *The Works of William Tyndale,* p. 111.

[32] John Milton, *The Reason of Church Government Urg'd against Prelaty,* in *Works* (New York: Columbia University Press, 1931), p. 196.

and so to have the law describe rather than govern him, to "be as it were an invariable Planet of joy and felicity . . ."[33] The psychological conception of conversion was allied with a cosmogony, since it explained what violated the whole and described the means of rectifying the jarred harmony.

For Cotton Mather, conversion and cosmogony were also allied with social theory. He believed that he lived in a society where divine law had been satisfactorily embodied in the social order, that the social order itself was allied with the divine law of which it was a sufficient image. Submission to divinity consequently took the form of submission to magistrate, minister, teacher, and father. In his *Magnalia Christi Americana*, Mather quotes at length, approvingly, from a speech that John Winthrop delivered to the General Court of Deputies in 1645:

> There is a *Liberty* of corrupt Nature, which is affected both by *Men* and *Beasts*, to do what they list; and this Liberty is inconsistent with *Authority*, impatient of all Restraint; by this *Liberty, Sumus Omnes Deteriores;* 'Tis the Grand Enemy of *Truth* and *Peace*, and all the *Ordinances* of God are bent against it. But there is a Civil, a Moral, a Federal *Liberty*, which is the proper End and Object of *Authority*; it is a *Liberty* for that only which is *just* and *good*; for this *Liberty* you are to stand with the hazard of your very *Lives*; and whatsoever Crosses it, is not *Authority*, but a *Distemper* thereof. This *Liberty* is maintained in a way of *Subjection* to *Authority*; and the Authority set over you, will in all *Administrations* for your good be quietly submitted unto, by all but such as have a Disposition to *shake off the Yoke*, and lost their true *Liberty*, by their murmuring at the Honour and Power of *Authority*. (*MCA*, I:127)

The authority of the magistrate, Winthrop went on to say (though Mather stopped his quotation here), is analogous to the authority of God over man and of husband over wife. It is a "sweet yoke" that does not constrain those who are devoid of the apostate inclination to the lower liberty. In a profane community, the authority of God is plainly distinct from social authority, as in the first generation's England, where, according to Roger Williams, the "fathers made the children heretics, and the children the fathers." This divergence legitimates separation. But in his New England, Mather believed, the authority of divinity was adequately extant in the prevailing order.

In this opinion he disagreed with Augustine's belief that divinity was always distinct from the city of man. But Augustine's psychological focus is preserved in Mather's notion that the law must be not simply obeyed, but also accepted as an interior voice at odds with self. Submission to objective social authority was thus a sign of this interior sovereign, rather than an autonomous activity. Consequently, Mather did waver on the

[33] Milton, *The Reason of Church Government*, p. 186.

issue of the civil enforcement of religious questions, especially after the
Salem debacle. Though order had to be maintained, external coercion
could only betoken either a devious insinuation of anti-Christian principles into the body of the law, or else a lapse in pious persuasion in the
community at large. At best, the magistrate and his allies would be a sort
of illustrative redundancy, an emblem of the sovereign fideism enthroned
within. But the historical specificity of the intentions, acts, and maxims
of these emblems mandated that the law Mather had to embody would
be clear, specific, and defined. Virtuousness would not be a general affective disposition, but an exact congruence with an articulated code that
neither required nor permitted creativity in its application. The law demanded exact observance, not only in conduct, but in the recesses of
emotion. The heart must be circumcised; "all that is improper" must be
amputated.[34]

In the series of worldly figures in which divine authority was illustrated, the father was for Mather the key term. In Mather's imagination,
the expression God the Father was never a commonplace or a merely
ornamental figure. Rather, it expressed the most profound analogy in the
whole of creation: it was the fulcrum of creation. In the *Duties of Children
to Their Parents,* he contended that all law emanated from the fifth commandment. If that law were broken, the rest of lawlessness would soon
follow. Consequently, a submissive family is the foundation for social
order: the authority of political, ecclesiastical, and scholastic parents flows
from the authority of the father.[35] A well-disposed family not only con-
tributes to order in any given moment of time, but, according to Mather's father, it perpetuates the continuous coherence of order through
time:

> A new heart shall be given to the house of *Israel,* i.e. the Elect, typified
> by the house of *Israel,* Gal. 6. 16. Now God hath seen good to cast the
> line of Election so, as it doth (though not wholly, and only, yet) for the
> most part, run through the loins of Godly parents . . . And there are
> some Families that the Lord hath chosen above others, and therefore
> poureth his spirit upon the off-spring in such Families successfully.[36]

The line of the sacred persists from Israel to certain modern families,
among them, certainly, the Mathers.

The assertion that the congregation was a vast body was a *topos* in
Puritan thought. In Mather's filiopiety, the family was a single body with
a collective identity, a superior intelligence to which each son was a
member. His task was to submit personal inclination – the self – to the

[34] Mather, *The Wonderful Works of God Commemorated,* p. 11.
[35] Cotton Mather, *A Family Well-Ordered* (Boston, 1699), pp. 45, 3–4.
[36] Increase Mather, *Pray for the Rising Generation* (Boston, 1679), p. 12.

larger dynastic intention, operating without personal purpose, preserving the family's eminent past and projecting it into the future. In his many tracts addressed to parents and children, he associated Adam's having been made in the image of God with the child's having been made in the image of the parent: the parents' word must be law, and the children must see an "awful *Image of God*" in their parents' superiority, and respect them as "the very *Deputies of God*."[37] The submission to pattern outlined in the theory of conversion, therefore, was also a submission to the paternal example (the pun pattern/paternal is at work in the title of Mather's autobiography, *Paterna*). Submission had a double effect: the will of the father was as unquestionable as the will of God and required a complete suppression of self; and the will of God was given an explicit articulation which did not require imaginative explication. Cotton Mather was suspicious of the vagaries of independent will, and his occasional calls for moderation do not severely mitigate his belief that the son must sacrifice self to the father in an acquiescence as profound as Christ's if the order of things was to be preserved. With this fealty, he would discard the self's "distemper of *Authority*" and pass into the larger supertemporal, transcendent, collective personality of the dynasty.

In these passages and the many others like them, Mather is exhorting the reader to an attitude that he sought in himself. His inheritance of the Cotton and Mather mantles gave him considerable prestige, but it also pressured him to demonstrate that his extinction of self was sufficient to entitle him to "the *Inheritance* of the Saints in Light," a phrase that recurs many times in his writings. In his remarks on family, remember, Increase Mather contended that election was cast through the loins of Godly parents *for the most part*: general probability, not certainty, was the best attitude. Membership in such a family could result in arrogance, but such arrogance would always be poised above, and spurred by, the terror of being the exception. In 1678, when Cotton Mather was fifteen, Increase Mather preached *Pray for the Rising Generation*, which included this exhortation:

> Let me exhort Children that are here before the Lord this day: *O do you go home, and pray earnestly for converting Grace.* Beg as for lives that the God of your Fathers would pour his Spirit upon you: Young ones hearken! In the Name of the Lord I speak to you; the Lord can pour his Spirit upon you betimes, then shall you be rich in Grace, let thise promise encourage you to look up to God through Jesus Christ. Go into secret corners, and plead it with God; say, Lord, thou hast promised to pour thy Spirit upon the Off-spring of thy Servants; I am (through thy Grace)

[37] Cotton Mather, *Duties of Children to Their Parents*, printed with "A Family Well-Ordered," p. 60.

among the Children of thy Servants; thou art the God of my Father, the God of my Grand-Father, oh! be my God also. If you seek God in earnest, he will be found of you, but if you forsake him, and breake his convenante sealed in your Baptisme, wo unto you.

The likelihood of holiness is great among the sons and grandsons of New England authority, but the pressure to make good on it is that much greater:

> If you dy and be not first new Creatures, better you had never been born: you will be left without excuse before the Lord, terrible witnesses shall rise up against you at the last day. Your godly Parents will testify against you before the Son of God at that day: and the Ministers of Christ will also be called in as witnesses against you for your condemnation, if you dy in your sins. As for many of you, I have treated with you privately and personally, I have told you, and I do tell you, that if you dy in a Christless, graceless estate, I will most certainly profess unto Jesus Christ at the day of Judgement, Lord, these are the Children, whom I spake often unto in thy Name, publickly and privately, and I told them, that if they did not make to themselves a new heart, and make sure of an interest in Christ, they should become damned creatures for evermore; and yet they would not repent and believe the Gospel. O why should I that can appeal to God, that I long for your Conversion, be your accuser before the Lord Jesus at the last day?[38]

Cotton Mather was a student at Harvard when this sermon was preached, but if he did not hear it, he would certainly have read it when it was printed shortly after. It must have seemed a personalized warning: some hundreds of judges, reluctant to anger, would have been willing to cast the boy off if necessary. His father preached other such sermons during Cotton Mather's adolescence, including the ominously titled *A Discourse Concerning the Danger of APOSTASY, Especially as to those that are the Children and Posterity of such as have been Eminent for God in their Generation* (1677, preached; 1679, printed). Increase Mather was challenging his son to equal his achievement just at the time in the son's life when Cotton was uncertain about what course that life was to take. Free choices were branded apostasies. The son must have felt he was in the presence of divinity itself. In his elegy for Increase, the sixty-year-old Cotton Mather recalled his father's awful power: "He rendred this Pulpit a *Flaming Mountain*, with his Warnings, Yea, with Mighty *Thundrings*, unto *Evil-Doers* of all sorts, to Repent of their *Evil-Doings;* and especially unto *Young People*, betimes to *know and serve the* GOD *of our Fathers.* If you have *sinfully forgotten the Exhortation*, How, How can you answer it!"[39]

---

[38] Increase Mather, *Pray for the Rising Generation*, p. 22.
[39] Cotton Mather, *A Father Departing* (Boston, 1723), p. 28.

Cotton Mather's language recalls the sermons of forty years earlier, and the charge they contained: and he continues to pose the challenge to himself.

In *Pray for the Rising Generation,* the most intimidating moment comes when Increase threatens to chasten his love and join the witnesses against the child. This action would not be in selfish anger: but instead a reluctant bowing to a necessity forced upon him by the miscreant child. But the absence of anger does not mitigate what is terrifying. Like the God of the conversion, the father/minister will turn his face from the child, resigning his role as special support in a forbidding world to join the uniform front of saints arrayed in witness against the child. At numerous points in his diary, Cotton Mather reveals his yearning for a god of unconditional care and love: "And now *my Father* is going to tell me, what He will do for me. *My Father* loves me, and will fill me with His *Love,* and will bring me to everlasting *Life. My Father* will never permit anything to befall me, but what shall be for *His Interest. My Father,* will make me a *chosen Vessel,* to do good in the World" (*D,* I:438). But, as the third and fourth sentences in this passage demonstrate, Cotton Mather had been convinced that the paternal love was rigidly exacting, and abundant only after its conditions had been met: if the son followed self, and so was not simply a receiving vessel for God the Father's intentions for him, the sustaining medium would withdraw, and the self – which is its own punishment – would be left alone in the *tenebrae exteriorae* where there is only bewilderment, vacuity, and the noise of the other damned. The uncircumcised heart – the unamputated self – would be cast out from the city of light, his own father pronouncing the sentence sadly. For Cotton Mather, the fear of being cast out was a deep and prerational terror, so when he deliberated on the most efficacious tool of discipline for use with his children, he chose withdrawal: "I would never come, to give a child a *Blow;* except in Case of *Obstinacy;* or some Gross Enormity. To be chased for a while out of *my Presence,* I would make to be look'd upon, as the sorest Punishment in the Family" (*D,* I:536). And when his son Increase seemed committed to being other than his father's chosen vessel, in 1721, Cotton Mather, wondering what was his "Duty in relation to the incorrigible Prodigal," chose this course: "My miserable son *Increase,* I must cast him and chase him out of my Sight; forbid him to see me, until there appear sensible Marks of Repentance upon him. Nevertheless I will entreat his Grandfather to take Pains for his Recovery" (*D,* II:612). Even the awesome grandfather seems to have failed with the prodigal, however, because one week later Cotton writes: "I will write a tremendous Letter to my wicked Son *Increase;* and after I have sett his Crime in order before his Eyes, I will tell him, that I will never own him or do for

him, or look on him, till the Characters of a Penitent are very conspicuous in him" (D, II:612).

We may take the measure of Cotton Mather's terror of banishment in
a letter he wrote to his father in May 1690, when he was twenty-seven.
In 1688 his father had narrowly eluded the agents of the governor, Sir
Edmund Andros, and he sailed to England to negotiate a new charter at
the court of James II which would restore New England's former liberties. Between the time of Increase Mather's departure and Cotton Mather's letter, the son had seen the publication of his first written works;
he had assisted in the resistance to Episcopal encroachments into Boston;
he had played a substantial part in the bold overthrow of Andros and in
the composition of the eloquent justification of the overthrow, and he
had studied and treated the extravagant symptoms of Martha Goodwin's
demonic possession. By spring 1689, as David Levin contends, Cotton
Mather's independent activity had resulted in the "highest popular recognition and public usefulness of his young life."[40]

But during the same time, Increase Mather failed to secure a complete
return of the old liberties, and he had settled for the best arrangement he
felt possible, the appointment of Sir William Phips as royal governor.
The citizens of New England – many of them, at least – felt that Increase
had compromised them, and this criticism piqued him. In early 1690
Increase, who had left England reluctantly in the 1660s, threatened to
remain. Cotton's response, in the letter, is very telling. He begins with a
bold challenging of the father's touchiness:

> Sir,
>   'Tis not a little trouble unto me to find your so speedy and sudden
> an inclination in you, to such a dishonorable thing as *Your not returning
> to New England* – where you have had such measures of respect and
> esteem, as no person in this part of America ever had before you, and
> where the slights which you have thought cast upon you are but so
> *imaginary*.

At the beginning and end of the sentence, the son finds the father dis-
honorably susceptible to imagined slights and to hasty resolution. He
proposes a higher standard of correct feeling against which his father can
be judged. But beneath this temerity is anxiety: he is troubled by his
father's threat to withdraw, and he protests that New England's filiopiety
has over the years been punctilious.

In the next paragraph save one listing the returns of other agents, this
anxiety comes to the fore:

> This distressed, enfeebled, ruined country have hitherto designed noth-
> ing but your honor; they celebrate you as their *deliverer*, and have all

---

[40] Levin, *Cotton Mather: The Young Life*, p. 172.

along resolved not only the repayment of our debts, which our affairs
in your hands have made, but also such a requital of all your pains to
us, as would have been proper when you should have arrived here, in
the way of receiving it.

New England, like the soul deserted by God, is desolate. Increase had
threatened to turn away his face because he suspected his costs and sti-
pends might not be paid. This pecuniary ingratitude, however, is for the
son only a symptom of a larger issue: New England has failed to repay
its father with the proper esteem and submission, the father has threatened to withhold affection, and New England is devastated. Notice that
"they" and "their" have changed to "us" and "our":

> Perhaps our delays have been imprudent and ungrateful things; but
> place them in a true light and you will see that they have been purely
> necessary. Nor have we forborne to give you and our friends with you,
> those assurances which you ought rather to complain for the miscar-
> rying, than the not-sending of.

Again, he grows bold, proposing a "true light" in which the father's
touchiness should be appraised. However, he persists with the "we," an
incongruous choice, since Cotton Mather was not among those who resented Increase's achievement. The son takes the father's decision personally: this reaction makes no sense, unless the son at some emotional level
suspected that Increase's resentment was directed at the independence the
son had enjoyed during the father's absence. In that case, the drama of
self-assertion, abandonment, and despair would be the depth below the
discussion of charter and monetary remuneration.

The next paragraph brings back the accusatory, challenging mood:

> But have you indeed come to resolutions of seeing New England no
> more? I am sorry for the country, the College, your own church, all
> which languishes for want for you. I am sorry for your family, which
> cannot but be exposed unto miserable inconvenience in transportation.
> I am sorry for myself, who am left alone in the midst of more cares,
> fears, anxieties, than, I believe, any one person in these territories, and
> who have just now been within a few minutes of death by a very dan-
> gerous fever, the relics whereof are yet upon me. But I am sorry for my
> dear father, too, who is *entered into temptation,* and will find snares in his
> resolutions. May the God of Heaven direct you, and prevent every step
> which may not be for the honor of His blessed name!

Cotton Mather represents his state as febrile and weak, rather than stressing the vigor that has characterized the time since they last talked. But
this weakness is in contrast with the boldness of the criticism: from hyperbolical abjectness (he is more anxious than anyone else in the territories) which balances with his father's prestige (Increase is more esteemed

than anyone else in that part of America), Cotton Mather moves toward a reversal; from destitution he rises to moral superiority, his italics echoing the Lord's Prayer in a challenge to the father's maturity. His final prayer is more like what a father would say to a son than vice versa.

But he is dolorous again in the next paragraph:

> I confess that I write with a most ill-boding jealousy that I shall never see you again in this evil world; and it overwhelms me into tears which cannot be dried up, unless by this consideration, That you will shortly find me among the spirits of the just men made perfect.
>
> Your Son,
Cotton Mather[41]

The mixture of assertion and capitulation shows again. He is weak to dying without the father, and unable to continue. However this plea is also a threat: the son, who is assured of his rectitude, will emigrate to death's kingdom if the father emigrates to England. He will turn his face from his father in retribution for his father's touchy self-indulgence.

David Levin has described the ambivalence in this letter: "The most rebellious letter that he ever wrote to his father begs him to come back before it is too late to help his desolate son."[42] Cotton Mather was not among those who had objected to Increase's settlement, so the vague guiltiness that pervades the letter is logically ungrounded. However, he had been successful in independent self-assertion during his father's absence and, even though he had been acting in service to his father's ideals, this independence may be the true reason he fears his father's ire and protests both his fidelity and his weakness. Despite the startlingly rebellious uprisings that implicitly protest that independent action and filiopiety are not incompatible, the letter's conclusion is Mather's lifelong conclusion: as his physical existence will cease without his father's physical presence, so his identity will flourish only in the favor of the paternal will that demands his submission and his amputation of the desire for independence.

The pressure of paternity had shown itself earlier, in Cotton Mather's adolescent stammer. While an undergraduate at Harvard between his eleventh and fifteenth years, he had grown interested in medicine, and considered it as a career. But he chose the ministry, perhaps because dutiful conformity to his father's vocation would testify more clearly to his exact filiopiety. However, he developed a stammer which threatened to interfere with the extensive verbal performance required of a minister. David Levin suspects that the family's vigorous anticipation of the son's

---

[41] Cotton Mather, *Selected Letters,* ed. Kenneth Silverman (Baton Rouge: Louisiana State University Press, 1971), pp. 25–6.

[42] Levin, *Cotton Mather: The Young Life,* p. 183.

ministry had "a choking effect."[43] When Mather writes of this episode in his later life, he tends to represent the stammer as a chastisement, as though the Lord, to teach new rigor, were interfering in his complacency. However, the description of the affliction in his diary, especially the description of the techniques he used to overcome it, suggests that the interference came from self, not God. One does not encounter, bind, and vanquish divine chastisements. The crucial part played by discipline directed against the stammer itself, rather than against the complacency for which it might be a punishment, reveals that Mather felt that the affliction displayed a tension between the words he should say, minister's words, words for the father, and the temptation to speak other words. The normal variety of utterance appeared to him in the form of a contradiction between duty and inclination, and the development of this tension into pathological failure indicates the intensity of the polarization of his consciousness into filiopiety and apostate self. Cotton Mather concluded that he must drive all words but the Father's words from his mouth: the dutiful son was to transcend the neighborhood of self, to scrutinize and govern it with an eye as perspicacious as the Lord's. If he did not do so, God would.

But the other words would not submit. They glutted his tongue, and violated the integrity of his utterance:

> Lord! Thou art Hee that *made man's Mouth!* and thou wast angry with Moses, because hee would not make that consideration, an Argument for *Faith,* that thou wouldest *bee with his Mouth.* And now, because I would not so sin, therefore I trust in thee! Thou dost send *mee* forth, as thou didst *Moses,* in service for thy Name among thy people; and thou who didst make *Mans Mouth* and make *My Mouth,* wilt bee with my Mouth. It was also once used, as a Bottom for Faith, *the Lord hath,* and therefore, *the Lord will.* Now tis a blessed Experience which I have already had of thy Help; yea, such an experience as hath caused mee to promise, *that I would never distrust thee more. Lord,* Thou saist, *None of them who trust in thee shall bee desolate.* But how *desolate* shall I bee, if I am left without *Speech* for thy *Work!* I trust in thee; and therefore it shall not bee. (*D,* I:2–3).

There is consolation in the thought that the great lawgiver suffered from a similar complaint. Mather presents Moses' affliction as a symptom of his obstinacy rather than as a punishment for it: the desert privation has reduced Moses' recalcitrant Egyptian pride to dust; the whole of Moses submits, being a blank tablet on which the Lord will write; but an iota of self remains, so he will need Aaron. God wants both Moses and Mather to speak, and he will allow them to if they can discipline the resistance. The interference comes from elsewhere, from self, so redoubled disci-

---

[43] Ibid., p. 32.

pline, not acquiescence, is in order. Infidelity, not complacent pride, is the culprit. The affliction is the sign of the wayward self's last obstinacy, and so it may be encircled and subdued, as divine acts may not:

II. As to my *Words*.

1. To bee not of many *Words*, and when I do speak, to do it with *Deliberation*.

2. To remember my obligations to use my *Tongue* as the *Lord's*, and not my own; and therefore, to promote *savoury Discourse*, if I can, wherever I come; and to discourse with such as come fairly in my way, about the *Things* of their everlasting *Peace*.

3. Never to answer any *weighty Question*, without lifting up my Heart unto God, in a Request, that Hee would help me to give a *Right Answer*.

4. To *speak Ill of no Man*; except, on a good *Ground*, and for a good *End*.

5. Seldome to make a Visit, without contriving, *what I may do for God, in that Visit*. (D, I:4)

Vigilant surveillance, pondering each sentence in advance and calculating its implications and likely effects, is the answer.

Mather's stammer was terminated by Elijah Corlet, who taught him to "drawl" rather than to speak quickly. Slowing the velocity of utterance down to the rate of vigilant supervision would help him calculate the nature of each sentence in advance. Because the interference is not from God but from self, it may be overcome. Carol Gay indicates the importance of this episode: "The family expected him to become a minister and he shared their hope. But his stuttering threatened to become an insurmountable obstacle." Her survey of modern speech therapy leads to her contention that Corlet's solution was no cure: "Mather's description of his cure, however, sounds more like a description of a masking device, the sign not of a cured stutterer but of a more intensely affected stutterer."[44] Gay contends that the cure was really an enhancement of the pressure that caused the affliction in the first place, and that, though it may have ended the stammer, it probably screwed tension tighter, and may have affected Mather's self-expression for the rest of his life. Mather did not cure the stammer by questioning the rigidity of the tension between what should be said and what wanted to be said, but by intensifying it, by acquiring a device that made his surveillance of the gusts of perverse impulse more adept.

The episode of the stammer, occurring at the beginning of his career and of his diary, serves as a kind of personal Genesis-myth. And it is a Manichean strife rather than an Augustinian creation *ex nihilo*: the ministerial word begins in victory over a now-silenced, aboriginal chaos that,

[44] Carol Gay, "The Fettered Tongue: A Study of the Speech Defect of Cotton Mather," *American Literature*, vol. 46, no. 4 (January 1975), pp. 451, 456.

like the Egyptian Moses, was antithetical to the piety that came to pre-
dominate. Though the primordial matter was largely silenced, the antithesis remained throughout the rest of Cotton Mather's life as an emotional tautness. Though he subdued the speech defect, and though several
of his acquaintances took note of his pleasant manner of speaking, the
tension persisted. In his 1717 diary, for instance, more than forty years
after Corlet's cure, the figure of Moses reappears in connection with the
disciplining of utterance: "O my Soul, Beware lest thy Temptations, (which
are wonderful!) discourage thee, from any suitable Activities in serving
the Kingdome of God, and good Interests. There is extreme Danger of
it! Lett *Moses* also make thee afraid of *speaking unadvisedly with thy Lips*"
(*D*, II:447). In his *Autobiography*, Franklin will record the close scrutiny
he gave his words, and he will call his departures from the elected way
errata, slips of the printer's hand, rather than of the tongue. But Franklin
implies with this figure that his slips are more a negligible carelessness
than revelations of recalcitrant parts of the self. Mather, on the other
hand, concedes that the slips have a center – self.

Augustine demanded that the Christian love the Creator above the
creature, and that the creature be loved as evidence of the Creator. In
many Christian writings, such as Jonathan Edwards's description of Sarah
Pierrepont, this concept is liberating and lovely. However, when the Creator to be loved is believed to be satisfactorily embodied in the specific
will of an authoritarian social code and of a looming father, it can be
oppressive. All enjoyment must be shown to be submissive; all joy in self
must be sacrificed on the altar of paternity; and the activity of varying
and modulating the sense of ought to suit the subtleties of experienced
emotion, if it is more than slight or ornamental, is an apostasy that would
chip away at the persistence of the sacred. Freud contended that the
members of modern society were scarcely aware of the repressions in
their sublimations. This observation cannot be made of Cotton Mather,
who made the holy war on self into the tense and exquisite center of his
writing.

In those moments when Mather felt he had purged all but the bit of
God the Father within himself, he felt an access of power: "My Mind,
and Voice and Strength, is evidently under some special Energy from the
invisible World; and a notable Fervency and Majesty and Powerful pun-
gency setts off my Discourses" (*D*, I:396). This was not self or personal
excellence, but self annihilated and an afflatus from elsewhere. With the
power came universality, the ability to apply this infused divinity to an
undetermined range of tasks – dogma, medicine, natural history, exor-
cism, and political theory, to name just a few. In this, the ministry proved
a happy career choice: in addition to allowing him to duplicate his father,
the ministry permitted Mather to involve himself in and speculate on the

full range of his parishioners' experience – as long as he was sure that the dutiful glorification of God the Father, rather than of an excellent self, was everywhere evident as the controlling purpose. At the end of conversion, after submission, he found a sublimated version of the personalized universality that, according to Peter Gay, was the common aspiration of Renaissance and Enlightenment.[45] But unlike Pico della Mirandola before him and Benjamin Franklin after, Mather did not believe that this achievement could be an immediate attribute of a harmonious self. Instead, such magnificence was God's, and could come to man only after the agony and from the wreckage of the gratefully crucified self.

[45] Peter Gay, *The Enlightenment: The Rise of Modern Paganism* (New York: Knopf, 1966), p. 267.

2

COTTON MATHER'S
WORK

Children, you set light by your Parents, if you don't *Requite* them, as
well as you can, and if you imagine that you can ever Requite them
enough.

Cotton Mather, *Duties of Children to Their Parents*

To be satisfying, work must be based on a secure epistemology. One
must feel that he knows what is needed of his talents; and the work must
cause him to feel that he has done well, that his character has achieved
sufficient expression in the action of remedying a need. To be satisfied in
work, he must believe he reads signs correctly, and that his deed is a
reliable sign of himself. The Puritan opposition to complacency and Arminianism complicated both of these requirements for satisfaction in work:
one had to work for the glorification of God, but the obscurity of God's
intentions kept him from knowing whether he was pursuing the right
course, or falling victim to a demonic monition; and the image of himself
generated in the deed bore no necessary relation to his spiritual estate,
since a seeming pious hypocrisy was easy and common. An epistemology that concentrated on uncertainty resulted in constant frustrations of
satisfaction.

The consequence of frustration might have been quietism or resignation were it not for the doctrine of the Covenant: Mather's god, for the
sake of his Elect, had condescended to objectify himself in apprehensible
signs, so that provisional insight was possible, if only approximate or
probable. Were the evidences of divinity either completely obscure or
completely lucid, there could be either resignation or confidence. But
the worldly media in which God expressed himself were variably ex-
pressive: there was a sure relation between the sign and the founding
intention of the covenant god, but human understanding could not discern it completely. Insight was, however, accurate enough that fathers,
masters, husbands, ministers, teachers, and magistrates could count

themselves divine trustees in their dealings with their respective depen-
dents, but to claim certainty was to reduce magnificent divinity to the
measure of sin-blighted man. Even among the most precisely contrite,
the approach to knowledge was asymptotic. Consequently, American
Puritanism is not so much a distinct epistemological position as it is a
field of tension between assurance and despair.

The entire field is reproduced in Cotton Mather's intellectual and emotional life, which oscillated between extremes of despair and of what
seems to be unparalleled egotism, but which Mather called victorious
self-annihilation. In the midst of profound dejection, he finds himself
called back to the task; in the midst of assertion, clarity crumbles and he
is lost. The resurrection of clarity is never strong enough to dispel dejection; but neither is the recurrence of dejection strong enough to allow
resignation, so work is interminable. Given this predicament, which leads
to an astonishing productivity, it is no surprise that Mather should have
spent a great deal of his time determining the extent to which signs *can*
be understood and explaining the origin and nature of the limit of understanding.

Satisfaction with the nature and the outcome of work is always complicated. Puritanism made this complication into a matter of explicit
principle, rather than divesting work of meaning completely. Luther argued that "good works do not make the good man, but the good man
does good works." In *The Old Paths Restored,* Mather agreed: "*Good Works*
are the *Fruit & Proof,* but not the *Cause* of his *Justification.*" A few pages
later, he adds "*Good Works* follow after Justification; and tho' they cannot
endure the *Severity* of Gods Judgements, yet they are *Acceptable* to God
and Christ, and they necessarily spring out of a *Lively Faith,* insomuch
that by them a Lively Faith may be evidently known, as a *Tree* discerned
by the *Fruits.*"[1] Mather's image is taken from the book of Matthew: "Even
so every good tree bringeth forth good fruit; but a corrupt tree bringeth
forth evil fruit." (7:17, also Luke 6:43) The fruit reveals but does not
cause the goodness of the tree. Even in *Bonifacius,* Mather's most renowned and extended treatise on good work, he is careful to claim that,
though good works are an essential part of the complete Christian, they
must follow from conversion: "The very *first-born* of all *devices* to *do good,*
is in being born again, and in *devising means, that a banished* soul may no
longer be *expelled* from the presence of God" (*B*:22). As in the writings
on conversion, the cure for banishment is self-annihilation: "Let the sense
of this cause us to *loathe* and *judge* ourselves before the Lord: let it fill us
with shame and abase us wonderfully!" (*B*:22). Works that do not pro-

---

[1] Cotton Mather, *The Old Paths Restored: The Apostasy of Innovation* (Boston,
1711), pp. 3, 7.

ceed from the abased self are *"dead works"* comparable to the literal observance of the Mosaic law among the Jews rather than the identification
with the law among the early Christians (B:27, 28).

To a pragmatist, the assertion that works signify rather than cause election would make little real difference. However, we must remember the
Puritan belief in the partial unreliability of signs. A hypocrite who feigns
goodness generates a sign – his works – that does not correspond with
the truth – his reprobate heart, and he may even deceive himself:

> There may be many savory *Frames* in an Unregenerate man, and mighty
> pangs of Mourning and Fearing, and Joying, and Hoping, about the
> Affairs of the Eternal World; yea, and he may continue in these his
> Frames all his days, and be in some sort of a *Religious* man, to his Dying
> Day. All this a man may do, and be but a Pharisee after all.[2]

The suspicion of hypocrisy – of literal but faithless observance – has an
important effect: though mischief would clearly signal reprobation, since
there would be no good reason to feign it, good works would not necessarily signify election. Consequently, the least slip would carry great
importance, and require vast amounts of good-doing to counterweight
it; in fact, no amount of good-doing would suffice for an exact observer.
As a result, the slightest suspicion of turpitude could cause enormous
edifices of good-doing to crumble, and it would provoke the construction of more and more enormous good-doing to compensate for it.

In Mather's scruple-shop, turpitude might be revealed by the failure *of*
good works as well as by the failure *to do* good works. His father had
contended that election probably ran through the loins of eminent families, but that it did not do so necessarily. We may detect the fear of being
the apostate exception at several points in Mather's writing: "what tho'
you are Descended of *Parents* that were the Favourites of Heaven? The
Jews bragg'd, *We have Abraham for our Father!* but our Lord could reply
upon them, *You are of your Father* the *Devil.*"[3] Mather never seems to have
doubted that his New England forebears were of the Elect, and that their
election was signified in their successful pastoral supervision of New
England piety, a victory he celebrates at great length in the *Magnalia
Christi Americana*. His failure to inspire a similar collective piety, therefore, might prove that his pastoral performance was merely rote, that it

[2] Cotton Mather, quoted in Richard F. Lovelace, *The American Pietism of Cotton
Mather: Origins of American Evangelicalism* (Grand Rapids, Mich.: Christian
University Press, 1979), p. 100. The same point is made in Mather's *The Armour of Christianity* (Boston, 1704), p. 102: "One Wile with which the Devil
hinders the Conversion of the Unregenerate, is, *By perswading the Unconverted,
that they are already and really converted.*" And p. 104: "*All is not Gold that Glitters;
and every seeming Conversion is not a sincere Conversion.*"
[3] Cotton Mather, *Unum Necessarium* (Boston, 1693), p. 60.

contained a halfheartedness or disinterest that showed itself in the flaccidity of his works' effect.

This fear would have redoubled his resolution to do more. Since good works, even when successful, would not signify clearly the *quality* of his soul, Mather seems to have been driven to seek some partial comfort in *quantity:* the greater the number of works and the amount of energy that goes into them, and the greater the resultant success in conversion of others to piety, the more probable his election would be. Quantitative performance is central to Mather's conception of his work. In his diary he resolves to write a book a month, and though many of his books are pamphlets or monographs, the total is nonetheless daunting. His longest work, the *Biblia Americana,* was to have been the *organon* of the whole *oeuvre,* but it was not published, and the six thousand pages of manuscript remain in the closed stacks of the Massachusetts Historical Society (though several American libraries have microfilm copies). This impulse to quantitative performance is evident in his description of the *Biblia Americana* in the "General Introduction" to the *Magnalia Christi Americana:*

> I considered, That all sort of *Learning* might be made gloriously Subservient unto the *Illustration* of the *Sacred Scripture;* and that *no professed Commentaries* had hitherto given a thousandth part of so much *Illustration,* as might be given . . . And I consider'd, That the *Treasures* of *Illustration* for the Bible, dispers'd in many many hundred Volumes, might be fetch'd all together by a Labour that would resolve to *Conquer all things;* and that all the *Improvements* which the *Later-ages* have made in the *Sciences,* might be also, with an inexpressible Pleasure, call'd in, to Assist the *Illustration* of the *Holy Oracles,* at a Rate that hath not been attempted in the vulgar Annotations . . . Certainly, it will not be ungrateful unto good Men . . . To have in *One Heap,* Thousands of those *Remarkable Discoveries of the deep things of the Spirit of God,* whereof *one* or *two,* or a few, sometimes, have been, with good Success accounted Materials enough to advance a Person into *Authorism . . . (MCA,* I:33)

Mather was widely read, and proud of the fact that he had the largest library in the New World, so that he was certainly aware of the magnitude of his ambition. His object, however, is not originality, since this is a "collection" or "heap" of materials already extant, a place where the "Giants of Knowledge" are "all set upon one Table" (*MCA,* I:33). Nor does he intend to surpass the past, really, but to offer the likelihood of election demonstrated in his huge labor in place of impossible certitude.

His aim as author was to instigate pious conversions. As minister, he worked throughout his life to accomplish conversions in Boston and in New England generally. But the extent of his writing and the diversity of topic reveal that his aim was larger: "The world has according to the computation of some, above seven hundreds of millions of people now living in it. What an ample field among all these, to *do good* upon! In a word, *the kingdom of God* in the world calls for innumerable *services* from us" (B:17). In the execution of these services, Mather acquired a correspondence that included English ministers and philosophers and German Pietists: Kenneth Silverman reports that he found Mather's letters in twenty-one different countries, and he contends that the correspondence, like the published work, demonstrates Mather's dedication to composing what he called "Libri Elephantini."[4] Mather wrote pamphlets for the conversion of Indians, Blacks, Jews, Catholics, mariners, farmers, soldiers, and those soon to be executed. He kept in touch with what he thought were the motions of reformation in England, France, and Turkey, and he wrote pamphlets such as *Une Grande Voix du Ciel à la France* (Boston, 1724) to expedite the chiliad. Though his chiliasm varied in intensity, it played a part in his thought throughout his life, and he envisioned his role to be not passive attendance but active catalyzation:

> Wherefore I now lamented before the Lord, the *Privateness* and *Selfishness* of Spirit, which in my former Devotion had attended mee; and I resolved, that I, as poor and as vile, as I am, would now become a *Remembrancer* unto the Lord, for no less than whole *Peoples, Nations,* and *Kingdomes.* I apprehended with myself that if I would thus lay to Heart the *Concerns* of the Lord Jesus Christ, and the State of whole Peoples, and continue, with extraordinary Supplications crying to Heaven, for mercy to them, I should be more *Angelically* disposed and employed, than I have been heretofore; and that I should prepare myself also for more *extensive Services* to bee done by mee; and I should enjoy unutterable Communications from the Holy Ghost then Delighting in mee; yea, and perhaps, *Manifestations* of what the Lord *is going to do in the Earth.* (D, I:199–200)

As Richard F. Lovelace argues, his resolution culminates in an ecumenical and evangelical spirit quite distant from the precise discrimination of Elect from Reprobate characteristic of earlier New England.[5] But if in its effect Mather's resolution was more liberal, it was not in its motivation: as the passage above suggests, Mather was prompted to such ambitious "extensive Services" by his need to demonstrate the success of the self-sacrificing stroke. This is arch-Calvinism screwed to its tightest.

To appeal to such a scope of humanity, Mather's devout intelligence would have to transcend intrinsic attachment to any particular part of the human scope and demonstrate instead a universal range. In Pico's de-

---

[4] Kenneth Silverman, introduction to Cotton Mather, *Selected Letters* (Baton Rouge: Louisiana State University Press, 1971), pp. ix–xx.
[5] Lovelace, *The American Pietism of Cotton Mather.* This is one of the major theses of Lovelace's book, and so it appears throughout.

scription of the dignity of man, *each* of the arts mastered by free intelligence is a practical achievement that testifies to its unique excellence: but
for Mather, as for Franklin after him, the universality is itself practical,
since it belongs to a personality that can bring coherence out of social
disparity. According to Mather's grandfather, John Cotton, the variety
of particular callings among men was a part of the same great law that
distributed variety of function among all the creatures. One's calling revealed the essential particularity that God had made as his nature: "Another thing to make a calling warrantable is, when God gives a man gifts
for it, he is acquainted with the mystery of it and hath gifts of body and
mind suitable for it."[6] The particular calling exhibits the specific gist of
one's personality: "The mind of man, as Philosophers have observed, is
somewhat assimilated into the nature of the Object which it studieth,
and is conversant about: as Mariners who are conversant about winds,
and seas, and storms are more boysterous. Shepherds and Herds-men
more brutish, Forresters more wild, Butchers more bloody."[7] This is an
extremely conservative doctrine meant to preserve station and degree
and to restrain restless mobility. To the generations of Americans who
have subscribed to the concept of the self-made man, it would be an
offensive dogma: from Cotton's perspective, however, such resentful
restlessness would be evidence of what Winthrop called natural liberty,
of the apostate self that wishes to be its own law and to define its own
cosmos.

Among the particular callings, ministry is an exception, a public particular calling: the "Object it studieth" is the trace of God in man, and if
the minister is "somewhat assimilated" to this trace, it will show a universality that transcends the particularities of its flock. The minister's
particular calling is to understand the goodness of the entire array of
particular callings and to be able to address each of them in a manner
suited to it. John Cotton himself, according to his grandson, was "a most
universal scholar, and a *living system* of the liberal arts, and a *walking library*" (*MCA*, I:273). This was not a particular talent, but a condensation
of mankind in one man:

> If it were a comparison sometimes made of the reformers, Pomeranus
> was a grammarian, Justus Jonas was an orator, Melancthon was a logi-
> cian, but Luther was *all*: even that proportion, it may without envy be
> acknowledged, that Cotton bore to the rest of our New-English di-
> vines; he that, whilst he was living, had this vertue extraordinarily con-
> spicuous in him, "that it was his delight always to acknowledge the gifts

[6] John Cotton, *The Way of Life* (London, 1641), pp. 104–5.
[7] John Cotton, quoted in Larzer Ziff, *The Career of John Cotton: Puritanism and
the American Experience* (Princeton, N.J.: Princeton University Press, 1962),
p. 12.

of God in other men," must, now he is dead, have other men to acknowledge of him what Erasmus does of Jerom, *In hoc uno conjunctum,
fuit et Eximium, quicquid in aliis partim admiratur* [in him were combined
all the excellences which we admire separately and singly in other men].
(*MCA*, II:253)

Such magnificence was required by the public particular calling. In his
Manuductio ad Ministerium, Mather told young ministers that they would
have to address parishioners of all conditions, and so he required them
to study theology, ancient and modern languages, logic, ethics, poetry,
natural philosophy, mathematics, judicial astrology, geography, history,
and music. The purpose of wide learning was not to demonstrate the
individual's excellence, but to free his thought of any provinciality that
might interfere with universal application.

This advice also appears in his chapter for ministers in *Bonifacius:*

It is needful, that you study the *condition* of your flocks; and bring them
such *truths*, as will notably *suit* their present circumstances. In order to
this, you will observe their *condition*, their faults, their snares, their griefs,
that you may *speak a word in season;* and if anything remarkable fall out,
you will suit the *words* to the *works* of God. You may divide your people
into *classes;* and think, what lessons of piety you are to dispense, unto
the *communicants;* what, unto all that are under the *bonds of the Covenant;*
what, unto the *aged;* what unto the *worldly;* what unto the *rich;* what
unto the *poor;* what unto them that are in *offices;* what unto them that
are under such, and such *afflictions;* what in regard of people's *personal
callings.* Above all, the *young* must not be forgotten: you will employ
all the *tunes* imaginable, to raise *early piety.* (*B:*72)

The minister will employ "all the tunes imaginable" as an author, too:

The *Tradesman's Library* needs to be more enriched. We have seen *Hus-
bandry Spiritualized;* and, *Shepherdy Spiritualized;* and, *Navigation Spiritualized;* we have seen, the *weaver* also accommodated, with agreeable
meditations. To spread the *nets of salvation* for men, in the ways of their
personal callings, and convey good thoughts unto them, in the *terms* and
steps, of their daily business, is a real service to the interests of piety.
(*B:*140–1)

The minister is "high Priest of the Creation": his charisma flows from
the fact that through him divine intentions are made manifest to all the
particular conditions and that in him the diversity of man is collected
into a universal *summa.*

Cotton Mather expresses his aspiration to such universal ability at many
points in his writings. In his diary he wrote, "I must again come to
consider distinctly the several Tribes and Sorts of People in my Flock,
and have my more explicit Contrivances ready for them" (*D*, II:528). He
expresses the aspiration figuratively in *The Christian Philosopher:* "But

sometimes the *Uses* of one *single Plant* are so many, so various, that a
wise Man can scarce behold it without some *Emulation* as well as *Admiration,* or without some wishing, that if a Metamorphosis were to befal
him, it might be into one of these" (*CP*:132). The same figure appears in
Bonifacius: "Of all the *trees in the garden of God;* which is there, that envies
not the *palm-tree,* out of which alone *Plutarch* tells us, the *Babylonians*
fetched more than three hundred commodities? Or the *cocoa-tree,* so ben-
eficial to man, that a vessel may be built, and rigged, and freighted and
victualled from that alone?" (*B*:8). In both *Bonifacius* and the "General
Introduction" to the *Magnalia Christi Americana* he compares himself to
the hundred-handed Briareus of Greek mythology, and in the latter he
promises that "(m)y reader will not find in me the Person intended in his
Littany, when he says, *Libera me ab homium unius Negotis* [deliver me from
a man of but one interest]" (*MCA*, I:32). Instead, he would "'love the
public, . . . study an universal good, and . . . promote the interest of the
whole world" (*B*:19). It is no wonder that Mather was stung when he
read (among other slanders) in the *New England Courant* that ministry
was only one among the many professions, and that ministers should
therefore abstain from statements of opinion about matters such as government or medicine.[8] This position directly controverted what he found
to be the vigor of ministry – a freedom from the specific forms of man
that allowed him to range over the whole and address each part specifically. His intelligence was to be versatile, general, and universal: surpassing intrinsic attachment to any one or several of the kinds of human
formation, it could address all of them.

But ministry was nonetheless a particular calling, and it was his father's
particular calling: though he could range over the entirety of human formation, his purpose in doing so was always to cultivate a self-annihilating
piety before the god of the fathers rather than to exercise speculative
secular interest or to demonstrate a free, loquacious, cheerful intelligence. The reason for addressing all the conditions of man was not to
exhibit the common reasonableness, but to induce the self-sacrificing stroke
that would level the pride of the men addressed. In the *Manuductio ad
Ministerium,* Mather told the young ministers that they had to learn the
"Universal Discipline" of self-annihilation before God the Father before
they could proceed to acquaintance with the "various *Tongues* and *Arts,*"
and that they must keep this discipline constantly at the front of their
thought: "Take a *proper season* for it, and *My Son,* the *present season;* I say,
Immediately! Therein, First, *Humbly* and indeed, *Lying in the Dust,* own

---

[8] *The New England Courant: A Selection of Certain Issues containing the Writings of
Benjamin Franklin* (Boston: American Academy of Arts and Sciences, 1956),
n.p. Issue no. 18.

your self unable to do any thing effectually of your self in *changing* of your Heart, and bringing your Soul to be *informed* and *affected* as it ought to be."[9] Whereas the self might aspire to a kind of spurious universality by denying that divinity has limited its excellence to a particular calling, piety amputates this ambition, submits selflessly, and receives the infusion of a universality that is the intellectual consequence of the heart's union with God. Should universality lapse into mere secular dexterity, it went apostate. In *Bonifacius,* he admires the universality of doctors: "*Physicians* often are *Men universally learned.* They have *treasure* enough, and sometimes *leisure* enough to write BOOKS, on a vast variety of subjects, whereby *knowledge* and *virtue* may be greatly advanced in the world" (*B:*100). He finds the same thing to admire among lawyers: "Your learning often qualifies you to *write excellent things,* not only in your own profession, but also on all the edifying themes in the world. The books that have been written by learned *lawyers,* would for number almost equal an *Alexandrian* library" (*B:*130–1). In both cases, however, Mather is careful to urge that this excellence must be subjugated by piety: it must proceed from self-annihilation and tend to encourage a selfless assent in the reader.

Once the minister has curbed self and received the infusion of a universal talent for disseminating piety, he can watch that talent take effect among his parishioners who head for conversion: "Your *Circles* will grow wider and wider; and anon expand unto Dimensions beyond what you could at first have imagined."[10] Here again Mather is concentrating on the *quantity* of communicants he can bring in as testimony to his own piety in place of the impossible certitude. The concept of numerically expansive influence predominates in this passage from *Bonifacius:*

> Behold, how *great a matter a little* of this heavenly *fire* may kindle! Five or six gentlemen in *London,* began with an heroic resolution, and association, to counter the torrent of wickedness, which was carrying all before it in the nation. Many were soon added unto them; and though they met with great opposition, from *wicked spirits,* and these *incarnate* as well as *invisible,* and some in *high places* too, yet they proceeded with a most honorable and invincible courage. Their *success,* if not proportionable to their *courage,* yet was far from *contemptible.* In the punishments inflicted on them who transgressed the laws of *good morality,* there were soon offered many thousands of *sacrifices,* unto the holiness of GOD. Hundreds of *houses* which were the *chambers* of Hell, and the *scandals* of earth, were soon extinguished. There was a remarkable check soon given to raging *profanity;* and the Lord's Day was not openly and horribly profaned as formerly. And among other *essays to do good,* they scattered thousands of *good books,* that had a tendency to reform the evil

---

[9] Cotton Mather, *Manuductio ad Ministerium* (Boston, 1726), pp. 8, 16.
[10] Ibid., p. 23.

manners of the people. It was not long before this excellent example was followed in other parts of the *British* Empire. Virtuous men of diverse qualities and persuasions, became the members of the *societies;* persons high and low, Con and Noncon, united; the union became formidable to the Kingdom of Darkness. The report of the *societies* flew over the seas; the pattern was followed in other countries; men of wisdom in remote parts of *Europe* have made their joyful remark upon them, *that they cause unspeakable good, and annunciate a more illustrious state of the Church of God, which is to be expected, in the conversion of Jews and gentiles.* America too, begins to be irradiated with them! (B:132–3)

The guiding metaphor in this passage is fire: the spirit is irresistibly inflaming, and a small spark soon ignites a conflagration of zeal across the known world that annihilates the differences between those who are ignited. The important things to note in this passage are Mather's emphases on quantitative accretion and on the annihilation of qualitative difference.

The metaphor of conflagration is compatible with the use of capital investment as a metaphor throughout *Bonifacius*. As a small spark can lead to a universal flame that burns off differences of heart, so a single dollar, as Franklin would say, can swell toward universal wealth if it is wisely invested. In both cases, the difference between the beginning and the end of the process is a difference of magnitude – the spark and the conflagration, the dollar and the fortune – and the nature of the process is the conversion of difference into uniformity – things into fires, commodities into sums of money. In his address to rich men, Mather urges that they not, like the Moguls of Hindustan, bury their gold, but instead invest it, put it in circulation (B:116–17). This call to investment is metaphoric: actual capital investment in search of profit would be a failure to invest the money in the spiritual growth of the community. As he had argued earlier, preoccupation with one's fortune is a way of turning from godliness (B:23). But the impious pursuit of wealth is suitable for figural improvement as a metaphor for piety: the things of the world may not be loved for themselves, but they may be loved as figures of higher things. So the danger of capital investment can be used as an illustration of investment in the community's goodness. At the end of the essay to rich men Mather extends the metaphor, urging them not to "bury their parts and gifts" (B:119), thus amplifying the buried Mogul gold into a figure for any talent that can be invested in an essay to do good. (Mather again associated the buried Mogul gold with uninvested talent in a 1712 letter to Dr. John Woodward, which is included in Kenneth Silverman's *Selected Letters of Cotton Mather.* This recurrence suggests that his use of money as a metaphor for personal capacity in *Bonifacius* was deliberate and, in his mind, important.) This metaphorical investment of metaphorical

money will not pay a dividend in the sense of yielding thanks or acclaim
to the investor's self: as long as selfishness is the prime motive, the investor will have to "*lend, hoping for nothing again*" (B:61). But once he realizes that the metaphorical money he is investing is the godliness within
him, not self, and that the return is a larger godliness in the human community, and not thanks or acclaim for his personal excellence, he will
receive his "*recompense*" and "*be enriched*" (B:20). Mather's use of capital
investment in *Bonifacius* is not what vulgar Marxism would call an unconscious reflection: rather, as in Emerson's concept of compensation, it
is a figural borrowing of properties from a potentially antispiritual process to illustrate a spiritual one.

As metaphors, conflagration and capital investment illustrate the two
effects Mather felt his work in the community of man would need to
have if it were to be judged successful – quantitative accretion and the
conversion of difference into unanimity. He did not seek a rigid identity
among men in all things, since the law stipulated a variety of particular
talents and callings. But he did seek a unanimity of heart based on a
common acceptance of and admiration for a superior law. Self-annihilation,
the key concept in Mather's psychology and private introspection, was
also the center of his social theory. The self's resentment of law could
show itself in different forms of varying degrees of extravagance: the
benign hypocrite, who acted piety but whose heart was untouched; the
bourgeois Arminian, who felt that his prosperity was proof of his election; the man who labored diligently at his calling but did not believe
that he was attending to a subordinate function in a vast plan, but instead
furnishing a discrete and whole personal world; the egoist, who felt that
his talent was proof of a personal excellence rather than of divine generosity; the self-fashioner, who resented the idea that he was innately bound
to a particular nature and a particular station in the order of things; the
diabolical hypocrite, who cloaked unholy intentions in a punctilious but
completely void literal piety; and the openly profligate: "There are knotts
of riotous Young Men in the Town. On purpose to insult Piety, they will
come under my Window in the Middle of the Night, and sing profane
and filthy Songs" (D, II:216–17). The common root of all these is self
that has not been sacrificed in a pure submission to the law of the fathers.

Once a general sacrifice of this nature was instigated in the human
community, the group would experience affective consensus while retaining the variety of their talents. The first duty of church elders, Mather
wrote in *Bonifacius,* was "to prevent the rise of strife, or of any sin"
(B:120), and the two are nearly synonymous, with self being an unnamed third. In **Brethren Dwelling Together in Unity**, he concedes that
there are differences among men and even that there are tolerable differences among precise definitions of the nature of godliness: the persecu-

tion of dissent in seventeenth-century New England, he admits, was an unhappy way to secure consensus. The tolerant tone that pervades the early pages of the pamphlet may be viewed as rhetorical judiciousness, since Brethren *Dwelling Together in* Unity was originally a sermon preached at a pastoral ordination in a Boston Baptist church. The genial latitude, however, disappears after the first few pages, when Mather comes to contend that such toleration does not include diversity of opinion about piety and utter submission. All damnable heresies must be abandoned, and "(a) Man who maintains *Errors,* that will prove mortal unto *Real* PIETY, must be treated by Good Men at that rate, Tit. III, 10. *After the first and second Admonition, Reject him.*" Toleration cannot extend to include the violation of purity. Premier among the mortal dangers is close and intense attachment to particularities that go contrary to, rather than cooperating in, the whole: "My Friend, Thy *Disputation* is but a *Litigious* Business and must be thrown among the *Works of the Flesh,* if a concern for PIETY be not the Thing that animates it." In a vital human group, all "Coalesce in the *Uniting Maxims* of PIETY."[11] The immediate result of a true submission of self to God was union among those who submitted, since self was the sole source of major discord.

His own self-annihilating piety, Mather believed, made him a useful vehicle for curing discord, because the universality it gave him allowed him to address men in all their conditions: "I am very much a Stranger to the clashing of particular Interests, and I have none of them to serve"; "one of the best Things that can be done for my poor Countrey is, to extinguish as far as tis possible, that cursed, and senseless Party-Spirit, which is now among us, in a most abominable Operation"; "there is an unhappy Discord, between some; for the Curing whereof, I would use all exquisite Methods of Prudence and Goodness" (*D, II*:419, 515, 555). Mather here shows his conviction that the discipline that lifts consciousness to universality can pay off in social consensus, a connection of psychology and social theory that also underlies what John Adams begrudgingly admired in Franklin:

> Franklin had a great genius, original, sagacious and inventive, capable of discoveries in science no less than of improvements in the fine arts and the mechanic arts. He had a vast imagination, equal to the comprehension of the greatest objects, and capable of a steady and cool comprehension of them.

As a result, his reputation

> was more universal than that of Leibniz or Newton, Frederick or Voltaire and his character was more beloved and esteemed than that of any

---

[11] Cotton Mather, **Brethren** *Dwelling Together in* **Unity**: *The True Basis for an Union among the People of God* (Boston, 1718), pp. 4, 18, 22, 25, 38–9.

of them . . . There was scarcely a peasant or a citizen, a valet de chambre, coachman or footman, a lady's chambermaid or a scullion who was not familiar with [his name], and who did not consider him as a friend to human kind. When they spoke of him they seemed to think he was to restore the Golden Age.[12]

The differences are plain, but they are modifications or revisions of the connection between universality and collective human wholeness that were already laid out in the work of Cotton Mather, from whom Franklin learned it.

All of Mather's inquiries into the universal range of topics to which he had access were disciplined to the glorification of the god of the fathers; and he was not friendly and congenial with men as they were, since the condition for joining him in consensus was a self-annihilating stroke comparable to his own. In an age convincing itself that progress toward collective secular happiness was more important than the advance of an austere godliness, and that the self was an orderly, legitimate, and productive entity that built society rather than eroding it, Mather's mode of conceiving the juncture between personal universality and social coherence was doomed to eventual eclipse, though this social development did not mean the palpable demise of Mather's power and prestige during his lifetime.

Mather viewed this new ideology as a deceiving simulacrum of true piety, as an idolatry among "People who terminate in Man, and sett man up in the Throne of GOD" (D, II:444). Though such people were not given to obvious impiety, obvious impiety was only an extreme manifestation of the fall from tense submission that they shared with it: Satan was adept at cloaking blasphemy in reasonableness, and obvious impiety had the advantage of candor and clarity. Diabolism and Enlightenment were related at the root: both were symptoms of what Mather labeled *declension,* of the quantitative *diminution* of rigorous self-sacrificing piety and of rising discord between the fallen-away and the diminishing number who remained. The lamentation of declension and the jeremiads that deplore it, begun in Increase Mather's sermons in the 1660s, are regular themes in Cotton Mather's writings from the first, but they reach levels of extreme bitterness and suppressed anger in the eighteenth-century diaries and tracts.

The diminution of piety did not, however, convince Mather that his piety was secretly halfhearted, and that he therefore fell short of his forefathers' eminence. Rather, though it balked and vexed him, it actually provided relief from self-doubt, because it allowed him to project the

[12] John Adams, quoted in Henry Steele Commager, *The Empire of Reason* (New York: Oxford University Press, 1977), pp. 252–3, 21.

inner tension between filiopiety and self outward as a tension between Cotton Mather and the tendency of the age, a projection that exonerated him by making him a pure agonist in the fight for the holy rather than a divided being imperfectly devoted to the bit of God within him. The declension converted him from the apostate scion to the Lord's Remembrancer: it allowed him to defer doubt about self and to treat his own conversion as an accomplished fact in striking contrast with the reprobation of the surrounding world. The satisfaction provided by this act of projection shows at several points in his diary. Though many of the entries lament his loathsomeness, those entries that record accusations made by others are completely free of self-doubt:

> I am especially sensible of the Divine Favour to mee in preserving for mee, *an unblemished Reputation*. I perceive myself by some Circumstances rendred so obnoxious to raging Envy, that if any *true* thing might be reported unto my Prejudice, or, if any *false* Thing might be invented, that would bee likely to stick upon mee, my Reputation would immediately find those that would ruine it. (*D*, I:319)

The argument here is not that the adversaries have failed to find the sinful self hypocritically concealed behind the works of piety. Rather, whenever external apostasy accuses him, his own self-accusation disappears:

> I acknowledged myself to bee *viler* before Him, than any of my causeless and cruel Adversaries could make mee, when they reviled mee. And I gave exceeding Thanks unto Him, for His praeserving mee, from the Unhappiness of being made obnoxious to their Malice, by any *real Blemish*, whereof if they could gett the least Notice, how wonderfully would they aggravate it! (*D*, I:338)

This passage reveals with special clarity the process of converting his inner tension between duty and inclination into the outer tension between himself and his adversaries: from the necessary confession of his selfishness, he moves quickly to the assertion that there is no real blemish, and that all contrary claims are slanders. Again, the two are logically compatible, since he might mean that his conduct is pure, and that the adversaries have no access to the true blasphemy only the Lord sees. But this logical compatability disguises the radically different emotional modes involved: on the one hand, a constraining panic at the thought of the self's monstrosity and of banishment from light; on the other, an unequivocal and unitary assertion of personal rectitude against the monsters engendered in the outside world. In their "unending efforts to feel at peace," according to Phillip Greven, many evangelicals became such "soldiers for Christ":

> The persistent feeling expressed by many evangelicals that other people were dangerous and aggressive, were intent upon doing harm to either their bodies or souls, could in extreme instances become a paranoid

vision of the outer world – a vision undoubtedly rooted in the denial of anger and the projection of inadmissible feelings within the self upon other people outside and beyond the self. Wherever evangelicals looked, they saw people who seemed to them to be the enemies of God's will and ways – and thus the enemies of themselves as well. Consequently, by becoming soldiers for Christ and warring against the unregenerated people of the world, evangelicals often demonstrated a remarkable capacity for vigorous and sustained aggressiveness in the outer world and for verbal and theological battles with their enemies.[13]

Fighting the father's enemies, the son exonerates himself from the charge of being his father's enemy: futility and depression are converted into vigor. Mather's most astute and humane apologists have demonstrated that he cannot be taken as a simple case study of paranoia and repression, but must instead be viewed as a complex, creative, and brilliant personality. It seems to me, however, that this need not be an either/or, and in fact should not be: as in Melville's creation of Ahab from the fabric of himself, Mather's creativity and brilliance lie in his literary development of a common personality type in the complexity of its consequences, rather than in his escape from it.

The shift from inner turmoil to outer combativeness involves a corresponding shift in Mather's explanation of the unreliability of signs. Whereas Calvinist doubt discredited the significance of his work by telling him that works were not completely credible signs, slander taught him that, though the true significance of his work was clear to him, it was not clear to the community, and so false significances could be attributed to it. Epistemological uncertainty is shifted from Mather to the human community: as the projection clears up his sense of personal apostasy, so too it clears up his sense that he does not understand the signs that God has provided; *other* men do not have proper understanding and are consequently vulnerable to believing *misconstructions* of the good man's good works.

Mather's theoretical position during the witch trials was that, though the tormenting spectres were quite real, they did not necessarily signify the diabolism of the persons of whom they were images, a position he took even before a young woman claimed to have been "threaten'd and molested" by a spectre resembling himself (*D*, I:178). Though for power of terror and urgency the Salem episode was unique, the general tendency to fail to see the true significance of his work and to be credulously susceptible to false representations was not. In 1683 his father had been called "*The Mahomet of New-England*,"[14] and Mather's diary for 1721 re-

---

[13] Phillip Greven, *The Protestant Temperament* (New York: Knopf, 1970), p. 110.
[14] Cotton Mather, *Parentator* (Boston, 1724), p. 90.

cords what he considered an equally insulting spectre: "A Lieutenant of a Man of War, whom I am a Stranger to, designing to put an Indignity upon me, has called his *Negro-Slave* by the Name of COTTON-MATHER" (*D*, II:663). To the modern reader, the difference between the Salem spectres and such satire is great, but to Cotton Mather they were together evidence of the fact that in other men's eyes the true significances of things were not clear, and that Satan could consequently disseminate lying simulacra in order to erode the effect of good work.

Mather's diary is a depository for his complaints that goodness is derided, a melancholy fact that assures him that he is certainly good, since he has attracted the devil's special spite and been compelled, like Job and Christ, to endure abuse for the sake of his excellence. Malicious misrepresentation is the climactic item in his extensive list of the symptoms of declension: "*Falsehood* and *Slander*, hath been continually carrying of *Darts* thro' the Land" (*D*, I:216). This misprision is so endemic that "I despair of any good Acceptance for any thing of mine" (*D*, II:385). The slander does not testify to any fault in Mather, but to the perfidy of the age: "if [Christ] were on Earth again, as once He was, Hee would be persecuted with wonderful *Malignity* from vast Numbers of people, that now go by the Name of Christians" (*D*, I:345). Quoting Baxter's *Christian Directory* to the effect that good work will be called covetousness, unkindness, or hard-dealing, Mather concludes that the remark is as good as a personal letter addressed to himself:

> It has, in some former Years commonly happened unto me, that when I visited, in the Way of my *pastoral Duty*, persons possessed with *evil Spirits*, the Persons, tho' they knew every one else in the Room, yett thro' the unaccountable Operation of the *evil Spirits* upon their Eyes, I must appear so dirty, so ugly, so *disguis'd* unto them, that they could have no Knowledge of me. I have a thousand times thought, that the Lord ordered this for some Intimation unto me, that when *Times of Temptation* come, wherein *evil Spirits* have as much Operation on the *Minds* of many People as they have on the *Eyes of Energumens*, a Minister of the Lord Jesus Christ that will be faithful unto His Interests, must look to be all over *disguis'd* by Misrepresentations, unto the *Minds* of them that are under the Power of *Temptation*." (*D*, I:412)

Though the topic of this entry in 1702 is not the events at Salem, the terminology and epistemology are similar. Because the good man's work does not clearly signify his goodness *to others*, they are susceptible to dissimulating misrepresentations of the nature of his work. At the same time, however, the meaning of his work is perfectly clear to him; he is faithful to the Lord's interests, and the episode is meant to teach him the power of slander, rather than to apprise him of his innate depravity. His image in their eyes is dirty, ugly, and *disguised*.

In the *Manuductio ad Ministerium* and *Bonifacius*, written to exhort the good to do good, Mather is careful to include a warning that their ortho-praxy will not necessarily yield the recompense of gratitude and acclaim, both of which would signify a union of heart between the converted piety of the good-doer and the contrite pleasure of the happy recipient of the deed. The recipients remain obstinate and unconverted, and so unable to see clearly the meaning of the good work done on their behalf. The doer's goodness will be seen "but at a *distance*" (B:8), a distance that obscures the truth and permits "MISCONSTRUCTION." He will be envied for his rectitude, and, because they are ashamed of the sin they cannot renounce, they will disparage him, accusing him of selfishness and con-triving:

> *Essays to do good* shall be derided, with all the *art* and *wit*, that he can inspire into his *Janizaries* (a *Yani-cheer*, or a *new order*, the Grand Seig-neur of Hell has instituted). Exquisite *profaneness* and *buffoonery* shall try their skill to laugh people out of them. The men who abound in them shall be exposed on the stage; *libels*, and *lampoons*, and satires the most poignant that ever were invented, shall be darted at them; and *pamphlets* full of lying stories, be scattered, with a design to make them *ridiculous*. *Hic se asperit Diabolus!* (B:11–12)

This exposure on the devil's stage, unlike the father's uncovering of the son on the stage before the saints, confirms the son's excellence. It is a crucifixion, not a damnification: "He that built a matchless castle for the *Poles*, for his reward, had his *eyes put out*, that he might not build such another" (B:10).

In *Blessed Unions* (1692) and *The Christian Philosopher* (1721), Cotton Mather argued that, in engendering Christ, God divided part of himself off from himself and made that part the Son. The perfect conformity between the divided parts is the source of divine "SATISFACTION," which is the Holy Ghost. The Paraclete, that is, is satisfaction in work, in the perfect match between the original intention of the worker and the ob-jective image of him which is the work. Man, too, is an image of God, potentially, but he is an "immorigerous," fractious matter, a primitive chaos upon which the hold of forming grace is tentative and always en-dangered. In his diary, Mather confessed his attraction to Paulicianism (D, II:282) and, though he managed to avoid any Manichean represen-tation of the creation as a whole, he did transfer Manichean renderings of the properties of darkness to the formless anarchy of self, which re-fuses to see the evidence of divinity in the surrounding world. Con-sciousness can rise above self to be an image of divinity in which divinity finds satisfaction for its work; but the residue of self or anarchy remains, and the imaging may always be broken by a diabolical resurrection of self-matter's inchoate license.

In his private humiliations, Mather lamented this gravitation within himself. In his work among men, however, he tended to treat himself as a satisfactory image of divine intentions. The matter of chaos then lay outside of him, in the human material upon which he worked, rather than within: and the task was not to make himself an image of God, but to make the external material an image of himself insofar as he was an image of God already. He sought to be mirrored, doubled, or imaged by the men around him, and thereby to have engendered a unanimity upon which could be founded social consensus. Hence his seeming vast egoism: but in his own eyes, what he wished to have doubled was his submission of self to superior power, to the example of Increase Mather. As he had, at great price and in huge struggle, so they should.

The object of his work as a minister and a godly citizen of New England was to convert the disparate into the one, and success would be satisfaction. In addition, Mather also sought to objectify or double himself in the smaller society of the family, as a father, in the precarious medium of women and children, and in the larger society of man, as an author, in the precarious medium of books. In both cases, the energumen was not the self, since the annihilation of self was a preparation for these works. It was instead the promiscuity of the external material, which could be bent toward godliness, but which always contained an awful, secret, residual proclivity to infidelity, and could betray the good man by unraveling all the patient and diligent work he had spent shaping it. In sons and in books, Mather hoped to double himself externally and so to pervade the human community in the future: but in both cases his attempts to construct satisfying, durable, and influential objectifications of his victory over self met with resistance that he feared would terminate his realization of his family's good name.

Such a disaster would waste three generations of labor. As both a son and a father, he had the dynastic task to maintain the reputation of the name *Mather* because the sons of the name seemed to him destined to cement the fideistic coherence of New England. His crucial central role as the community's modern Mather meant that the decline of the Mathers would contribute to the decline of New England; and, conversely, the decline of New England would signify the decline of the Mathers, suggesting that Cotton Mather had perhaps failed to act effectively on his inheritance. He wrote the *Magnalia Christi Americana* to embody the generational continuity of piety in New England, as if it were not Cotton Mather writing, but the genius of Cotton and Mather directing his servile pen:

> Reader, the book now in thy hands is to manage the design of a John Baptist, and convey the *hearts* of the *fathers* unto the *children.* Archilochus being desirous to give prevailing and effectual advice unto Lycambes, by an elegant *Prosopopeia,* brought in his *dead father,* as giving

the advice he was now writing, and as it were putting the pen into his *father's hands*. Cicero being to read a lecture of temperance and modesty unto Clodia, raised up her father Appius Caius from the grave, and in his name delivered his directions. And now by introducing the *fathers of New-England*, without the least fiction, or figure of rhetorick, I hope the plain history of their lives will be a powerful way of propounding their fatherly counsels to their posterity. A stroke with the hand of a *dead man*, has before now been a remedy for a malady not easily remedied. (*MCA*, I:234)

Purged of all inventive or transformative independence, all *self*, the writer is an *actual prosopopeia*, a pure medium for that angelic energumen, the father. He is a perfect objective image of the dynasty's invisible piety that propels it from its past excellence to its future success. In this framework, *Cotton Mather's self had no name*: given name and surname signifying dynasty, the prodigal part that might rebel was a bastard, unfathered. The son's duty was to perpetuate the father, restoring what time and the devil diminish. He is to vindicate by repeating, vociferously, eloquently, exactly. The son of Scipio Africanus, according to Mather, "proved a degenerate person and the *people* forced him to pluck off a signet-ring which he wore with his father's face engraven on it" (*MCA*, I:158). The human father's image is *impressed* on the son's metal as God is impressed on man: "The GOD who *forms the Spirit of Man* within him, has imprinted on your *Spirit, a Tendency of Return unto Him*. This *Impression* is wretchedly Suppressed, and Sinned away, in your fall from GOD, and the *Tendency* wofully diverted and enfeebled."[15] Strictly speaking, the son is not to be a remembrancer or repeater, but a remembrance or repetition, a personification of the dynasty. Like Christ, he is to be the *hypostasis* of the father.

If he succeeds in this, he will be a walking sign of the father's election:

> I may add, that some of our ministers, having their sons comfortably settled, at or near the place of their own ministry, the people have thereby seen a comfortable *succession* in the affairs of Christianity; thus, the writer of this history hath, he knows not how often, seen it; that his *grandfather* baptized the *grand-parent*, his *father* baptized the *parent*, and he himself has baptized the *children* in the same family. (*MCA*, I:241)

Sharing the pulpit of the North Church with his father, Cotton Mather was his father born again and so a sign of his father's election: "It was a problem among the ancient philosophers, 'Whether a child may not confer more benefits on his father than he has received from him?' This hath been sometimes bravely determined in the affirmative among us, when fathers have by the means of their own children been born again" (*MCA*, II:373). Such an excellent son legitimates his father by signifying him, to the point where each may signify the other and both signify the family:

[15] Mather, *Manuductio ad Ministerium*, p. 6.

"Among the Arabians, a father sometimes takes his name from an eminent SON, as well as a son from his reputed father. A man is called with an *Abu*, as well as an *Ebn*. Verily, a son may be such a blessing to his father that the best surname for the glad father would be, *the father of such a one*" (*B*:52).

In *Pray for the Rising Generation*, Increase Mather contended that a prodigal son would be an exception to his predecessors' holiness. At several points in his own writing, however, Cotton Mather contends that a prodigal son might signify the father's secret reprobation, just as a good son signifies a father's election. A prodigal might be a *prosopopeia* of the father's secret lapse. Using an allegory from the *Nichomachean Ethics*, which Gertrude Stein would later employ in *The Making of Americans*, he illustrates such a revelation:

> You have doubtless been inform'd of that famous History, in the *Theatrum Historiae:* A vile Son did once beat his old *Father*, and then drag him to the Threshold of the House, by the Hair of the Head. Afterwards, when he grew *Old himself* (which by the way, was a *Rare Thing!*) his own Son did in like manner beat *him,* and then Drag him also, by the Hair of the Head, not only to the Threshold, but out of the Doors, into the *Dirt.* Hereupon he cryed out with Anguish, *Ah! If this Varlet had pull'd me only to the Threshold, I had been serv'd, but just as my Father was by me!*"[16]

The crime of the son is a manifestation of the father's turpitude. This paragraph, published the year Cotton Mather's first son was born, expresses an anxiety that his own shortcomings will become visible in Increase's grandson, Increase Mather, or, to use Cotton's nickname for him, Creasy.

In the biography he wrote of his father, *Parentator,* Cotton Mather called the book an appendix for the *Magnalia Christi Americana,* implying that his labor as a son justified his father's inclusion in the pantheon.[17] In 1699, the year of Creasy's birth, he began his autobiography, *Paterna,* addressing it to the infant for exemplary instruction, and implying that Creasy's ascent to piety would signify Cotton Mather's place in the pantheon. His tense hope is evident in the diary entry recording Creasy's birth:

> While my Faith was pleading that the Saviour who was *born of a Woman,* would send his good Angel to releeve my Consort, the People ran to my Study-door with Tidings, *that a Son was born unto mee.* I continued then on my Knees, praising the Lord; and I received a wonderful Ad-

[16] Cotton Mather, *Duties of Children to Their Parents,* printed with "A Family Well-Order'd" (Boston, 1699), p. 47.
[17] Mather, *Parentator,* p. vi.

> vice from Heaven, that this my Son, shall bee a Servant of my Lord
> Jesus Christ throughout eternal Ages. (D, I:307)

This particular anticipation, like so many others, miscarried. At its conclusion, *Paterna* was addressed to the second son, Samuel, Franklin's correspondent, Creasy having strayed and died.

As early as 1711, when Creasy was twelve, Mather began to worry for
him, being distressed "lest some vicious and wicked Lads do corrupt and
ensnare him" (D, II:76). In his diary, he records constant concern over
Creasy's piety, praying that the Lord will give Creasy a new heart, and
instructing his son diligently in the ways of zeal. By 1713, he has given
up the idea that Creasy will be a minister, and he begins to seek some
reputable secular particular calling for him. But Creasy resists even this
fastidiousness, and the horror breaks in November 1717:

> The Evil that I greatly feared is come upon me. I am within these few
> hours, astonished with an Information, that an Harlot big with a Bas-
> tard, Accuses my poor son Cressy, and Lays her Belly to him. The most
> sensible judges, upon the strictest Enquiry, beleeve the youth to be In-
> nocent. But yett, oh! the Humiliation!—Oh! Dreadful Case! O sorrow
> beyond any that I have met withal! What shall I do for the foolish youth!
> What for my Afflicted and Abased family! (D, II:484)

The despair is deep in this case because a bastard, for a dynastic purist
like Cotton Mather, would be a waste of seed, an outlaw product, and
like Edmund in *King Lear*, a cosmic irritant.

Creasy's profligacy did not end with this: "My miserable, miserable,
miserable Son *Increase!* The wretch has brought himself under public
trouble and Infamy by bearing a Part in a Night-Riot, with some detest-
able Rakes in the Town" (D, II:611). During the next two weeks Cotton
Mather asks his father to intercede, and finally he resolves to turn his face
from Creasy. Continuing to resist his father's instructions, Creasy went
to sea, where he was drowned in 1724. His son's death, coinciding with
a resurgence of his wife's paroxysms, and following a year after his father's death, must have struck Mather with the force of a providential
judgment: the first rumor of the loss of Creasy's ship was reversed by a
rumor that the ship had been diverted to Newfoundland, but it was then
reversed again; the days of uncertainty exacted their price; his diary shows
great stress and weariness. In *Tela Praevisa,* the sermon he preached on
the occasion of his son's death, Mather returns to the verse from Job that
began his 1717 diary entry concerning the harlot big with bastard: "The
Thing which I greatly Feared, is come upon me." Echoing Heraclitus,
he announces that "Nothing in this World is *Constant,* but the *Inconstancy*
of the World," and he advises his auditors to live so that the world never
proves worse than they fear: "This *present Evil World,* has in it a World of

Evil, *Every Day* will bring a *Sufficient Evil* with it. All *Sublunary* Things are full of Changes."[18]

This mutability complaint is rhetorically important, since it attributes Creasy's death to a cause other than the punishment of the sins of the father that were made manifest in the son. The affiliation of his suffering with Job's reinforces this exoneration: "That *Piety* would signify little to bring him *out of Trouble;* inasmuch as it had not prevented him coming *into* Trouble."[19] By connecting his suffering with Job's, Mather is able to believe that Creasy's death is a sore test of his excellence, rather than evidence of his secret blasphemy. At several points during his son's prodigal career, Mather had worried that Creasy's abominations – as in the anecdote of the father dragged by the hair past the threshold – were signs of his own: "I considered the Sins of my Son, as being my own; and as also calling to Remembrance the Sins of my former Years; for all which I renewed my Repentance, with all Abasement of Soul, in the Sight of GOD" (*D,* II:485). Hence his repeated concern with the ways in which Creasy had damaged his reputation, an injury to *Mather* as well as to *Creasy.* This concern may also explain Mather's emphasis on the company Creasy kept. The son was unfledged, and susceptible; he was receptive to temptations that originated outside him; the paternal satisfaction was thus disrupted by exterior antagonists, who inserted themselves between the father the original and the son the sign.

The advantage of an exterior antagonist is especially clear in the case of the harlot big with bastard, whose promiscuity was accompanied by perfidy. Like the "pharaoh of hell" at Salem, she manufactured a lying spectre of a good person. Mather's horrification during that episode is a part of his general wariness of women's power to seduce fathers and sons into loving the things of the world for their own sakes, rather than for the glorification of God. Mather's assumptions led inevitably to what Michael Colacurcio has called his "theological antifeminism":[20] the continuity of the sacred in general was founded on the continuity of sons doubling fathers in those families through whose loins God had cast election; the severance of the line could mean either that its apparent election had been a delusion, or that a corrupting foreign element had been introduced from outside the line. Caution was thus imperative: Richard Mather married John Cotton's widow, and Increase Mather married John Cotton's daughter.

[18] Cotton Mather, Tela Praevisa: *A Short Essay on Troubles to Be Look'd For* (Boston, 1724), pp. 1, 4.

[19] Ibid., p. 2.

[20] Michael Colacurcio, "Footsteps of Anne Hutchinson: The Context of *The Scarlet Letter,*" ELH 39, no. 3 (September 1972), p. 475.

This is not to say that, in general, Mather believed that all women were actively sinful or even that they were more frequently sinful than men. He often praised feminine godliness, for example in his funeral sermons for Mary Brown and Sarah Leverett – *Eureka: the Vertuous Woman Found* and *Monica Americana: Female Piety Exemplified* – or in his encomia for his mother and his first two wives. Of the first, Abigail Phillips, he wrote:

> But there was another signal Article of my *Praises* to the Lord, on this Day; and this was, the Confluence of *Blessings*, which I enjoy in my dearest *Consort*, who bore me company in some of the Duties of the Day. Her *Piety*, the agreeable Charms of her *Person*, her obliging Deportment unto *me*, her *Discretion* in ordering my and her Affairs, and avoiding every thing that might be dishonourable to either of us, and the lovely *Off-Spring* that I have received by her, and her being spared unto me for now more than *Fifteen Years;* these are things that I should thankfully acknowledge before the Lord. (*D*, I:405)

But Mather's tone of wonder reveals his conviction that such domestic conformity was far from automatic. Eighteen months after this entry was made in the diary, Abigail Phillips miscarried, and she died after six months of terrible sickness which exhausted her husband and left him bereft. At her funeral he distributed a pamphlet entitled *Ornaments for the Daughters of Zion*: but in his diary, he reveals that, had she lived, she would have been sickly and she would have "run [him] into a consumption" had he "run the venture of sleeping with her"; and, if she had lived, subsequent sorrows in her father's family would have brought "a Disorder of Mind" upon her because she had always been of a "melancholy Temper" (*D*, I:451–2).

Two months later, his affections gravitated to a forward "ingenious Child." But the unnamed suitor's reputation was not good, and Mather's began to suffer after the audiences he had granted her in his study, the same room in which he groveled before the Lord: "I struck my Knife, into the Heart of my Sacrifice, by a letter to her Mother" (*D*, I:474). The repudiated suitor planned "exquisite revenges," but finally left off and testified that Mather's conduct had been entirely reputable. He found a more respectable object of affection, and, seven months after the death of Abigail Phillips, Increase Mather married his son to Elizabeth Hubbard: "I am satisfied, if the Spirit of my departed Consort now in the Kingdome of God, were advized, that her children were falling into the Hands of this Gentlewoman, it would be a Consolation unto her" (*D*, I:491). The time between the two compatible domestic regimes was a problematic interlude in which the health and reputation of the dynasty were endangered.

Though Mather did not consider women more sinful than men, his

reaction to the form female impiety took was noticeably intense and horrified:

> *What has a gracious Lord given me to do,* for the Profit and Honour of the
> *Female Sex,* especially in publishing the vertuous and laudable Charac-
> ters of *holy Women?* AND YETT, where is the Man, whom the *female
> Sex* have spitt more of their Venom at? I have cause to Quaestion, whether
> there are twice Ten in the Town, but what have at some time or other
> spoken basely of me. (*D,* II:706).

This entire diary entry is hyperbolical, and the last sentence above is no
exception, since Mather had elsewhere congratulated the godly women
of Boston on their number.

Mather's meditations on female aberration, however, frequently attribute to it a power of epidemical contagion and of damnable multiplication, a kind of perverse or inverse double of the quantitative increase of
piety to which he had dedicated his work:

> A very wicked Woman is found in the Church whereof I am the Ser-
> vant. She not only had an unlawful Offspring a few Years ago, which
> is now discovered, but her Impenitence has provoked her Neighbours
> to come in with Testimonies of a very lewd Conversation, that she has
> carried on. The Work of God in bringing forth her Wickedness is to be
> wondred at, to be trembled at. But her Father, who is an old and great
> Professor of Religion, does most grievously misbehave himself on this
> Occasion. He, and his foolish Family do not only treat me very ill, and
> with a strange Malice and Revenge for the doing of my Duty, and the
> poor Man is dreadfully forsaken of God: but also, they use violent Wayes
> to sow Discord among the Neighbours, and the Peace of the Church is
> threatened. (*D,* II:531)

The diabolical doubling is plain: as Mather works in a paternal way to
convert his parishioners to godliness, she converts her father from godliness; as his pious influence spreads through the group and unites it in
humility, her influence rouses the fractiousness of self and spreads strife;
and, as his exemplary godliness reveals his interior justification in work,
her misconstruction dims the light of his name. She is an anti-Mather.

It is noteworthy that her contagion begins with lewdness, since it shows
that an abuse of proper maternity is at the root of all this discord: the
actual bastard is the first of many bastard deeds and words. Though all
persons are susceptible to abusing their callings, the calling of woman –
wife and mother – is dynasty, the primal continuity upon which the others are founded. In Mather's Trinity, the Father does not objectify himself
in the Son through the medium of woman, and this may be why his
Satisfaction, the Holy Ghost, is complete and intact: but mortal fathers
must employ women, and so the line of spirit is ineluctably detoured

through a precarious interregnum. In his sermons and in pamphlets such as *The Pure Nazarite: Advice to a Young Man, concerning an* Impiety *and* Impurity *(not easily to be spoken of)* (1723), Mather cautioned young men about inclinations to masturbation: but perhaps he understood the inclination, since it converted the turmoil of real objects of affection into the conformity of imaginative objects. For Mather, woman continues to be a type of Eve, who first shattered God's satisfaction in his image, humanity. Whether through the abuse of maternal or domestic duties, or through enticing the father or son to an unheeding sensuality, the woman who did forsake her particular calling received from Mather a close, eloquent, and vividly dismayed condemnation. If the order of the family through time is the foundation of the human order in general, then feminine unruliness has the contagious power to expand toward an unraveling of the whole.

This power is the topic of Mather's chapter on Anne Hutchinson and Antinomianism in the *Magnalia Christi Americana*. The title itself is richly significant – "Hydra Decapitata": as Mather argued in his writings on self, the heart must be circumcised and all that is improper must be amputated; the appearance of virile, fractious assertion in a woman is doubly offensive; and the offense is compounded by her heresy's power to multiply, like the hydra's heads. Mather is particularly interested in the relationship between Hutchinson and his grandfather John Cotton, whose doctrinal scruples concerning the Congregational search for signs of conversion in the narratives of applicants grew into her rampant assertion that the private soul was inaccessible to group scrutiny and so endangered the foundation of theocratic authority. In his biography of Cotton, Mather reveals that Cotton and Hutchinson were called a "Montanus and Maxilla" (*MCA*, I:268), referring to the second-century heretic who believed in demoniac possession by the Paraclete and in charismatic prophesying, and to Maximilla, who, with Prisca, left her husband to join Montanus. In the eyes of Tertullian and Eusebius, Maximilla's prime transgression seems to have been her belief that woman could participate in ministry, a practice common among the Quakers, who were the other great enemy to Massachusetts theocracy. Mather does not wish to deny that Hutchinson was a Maximilla, but that Cotton was a Montanus: their intellectual affinity must be severed so that the pious grandson may exonerate his dynastic predecessor by vitiating Hutchinson. Mather details the circumstances of Hutchinson's presumptive quasi-ministry: "She set up weekly meetings at her house, whereto threescore or fourscore people would resort, that they might hear the sermons of Mr. Cotton repeated, but in such a sort that after the repetition, she would make her explicatory and applicatory declamations, wherein what she confirmed of the sermons must be *canonical*, but what she omitted all *Apocrypha*" (*MCA*,

II:517). Her repetition of the sermons, that is, is no repetition at all, but a revision based on unjustified accentuation and suppression. It is a misrepresenting simulacrum of truth constructed with diabolical ingenuity. The abomination lies not in Cotton's sermon, but in her distortion.

This intellectual offense is a development from a sexual contortion:

> Within a year after the gathering of the church at Cambridge, and the ordaining of Mr. Shepard in that church, the country was miserably distracted by a storm of Antinomian and Familistical opinions then raised. The *mother opinion* of all the rest was, "That a Christian should not fetch any evidence of his good state before God, from the sight of any inherent qualification in him; or from any conditional promise made unto such a qualification." From the womb of this *fruitful opinion*, and from the countenance hereby given to immediate and unwarranted revelations, 'tis not easie to relate how many monsters, worse than African, arose in these regions of America: but a synod, assembled at Cambridge, whereof Mr. Shepard was no small part, most happily crushed them all. (*MCA*, I:385–6)

The misconception of theology is closely analogous to the formulation of a monster in the womb, a *topos* of Renaissance demonology perpetuated in Winthrop's journal, in Bradstreet's "Author to her Book," and in Mather's *Elizabeth in Her Holy Retirement: An Essay to Prepare a Pious Woman for Her Lying in* (1710), where pregnant women are asked to compare the fetus to sins that may still be growing in them. In Hutchinson's case, the connection between monstrous opinions and monstrous sexuality was not figural, as Mather saw it. Hutchinson's sins, as they are chronicled in Mather's writing, are twofold: she perverted Cotton's truth, deforming it with heretical exegeses, and she was licentious, having borne several illegitimate children before she was killed by Indians while in exile. The two motives, intellectual aberration and sexual promiscuity, are so tightly woven in "Hydra Decapitata" that they are, finally, inseparable. Mather implies that Antinomianism, a compilation of "scandalous, dangerous, and *enchanting* extravagancies" (*MCA*, II:518) is the monster (and bastard) son of a Cotton sermon, analogous to the Hydatiform mole – a linked series of unfinished organic lumps (one lump for each of her heretical opinions, according to Mather) – to which Hutchinson gave birth before she died; or to the "Monstrum, horrendum, in forme, ingens" to which Mary Dyer (who was later hanged during the Quaker persecutions) gave birth after being infected with Hutchinson's heresies. Mather borrows from Winthrop's journal to describe this more articulated monster:

> It had no head: the face was below the breast: the ears were like an ape's, and grew upon the shoulders; the eyes and mouth stood far out; the nose was hooking upwards; the breast and back were full of short prickles,

like a thorn-back; the navel, belly, and the distinction of sex, which was female, were in the place of hips; and those back-parts were on the same side with the face; the arms, hands, thighs and legs, were as other childrens; but instead of toes, it had on each foot three claws, with taleons _like a fowl: upon the back above the belly it had a couple of great holes like mouths; and in each of them stood out a couple of pieces of flesh; it had no forehead, but above the eyes it had four horns; two of above an inch long, hard and sharp; and the other two somewhat less. (*MCA*, II:519)

We may contrast this with the rectitude Mather expected from his own body:

I would anatomically and particularly consider, every Part of my Body, and with as explicit an Ingenuity as may be, consider the several Actions, and uses thereof; and then go on to consider, on what Methods I may serve my glorious Lord with them, and in what Regards the Service done by them, is to be a Service for the Lord. These Considerations must be accomplished with Consecrations, and Satisfactions, entreating the Lord, that He would accept my Body, as being employ'd for Him, in these Applications, and preserve me from ever Perverting my Body, unto any Employments forbidden by Him. As I would sett apart some Times for an effectual Management of this holy Exercise, thus I would occasionally be awakened unto something of it, when I suffer any Pain or Disorder in any Parts of my Body. Herein I would propose, not only to have my Body more notably, made a Temple of God, but also to praepare for a blessed Resurrection of this Body from the Dead by the Saviour of the Body. (*D*, II:75)

The body is not a thing indifferent: whether in ordinary or monstrous form, it must be meticulously scrutinized as a sign from the Lord; and wherever possible, it must be consecrated, or made into a sign of the Lord, though this would seem to be impossible among the children of Antinomianism. Whether in horror or satisfaction, these passages show a close fascination with the unknown wilderness of the body, the promiscuous and dark region that may be made a medium for the expression of divinity, but may also engulf form.

We should remember that Hutchinson's Antinomianism was a theory of the extraordinary: she contended that soul-experience escaped objective measure, and could not be appraised for the sake of admitting to or excluding from church membership and (as a result) social legitimacy. The individual's essential, defining experience transcended the purview of ecclesiastical authority, and that power was therefore not entitled to form a judicial representation of it. Winthrop's and Mather's concentration on the physiologically monstrous assumes that an extraordinary and extravagant psyche is just as aberrant as an extraordinary and extravagant physique: the regularity and rectitude of psychological experience as it was defined and legislated by the paternal authority of the theocratic community was no more eligible for variation or transformation than the obvious regularity and rectitude of the human torso. Both were nature.

If Mather's remarks in "Hydra Decapitata" show an uncharacteristically extreme antifeminism, it is because Hutchinson represents for him a sort of limit-case of what happens when woman neglects her calling. All women are not Hutchinson: but the potential for straying that exists in all humans, together with the especially disastrous effects of feminine disorder, meant that Hutchinson lurked in all women – as a potentiality that a great many women, Mather thought, had governed successfully. But the awful possibility remained: Hutchinson was promiscuous; her accompanying promiscuous theology endangered the reputation of John Cotton, and with it the reputation of the Mather dynasty; and she sought to unsettle the founding premise of New England Puritanism – that human knowledge of the ways of God could be sufficient to judge and regulate the motions of the private man. Her contempt for legal paternity per se led contagiously to disregard for the paternal wisdom of her minister and to opposition to patriarchy. She, too, is a dark double of Cotton Mather, who governed his body, submitted self to dynasty, and wrote the massive *Magnalia Christi Americana* to vindicate and revive the primitive foundations of New England Calvinism: "'Tis noted of seducers that, like their father the devil, the old, the first seducer, they usually have a design upon the *weaker sex*, who are more easily gained themselves, and then are fit instruments for the gaining of their husbands unto such *errors* as will cause them to *lose* their souls at last" (*MCA*, II:516).

Mather's concentration on the unfledged frailty of the son and on the potential for epidemical abomination in the woman allowed him to conclude that failure to objectify himself in his work as a father would derive from the instability of the material with which he had to work, rather than from some deficiency of intelligence or will. This is a paradigm for his understanding of failure in general: as he argued in *A Family Well-Ordered*, the activity of the father is the analogical type for the activities of the minister, the teacher, and the magistrate; consequently, his comprehension of his failures in those analogical endeavors also drew upon the theory of the promiscuity of the material medium.

Mather's attention to the unreliability of the medium is particularly clear in his comprehension of his fate as an author. His commitment to writing, to repeat, was enormous. In his *Phaedrus*, Plato deplores writing because it insistently repeats the same statement and so sabotages living memory. Suspicious as he was of the transformative creativity of living memory, Mather valued writing for the repetition that Plato's Thamus rejected. A book was faith made into perdurable monument, a belief that

Mather reveals in his choice of objects such as statues and memorial stones as figures for written memory. The book is faith objectified and ready to survive.

In this, it is analogous to a son. Perry Miller referred to Mather's "monstrous lust for publication" and thus (perhaps inadvertently) recapitulated a metaphor with which Mather was intrigued. In his 1712 diary he records having compiled "the Catalogue of Books which I have been the Father of" (D, II:157), a figure he had developed at greater length in the *Magnalia Christi Americana:*

> It was the honour of [Robert Parker] to be the *father* of such learned books as that of his *"De Politia Ecclesiastica,"* and that *"Of the Cross,"* as well as the *foster father* to that of Sandford's *"De Descensu Christi ad Inferos,"* yea, to be in some sort the *father* of all the *non-conformists* in our age, who yet would not call any man their father. But let it not be counted any *dishonour* unto him that he was also the natural *father* of our Thomas Parker. (*MCA*, I:480)

This argument is not idle ornamentation: he wrote the *Magnalia Christi Americana* as a part of his duty as a son, and he wrote *Paterna* as a part of his duty as a father: book-writing was for him an essential part of his dynastic obligation, so it is not surprising that this paternal duty should appear to him as a form of paternity.

As has been frequently noted, Mather was proud of his record of publication: "[I must thank the Lord] For His favouring mee, with the *Liberty of the Press*, and publishing more of my Composures than any Man's, that ever was in *America*, while I am yett a young Man" (D, I:228). "There are many Favours of Heaven, wherein I have been *singular*. Especially . . . that I should bee a more silly and shallow Person, than most in this Countrey; and yett write and print more Books, and have greater Opportunities to do good by my published Composures, than any Man that ever was in this Countrey, or indeed in all *America*" (D, I:311). According to Mather, this success did not derive from self, but from God operating over the ruins of a worthless self:

> If the *God of my Life* will please to spare my Life (my yet Sinful, and Slothful, and thereby Forfeited Life!) as many years longer as the *Barren Fig-tree* had in the Parable, I may make unto the Church of God, an humble Tender of our BIBLIA AMERICANA, a Volumn enrich'd with better things than all the Plate of the *Indies;* YET NOT I, BUT THE GRACE OF CHRIST WITH ME. (*MCA*, I:34)

Since the *I* was silly, shallow, sinful, slothful and barren, the publication of so many books notable for spiritual excellence must testify not to self, but to a perfectly submissive son through whom God the Father writes. But the intensity of his disavowals of egotism only show how strong the egotism was:

Looking over a Catalogue of the Books, published, whereof the Grace of GOD has made poor me the Writer, I must in the first place loathe and Judge myself exceedingly before the Lord, for the sinful Corruptions, and especially the selfish Intentions, which have defiled all these Publications. And I must exceedingly watch against all Vanity of Mind, even the least Motion that way, from the Number of the Publications, which amounts to near two hundred and fourscore, so I must admire the Goodness and Mercy of a sovereign GOD, who has herein distinguished the Chief of Sinners, and might have employ'd any one else, as well as this Vilest of Men, in this Variety of Services. (*D*, II:505)

Condemned to uncertainty about the worthiness of his work, Mather was driven to a desperately energetic concentration on the quantity of work, since its quality could not be known: but if any one of these textual sons shows the prodigality of defilement by self, then it puts the father's sin in public view and cancels the rest.

Consequently, as textual father, Mather concentrated on the instability of the media in which the author expressed himself, again because such attention offered relief from doubt about the founding intention. On the most literal level, this anxiety appears in diary entries where Mather agonizes over the necessity of shipping his longer manuscripts to England for publication. But the sea was not the only hideous variable he had to accept: language itself was unstable; it could be pared to an austere transparency that submitted to divinity, as in the plain style of the sermon; or it could irrupt with a diabolical independence, as in the Anglican sermons or in the seductions of pagan poetry. Commenting on the rhetorical sophistication of Laudian ministers such as Lancelot Andrewes, Thomas Hooker had explained their popularity: "The reason is, because *all this stings not*, they may sit and sleepe in their sinnes, and *go to hell hood-winckt.*"[21] Cotton Mather reports that, when John Cotton decided to govern his language, he suffered a diminution of popularity among the profane:

> Many difficulties had Mr. Cotton in his own mind now what course to steer. On the one side, he considered that if he should preach with a scriptural and Christian *plainness*, he should not only wound his own fame exceedingly, but also tempt carnal man to revive an old cavil, "that religion made scholars turn dunces," whereby the name of God might suffer not a little. On the other side, he considered that it was his duty to preach with such a plainness, as became the oracles of God, which are intended for the conduct of men in the paths of life, and not for *theatrical* ostentations and entertainments, and the Lord needed not for any sin of ours to maintain his own glory . . . The vain wits of the university, disappointed thus, with a more excellent sermon, that shot

---

[21] Thomas Hooker, quoted in Carl Bridenbaugh, *Vexed and Troubled Englishmen, 1590–1642* (New York: Oxford University Press, 1968), p. 293.

some troublesome admonitions into their consciences, discovered their
vexation at this disappointment by their not *humming,* as according to
their sinful and absurd custom they had formerly done; and the Vice-
Chancellor, for the very same reason also, graced him not, as he did
others that pleased him. Nevertheless, the satisfaction which he enjoyed
in his own faithful soul, abundantly compensated unto him the loss of
any human favour or honour; nor did he go without many encourage-
ments from some doctors, then having a better sence of *religion* upon
them, who prayed him to persevere in the *good way of preaching,* which
he had now taken. (*MCA,* I:256)

Self, rich expressiveness, and the evasion of conscience are bound together: echoing Jerome's hesitations about rhetoric, Mather felt that language, like women, rested in the ambiguous space between man and
God; he felt that it could be disciplined to speak truth, or that it could
become a crazed wife, stealing, seducing, perverting, leading the writer
or speaker into ostentations and entertainments. Consequently, he resolved to write the *Magnalia Christi Americana* in a "Simple, Submiss,
Humble *Style*" (*MCA,* I:31) free of self-celebrating eloquence.

But governing his own style was not the end of his problem with
language. To the Puritan, the true significances of things were not certain
and clear, though there were degrees of insight. Consequently, articles
and books could be written about his books that would *misrepresent* his
motives, disguising the true meaning and replacing it with a false one,
as Hutchinson had done with Cotton's sermons even after he had castigated his extravagance. Though Mather might console himself that these
were false slanders, they still had the power, if they were eloquent, to
injure his books' power to do good, and so to cause his work to *miscarry.*
In this case, the failure of his books to do their job would not be due to
their secret egotism, but to the egotism that was falsely attributed to
them by those caught by "the black Fowler of Hell."

In the "General Introduction" to the *Magnalia Christi Americana,* Mather
credits the invention of printing with a large part of the success of Puritanism, and Larzer Ziff agrees, arguing that Puritan resentments would
have remained at the level of folk mythology rather than coalescing into
a coherent movement were it not for the power of the printed word to
unify the scattered dissenters.[22] Ziff is certainly correct, but he draws his
argument and his examples from the history of Puritanism in England,
and so neglects how vexing free printing was to the American Puritans,
who had become the ruling party and had to put up with the likes of
Morton's *New English Canaan.* Because of freedom to print, the pious
man's government of his own style could not be repeated in the world at
large. Satan got published: and the abominations expelled from the good

[22] Larzer Ziff, *Puritanism in America* (New York: Viking Press, 1973), pp. 3–26.

book could appear in evil books that disparaged the good book and restricted its efficacy. This predicament reached epidemic proportions in
Mather's time, when his written works were impugned by writers big
with falsehood, such as Robert Calef or James and Benjamin Franklin,
as Creasy had been impugned by the harlot big with bastard. If the work
were to fail – if the truth did not go out and increase – this was the fault
of the demonic dissemblers, rather than a result of the flaw that lay in the
work itself.

Calef's *More Wonders of the Invisible World* was published in London in
1700. Inside the cover of his copy, opposite the title, Cotton Mather wrote
"Job xxxi. 35, 36. My desire is that mine Adversary had written a Book.
Surely I would take it upon my Shoulder, and bind it as a Crown to me.
Co: Mather." [23] Like the death of Creasy, Calef's book is an affliction, but
an affliction to test Mather's excellence, rather than a revelation of his
error. This reaction spares him from giving credence to Calef's book,
which is a sort of proto-rationalist critique of the mixture of what Calef
called superstition and venery in the Mathers' behavior during the period
of the witch trials that anticipates Franklin's "A Witch Trial at Mount
Holly." If the witch trials were the expression of a collective attempt to
surmount obsolete, mysterious folk-technologies, Calef (or "Calf," as
Mather calls him in his diary), like Franklin, argues that the Mathers'
mistake was to take witches seriously: ridicule, rather than juridical combat, was the proper mode. *More Wonders of the Invisible World*, then, scoffs
at the horrification of the Salem judges, divests unreason of gravity and
density, and implicitly criticizes theocracy in general for its assertion that
the careful differentiation of spiritualities belongs in public policy rather
than deluded fancies; and a reader as perspicacious and as attuned to the
new science of Newton as Cotton Mather was would not have missed
the fact that *More Wonders of the Invisible World* was an attack on his entire
worldview rather than an exposé concerned merely with one quirk of his
career.

Calef's salvos against the Mathers' way were directed not so much
against their behavior and the intellectual assumptions that lay behind it
as they were against the books the Mathers wrote to justify their behavior, as if Calef realized the crucial place of book-writing in their self-
conception. *More Wonders of the Invisible World* was a counter-book, a near
namesake or rebellious son that doubled its father satirically with the
addition of a single snidely hyperbolical word to its parent's title: *More
Wonders of the Invisible World* was not a direct response to Mather at Salem
but a rejoinder to Mather's representation of the nature of his work among

[23] Julius Herbert Tuttle, "The Libraries of the Mathers," *American Antiquarian
Society Proceedings* 20 (April 1910), p. 302.

the witches in *Wonders of the Invisible World, Memorable Providences,* and in the biography of Phips. The issue of the proper significance of witches was subordinate to the issue of the proper significance of the Mathers as enemies of the demon. Calef's book is an attempted exposé of the Mathers' exposition of their own assumptions and motives.

Mather was stung not only by what was said in the book but also by the fact that Calef had been able to find a willing publisher. He believed that material for the book had been given to Calef by Benjamin Colman, pastor of the rival Brattle Street Church, which had dispensed with conversion narrative and promoted a somewhat more latitudinarian way. In later years, the tension between Mather and Colman eased, to the point that Colman preached the funeral sermon for Mather. But at the turn of the eighteenth century, Mather considered Colman an enemy to faith: in 1700, the year Calef published *More Wonders,* Colman published a book that Mather claimed was full of the "devices of Satan," but Mather's own *Magnalia Christi Americana* was still without a publisher. Mather assembled Calef and Colman (together with the Brattles and Leverett, who were founders of Colman's church) into a single coherent front directed against himself: "All the Adversaries of the Churches Lay their Hands together as if by Blasting of us they hoped utterly to blow up all" (*D,* I:377). Increase Mather is reported to have had *More Wonders of the Invisible World* burned in Harvard Yard.

Calef's book nettled Mather because Calef contended that Mather's opinions were demented inventions that had nothing to do with scripture. He accused Mather of breaking from the textual dynasty that stretched from the patriarch, the Bible, through the works of Tertullian, Eusebius, Augustine, Luther, Calvin, the English Reformers, and the fathers of New England to his own *Biblia Americana,* which, he claimed, transumed the entirety of its tradition. As Mather repeatedly emphasized, these writers were church *fathers,* and the sequence of their books was a dynasty to which his books were the latest members, and, like all good sons, his books doubled exactly, exceeding the tradition only in quantitative intensity. Hence Mather's frequently irritating inclination to ground every observation in a citation:

> But in these *Quotations,* there had been proposed, first, a due *Gratitude* unto those, who have been my *Instructors;* and indeed, *something within me* would have led me to it, if *Pliny,* who is one of them, had not given me a Rule; *Ingenuum est profiteri per quos profeceris* [It is noble to acknowledge by whom you have profited.] It appears but a piece of *Justice,* that the *Names* of those whom the Great God has distinguished, by employing them to make those *Discoveries,* which are here collected, should live and shine in every such Collection. (*Cp:*3)

The fifth commandment applies to authors: Mather does homage to his fathers by citing them, by acknowledging that his own work is a collec-

tion rather than a discovery, and by making them live again. He is a
prosopopeia of his textual dynasty, so earnestly so that he even employs a
quotation to justify the inclusion of quotations, in order that the authority of the work not depend on something within *him*.

This is the target of Calef's bolts. Insofar as he ridiculed the tradition
itself, Calef would be merely vile. But insofar as he implied Mather went
against the tradition, he would be truly maddening. By arguing that Mather
foisted superstition onto scripture, Calef accused Mather of doing what
Mather accused Hutchinson and Satan of doing – constructing simulacra
that looked like truth, but were actually traductions meant to interrupt
the tradition of piety: "When the *Devil* comes to us with *Scripture* in his
mouth, he comes with a *Thus saith the Lord.* The *Devil* then speaks dread-
ful things to us with the *Voice of the Lord.*"[24] When Calef's book was
published, Mather had been assembling the *Biblia Americana* for seven
years, so we may imagine the severity of his reaction to Calef's assertion
that (as Perry Miller puts it) "all learned theories concerning the nature
of sin or its evidence are 'human invention' – mere 'traditions' foisted
onto scripture on a par with the superstitions of Rome."[25] By including
Mather's tradition under the heading of superstition, Calef inverted Mather's belief in a tradition that had preceded, been eclipsed by, and then
struggled free from the Roman Babylon. Calef's argument cut Massachusetts' great tradition loose from its biblical and patristic anchor, leaving it to "be exiled into the confusions of them that are to be without"
(*MCA*, I:509–10).

Calef's implications that Mather's books were full of inventions would
have struck at the heart of his anxieties about the self and its abominable
proclivity to adulterate rather than duplicate the great tradition. The tension between repetition of truth and creative but sterile invention pervades his writing: virtually every biography in the *Magnalia Christi Americana*, for example, begins with a figural improvement of the life of the
person at hand, and Mather's understanding of this activity seems to me
to be exactly balanced between perceiving these figures as discoveries of
some type of allegory innate to the order of things and perceiving these
figures as free flights of wit. In the fourth chapter, I will discuss Mather's
contention in the *Manuductio ad Ministerium* that creative innovation can
poison the tradition, but that, used judiciously, it can be a fine medicine.
According to Calef, however, Mather's inventions were not judicious or-
namentations of truth, but a complete eclipse of it. Consequently, Mather's logic compelled him to conclude that Calef's book was one of Satan's poisons, a fair-seeming simulacrum that impugned the goodness of

---

[24] Cotton Mather, *The Armour of Christianity* (Boston, 1704), p. 209.
[25] Perry Miller, *The New England Mind: From Colony to Province* (Boston: Beacon
Press, 1961), p. 250.

good work. Mather knew his writings demonstrated his piety, but because this conjunction of production and virtue might not be clear to
man at large, Satan could insert himself between truth and appearance
and waylay the credulous.

At several points in his diary, Mather shows a general worry about the
devil's books:

> What has a gracious Lord given me to do, in the *Writing of many Books*, for
> the Advancing of Piety, and the Promoting of his Kingdome, *Glory to
> GOD in the Highest and Good will among men?* There are, I sup-
> pose, more than three Hundred and thirty of them. AND YETT, I
> have had more *Books* written against me; more Pamphlets to
> traduce me, and reproach me, than any man that I know in the
> world. (*D*, II:707)

Since Mather is the personification of New England piety, Satan's general
hatred of piety culminates in a specific hostility to Mather, and commits
him to an inverting mimesis of Mather: as Mather writes many books to
spread piety, Satan writes many books to malign Mather and so spread
impiety. He even imitates Mather's power of universal address to men in
all their situations: "There is no sort of *Men*, but the *Devil* has many
wiles to come at them. Whatever be our *Tempers*, there are *many wiles* of
the Devil to fit them."[26] The most egregious among the devil's ventril-
oquizing counter-books was the anti-Bible circulated in Salem in search
of signatures. Notice Mather's insinuation that there is an occult, hostile
connection between this book and his own publications:

> I had filled my Countrey with little BOOKS, in several whereof, I had,
> with a Variety of Entertainment, offered the *New Covenant* formally
> drawn up, unto my Neighbours: hoping to engage them eternally unto
> the Lord, by their subscribing with *Heart* and *Hand,* unto the *Covenant.*
> Now in the late horrid *Witchcraft,* the manner of the Spectres was to
> tender BOOKS unto a *League* with the Divel therein exhibited, and so
> become the Servants of the Divil forever; which when they refused, the
> Spectres would proceed to wound them with Scalding, Burning,
> Pinching, Pricking, Twisting, Choaking, and a thousand preternatural
> Vexations. (*D*, I:155)

Again, there is the diabolical doubling: the covenant of light is opposed
by the covenant of darkness; and the agent of light, Cotton Mather, who
possesses a universalist capacity to "engage" the full range of his neighbors with a "Variety of Entertainment," is opposed by an agent of darkness who likewise has an armory of persuasive devices for the array of
man. Mather's theological epistemology denied him certain knowledge
of the quality of his soul, and led him to work that would provide approximate certainty but could never really reassure him, because the

[26] Mather, *The Armour of Christianity,* p. 20.

slightest slip was extremely significant. He set himself an infinite task –
complete freedom from any taint of self, a purely universal piety, and a
universal conversion of man – at the time that he believed that the failure
of his work would testify to the failure of his piety. The screw can be
turned no tighter: so when his work did fail, he needed an explanation
that offered relief from doubt about himself. He found relief by projecting the inner tension outward as the combat between himself and the
pharaoh of hell: and it is therefore no coincidence that he found Satan to
be an uncannily specific inversion of the nature and method of his own
piety.

This is not to say that Cotton Mather was a failure by objective standards, but that he was a failure at the infinite task he set for himself as
the only sufficient surrogate for impossible certainty. Until his death, he
retained a great deal of influence among the citizens of Boston. His correspondence and his renown reached beyond his locale, and he was one
of the first colonials elected to the Royal Society. It is at least within the
range of debatable feasibility that, as John Bach McMaster argued, "the
greatest American then living [during the period of Franklin's early man-
hood] was Cotton Mather."[27] Colman summarized his eminence after
Mather's funeral:

> His Name is to live a great while among us in his *printed Works;* but yet
> these will not convey to Posterity, nor give to Strangers, a just Idea of
> the real *Worth* and great Learning of the Man. His *Works* will indeed
> inform all that read them of his great Knowledge, and singular Piety,
> his Zeal for God, and Holiness and Truth; and his desire of the Salva-
> tion of precious Souls; but it was *Conversation* and Acquaintance with
> him, in his familiar and occasional Discourses and private Communi-
> cations, that discovered the vast compass of his Knowledge and the
> Projections of his Piety; more I have sometimes thought than all his
> *Pulpit* exercises.[28]

Colman correctly identifies Mather's trio of ambitions: piety, or the annihilation of self; a consciousness of vast compass; and a large posterity
recruited by his work. If Mather considered his work a failure, therefore,
it is only partly because he saw the beginning of a rising generation closer
to Franklin than to filiopiety: it is also because of the magnitude of the
task to which the epistemology he inherited condemned him. Given this
task, he was invigorated to *go on,* if not succeed, by the thought of the
dark double.

[27] John Bach McMaster, *Benjamin Franklin as a Man of Letters* (Boston: Houghton
Mifflin, 1893), p. 9.
[28] Benjamin Colman, quoted in David Levin, *Cotton Mather: The Young Life of
the Lord's Remembrancer* (Cambridge, Mass.: Harvard University Press, 1978),
p. ix.

The perseverance afforded him by the concept of the exterior apostasy is quite clear in the vexation he encountered in his third marriage. In his diary for 1716, he reveals a startling discovery. Several earlier passages of "Good Devised" had been so completely inked out that they were unintelligible and, consequently, lost from the good. A "Good Devised," noted by G.D. at the beginning of an entry, was a resolution to good work addressed to some particular part of his audience, and it was also a note that might be used in a later tract on pious activity. The cancellation of several of these consequently caused him great consternation, because it interfered irreparably with the part of his life so central to his self-conception – writing.

"I could never learn How or Why the Blotts were made" (D, II:384). He must, however, have had suspicions, because this was not the first occult interference with his textual production. In September 1693, Mather was beginning his great authorial labor, working on the first conceptions of *The Wonders of the Invisible World*, the *Magnalia Christi Americana*, and the *Biblia Americana*. But he interrupted this work to write sermons to preach at Salem, which had recovered from the witch trials but was experiencing sore division as an aftermath:

> But I had one singular Unhappiness, which befel mee, in this Journey [to Salem]. I had largely written three Discourses, which I designed both to *preach* at Salem, and hereafter to *print*. These *Notes*, were before the Sabbath, *stolen* from mee, with such Circumstances, that I am somewhat satisfied, The Spectres, or Agents in the *invisible World*, were the *Robbers*. This Disaster, had like to have disturbed my Designs for the Sabbath; but God helped me to *remember* a great part of what I had written, and to *deliver* also many other Things, which else I had not now made use of. So that Divel got nothing! (D, I:172)

When he returned to Boston, he discovered that Satan had arrested and possessed a neighbor, Margaret Rule. Mather treated her possession (according to Calef, this treatment included soothing by stroking her face and naked breast), and, after six weeks, he noticed a diminution of the affliction. As her madness passed, she explained the loss of his notes: "As for my missing Notes, the possessed young Woman, of her own Accord, enquir'd whether I missed them not? Shee told mee, the *Spectres* bragg'd in her hearing, that they had rob'd mee of them; shee added, *Bee n't concern'd; for they confess, they can't keep them always from you; you shall have them all brought you again*." One of the verses with which the notes were concerned, Haggai 1:9, concerns the destruction of vain work: "Ye looked for much, and, lo, it came to little; and when ye brought it home, I did blow upon it." But Mather's work had been blown away by Satan, not God, and the fact that it was not vain work was proved when God returned it to him: "On the fifth of *October* following, every Leaf of my

Notes came again into my Hands, tho' they were in eighteen separate
Quarters of Sheets. They were found drop't here and there, about the
Streets of *Lyn;* but how they came to bee so drop't I cannot imagine; and
I as much wonder at the Exactness of their Praeservation" (*D,* I:173).
"I could never learn How or Why the Blotts were made." Two years
later, in 1718, he did discover. His third wife, he asserts, had gradually
gone mad. After only a year of marriage, Ronald Bosco contends, Mather
was already suspecting her "pretenses of religion and maternal affection";[29] by 1718, he had concluded that, though she had been at first
content with crossing out Good Devised on the sly, her madness had
worsened until she delighted in stealing some of the yearly diaries, and
refusing to return them. It is impossible to judge if Lydia George was
insane, rather than angry, or, if she was insane, what the root of her
illness was. It seems to me that the best hypothesis is that she was caught
– as he was – between his ardor and his determination to filiopiety. After
his second wife, Elizabeth Hubbard, died from measles shortly after giving birth to twins in November 1713, Mather vowed to glorify God with
widowhood for the rest of his life (*D,* II:281). But he married Lydia
George, who had herself been widowed in November 1714, in July 1715,
when he was fifty-two. She seems to have been the reluctant partner
during the courtship, forbidding his attentions on several occasions while
his importunities were fervent, in a pious way. In one letter, he wishes
her sweet interviews with Christ, "whom your soul loveth!"

> What is He, more than any other Beloved! O infinitely more! All oth-
> ers, pretenders in your esteem and I among the rest, are black and base
> and vile things, yea, and the brightest Angels in Heaven, are mean things
> in Comparison of Him. O Sun in the Firmament; Thou too art all
> Blackness, before that Sun of Righteousness.

He hopes, however, that, though she may scorn his vile self, she might
see that he is a son of righteousness and a fair facsimile of Christ the
bridegroom: "I mightily wish, That you may love nothing that is Mine.
My wishes are, That I may be so Happy as to exhibit unto you some
Reflections of his Image" (letter in *D,* II:308–9).
During their marriage, he resolves to govern her soul:

> My religious and excellent Consort meets with some Exercises, which
> oblige me, (and, oh! how happy am I, in the Conversion of so fine a
> Soul, and one so capable of rising and soaring to the higher Flights of
> Piety!) to treat her very much on the Point of having a Soul, wherein
> GOD alone shall be enthroned, and all the Creatures that have usurped

---

[29] Ronald A. Bosco, "A Chronological Chart of Significant Dates and Events in
the Life of Cotton Mather," in his edition of Cotton Mather, *Paterna* (Delmar,
N.Y.: Scholars' Facsimiles and Reprints, 1976), p. viii.

His Throne ejected and banished, and having a Will utterly annihilated before the Will of God! (*D*, II:346)

He urges her to reject governance by any creatures, including her own will and, implicitly, himself, but the act of urging is itself an act of governance. His recommendations reproduce a discipline he required in himself:

> I do not apprehend, that Heaven requires me utterlie to lay aside my fondness for my Lovelie Consort.
> But I must mourn most bitterlie and walk humblie all my Daies for my former pollutions. I must abhor the least tho't of regard unto anie other Person but this dearlie beloved of my soul. I must be temperate in my Conversation with her. And I must alwaies propose a good and an high End in it; something that mai be an Expression or an Evidence of my Obedience to God. (*D*, II:523)

But one of the evidences of her madness is her decision to govern his ardor for him:

> Moreover, my Consort's leaving of my Bed, when I am a Person of whom there cannot be the least Pretence of my being a Person universally acceptable, affords me Occasion of particular Supplications, that the Holiness and Purity whereto I am so singularly called of GOD, may have its perfect Work, and that I may no longer so foolishly dote as I have done, upon a Person who treats me with such a matchless Ingratitude, and Malignity. (*D*, II:752–3)

Mather's remark that he is not universally acceptable does not refer to his pastoral capacity in this case; but his affliction does refer him to his duty to the Creator by denying him the enjoyment of the creature. The sign of her return to domestic conformity is the end of the harsh regime:

> In the Evening of this Day, my poor Wife, returning to a right Mind, came to me in my Study, entreating that there might be an eternal Oblivion of every thing that has been out of Joint, and an eternal Harmony in our future Conversation; and that for the expressing and further obtaining of this Foelicity, I would now join with her, in pouring out Supplications to the Lord; and resolve to pray oftener with her, than ever heretofore. I did accordingly. And the Tokens of the greatest Inamoration on her part ensued upon it. (*D*, II:755)

From the love letters through this entry, the language of pious rapture and the language of erotic rapture are close, as in the Song of Solomon and in Edward Taylor's poems: Mather's thought meshes the two at the same time that it insists that they must not be confused – a fine and easily bewildering distinction in practice, which may have aggravated Lydia George's madness, if she was mad.

Her third recorded bout of paroxysm coincided with the death of Creasy, and it must have seemed to Mather to be evidence of epidemic, of the hand of the single antagonist behind the proliferation of diffuse balkings. When he married Lydia George, he assumed responsibility for her late son-in-law's estate, and he was threatened with financial ruin until his congregation saved him. He also took her niece into his house, but the niece proved to be "a very wicked Creature, and not only utterly deaf to all Proposals of Piety, but also a monstrous Lyar and a very mischievous Person, and a Sower of Discord, and a Monster of Ingratitude. The Un-easiness that by her vile Tricks is caused in my Family, is a sore Trial to me" (D, II:709). The reference to ingratitude, discord, and monstrosity, like the references to ingratitude and malignity in the entry concerning his wife's having left his bed, employ the language he saved for Satan: misrepresentation, deformation, strife, slander. It was therefore uncan-nily and diabolically appropriate that the epidemic should also reach to an actual physical assault on the production of truth in writing.

In a long diary meditation, he speculates on the origin of Lydia George's affliction, and wonders if there is a demonic seducer. He begins by in-quiring whether her affliction might be a punishment of a failure of piety within himself: "My glorious LORD, has inflicted a new and sharp Chas-tisement upon me. The Consort, in whom I flattered myself with the View and Hopes of an uncommon Enjoyment, has dismally confirmed it unto me, that our *Idols* must prove our *Sorrows*." But he is quick to note that, even if this is a chastisement of excessive love on his part, it is not a product of cruelty to her:

> Now and then, in some of the former Years, I observed and suffered grievous Outbreakings of her proud Passions; but I quickly overcame them, with my victorious Love, and in the Methods of Meekness and Goodness. *And, O my SAVIOUR, I ascribe unto thee all the Glory of it, and I wondrously praise thee for it;* I do not know, that I have to this Day spoke one impatient or unbecoming Word unto her; tho' my Provoca-tions have been unspeakable; and, it may be, few Men in the World, would have born them as I have done.

The locus of error is shifting from his idolatry to her mad pride. As he reexamines their time together, he realizes the insuperable periodicity of her complaint's recurrence. Holy work may fail to secure its end, but the flaw lies in the instability of the material, not in the worker: "But this last Year has been full of her prodigious Paroxysms; which have made it a Year of such Distresses with me, as I have never seen in my Life before."

Once error has been transferred from self to antagonist, Mather begins to inquire into the origin of this periodic affliction:

> When the Paroxysms have gone off, she has treated me still with a Fondness, that it may be, few Wives in the World have arriv'd unto. But in the Returns of them (which of late still grow more and more frequent,) she has insulted me with such Outrages, that I am at a Loss,

> which I should ascribe them to; whether a Distraction, (which may be
> somewhat Haereditary,) or to a Possession; (whereof the Symptoms
> may have been too direful to be mentioned). (*D*, II:584–5)

Here he forbears, and does not unequivocally enlist his antagonist the
demon. He would not forbear in this manner when the complaint re-
curred in 1724, shortly before Creasy's death:

> This Night my unaccountable Consort, had a prodigious Return of her
> Pangs upon her; that seemed little short of a proper Satanical Posses-
> sion. After a thousand unrepeatable Invectives, compelling me to rise
> at Midnight, and retire to my Study that I might there pour out my
> Soul unto the Lord; she also gott up in an horrid Rage, protesting that
> she would not live or stay with me; and calling up her wicked Niece
> and Maid, she went over to a Neighbour's house for a Lodging; Doubt-
> less with numberless Lies, which a Tongue sett on Fire of Hell, would
> make no Conscience of . . . I verily beleeve, there is not in all these
> Regions an Husband, who treats a Wife, with more continual and
> exquisite Endeavours, to please her and serve her, and make her com-
> fortable at home, and reputable abroad. And it is astonishing, how she
> can invent Occasions for the Outrages that she will fall into, after the
> lucid Intervals which are filled with Expressions of the most enamoured
> Fondness for me. (*D*, II:749–50)

As in the 1718 entry, Mather lays heavy stress on the periodicity of deformation: the matter of woman can be governed so that it assumes form,
but form's purchase is always precarious, and the matter is ineluctably
liable to slipping free.

In the 1718 entry, he moves from his contemplation of the origin of
her affliction to her anger at his writing: "But, what I have here to relate,
is; that she expressed such a Venome, against my reserved Memorials, of
Experiences in, and Projections for, the Kingdome of GOD, as has obliged
me to lay the Memorials of this Year, I thought, where she would not
find them." During this year, he adds, he had hoped to rest in work
accomplished: "It has been a Year, wherein I have made more Advances
in Piety, than in many former Years. Perhaps, my Journey thro' the Wilderness just expiring, I must rid more way in one year now, than in forty
before." He records the diligence with which he has continued in piety
without hoping for rest, and he concludes that the Lord has smiled upon
him not by terminating her paroxysms – labor is never done – but by
maintaining his reputation in the public eye as a sign of his excellence:

> I have lived for near a Year in a continual Anguish of Expectation, that
> my poor Wife, by exposing her Madness, would bring a Ruine on my
> Ministry. But now it is exposed, my Reputation is marvellously prae-
> served among the People of GOD, and there is come such a general and
> violent Blast upon her own, as I cannot but be greatly troubled at.

The failure in his holy work does not testify to his own turpitude, but to the insurmountable profligacy of his material, which condemns him to incessant and infinite labor, but does not condemn *him:* "I will now go on" (*D*, II:584–6).

The succinct conjunction of Mather's key themes – fear of personal shortcoming, labor, women, writing, slander, the demon, projection, incessant dissatisfaction, and reputation – makes Mather's encounter with Lydia George, as he implies in his comment on the forty previous years of work, a brief image of his life as a whole. Despite his obsessively pertinacious labors, the "Methods of Meekness and Goodness," delirium always found him, but he went on:

> And that which more afflicts me is; that tho' I cry to God in the Battel, and plead the Sacrifice of a Glorious Christ, and His Compassion and Ability to succour the Tempted, for my Deliverance; yett the Uttermost that I can obtain is, for the Tempter to depart but for a Season; returns again to me, in a Month or two, with more efficacy than before. (*D*, I:586).

3

DECLINE AND REMEMBRANCE

The deepest form of fascination, that of the artist, derives its strength from being [an expression of] both horror and the possibility of conceiving horror.

André Malraux, A Preface for Faulkner's *Sanctuary*

If we were to itemize the varieties of sin that Cotton Mather put into the category of the abominable, we would find, among many others: Hutchinson, her licentious heterodoxies, and the deformities she engendered; the devil(s) behind the spectres at Salem; the theology that sought to do away with public conversion narratives; Anglican surplices; and the kind of life that Benjamin Franklin made for himself even after he had progressed from slanderous satirist to venerable philosophe. This may seem a miscellaneous grouping of things that happened to irritate Mather; but we should not divide his thought along lines native to our own assumptions rather than to his if we wish to understand him. Mather's categorization of the abominable is coherent, and it plays an important part in his self-conception.

His Calvinism led him to an incessant war on the self's vigorous resistance to pattern: and if the pressure of this inner strife led him to seek relief by projecting it outward as a combat between himself and a diabolical antagonist, then the antagonist would be a fabulous and magnified representation of the self's own vigor – a repellent picture of what the self would be if it ever really got out. This conviction would explain his recurring intuition that the devil was a specifically inverse double of himself, uncannily miming his universal, self-annihilating labor as a father, a minister, and an author. It would also explain why Mather was imaginatively meticulous (rather than just condemnatory) in his anatomy of the kinds and techniques of evil, as he would not be if there were no secret fascination.

Unlike the self, however, these doubles were opposed only by Cotton

Mather: in their deeds, their imaginations, and their self-conceptions, the doubles who meddled in the universal effect of his talent were not internally diverted by a compelling voice that interrupted and checked the self's complacent procedure. If, therefore, Mather were to have argued that some of these blithe sinners' methods might be borrowed for use against them, that things rightly called hostile to piety might nonetheless, if delicately employed, actually invigorate it, this homeopathy would also be evidence of the secret fascination. And if Mather were to have written a biography of a man unvexed by piety, but not demonically antipious, and if for once he did not castigate such relaxation, this biography would be further evidence. Such a biography would be a declaration of independence from filiopiety, a vindication of the self on its own terms, though still in the projected form of another's life. Such a biography would adumbrate a secular doubling of Mather's ministry – a universal aptitude indigenous to the self, capable of eliciting wide assent for its universal capacity, but neither especially pious nor dedicated to the spread of piety. In such a rare liberal climate, the double could be seen, not as a diabolical simulacrum, but as a modernizing revision – the universal self released from service to the father into its own service. Rather than a sheer negation, therefore, such a double would be an antithesis that negated the filiopious form of universality in the interest of preserving universality in a new form. One member of the category of the abominable would have seceded: and, insofar as its self-vindication did have wide appeal, heirs such as ourselves would conclude that it had not belonged in the category of monstrosity to begin with.

In subsequent chapters, I will follow this development through Mather's advocacy of smallpox inoculation and his biography of Sir William Phips to Franklin's writings. For the present, however, I will remain with Mather's anatomy of what Perry Miller called the Great Declension of faith to show how, even when he is condemning abomination, we may detect the self murmuring in its internment in the dynastic past.

Robert Middlekauff offers a way to understand the unity of Mather's categorization of the monstrous:

> A Puritan layman recognized the special horror of any defense described as "unclean" or "filthy." Richard Mather, like every minister, used these words to describe sins such as fornication or adultery. Increase Mather pushed this terminology further, using these words to describe offenses having no connection with sex. These rhetorical, or stylistic, choices suggest a character less confident of itself, less sure of its goodness perhaps, and striving for reassurance that it measures up to the best of the past.[1]

[1] Robert Middlekauff, *The Mathers: Three Generations of Puritan Intellectuals* (New York: Oxford University Press, 1971), p. 92.

The special horror, that is, was expanded from the self's sexuality to the whole self as the sense of dynastic obligation began to put pressure on the self's whole worldly being.

But Middlekauff is wrong to claim that these sins have *nothing* to do with sexuality. The expansion of the category of the abominable is not simply a rhetorical or stylistic transfer of adjectives, but instead the product of a philosophical fusion of the filiopiety prescribed in the fifth commandment with the iconoclasm prescribed in the second commandment: eros is not to be tolerated if it is not subdued to the form of marriage and progeny; the assertion of the individual is not to be tolerated if the self is not subdued to the paternal pattern; and any affection for worldly things in any way is impermissible unless it is capped by a conscious glorification of the god who made them. Sexual aberration, perhaps by virtue of its intensity, is the most conspicuous case of a more general tendency to take lesser things as opaque delights rather than as translucent revelations of the divinity that lies behind. The extension of the special horror is thus not logically incongruous: rather, it is an implicit contention that sins now included as special horrors are perhaps subtler than rampant eros, or less pressing, but not less severe. The self, and all of the interests and affections that compose it, is the locus of potential declension: it must be interrupted in its rush to damnation, and subordinated to paternity.

The tendency Middlekauff attributes to Increase Mather was carried still further by Cotton Mather, whose use of the adjectives *licentious* and *adulterous* (among others) to condemn activities other than sexuality is frequent. We should remember that the roots of these adjectives – license and adulterate – have a more general denotation: Mather wishes to employ both the larger significance of the roots and the anti-erotic connotations of the adjectives to spread the force of Christian anti-erotic rhetoric over the whole field of richly imagined apostasies, as he did when he followed Winthrop in connecting Hutchinson's heterodoxy with her promiscuity.

In *Icono-clastes: An Essay upon the Idolatry too often committed under the Profession of the most Reformed Christianity,* Mather contends that there are grosser and finer sorts of idolatry. The grosser sort, described in the original Hebrew opposition to Canaanite worship and still practiced, according to Mather, in Spain, Italy, China, and Japan, consists of worshiping manufactured material images. The finer sort consists of the mental failure to subordinate the love of the creature to the love of the Creator even if physical images are not involved: "There is an *Idolatry* in our *Apostasy.* Self is now set up in the throne of God. Our Chief Aim, now is, to Gratify and Aggrandize our *Self,* without a due Subordination unto GOD, That our usurping *Self* may accommodated, we go to *Creatures* for

Succours, and Supplies, instead of going unto GOD, for relief of our wants."
Self is the locus of usurpation, and all of its uses of the creature for succor
or supply are fornications: "Be sure, all such Idolatry in us, will be a
perfidious breach of our Covenant. It will be a *Spiritual Adultery*. The
Jealous GOD will upon it, proceed against us as adulterers."[2] In Cotton
Mather's thought, as in his father's, the usurping failure of subjugation
and subordination that occurs in fornication is distilled from the literal
act and generalized to include all enjoyments that are not mindful of the
will of the father.

Mather's category of the abominable is thus not a miscellaneous amalgam, but a logically whole hermeneutic theory, with the world rather
than a book being the text at hand:

> *Chrysostom,* I remember, mentions a *Twofold Book* of GOD, the Book of
> the *Creatures,* and the Book of the *Scriptures . . .* We will now for a
> while read the *Former* of these Books, 'twill help us in reading the *Latter:*
> They will admirably assist one another. The Philosopher being asked
> What his *Books* were; answered *Totius Entis Naturalis Universitas* [the
> natural university of all the existing universe]. All Men are accommo-
> dated with that *Publick Library. Reader,* walk with me into it, and see
> what we shall find so legible there, *that he that runs may read it.* Behold
> a Book, whereof we may agreeably enough use the words of honest
> *Aegardus; Lectu hic omnibus facilis, esti nunquam legere dedicerint, et com-
> munic est omnibus, omniumque oculis expositus* [here is easy reading for
> everyone even when they have not learned to read, and it is open to all,
> and set out before everyone's eyes]. (*CP:* 8)

Here, in the introduction to *The Christian Philosopher,* Mather attempts
to encourage the fledgling by claiming that reading the creature is just
plain seeing, and not reading at all. But if this were so there would be no
need for *The Christian Philosopher,* which is a manual on the proper reading of nature; and as the reader progresses through the dense argumentation of *The Christian Philosopher* he will realize that the reading of the
creature is closer to the arduous reading of scripture that Augustine describes in *De Doctrina Christiani* than it is to plain seeing. To read properly, the observer of the creature must overcome his own idolatry and his
susceptibility to demonic misconstructions. If he is persuaded that the
creature gives evidence of what the minister knows is a falsehood, or if
his hermeneutical endeavor stops short of glorifying God to marvel at
commodity or reason, he will have misread, and mistaken quicksand for
a sure foundation. Piety must combat false readings and absorb subordinate readings, which become damnable competitors if they are not so
absorbed.

---

[2] Cotton Mather, *Icono-clastes: An Essay upon the Idolatry too often committed under
the Profession of the most Reformed Christianity* (Boston, 1717), pp. 1, 5, 11.

Mather did distinguish between various kinds of abominable misreadings. In a suggestive passage in his diary, he divided abomination into base thoughts, vile thoughts, and vain thoughts (*D*, II:207). Base thoughts would be specimens of appetite, the interpretation of the creature as a source of physical comfort or sensual gratification that was not accompanied by gratitude to the provider. Among vile thoughts, Mather includes popery, Quakerism, and Arminianism; vileness consists of explicit distortions of true theology, or true reading. Vain thoughts would be pride, satisfaction with self, its unique excellence, its reason and its achievement without the thought of self-annihilation before the father. In this trio of sins, vileness would be an exacerbation of the other two: a vile doctrine would try to assure a base or vain person that his baseness or vanity was justifiable; thus though a vain person might tend to be Arminian, Arminianism would be vile. All three sorts of error are failures to read the world correctly, but they have distinct characteristics, and they call forth different modes of opposition from the minister's armory of abilities.

In general, Mather associates vile thoughts, or deliberate misreadings of the truth, with Satan, calling them intentional acts committed by a coherent antagonist and hence requiring an aggressively militant demeanor. In *The Armour of Christianity,* his most developed tract on the demon, Mather contends that "The *Work* of a Christian in this world, has in it very much of a Warfare." The martial images that pervade the essay underscore his conviction that in the battle with outright misrepresentation he was arrayed against an apprehensible personality. The forces of evil are persons:

> The Sovereign GOD hath, with infinite *Wisdom* & *Justice,* confined the *Fallen Spirits* unto this *Atmosphere;* but with their *Confinement,* they have so much *Liberty,* that until the *Second Coming* of the *Messiah* into this lower world, they may range and rove about, and molest the poor Children of men. Our *Air* is filled with them, as with *Flies* in Mid-summer. We draw our breath in the *place of Dragons.*[3]

The tract wavers on whether Satan is one person or a collective name for many spirits, but it leaves no room to doubt the author's conviction that he is engaged in holy war with clever and eloquent adversaries for the possession of souls.

But the vile thoughts promoted by the demon(s) were exacerbations of base thoughts and vain thoughts, both of which preexisted demonic temptation and both of which required other modes of pastoral opposition, since they were ways of falling short of the full truth rather than outright falsehoods. As long as Mather was confronting a willful and active distortion, he assumed the martial stance and anticipated victory,

---

[3] Cotton Mather, *The Armour of Christianity* (Boston, 1704), pp. 2, 6.

as in his discussions of the coming chiliad, which frequently include references to satanism, because the concept of an antagonist carries with it the thought of the antagonist's defeat and of the restoration of pure lucidity. At several points in his writing, for example in his diary for the months before Satan's appearance at Salem, Mather seems even to welcome demonic vileness, perhaps because combat and the possibility of victory offer more clarity than the slow pedagogy of rectifying men's torpor. Nonetheless, Mather realized that when he confronted men not seduced by falsehood but guilty of a sagged piety, he would have to adopt a less martial and more pedagogical mode of approach. Such men were stopping their reading of the creature at appetite or reason: this was not an explicit contradiction of truth, but a failure to reach high enough, a termination at one of the inferior steps of the ascent.

Mather was likely to see this sag as original sin, a heaviness or torpor which Satan might exploit, since falsehoods gain currency easily among those who do not see clearly, but which was distinct from Satan: "There may be some Feebleness, and Heaviness in our Natural Constitution, or some tiresome Accident, sometimes betraying us into [spiritual lethargy]."[4] Despite the obvious differences, Mather's argument resembles Gibbon's contention that the Christian abuse of reason was able to flourish because the Romans had already sunk from their virile republicanism into uxoriousness and submission. Because they had lapsed from the conspicuous excellence of the earlier generations, the tarnished saints of Mather's New England might be more susceptible to agile falsehood, but the decline to lethargy happened independently of the falsehood. Such a predicament required ministers and authors that were pedagogues and remembrancers, rather than soldiers of Christ. The distinction is important because the virtues celebrated by the Enlightenment – commodity and practical reason – were not the tools of heresiarchs who hated the faith, but instead shortfalls: the men of Enlightenment had to be shown not that they had taken the wrong path, but that they were only part way there, and so could not stop to build a house. Mather's ambition, like Edwards's, was not to castigate Enlightenment, since the virtues it extolled were gifts of God, but to absorb it; or, rather, to prevent revisionary thinkers such as Franklin from taking piety off the top of commodity and practical reason in order to call them sufficient in themselves.

Mather's most extensive published contribution to the cure of forgetfulness was the *Magnalia Christi Americana,* which Perry Miller called a "colossal jeremiad."[5] This book may be read with an antiquarian or scholarly interest; and readers of a Borgesian or Melvillian bent may also

---

[4] Ibid., p. 75.
[5] Perry Miller, *The New England Mind: From Colony to Province* (Boston: Beacon Press, 1961), p. 33.

find in it the curious, compendious zest of *The Anatomy of Melancholy* or *Pseudodoxia Epidemica*. I think that Mather would not repudiate such readings, since he seems often to have read in these ways himself. But they would be *preparations,* and not memory itself. Remembrance requires a reproduction of the excellence of the past in the person of the contemporary reader, a method he practiced in his reading of scripture:

> The Holy Spirit of GOD who inspired His Chosen Servants to write the Oracles he has given us in the Scriptures, made heavenly Impressions on the Minds of the Writers, which raised Heavenly Affections in them. When I take a Passage of the Bible under my Consideration, I will nicely observe, what Affection of Piety appears in the Passage, and press after the raising of the same Affection in myself, and not count that I have the full Meaning of the Text until I have done.[6]

The task of reading is an exact reproduction of the piety of the past in the present, in the son, which makes him a visible monument to the living tradition, rather than a sepulchre that records its demise.

Mather's key figure for his writing of the *Magnalia Christi Americana* is the erection of the stone Ebenezer in 1 Samuel 7:12: "Then Samuel took a stone, and set it between Mizpeh and Shen, and called the name of it Ebenezer, saying, Hitherto hath the LORD helped us." The *Magnalia Christi Americana* is Cotton Mather's Ebenezer (eben ha-ezer: stone of help), a perdurable reminder of the Lord's impression of faith on the souls of New England's past greats. It is not an *ubi sunt,* but instead a persisting standard against which the drift of the present can be measured in the interest of rectification. The book has many references to funerary and other monuments that symbolize the book itself, a persevering memory that contrasts with the vagaries, the countless infidelities, and the constant defections of human experience. Mather's references to edifices, columns, candelabra, even the signet ring taken from the son of Scipio Africanus, are figures for his dedication to writing as a cure for forgetfulness: when discussing his own writing, he emphasizes its permanence; the writing is directed primarily against the ephemerality of human allegiance, rather than against malevolence. The contrast between the monument and the busy human community that goes on around it is a visual emblem of his lifelong preoccupation with the disparity between the *ought* of inheritance and the *is* of actual experience.

The figure of the Ebenezer is first introduced at the end of Book I, in the "Historical Remarks on the State of Boston," a rather caustic diatribe against contemporary turpitude which takes note of the proliferation of

---

[6] Cotton Mather, *Diary* II, 479, as quoted in Richard F. Lovelace, *The American Pietism of Cotton Mather: Origins of American Evangelicalism* (Grand Rapids, Mich.: Christian University Press, 1979), p. 115.

alehouses, likens Boston to Sodom, and points to a recent earthquake in
Jamaica as an omen of what might happen should piety not grow quick
again. Boston has lapsed: "Shall I tell you where that Utopia was? 'Twas
NEW-ENGLAND! But they that go from hence must now tell another story"
(*MCA*, I:103).

But Mather includes an interesting variation on the usual themes of
the jeremiad. Whereas the jeremiads that Perry Miller discusses in *The
New England Mind* had been based on the assumption that the declensions
that were regular in profane communities were infallible signs of failure
in the community of the Elect, Mather's "Historical Remarks on the State
of Boston" assumes that periods of decline are inevitable in *all* communities. New England is to be congratulated not for the absence of declension, but for the fact that declension has been minimized:

> What changes have we seen in point of *religion?* It was noted by *Luther,*
> *he could never see good order in the church last more than fifteen years together*
> *in the purity of it.* Blessed be God, *religion* hath here flourished in the
> purity of it more than fifteen years together. But certainly the *power of*
> *Godliness* is now grievously decayed among us. (*MCA*, I:103)

As the last sentence suggests, Mather's purpose in making the assertion
is not to promote a more forgiving attitude in the face of human fallibility but to alter the significance of the declension that is here deplored as
vehemently as in any other jeremiad. Mather is contending, as he did in
his accounts of his wife's madness and in his funeral sermon for his son,
that faith's purchase on its human material is always precarious, even in
New England, and that slippage does not connote a weakness of faith.
Given the lurking promiscuity of the medium in which faith must work,
periodic explosions are to be expected, and they do not reveal the insufficiency of the worker.

Robert Middlekauff contends that Richard Mather had seen such periodicity in the history of the English Church: "As part of the old order
of Christ, the English Church experienced the long cycles of purity and
decay that supplied the common pattern of history."[7] In the "Historical
Remarks on the State of Boston," Cotton Mather implies that this periodicity afflicts the new order as well as the old. Though this does not
relax the sense of the awfulness of declension or of the severity that op-
posing declension requires, it does exonerate the diligent monument-
maker and allow him to confront the present with vigor rather than with
the depressed fatigue that would come from self-suspicion: "*Lord, help*
us to remember whence we are fallen, and to repent, and to do the first works."
As in his encounters with Lydia George, no achievement is got once and
then safe. Holiness – the "first works" – requires constant revival in later

[7] Middlekauff, *The Mathers*, p. 24.

works, such as the *Magnalia Christi Americana* and other Ebenezers, which repair the nearly forgotten by measuring the extent of forgetfulness.

Mather's remarks on the insuperable periodicity of declension are an interesting moment in filiopiety's war to annihilate the self. By projecting the self's aberration outward as the external demon, Mather finds some relief from shame. By claiming that the exterior declension is insurmountable even in New England, he exonerates his failures as well as his motives. He asserts that the dynasty is vulnerable, and that its name depends on him, rather than being endangered by him. The father's word changes from a condemnation to a plea. Once abomination is projected outward as a perpetual fallibility in men in all communities, Cotton Mather is transformed from the wayward, damnably innovative son into the stalwart remembrancer without whose pertinacity the words and deeds of the father and of the father's fathers will sink into oblivion. This projection may explain the fact that in Mather's *Diary*, the yahwistic Increase Mather of *Pray for the Rising Generation*, *A Father Departing*, and *Parentator* appears much less frequently than the beset, victimized, and distressed Increase Mather who had resolved to remain in England after suffering New England's ingratitude. In such passages from the diary, however, Cotton Mather does not guiltily include himself among the ingrates: the point is not that the angry father has turned his face from the son, but that a diligent old man has been stung by the unceasing ingratitude of the world and needs to be recalled to his commitment – or to have his mantle assumed by his still-vigorous son.

In these diary entries, Cotton Mather shows us his father hurt and withdrawing for self-protection rather than angry and withdrawing for punishment:

> G.D. Still my aged Parent must be the Object of my Cares. To make him easy, under his Resentments of the Proceedings about our New Church; and to procure him Releefs against bodily Distempers that somewhat incommode him; and to gett his Mind raised unto the Points of Resignation to God and Satisfaction in His Will, which become us in the Suburbs of Heaven. (*D*, II:194)

As in the 1690 letter, the son sees his father's touchiness as a moral shortcoming: but his reprimand is less precarious because he has exonerated himself from complicity in the ingratitude that instigated the distress. In 1700 the Mathers' opponents sought to block Increase's appointment as president of Harvard by requiring that the president reside in Cambridge, a requirement that would keep Increase from his pastoral duties in Boston. He did move to Cambridge briefly without his family, but returned to Boston after a few months. While his father lived in Cambridge, Cotton Mather complained that his father's removal caused him two kinds of distress. First, his father was plunged into a "strangely melancholy, and disconsolate, Condition of mind," he was "prodigiously unfram'd, unhing'd, and broken," and he was in danger of dishonoring the name of Christ. Cotton Mather's second distress was having to work alone: "I am now left alone, in the Care of a vast Congregation, the largest in all these Parts of the World . . . And, I am feeble; and in this Town, I have many Enemies; indeed, all the Enemies of the evangelical Interests, are mine" (D, II:360). This is not to say that Cotton Mather delighted in his father's misfortunes, but that, by stressing the deplorable power of the enemy to interfere in the father's efficacy, the son could emphasize the father's need for him rather than the father's disapproval of him.

Mather's remark that his enemies are also the enemies of the evangelical interest reminds us that the hazards of his father's career were not a private distress. Because Cotton Mather identified his family's interests with New England's great tradition, the decline of Increase's influence would be a prime symptom of the declension at large. This in turn invites us to wonder whether Mather's judgment that New England *was* experiencing a declension might not stem from the psychomachy between filiopiety and self as well as from cool appraisal of the condition of faith among his contemporaries. This consideration does not enter into Perry Miller's analysis of decline: "The code resisted change, and therefore change became declension."[8] As New England grew secular and commercial, according to Miller, the love of the creature – base thoughts and vain thoughts – declared independence from the love of the Creator. Those still emotionally allied to the old way composed jeremiads lamenting the change; those in the front of change attended to the jeremiads as a self-castigating ritual homage to the past that purged guilt and released them to their innovations. The society thus enjoyed a sense of continuity while in the midst of alteration.

The problem with Miller's argument is that the suspicious inquiry he directs at the rhetoric of the jeremiad is not directed at the initial assumption that a declension had begun by the middle of the seventeenth century. The jeremiads declared that a declension had begun, and Miller took them at their word. However, Kenneth Murdock, Robert G. Pope, Emory Elliott, and Sacvan Bercovitch have disputed the assumption that a declension began before the second or third decades of the eighteenth century, some seventy years after the New England divines began to deplore it, and Elliott and Bercovitch have suggested that the motivation for the assumption that there was a declension might itself be scruti-

---

[8] Miller, *The New England Mind*, p. 48. Miller's explication of declension and jeremiad runs from page 19 to page 149, though in a sense it is the topic of the whole volume.

nized.[9] The point of questioning the assumption that declension was occurring is not to prove it was not, or to challenge the dates, but to establish that the act of declaring that a decline is underway is not an act of
pure observation. A declension of faith is not an event in the way King
Philip's War or the installation of Andros were. There *were* conspicuous
abuses of morality such as the brothel that Alice Thomas opened in Boston in 1672. Miller concedes, however, that rampant vice was only a
froth on the true problem – spiritual lethargy. As Mather wrote in 1724,
"the epidemical Malady of the Time" was "a woful Indifferency and Formality in the grand Business of Religion" (*D*, II: 747).

But there is no yardstick to measure the extent to which a man's gratitude toward the Creator is only a perfunctory appendix to his sensual
enjoyment of the creature or whether thanks for the power of reason are
a mere formality covering the love of the self's rational power. Consequently, the postulation of a historical trend is an *interested* act: conver-
sations in the street, book sales, the tone of voice during a pastoral visit,
naps in church, the timbre of participation, and a host of other subtle
phenomena must be declared significant and assembled as symptoms of
a single, coherent trend. This is not to say that the declension was a
fantasy, but that the declaration that there was a declension could contain
complex motivation in addition to observation.

Among the motives might be the enhancement of the power and significance of the present generation. As heirs to the first generation, they
were taught to admire the vigor with which the first generation had declared independence from the corruption of Anglican England, a vigor
that is treated in every one of Mather's biographies of the members of
the first generation in the *Magnalia Christi Americana*. At the same time,
however, they were urged to an exact emulating admiration for Puritan
Massachusetts. Elliott has described this predicament:

> As young Englishmen, the founders had been pioneering and adven-
> turous themselves. They had been outspoken and daring non-con-
> formists, revolutionaries, and virile planters of a new society in a virgin
> land. But they did not want their children to imitate these qualities.
> They told their children that in New England they should be conform-

[9] Kenneth Murdock, *Increase Mather* (Cambridge, Mass.: Harvard University
Press, 1925), p. 319; Robert G. Pope, *The Half-Way Covenant: Church Member-
ship in Puritan New England* (Princeton, N.J.: Princeton University Press, 1969);
Emory Elliott, *Power and the Pulpit in Puritan New England* (Princeton, N.J.:
Princeton University Press, 1975), esp. p. 4; Sacvan Bercovitch, *The American
Jeremiad* (Madison: University of Wisconsin Press, 1978), esp. pp. 3–30. As
Bercovitch argues, a jeremiad requires a declension, and so if the jeremiad can
be viewed as a genre older than the American Puritans, so too can the act of
observing a declension.

ists and submissive laborers in the new society and leave leadership to the elders. The first fathers could not raise their children to reenact their own liberating rebellion, and perhaps by suppressing the young they were attempting to expiate their guilt for their own revolt against authority. Thus in their tales of their flight from persecution and the founding of the colony, the fathers presented to their children an image of vigorous independence, but in their directions to the young they preached submissiveness and obedience.[10]

If, however, as Mather asserts in his "Historical Remarks on the State of Boston," periodic declension did not cease with the American emigration, then the fathers' way could sink into corruption as primitive Christianity had sunk into the Roman Babylon; and the sons would have to declare independence from a corrupt world as their fathers had in England, as a gesture of fidelity to the fathers' way, as the fathers' rebellion had been faithful to the model of primitive Christianity. This action would not liberate the creative potential of the self, since self-annihilating and exact repetition were still in order: but by castigating the self, projecting its danger outward as an adversary that could – and had – constrained the power of the father's name, the son could make his job as remembrancer cosmically significant and he could use his fidelity to the father to justify his self-asserting rebellion against a corrupt world, as Mather had done in his participation in the overthrow of Andros. The act of declaring a declension to be underway limited the father's power, converted condemnation into plea, and justified self-assertion.

Therefore, though remembrance represented itself as being in opposition to transformation, innovation, and self, if it were coupled with the declaration of declension, it could provide the desire for self-shaping independence with partial and disguised expression. Again, there is an uncanny resemblance between piety and what it opposes, though in this case Mather would not acknowledge the resemblance because it is not an inversion, but a real similitude. At several points in his writing, however, the affinity between remembrance and independence shows through his resolution to maintain their polarity. For example, in the figural treatment of remembrance that begins the biography of Phips in the *Magnalia Christi Americana*:

> If such a Renowned Chymist, as *Quercetanus*, with a whole Tribe of *Labourers in the Fire*, since that Learned Man, find it no easie thing to make the common part of Mankind believe, That they can take a *Plant* in its more vigorous Consistence, and after a due *Maceration, Fermentation* and *Separation*, extract the *Salt* of that *Plant*, which, as it were, in a *Chaos*, invisibly reserves the *Form* of the whole, with its vital Principle; and, that keeping the *Salt* in a *Glass* Hermetically sealed, they can, by

10 Elliott, *Power and the Pulpit in Puritan New England*, pp. 78–9.

> applying a *Soft Fire* to the *Glass,* make the *Vegetable* rise by little and
> little out of its *Ashes,* to surprize the Spectators with a notable Illustra-
> tion of that *Resurrection,* in the Faith whereof the *Jews* returning from
> the Graves of their Friends, pluck up the *Grass* from the *Earth,* using
> those Words of the Scripture thereupon, *Your Bones shall flourish like an*
> *Herb.*

There is one tenor in this figural passage – the writer's remembrance –
but there are two vehicles, and they conflict. In the the alchemical resti-
tution of the plant from its salts, that which is restored is identical with
that which was reduced: "invisibly reserves the *Form* of the whole." But
the resurrection of the dead, whether as spirits or as herbs, transforms
them into something radically different from what they were before they
were reduced. If written remembrance is like the plant from the salts, it
is an exact repetition; but if it is like the herb from the corpse, it is a
significant revision.

Mather attempts to disguise this conflict by having plants in both
metaphors, but the ambiguity persists through the rest of the passage:

> The *Resurrection of the Dead* will be as Just, as Great an Article of our
> *Creed,* although the *Relations* of these Learned Men should pass for *In-*
> *credible Romances:* But yet there is an *Anticipation* of that Blessed *Resur-*
> *rection,* carrying in it some Resemblance of these *Curiosities,* which is
> performed, when we do in a *Book,* as in a *Glass,* reserve the History of
> our Departed *Friends;* and by bringing our *Warm Affections* unto such an
> History, we revive, as it were, out of their *Ashes,* the true *Shape* of those
> Friends, and bring to a fresh View, what was *Memorable* and *Imitable* in
> them. (*MCA,* I:165)

Mather would have been familiar with the Pauline doctrine of the letter
and the spirit, and consequently would have known that resurrection is
a transfiguration of the dead weight of the past that changes ponderous
dogma into vital new form. But the implications of the metaphor of the
resurrection of the dead are subdued by the implications of the metaphor
of the plant reconstituted from its salts: he goes out of his way to announce that his revival is a pure mirroring of the true shape of the past,
rather than an inventive romance; his preservation of what is memorable
or imitable is not selective or revisionary, but instead filiopious. But,
though he does not transform the original in the act of remembering, he
does transform the "chaos" to which the original has been reduced: once
he has disavowed any attraction to transforming the excellence of the
past, he can announce that the past is subject to degradation and dedicate
himself to transforming the degradation of the excellence of the past.
The transformative creativity of self is denied in the passage, but it reappears in disguised form as faithful remembrance.

Self is projected outward as declension, and then sublimated as remembrance. But, though this process reduces the pressure of paternity to a plea, confers significance on the son's historical mission, and justifies gestures of offended separation, it is nonetheless a disguised and partial gratification: pressure remains. Though the concept of declension might allow Mather to imagine himself in a situation similar to that of the first generation in the midst of the apostasies of the English Church, there is an important difference: the members of the first generation justified their severance of allegiances to their world on the grounds of their allegiance to the model of primitive Christianity; but the model to which Cotton Mather adhered in resisting declension was not separated from him by a vast historical distance, and so it did not require much modern adaptation. Whereas John Cotton and Richard Mather were following the example of the Christian communities of the first centuries after Christ, Cotton Mather was following an example developed only three decades before his birth. Consequently, his opposition to declension could not include creativity in the description of the model of piety from which the world had declined, and the relationship between his sense of obligation and the potential apostasy of his imaginative interest in the actual world remained tense.

This tension can be seen in *The Christian Philosopher,* where Mather is plainly attracted by Enlightenment modes of describing the world – commodity and rational causality – but where filiopiety repeatedly breaks in, labels these attractions base and vain thoughts, and subjugates them to Calvinism. Consequently, the structure of the argument of the book is dialectical rather than logical: Mather first delineates the appeal of one of the subordinate, inferior modes of reading the world, and then demolishes it so that the reader will not remain content in the subordinate position but will progress toward true virtue: *"Lord, I hope for an eternally progressive Knowledge, from the Lamb of God successively leading me to the Fountains of it!" (CP:*303). The rhetorical relation between the writer and the reader, a series of offered positions followed by undermining negations, thus mirrors the effect of piety on self within Mather's own consciousness.

The dialectical structure of the argument, however, is not reflected in the book's actual sequence. In his diary of 1716 Mather asks, "Is there no Possibility, for me, to find the Time, that I may contrive a System of the Sciences wherein they shall be rescued from Vanity and Corruption, and become consecrated unto the glorious Intention of *living unto God,* and the real and only Wisdome?" (*D,* II:339). He had contrived such a system in the massive *Biblia Americana,* but it had not been published. So he culled wisdom from several works, *Curiosa Americana, The Christian Virtuoso,* and, perhaps, the *Biblia Americana,* rearranged the material in topical chapters – "Of the Vegetables," "Of the Minerals," and so on – and published the new work as *The Christian Philosopher* in 1721. The heterogeneous origin of the material and the choice of topical chapters for convenient reference affected the sequence of the book. The "progressive" argument that moves from lamb to the fountains, from the type to the archetype, from vanity and corruption to the real and only wisdom is dispersed through the various topical chapters, rather than structuring the actual sequence. This dispersion has led Bercovitch to contend that *The Christian Philosopher* is a "haphazard proliferation of literary modes," a "chaos" that "palpably betokens a dissolution of external controls." He sees this chaos as a confusion that "appears in every Bible culture."[11] It seems to me, however, that the *appearance* of chaos can be attributed to the choice of topical chapters, and that, if the topical sequence is overlooked, the progressive argument can be reconstructed. The "haphazard proliferation" of modes can be seen as a dialectical sequence of subordinate epistemologies of reading the world and subsequent negations on the way to the real and only wisdom.

Reconstructed in this way, Mather's argument anticipates later American meditative structures such as "Nature" and *Walden*. Like Emerson and Thoreau, Mather is addressing men whose forgetfulness has shrunk nature to satisfaction, commodity, and rational causality, and who need to be reminded that nature is an extensive spiritual text that surpasses the paltry egocentric and utilitarian readings they have foisted upon it in their pursuit of comfort. According to the Covenant theology, nature's god had generously contracted himself into a provisional calculability, but he was not confined to it. Mather's aim was to return men from credulous infatuated forgetfulness to the awareness of the inscrutable superintending power of the god of the fathers, an aim we might also see as returning Cotton Mather from self to the example of the father: the author's attraction to modes of knowing the world which he must nevertheless negate is quite strong. To the end of curing amnesia, both in the reader and in the writer's self, *The Christian Philosopher* is a meditative ascent through five steps that identifies the allure of declension / Enlightenment, negates that allure, and then absorbs it as a subordinate moment in the faith of the fathers.

First, there is gratitude that the world ministers to human need: "how amazingly serviceable is our *Iron* to us" (*CP*:120); "every particular *part* of the Plant has its astonishing Uses" (*CP*:125); "even the most *noxious* and most *abject* of the vegetables, how useful are they!" (*CP*:129). Of course Mather does not consider that the human is genetically adapted to its surroundings, since man was made in the divine image, so the

---

[11] Sacvan Bercovitch, "Cotton Mather," in Everett Emerson, ed., *Major Writers of Early American Literature* (Madison: University of Wisconsin Press, 1972), p. 133.

conformity of things to human use signifies the validity of man's presence in the creation: "how nice the provision of Nature for their Support
in *standing* and growing, that they may keep their Heads above ground,
and administer to our Intentions!" (*CP*:131). The things of the world
thus refer to the validity of human worldly activity: "our compassionate
God has furnish'd all Regions with *Plants* peculiarly adapted for the relief
of the Diseases that are most common in those regions" (*CP*:136). Thus
signifying their service to the human, the things of the world testify to
design, and a designer, if men will pause from using, and reflect.

     This first step of realization is an advance beyond blind consumption
into reflection on consumption, and it thus implies at least, like the act
of picking up *Walden* and reading it, a *pause* in spiritual declension. Mather's italics and exclamation marks indicate that the common is a wonder, but only if the reader pauses from using it to reflect on the fact that
it can be used.

     However, the first step is based on an insufficient premise, because it
considers only nature's ministration to physical use and because it is an-
thropocentric. For Mather, man is not the measure of things: to say otherwise is idolatry. And so the second step in the meditation is antithetical
to the first, a reminder of nature's hostility to man:

> The History of Earthquakes would be a large, as well as sad Volume.
> Whether a *Colluctation of Minerals* in the Bowels of the Earth is the cause
> of those direful Convulsions, may be considered . . . But Mankind ought
> herein to tremble before the Justice of God. Particular *Cities* and *Coun-
> tries*, what fearful Desolations have been by Earthquakes brought upon
> them! (*CP*:101)

Nature does not nourish and revive man's body in order to leave him free
to do as self pleases. Should healthy men choose to obey self, their collective self-centeredness would ignore their subordination in the moral
whole of nature's order. Their concentration on the secular development
of their corner of the creation, without any attention to the plan of the
entirety, will cause the remainder of the whole to appear to them as a
jealous and hostile alterity – God's justice – inimical to their cultivated
cities and countries. In the *Magnalia Christi Americana,* Mather had used
the Jamaican earthquake to admonish Boston for its forgetfulness: the
love of the creator in the creature had shrunk to the love of the creature,
to human instrumentality, so when the forgotten larger dimension of
nature asserted itself, it did so as cataclysm – as forcible reminder. Disaster is the alternative to remembrance: the repression of the glorious God
compels his resurgence to be violent.

     Mather continues this argument in *The Christian Philosopher:*

> A modern Philosopher speaks at this rate, "We do not know when and
> where we stand upon *good Ground:* it would amaze the stoutest Heart,
> and make him ready to die with Fear, if he could see into the *subterra-*

> *neous World,* and view the dark Recesses of Nature under ground; and
> behold, that even the strongest of our Piles of Building, whose Foun-
> dation we think is laid firm and fast, yet are set upon an Arch or Bridge,
> made by the bending Parts of the Earth one upon another, over a pro-
> digious Vault, at the bottom of which lies an unfathomable Sea, but its
> upper Hollows are filled with stagnating Air, and with Expirations of
> sulphureous and bituminous Matter. Upon such a *dreadful Abyss* we
> walk, and ride, and sleep; and are sustained only by an *arched Roof,*
> which also is not in all places of an equal Thickness." (*CP:*102)

Human art ("the strongest of our Piles of Building") and human commerce ("we walk, and ride, and sleep") are situated over a cavity that
wants their collapse, and the demise is restrained only by God. Mather's
imagery anticipates *Sinners in the Hands of an Angry God* because, like
Edwards, he intends to persuade forgetful men that

> the sun don't willingly shine upon you to give you light to serve Sin
> and Satan; the earth don't willingly yield her increase to satisfy your
> lusts; nor is it willingly a stage for your wickedness to be acted upon;
> the air don't willingly serve you to breathe to maintain the flame of life
> in your vitals, while you spend your life in the service of God's enemies.

The second step in Mather's meditation is antithetical to the contentment
and gratification enjoyed in the first, not because Mather is inconsistent,
but because the self-centered or anthropocentrically centered vision of
the order of nature is complacent and contracted. The sense of God's
design, combined with the assertion of divine hostility to human self-
centeredness, yields the wisdom of the third step, a feeling for man's
devout participation in a designed whole as a subordinated part rather
than as the capital.

This meditative advance is recommended in *The Wonderful Works of
God Commemorated*; Mather urges the reader to stop building his little
house in order to experience the design of the whole and become the
high priest of creation. "(O)ur Grand, our chief Errand into the World,"
as he wrote there, "is, that our God may have a Number of *Rational
Beholders* to be sensible of his Excellencies."[12] Natural ministrations to
the physical needs of man are one aspect of the whole in which all parts
tend and are tended to. The discovery of this order, which is not centered
around any of the parts, is the job of reason, which is "the power by
which *we* discern the *Connexion* and *Relation* of things to one another."[13]
Man's physical existence and comfort are only two of the possibilities
adumbrated in the divine fecundity: "The various Moulds and Soils of
the Earth declare the admirable Wisdom of the Creator, in making such

[12] Cotton Mather, *The Wonderful Works of God Commemorated* (Boston, 1690),
p. 22.
[13] Mather, *Icono-clastes,* p. 16.

a provision for a vast Variety of Intentions" (*CP*:96). The human use of
plants seems like an almost incidental, but certainly subordinate, effect
of a system whose beauty is not its ministration to man, but its maintenance of the whole, which is a hymn to the Creator:

> There is a Curiosity observed by Mr. *Robinson* of Ousby, that should
> not be left unmentioned: it is, that *Birds* are the *natural Planters* of all
> sorts of *Trees;* they disseminate the *Kernels* on the Earth, which brings
> them forth to perfection. Yea, he affirms, that he hath actually seen a
> great Number of *Crows* together planting a Grove of *Oaks;* they first
> made little Holes in the Earth with their Bills, going about and about,
> till the hole was deep enough, and then they dropped in the *Acorn,* and
> cover'd it with Earth and Moss. At the time of his writing, this young
> Plantation was growing up towards a *Grove of Oaks,* and of an height
> for the Crows to build their Nests in. (*CP*:138)

The evidence of plan and intelligence does not refer to any human employments of either oaks or crows. Man is crown of creation by virtue
of his part as observer, not user, as Mather contends in *Reasonable Religion:*

> Let *Reason* look upon the *World,* the various *Parts* of it, the curious *Ends*
> of it, the incomparable *Order* of it. It will see a *World* of *Reason* to Con-
> clude, *That there is a* GOD, *who made such a World.* There are the
> sensible stamps of an Immense *Power,* and *Wisdom,* and *Goodness,*
> to be seen everywhere throughout the world; *there is no Lan-
> guage,* or Creature, *where the voice thereof is not heard.*[14]

The problem with this third step is that it is an argument from design:
as Mather contends on the next page of *Reasonable Religion,* the creation
testifies to a god as a well-built house or a ship testify to a builder. Though
it testifies to a god, therefore, it does not necessarily testify to Mather's
god. It suggests a divinity that is regular and apprehensible to human
intelligence. But Mather contends that his reader should not confuse the
condescending generosity of a god who agrees to operate apprehensibly
with the intrinsic nature of divinity itself. To do so is to make reason an
idol:

> To make an *Idol* of our own REASON; This is that, from which we are
> to *flee,* as from an *Idolatry* that will be found *Unreasonable.* Christians,
> do not *Idolize* your own *Reason;* But humbly bewail the *Darkness,* which
> our Fall from GOD has brought upon it. *Reason* is, indeed, an Excellent
> Faculty; a Surprizing Faculty: *Understanding,* 'Tis the *Inspiration of the
> Almighty that gives it. Reason* is an admirable work of the *God that forms
> the Spirit of Man within him.* However, we may not make a GOD of it.[15]

---

[14] Cotton Mather, *Reasonable Religion, or, the Truth of the Christian Religion, Demonstrated* (Boston, 1700), p. 15.
[15] Mather, *Icono-clastes,* p. 15.

As the first step had unduly emphasized man the user rather than man the observer, so the third step unduly emphasizes the discernment of connections and relations as a sufficient apprehension of God, rather than of God's generosity: as he tends to human physical needs, so he presents order to the faculty of reason. Though the creatures are evidence of plan, therefore, the plan itself is a message: nature signifies divinity not as a ship signifies a shipbuilder but as a book signifies an author, not, primarily, through the order of its parts, but through the constant broadcast of intention.

Consequently, the fourth step, like the second, is negative, stressing events in nature that escape rational comprehension, as the second step had stressed events in nature that were hostile to human comfort. This progression is foreshadowed in both *The Wonderful Works of God Commemorated* and in *Reasonable Religion,* where the remark that nature is like a house or ship is followed immediately by a discussion of extraordinary occurrences, as if, while wandering through the house, we were to encounter odd tokens left there to be explicated as messages as well as the indirect evidence of the house itself. At several points in *The Christian Philosopher,* Mather includes phenomena that testify to the inscrutability of the founding intention. Pondering the movement of the magnetic pole, for example, Mather suggests that the surface of the earth is an outer shell, that there is another globe within, and that the differential movements of the two spheres account for the motion of the pole on the outer sphere. But this attenuated speculation is revealed as airy conceit and deftly converted into a meditation on the absence of surety in speculations on the causes of things:

> The Diameter of the Earth being about eight thousand *English* miles, how easy 'tis to allow five hundred Miles for the Thickness of the Shell! And another five hundred Miles for a Medium capable of a vast Atmosphere, for the Globe contained within it! – But it's time to stop, we are got beyond *Human Penetration;* we have dug as far as 'tis fit any Conjecture should carry us! (*CP*:110)

Mather reveals that his conjecture about the earth's core was fanciful so that the fancifulness inherent in all conjecture can be seen. Imponderables such as the movement of the magnetic pole teach man that he can penetrate so far toward the core of things, and no farther, with simple reason:

> It shall then be no indecent *Anticipation* of what should have been observed at the Conclusion of this Collection, here to demand of you, that you glorify the infinite Creator of this, and of all things, as incomprehensible. You must acknowledge that *Human Reason* is too feeble, too narrow a thing to comprehend the *infinite* God. (*CP*:111)

As the vision of divine hostility had purged the reader of his attachment to human need as an interpretive principle, so the vision of divine incomprehensibility is meant to purge the reader of his overinfatuation with the human power to probe the causes of things.

The intention behind the assertion of incomprehensibility, as the quotation above suggests, is not to provoke the despair of ignorance, but to provoke glorification. Specifically, the reader, purified of his rational overconfidence, should look past the surface coherence of patterned causes for deeper significations. Disabused of his obstructive belief in his own power to comprehend nature as a perfect machine, he is to look to nature as a physical allegory for invisible spiritual prescriptions. This is the fifth step. Though physically man is a subordinate part of nature among others, he is spiritually exceptional in his power to see past things as physical causes and proceed into allegorical interpretations. Man is that part of the creation that is able to see that the things of the world are "field preachers," rather than simply so much nourishment, protection from the elements, or links in a system that never transcends itself.

This perception is most clear when Mather discusses the "vegetables." He admires the way plants persist in their structure throughout their successive generations: "An ingenious Observer upon this one Circumstance, cannot forbear this just Reflection: *A visible Argument that the plastick Capacities of Matter are govern'd by all-wise and infinite Agent, the native Strictnesses and Regularities of them plainly shewing from whose Hand they come*" (CP:131). The persistence of pattern is evidence of intelligence: "How unaccountably is the *Figure* of *Plants* preserved? And how unaccountably their *Growth* determined? Our excellent *Ray* flies to an intelligent *plastick Nature*, which must understand and regulate the whole *Oeconomy*" (CP:135). The intelligence of each mortal, single plant, though capable of some plastic adaptability, surveys the whole economy, compelling it to observe native strictnesses and fastnesses, thereby insuring that its generation duplicates the preceding generations and adheres to the perpetual return to the same which keeps the species constant. The plants provoke Mather to emulation as well as admiration: his description of the plants' plastic intelligence is a plain allegory for his duty as a son. The plants teach filiopiety. Mather looks at them and finds validation for his own compulsion to observe native, inherited strictnesses and fastnesses, and he notices that sexual delight exists for this end among the plants as well as among the Mathers. The plants are female:

> The *Flowers*, their Gaiety and Fragrancy; the *Perianthium* or *Empalement* of them; their curious Foldings in the *Calyx* before their Expansion, with a *close Couch* or a *concave Couch*, a *single Plait* or a *double Plait*, or a *Plait* and a *Couch* together, or a *Rowl*, or a *Spire*, or *Plait* and *Spire* together; and their luxuriant Colours after their *Foliation*, and the expanding of their *Petals!* (CP:127)

and male: "The *Stamina*, with their *Apices;* and the *Stylus* (called the *At-*

tire by Dr. *Grew*) which is found a sort of *Male Sperm,* to impregnate and fructify the Seed!" (*CP:*127). The plants, "plainly shewing from whose Hand they come," possess sexuality entirely for the perpetuation of the intelligent economy of the species. Their sexuality is not potentially aberrant, it cannot distract from perpetuation, as Mather found it could for men: "The Analogy between their States and ours would be also as *profitable* as *reasonable* a Subject of Contemplation" (*CP:*139). The plants do not lapse from piety, as do the men to whose remiss understandings *The Christian Philosopher* is addressed: in other words, Mather is performing his version of the plants' piety by writing the book in which the plants' piety is explained; hence, perhaps, his comparison of the plants' male organ to a *stylus,* or pen, a tool for mastering the feminine variability of language, which is prone to atheistic forgetfulness, in the service of the restoration of his predecessors' wisdom. Nature satisfies Mather because it allows him to find, not chaotic extravagance, but a vindication of his own self-sacrifice to dynasty. The creatures do not have selves.

But, though the plants observe their native strictnesses and regularities, and are not vexed with selfhood, there is a plant, the Jamestown Weed, which, when men eat it, provides a lively emblem of degeneracy:

> In *Virginia* there is a Plant called the *James-Town-Weed,* whereof some having eaten plentifully, turn'd *Fools* upon it for several Days; one would blow up a Feather in the Air, another dart Straws at it; a third sit stark naked, like a Monkey, grinning at the rest; a fourth fondly kiss and paw his Companions, and snear in their Faces. In this Frantick State they were confined, lest they shuld kill themselves, tho there appear'd nothing but Innocence in all their Actions. After eleven Days they return'd to themselves, not remembering any thing that had pass'd. (*CP:*138)

The Jamestown Weed does not fail to observe its native strictnesses and regularities, and so it does not refute the lesson of piety Mather finds in nature. But, when eaten by men, its berries, which contain solanine, a narcotic that can prove deadly, incite a kind of behavior that epitomizes atheism, the belief that nature does not provide evidence of God: "My Friend, a Madness more senseless than that with which this *Vegetable* envenoms the Eaters of it, holds thee in stupefying Chains thereof, if thou dost not behold in the whole *Vegetable Kingdom* such Works of the glorious Creator, as call for a continual Admiration" (*CP:*138–9). To look at the Jamestown Weed is to see an allegory of the piety God requires of man; to eat the berries of the Jamestown Weed is to fall into a delirium that is like atheism; to look at those who have eaten the berries of the Jamestown Weed is to see an allegory of those who fail to see allegory in nature. Nature, then, includes an anticipatory rebuttal of its own misreading.

The first and third steps in the meditation are potential allies to piety:
Mather's god does tend to the needs of the creatures, and he does con-
descend to maintain a generally rational operational creation. But, should
commodity or reason forget their subordination to the direct messages
of an aloof god, they would make comfort or understanding into idols,
they would become competitors to piety, and they would be specimens
of the foolish frenzy illustrated in the behavior of those who eat the
Jamestown Weed. Hence the crucial part played by the second and fourth
steps, which do not destroy the first and third, but interfere to prevent
their becoming autonomous and self-sufficient. The negative steps are
intrusions of the paternal pattern into the complacency of the self's love
of the other creatures and into the self's love of itself.

   Insofar as *The Christian Philosopher* contains modes of thought that are
recognizably characteristic of the Enlightenment, therefore, it does so
with a full awareness of their explosive potential. The antipious potential
of Enlightenment thought is recognized, circumscribed by negation, and
absorbed by piety. The Enlightenment is present in the book as a dialec-
tically governed danger. Piety and Enlightenment are not simply mixed
together, as Joseph Ellis contends is the case in the writings of Mather's
contemporary, Samuel Johnson of Connecticut:

> The available evidence is sparse, but it is sufficient to show that Johnson
> was too cautious and common a man to lead New England into the
> eighteenth century. He did recognize that the New Learning outmoded
> the lessons of the Saybrook curriculum and that the metaphysics of his
> *Technologia* was hopelessly outdated. But the philosophical treatises he
> composed during the period from 1715 to 1720 also reveal that Johnson
> did not comprehend the import of the new science or philosophy. The
> New Learning was a name he used rather than a coherent system he
> understood. His ideas contain a hodgepodge of old and new ideas, a
> blend of Puritan technologia and English empiricism that represents his
> attempt not to champion new discoveries, but to integrate them with
> the comfortable certainties learned in college. Johnson may have de-
> nounced the old learning of Puritan New England, but he devoted the
> bulk of his intellectual energies to a synthesis of Ames and Ramus with
> Locke and Newton. If his experience is an accurate measure of the way
> enlightened ideas established themselves in America, it is clear that this
> was a phase of American intellectual history fraught with confusion and
> inconsistency.[16]

In *The Christian Philosopher,* however, piety and Enlightenment are combined in a dialectical progression rather than in a confused mélange. If,

[16] Joseph Ellis, *The New England Mind in Transition: Samuel Johnson of Connecticut,*
   1696–1772 (New Haven, Conn.: Yale University Press, 1973), p. 37.

in general, there "was as yet no sense of tension between science and Scripture,"[17] there was in Mather's thought, where the implications of Enlightenment are realized, and where there is a brilliant and systematic attempt to circumscribe and incorporate Enlightenment into devotion despite its danger, rather than a simple attempt to have both at once. Like Franklin, Mather realized that piety and Enlightenment were at heart antithetical, and that one could be subordinated to the other only by negating its autonomous power.

The intrusions of negation into commodity and reason in *The Christian Philosopher* are paternal intrusions into the incipient apostasy of the self, both in the abstract sense of paternity as the authority of universal dynasty and in the specific sense of the example of Increase Mather. Robert Middlekauff has contended that Cotton Mather's works on natural observation follow in the footsteps of several of his father's treatises which stress empirical observation. However, as Middlekauff shows, there is an important difference.[18] Increase Mather's *Illustrious Providences* (1684) is primarily concerned with cataclysms that destroy social tranquillity, and the major thesis of his *Kometographia* (1683) is that the appearances of comets cannot be rationally predicted and that they must be taken as direct messages. Increase Mather's works on natural observation, in other words, anticipate the second and fourth steps of *The Christian Philosopher*, and suggest that the dialectic in the book is a dialectic between father and son, between self and filiopiety. Increase's emphasis on the cataclysmic and the astounding in nature implicitly states his conviction that a fascination with the detail of regular natural operation tends to distract from zeal. Though the fascination with the comfortable and the regular *is* governed in *The Christian Philosopher*, however, the delineation of nature in itself, rather than as allegory, occupies Cotton Mather a great deal, and he threatens to forget its subordination to allegory, as an eager man might forget the purposes of sexual delight. In this context, the attentiveness and modernity of Increase Mather's scientific works are less important than his choice of what to observe, a choice that expresses his distrust of the observation of the regular in nature and that consequently provides more of a reproof than of a sanction for Cotton Mather's fascination with the structures of the flowers, the legs of the insects, and the behavior of the four-footed. The government of Enlightenment by piety, of the first and third steps by the second and fourth, is a government of Cotton Mather by the voice of Increase Mather within him: and his castigations of declension/Enlightenment originate (though Mather does not admit this) in his horrified imagination of what would happen if the son ever repudiated the father who negates the son's self and absorbs him

[17] Ibid., p. 5.   [18] Middlekauff, *The Mathers*, pp. 143, 281.

into the piety of dynasty. Once this imagined apostasy is projected outward, as *the reader's* powerful desire to remain complacently at the first
or third step, then the exonerated *author* can associate himself with the
severe negations of the second and fourth steps.

This association is clear in the last chapter of *The Christian Philosopher*,
"Of Man," which explains the allegorical or analogical structure of the
creation in terms of the relation of Son to Father in the Trinity. Mather
contends that the complacent reader has forgotten the example of Christ,
the mediator, or ladder, between the minuscule natural understanding
and the manifold mysterious god. Mather makes no reference to the man
Jesus in this chapter because he is presenting Christ as a divine principle,
the infusion of significance into sagged understanding. Emory Elliott
and Jay Fliegelman have argued that the eighteenth century saw an increased emphasis on Christic forgiveness and mitigation of the law derived from an enhanced sense of the abuses and arbitrariness possible in
human law.[19] Mather's Christ, however, does not shape the law to a kindly
conformity with human faultiness but instead asserts that the law is not
so distant that all improvement is inconsequential. Christ, after all, was
not without severity: though he forgave the natural man, he demanded
the sacrifices of possessions, family, and self-love, as he denied his mother
special love. The approach to divinity made possible by Mather's Christ
requires similar progressive negations of self-priority. The aim is to practice selfless piety as spontaneously as the plants do, to have the law describe rather than oppose the individual's life.

The cancellation of narrow hermeneutics based on self that is prescribed in *The Christian Philosopher* and *Sinners in the Hands of an Angry
God* permits the influx of what Edwards calls a general, rather than particular, virtue:

> If any such thing can be supposed as a union of heart to some particular
> being, or number of beings, disposing it to benevolence to a private
> circle or system of beings which are but a small part of the whole, not
> implying a tendency to a union with the great system, and not at all
> inconsistent with enmity towards being in general, this I suppose not
> to be of the nature of true virtue, although it may in some respects be
> good, and may appear beautiful in a confined and contracted view of
> things.[20]

The negative moments in the meditative progress of the soul allow the
soul to surpass the confinement and contraction of vision – including the

---

[19] Elliott, *Power and the Pulpit in Puritan New England*, chaps. 4 and 5; Jay Fliegelman, *Prodigals and Pilgrims: The American Revolution against Patriarchal Authority, 1750–1800* (Cambridge: Cambridge University Press, 1982).

[20] Jonathan Edwards, *The Nature of True Virtue*, in *Works* (New York: G. & C. &
H. Carvill, 1830), vol. 3, p. 95.

rationalism Mather and Edwards attempted to include and transcend in their writings – in the interest of a general virtue not warped to the shape of particular affection, complacent reason, or commodity. For Mather, then, Christ made the law mild not by mitigating it but by providing the ladder whereby a man might overcome the parts of thought that were alien to the intention of the law and come to feel it more as an expression of himself than as an adversary. Christ's sonship represented for Mather the theoretical possibility of the progress followed in *The Christian Philosopher*: Christ's sonship was a map showing sons how to get from their forgetful wish for an independent life in a novel modernity to acquiescence in the will of the father by exposing the specious allure of reason as a degenerate, contracted view of the actual structure of the present.

Christ represents for Mather the infusion of some degree of paternal intelligibility into a universe in which sons are liable to find dogma irrelevant:

> And certainly he that as a *Father* does produce a *Son*, but as an *Artist* only produce a *House*, has a Value for the *Son* which he has not for the *House;* yea, we may say, if GOD had not first, and from Eternity, been a *Father* to our *Saviour*, He would never have exerted Himself as an *Artist* in that *Fabrick*, which He has built *by the Might of his Power, and for the Honour of his Majesty!* (CP:299)

The plants automatically signify piety, because they have no selves, unlike men, who may or may not adhere to law; nevertheless, they are inferior to man, because they are part of the house, and he is the son who lives in it. Nature is a habitation, a manufactured world constantly signifying its maker, though the son is liable to be oblivious of that fact; but if he does awaken to the father's beneficence, his piety satisfies God more than the plants' piety, because theirs is no feat. The house does not know it is a house or who made it; it requires an inhabitant to wander through it, to admire, to be grateful for its magnificence, and to achieve selfless assent. In the "Prologue" to the first series of his *Preparatory Meditations*, Edward Taylor, like Cotton Mather in "Of the Vegetables," fears that his praise falls short of the creatures' praise. But he concludes by implying that, once man has admitted that his selfhood is completely vacuous, human art will surpass the creature: "And then Thy works will shine as flowers on stems / Or as in jewelry shops do gems."[21] The creature is perfected when it is gathered and improved in human praise. In his advertisement for the *Biblia Americana* in the introduction to the *Magnalia Christi Americana*, Mather calls the book a "Collection," and this designation may apply to *The Christian Philosopher* as well. The word

[21] Edward Taylor, *Poems*, ed. Donald E. Stanford (New Haven, Conn.: Yale University Press, 1960), p. 1.

Collection here has in its background the patristic synonym for Christ, *Logos:*

> Hence arises Justin's one original contribution to Christian thought, the conception of the "Spermatic Logos." Before the coming of Christ men had been enabled to attain to bits and pieces of the truth through possession of "seeds" of the Divine Reason; at Christ's coming the whole *Logos* took shape and was made man.[22]

Henry Bettenson is here referring to Justin's *Second Apology,* which would have been included in Increase Mather's copy of Justin's *Opera Graeco-Lat.*[23] Commenting on the recommendation in James 1:21, that the Christian "receive with meekness the implanted word, which is able to save your souls," Justin wrote: "For each man spoke well in proportion to the share he had of the spermatic word, seeing what was related to it."[24] Cotton Mather's collection of the evidences and messages of God would be a recollection, a filiopious repair of the father's impregnation of the world. Christ the son is the unifying point of view that reveals the divinity of the world's design – a son who is a *gathering* of the *meaning disseminated* by the father. "The whole *Plant,*" Mather contends, "is actually in the *Seed*" (*CP*:128), and he exclaims: "What various ways has Nature for the *scattering* and *sowing* of the Seed!" (*CP*:130). *The Christian Philosopher* is a son's gathering of the seeds of meaning sprayed across nature: and his "improvement" does not alter the meaning which is extant and complete from the time of finding.

This vision leads Mather to an Augustinian Platonism:

> All *intelligent compound Beings* have their whole Entertainment in these three Principles, the DESIRE, the OBJECT, and the SENSATION arising from the *Congruity* between them; this *Analogy* is preserved full and clear thro the *Spiritual World,* yea, and thro the material also; so *universal* and *perpetual* an Analogy can arise from nothing but its *Pattern* and *Archetype* in the infinite God or Maker; and could we carry it up to the Source of it, we should find the Trinity of Persons in the eternal GODHEAD admirably exhibited to us. (*CP*:303)

"Compound beings," part mortal, marred by death and declension, and part heavenly, long to transcend their mortality by duplicating the pattern of past generations – as sons – and by having themselves duplicated in new generations – as fathers. Mather had detected this desire in the

---

[22] Henry Bettenson, Introduction to *The Early Christian Fathers* (New York: Oxford University Press, 1956), p. 10.

[23] Julius Herbert Tuttle, "The Libraries of the Mathers," *American Antiquarian Society Proceedings* 20 (April 1910), p. 280.

[24] Justin Martyr, *Second Apology,* in Alexander Roberts and James Donaldson, eds., *The Ante-Nicene Fathers* (Buffalo, N.Y.: The Christian Literature Publishing Co., 1885), vol. 1, p. 193.

plants' intelligence, as well as in his own submission of self to his father's dynasty and in his disappointment over his son's prodigality and demise. The self-negations required by the meditation permit the individual member's entry into the sequence of eminent self-negations that comprise his illustrious ancestry. The analogy between Mather's maintenance of dogma, the plants' fidelity to pattern, and all other dynastic aspirations among the "intelligent compound Beings" suggests an original paradigm upon which these are all variations.

The pattern is the self-duplication of God in the Trinity:

> In the GODHEAD we may first apprehend a *Desire,* an infinitely active, ardent, powerful *Thought,* proposing a *Satisfaction;* let this represent GOD the FATHER: but it is not possible for any Object but God Himself to *satisfy* Himself, and fill his *Desire* of Happiness; therefore HE Himself *reflected* in upon *Himself,* and contemplating His own infinite Perfections, even the *Brightness of His Glory,* and the *express Image of His Person,* must answer this glorious Intention; and this may represent to us GOD the SON. Upon this Contemplation, wherein GOD Himself does behold, and possess, and enjoy Himself, there cannot but arise a *Love,* a *Joy,* an *Acquiescence* of God Himself within Himself, and worthy of a God; this may shadow out to us the third and last of the Principles in this *mysterious Ternary,* that is to say, the Holy SPIRIT. (*CP:*303–4)

To reflect in upon himself, God must first divide himself, and then have the world he divides from him conform to him. To achieve this conformity between the two moieties of the self-severed God, Christ, or mediation, is required, and the conformity itself is the Paraclete.

This "archetype" for the analogies among the paternal impulses of the "intelligent compound Beings" is the reason why those analogies exist: that is, God's paternal desire to duplicate himself in the creation he has severed from out of himself is satisfied by having the intelligent members of that creation desire to duplicate themselves. The dynastic desire of the creatures – including the dynastic desire of the Mathers – is an imperfect microcosm of God's dynastic desire, which is gratified to have made a world that is separate, but not alien, because its structure is a fullness of analogous microcosms of himself. In writing *The Christian Philosopher,* Mather collects and exhibits those microcosms disseminated in nature: *The Christian Philosopher* is a sophisticated return to the same – of Christic nature to the paternal whole from which it was severed, and of Cotton Mather to the Mather tradition from which the selfishness of creative originality might lure him. The anchoring of his filiopietistic duty to John Cotton and Richard and Increase Mather in the archetype of the Trinity is Cotton Mather's definitive repudiation of the Enlightenment's assertion that the world is an excellent machine apprehensible and available to secular, innovative, and independent selves. As the creation is the house built by Christ's father for him to live in and appreciate, so the world of 1721 is still Increase Mather's house; truth, as Nathaniel Ward contended, is evergreen, it grows no gray hair, and never shows "wrinckle" or "morphew."

Its defenders, however, do die, and their wisdom is vulnerable to declension. Hence "intelligent compound Beings" long to extend themselves in new generations, as they had extended previous generations. Their desire suffices to begin the meditation toward the divine archetype, but it is, finally, an insufficient vehicle. Where they are divided between mortality (and its flaws) and heavenly inspiration – as it is embodied in a successful dynasty – God is self-divided, for no apprehensible reason. Once God "*reflected* in upon Himself," his desire became explicable. But the self-severance remains mystery: certainly he does not require the Son to extend him past his death. We may discern the pattern in the creature, and the reason for the pattern, but as the meditation ascends from the analogy to its source, comprehension drops away. Hence Mather's cautious warning that his portrait of the Trinity is a rough sketch: "*let* this represent . . . ," "this may shadow out to us." The recurrence of pattern in the creature adumbrates the archetypal Creator, but the motive for the archetype remains unavailable:

> Tho these *three Relations* of the Godhead in itself, when derived analogically down to Creatures may appear but *Modifications* of a *real subsistence,* yet in the supreme Infinitude of the Divine Nature, they must be infinitely *real* and *living Principles.* Those which are but *Relations* when transferred to *created Beings,* are glorious REALITIES in the infinite God. And in this View of the Holy Trinity, low as it is, it is impossible the SON should be without the FATHER, or the FATHER without the SON, or both without the Holy SPIRIT; it is impossible the SON should not be necessarily and eternally begotten of the FATHER, or that the Holy SPIRIT should not necessarily and eternally proceed both from Him and from the SON. Thus from what occurs throughout the whole Creation, *Reason* forms an imperfect Idea of this incomprehensible Mystery.

One sentence more, and the book is completed: "But it is time to stop here, and indeed how can we go any further!" (*CP*:304). That which illuminates cannot itself be seen, a conclusion that Anne Bradstreet also reaches in "Contemplations": "Art thou so full of glory that no eye / Hath strength thy shining rays once to behold?" [25]

The assertion of the unknowable is the final subjugation of vain reason by the remembrance of paternity. However, *The Christian Philosopher* and related works such as *The Wonderful Works of God* and *Reasonable Religion* are remarkable members of Mather's canon not because in the end they

[25] Anne Bradstreet, *Works in Prose and Verse,* ed. John Harvard Ellis (Gloucester, Mass.: Peter Smith, 1962), p. 372.

agree with works such as *Unum Necessarium* or *Icono-clastes*. They are remarkable because they show Mather trying to absorb rather than to lambaste piety's competitors, and because to absorb their appeal he must concede it: in the moments before the transuming negations, these writings allow piety's competitors, the forces of declension/Enlightenment, to attain to full and sympathetic expression, and thus to approach secession from the category of the abominable. But, finally, this incipient plurivocity is always reined in by the negations that follow the model of Increase Mather's science of physical and rational cataclysm. It is important to note that these negations do not happen only twice in the book as it is read: because the meditative pattern is distributed throughout the topical chapters, the assertions of independence followed by negation are numerous and repeated, making the book a structural mimesis of the oscillation between standing up and being tripped again that was the recurring unit of Mather's emotional life.

In the magisterial-paternal final chapter, the negation of the self's interests is the full voice that preempts the self-expression of piety's competitors, brands them incipient atheists, and returns them to the category of awful things exiled from the universality of divinity: "*Atheism* is now for ever chased and hissed out of the World, every thing in the World concurs to a Sentence of *Banishment* upon it. *Fly, thou Monster, and hide, and let not the darkest Recesses of* Africa *itself be able to cherish Thee; never dare to shew thyself in a World where every thing stands ready to overwhelm thee!*" (*CP*:294); "Men would soon become *Canibals* to one another by embracing [atheism]; Men being utterly destitute of any Principle to keep them *honest in the Dark,* there would be no *Integrity* left in the World, but they would be as the *Fishes of the Sea to one another,* and worse than *the creeping Things, that have no Ruler over them*" (*CP*:295); "[until atheism is banished] the World continues in a wretched Condition, *full of doleful Creatures,* with *wild Beasts crying* in its *desolate Houses, Dragons* in its most *pleasant Palaces*" (*CP*:295). Recollecting the father, Mather divests piety's competitors of their eloquence, and once again arrays himself against his father's enemies. But do we ever imagine a life that is completely devoid of secret luster?

4
PHARMACEUTICAL
INNOVATION

In some *Reformed churches,* they do not permit a *minister* of the Gospel,
to practice as a *physician,* because either of those callings is ordinarily
enough to find full employment for him that faithfully follows it. But,
the *priests* of old, who reserved in the archives of their temples, the
stories of the cures thankfully acknowledged there, communicated from
thence directions for cures in such cases among their neighbors.

Cotton Mather, Bonifacius

In *The Christian Philosopher* and related works, the sheer polarity between
the self's banished solitude and the city of dynastic piety is replaced with
a more graded or mediated scheme. Though the steps between spiritual
indigence and perfect saintliness represent poison if taken as sufficient in
themselves, they are not automatically intolerable so long as they are
clearly subordinated. Some of the self's enjoyments are allowed a con-
ditional permissibility: they do not necessarily drag a man from the light
if the awareness of their secondary, ornamental nature is constant, and if
their dangerous potency is never forgotten. In the last chapter of *The
Christian Philosopher,* however, polarity is reinvoked: the potential for
idolatrous apostasy lurking in the self's enjoyments is again stressed, and
the self is warned that it may degenerate to the chaos of the cannibal
fishes, or of the dragons who squat in the pleasant palaces of creation.
This last chapter is stern allegory: all things of the world are only to be
viewed as expressions of the divine creative intention, and the self must
be considered an allegorical sign of the dynasty that encloses it.

But before this severity is invoked in the last chapter, piety's sometime
competitors achieve provisionally valid articulation, despite their dangerous potential. Mather's announced purpose is rhetorical: to "challenge
all possible Regards from the *High,* as well as the *Low,* among the People"
(*CP*:2), piety must acknowledge the competitors' allure, circumscribe
that allure by negating its tendency to an assertion of self-sufficiency, and
then absorb the competitors into itself as subordinate moments. If piety

can do this, it will be more vigorous than a theology that dissociates itself completely from its competitors by attempting to quarantine them. However, to concede the competitors' allure, Mather must characterize it, to characterize it well he must feel it, and so there is a certain permitted exhilaration. To fetch Enlightenment back into piety, the writer must be let loose to go after Enlightenment. If at the end self and Enlightenment are both back in the father's house, during the errand self has been at play. By asserting that it is going out to fetch the prodigal home, Cotton Mather's unnamed self follows the prodigal out into a loose world, and even constructs a congenial abode, though this abode is temporary, to be dismantled again in the splendor of reabsorption.

These competitors to piety are similar to the "things Indifferent" postulated in Anglican theory, but with an important difference. Rather than being neither dangerous nor helpful to faith, they are both dangerous and helpful. Their "indifference" comes from being doubly charged, rather than not charged at all. This is not the mix of submission and rebellion Mather detected in all human matter: rebellion itself is ambiguous, since, in limited doses, it can prove even more evangelically efficacious than plain literal submission would.

Consequently, Mather's liberalizations of seventeenth-century Congregationalism do not proceed from liberality or equanimity, from a reduced sense of danger. They do not grow from the moderation recommended by Terence, who announced that nothing human was alien to him because he was a man. On the contrary, Mather's liberalizations rely on an anxious, close, and continuous supervision and circumscription of the danger he looses. Mather does not open Pandora's box because he has concluded that the energumens within are only harmless sprites: he opens it hoping that, like an unflagging Maxwell's demon, he can let loose the good while stopping the bad. An anxious surveillance seeks to ensure that danger does not pass the point of excess, mindful that disaster can irrupt from a moment's relaxation. As Kierkegaard remarked in *The Point of View for My Work as an Author,* Christian rhetoric sent out to fetch the reprobate is always in danger of going reprobate; like Henry James's Strether, piety sent to reclaim the prodigal might decide to stay. So it may listen, but it must be tied to the mast.

Mather's anxious liberality provides the intellectual and emotional milieu in which he discovered the virtue of smallpox inoculation. Several of Mather's apologists have defended him from Calef and Calef's heirs by pointing to Mather's enlightened advocacy of inoculation despite skeptical, even hostile public opinion.[1] The apologists would have it that, in this one respect at least, Mather was ahead of his age because, like

[1] See Otho T. Beall and Richard H. Shryock, *Cotton Mather: First Significant Figure in American Medicine* (Baltimore: The Johns Hopkins University Press,

Voltaire, he divined the good hidden in the obscure workings of the pox. But to present Mather's interest in this way, though it may do his maligned memory some service, is, finally, to say more about oneself than about Mather, because it implies that Mather's interest is a bizarre, extrinsic member of his thought as a whole. In so detaching inoculation from the body of Mather's thought, such apologists do exonerate him from pure anachronism, but they yield to Perry Miller's accusation, that Mather's advocacy of inoculation was an adventitious discovery, happened upon by a disoriented and second-rate intelligence with a Burtonian interest in quirky knowledge. Mather's attention to inoculation, according to Miller, had two sources, a "fantastic story" told by his slave Onesimus about medicine in North Africa, and essays on Turkish medicine by Timonius and Pylarinus. This combination of happenstance and peripatetic research led Mather to his fortuitous celebration of smallpox inoculation, which is therefore not part of an integrated whole, but instead a stray morsel in an erratic extravaganza of miscellaneous oddities: "By a lucky shot – almost, one might say, in the dark – Cotton Mather came up with an idea which all of us nowadays believe correct."[2]

But Miller's contention that Mather's interest in smallpox was a mere curio cannot explain Mather's brave and constant advocacy: Mather's elephantine reading led him through thousands of odd ideas that did not inspire resolute commitment in him. To explain the commitment, we must note both Mather's humane discontent with the effects of smallpox on New England and the figural consonance between the idea of smallpox inoculation and the idea of perilous liberalization. The intermingling of medical and theological issues in Mather's thought, according to David Levin, was lifelong, beginning even before his enrollment at Harvard. Levin suggests that Mather's early interest in medicine was both a response to and a contributing cause of the hypochondria he shared with his father, a hypochondria that develops from a horrified fascination with what lurks in the deep recesses of the body; and Levin implies that it was a theological hypochondria based on the assumption that the body is analogous to the soul and the human community, all three of which were fields in which one might inquire into the etiology of the Lord's wrath. Levin reminds us, in other words, of Mather's penchant for analogy and allegory, which he thought structured the creation, and Levin thus provides a context in which to challenge Miller's assertion that inoculation was for Mather some sort of free-floating, extrinsic interest. Armed with

1954) and Kenneth B. Murdock, *Increase Mather* (Cambridge, Mass.: Harvard University Press, 1925), pp. 386–7.
[2] Perry Miller, "The Judgement of the Smallpox," in *The New England Mind: From Colony to Province* (Boston: Beacon Press, 1953), pp. 345–66. Mather's "lucky shot" is discussed on page 348.

his interested reading in medicine, Mather was able to comprehend the meaningful origin of the smallpox epidemics that devastated Boston. And, as the onslaught of smallpox was a symbolic event (which is not to say it was not a real event), so too his view of the cure for smallpox was also symbol-fraught. As Levin writes, "He already knew something about the method of Petrus Ramus, which was dogmatic but almost unlimited in its inclusiveness."[3]

The semantic history of the word *inoculation* provides more reason to doubt that Mather's interest in inoculation was simply miscellaneous. The *Oxford English Dictionary* reveals that the modern, medical use of the word dates from approximately 1714, when Mather was fifty-one, seven years before he and his father completed a pamphlet on the subject.[4] We may assume, therefore, that in those early years of the eighteenth century the medical sense of the word was still figural, still drawing from and setting itself off from what was then the established meaning – the grafting of a new bud onto an old plant, or to "join or unite by insertion (as the scion is inserted into the stock so as to become one with it)." We might correctly say that Cotton Mather inoculated the Mather tradition insofar as he was a scion who became one with it – that is, insofar as he suppressed his transformative impulses. But the transition from the established to the medical meaning imports a new connotation: with the new meaning, inoculation involves inserting something that is alien or even hostile to the host stock, though the end is still the regeneration of the original. This new meaning is intriguing because in those years it must have resonated in contrast with the older meaning, but also drawn on the older meaning in order to assert that the overall purpose of the activity was still continuity and preservation. Though continuity is still conceived of as untransforming repetition – the health of the inoculated man is identical with the health of the noninoculated but uninfected man – continuity is nevertheless complicated by these injections of danger that will eventually refurbish health after a short fever. The new member

---

[3] David Levin, *Cotton Mather: The Young Life of the Lord's Remembrancer* (Cambridge, Mass.: Harvard University Press, 1978), p. 27.

[4] Increase Mather, *Several Reasons Proving that Inoculating or Transplanting the Small Pox is a Lawful Practice, and that it has Been Blessed by God for the Saving of Many a Life* (Boston, 1721). This is a two-paged pamphlet. After his own essay, which takes up most of the first page, Increase Mather "subjoyn(s)" an essay by Cotton Mather – "the Sentiments of another, well known in our Churches, of which I declare my hearty Approbation" – so that "the Cause may have Two Witnesses." Cotton Mather's essay is entitled "Sentiments on the Small Pox Inoculated," implying, perhaps, that his father's sentiments are "inoculated" by his own.

arrives to continue the old order, which is liable to sickness: but, to the shortsighted, he might seem to oppose the old health.

Mather hints at such a figural improvement of inoculation in *The Christian Philosopher*, where among the many "field preachers" we find homeopathic herbs:

> What though there are Venomous Plants? An excellent *Fellow of the College of Physicians* makes a just remark: "*Aloes* has the property of promoting *Haemorrhages*; but the Property is good or bad, as it is used; a *Medicine* or a *Poison*; and it is very probable that the most dangerous *Poisons*, skilfully managed, may not only be innocuous, but of all other Medicines the most effectual." (*CP*:134)

Mather, who puns frequently, may have meant the reader to hear *inoculation* in *innocuous*. But the connection does not rest on the pun. In his addition to his father's pamphlet on smallpox inoculation, Mather writes: "A Physician is Master of a *Purge;* which whosoever takes it, is in an ordinary way, delivered from the danger of that Mortal Distemper. An *Artificial Purge* seasonably taken saves him from Death by the *Natural Purge*, which he is exposed unto. Will any scruple the taking of this *Artificial Purge?*"[5] Herbal cathartics such as aloes or hellebore are analogies and precedents for the technology of vaccination, divinely planted proofs that there are many things that, though poisonous in excess, are superbly invigorating if "skilfully managed." In his address to physicians in *Bonifacius,* Mather notes that in much of the world medicine is still "*a thing horribly magical.*" Describing some of the abominations of the Egyptian magi, Mather writes that other "countries were from *Egypt* infected with them. Hence medicines were called, *pharmaca.*" Concerning this cryptic remark, Levin speculates that perhaps "Mather's reason for saying 'Hence' is that the Greek word 'pharmaca' meant *poison* as well as *drug,* and that it might thus be associated with magic" (*B*:105, 175). Or perhaps because, as inoculation is a seeming poison that is in fact a cure, so the *pharmaca* of the Egyptians are seeming cures that are in fact poisons.

The doctor, then, administering such a perilous cure, impersonates death, "seasonably" imitating the affliction that, coming at its own time, would kill. Thus impersonating death, staging a simulation of death, the doctor vanquishes it. This risky business puts a heavy test to the doctor's posological skill: the administration of too much poison will metamorphose him from an impersonating enemy to an agent of the adversity he is attempting to oppose. In "Plato's Pharmacy," Jacques Derrida contends that the precarious ambiguity of the word *pharmakon* plays an important part in Plato's writing, provoking a daring recommendation that, with

[5] Mather, "Sentiments on the Small Pox Inoculated," p. 2.

due vigilance, the remedial potential for regeneration should not be neglected, despite massive risk. Eventually, according to Derrida, Plato proves
unable to sustain a mastery of the *pharmakon*, to secure the thin line between the preventive staging of death and death itself.[6] Mather's figural-
izing interest in natural and man-made homeopathics taps into this ancient anxiety, and informs his thinking on liberalization. For both Derrida's
Plato and Mather, the crucial question is: where does preventive imper-
sonation turn into complicity? how to draw the line?

The terms Mather uses in his addition to his father's pamphlet – "salvation" and "purge" for example – together with medical terms such as
"infection" that are commonly used in nonmedical contexts in Puritan
writing, have supermedical connotations that indicate Mather's general
sense that the medical preservation of the body's health through all hazards is analogous to the preservation of the dynasty and of the congregation through the temptations to forgetfulness that prey on successive
generations. And within this general correspondence, Mather recommends specific devices for the communal maintenance of faithful memory that are analogous to the helpful alterity of the cautiously inserted
smallpox.

Among these is classical poetry, as he discusses it in *Manuductio ad
Ministerium*. Seeking to promote some relaxation of the stringent discipline of the plain style, an inherited compositional requirement, he writes:

> Though some have a soul so unmusical that they have decried all verse
> as being but mere playing and fiddling upon words, all versifying as if
> it were more unnatural than if we should choose dancing instead of
> walking, and rhyme as if it were but a sort of Morisco dancing with
> bells, yet I cannot wish you a soul that shall be wholly unpoetical.

The danger, or *poison*, in poetry, as in the dancing of the Spanish Moors,
is that things meant to be vehicular – sound and motion – are enjoyed for
themselves, thereby violating the Augustinian injunction that the things

---

[6] Jacques Derrida, "Plato's Pharmacy," in *Dissemination* (Chicago: University of
Chicago Press, 1981), pp. 61–173. My one-page summary of Derrida's long
and dense essay is necessarily simplistic: the reader is encouraged to explore the
essay for himself, because it is a truly remarkable and profoundly suggestive
reading of Plato. In addition to simplifying Derrida's essay, I have twisted it to
suit my purposes in two ways: first, since my argument is dialectical rather
than deconstructive, I contend that what Mather perceives as an absolute otherness – independent originality – is for Derrida's Plato an irrecuperable nonsense that cannot be made lucid in the way that I will attempt to elucidate the
objects of Mather's disapproval; and second, I emphasize Plato's daring willingness to be open to the pharmakon's ambivalence, but Derrida would suspect
the intentionality implied in my assertion of Plato's temerity.

of the world are to be enjoyed for their contribution to supermundane ends. As supplements to truth, they are useful, so long as they do not replace truth. But, eager to assure the cautious critic that such a liberalization is not an irrecuperable departure from health in style, Mather cautions against overindulgence or unsupervised doses. Note the presence of metaphors that suggest a doctor's opinion of culinary habits: "Be not so set on poetry to be always poring on the passionate and measured pages. Let not what should be sauce rather than food for you engross all your applications. Beware of a boundless and sickly appetite for the reading of poems, which now the rickety nation swarms withal; and let not the Circean cup intoxicate you."[7] Sauce, eaten as food, drains vigor; but, as sauce, it improves the meal. So, in this diatribe against classical verse, he may employ classical allusion – Circe's cup converted to Christian allegory.

The recommendation for moderation is therefore not a slight philosophical commonplace: the stylistic dietician must distinguish between a safe dose, which enhances the flavor of the meal and thereby remains extrinsic, and an excessive dose, which replaces the nourishment by becoming an intrinsic end in itself rather than remaining an extrinsic vehicle. Consequently, the plea for moderation is less an ad hoc experiential commonplace than a theoretical explication of overdose based on a discrimination between ornament and argument, between the extrinsic and the intrinsic. This discrimination, which *restrains* the dose of transformative innovation, might also be said to *permit* it: Mather's plea for moderation, by warning us to poison cautiously, nonetheless licenses us to poison.

The use of the concept of homeopathy to justify strategically the exercise of liberality is also at work in the *Magnalia Christi Americana*. Forgetfulness, in that book, is represented as a sort of plague infecting the community: suppressing their remembrance of duty to the sacred inheritance, the citizens of New England have rushed off after cheap attractions and contributed to the waning of faith. Mather's most frequent response, as I argued in the last chapter, is strict, literal, dutiful remembrance, figuratively represented in the raising of the stone Ebenezer. However, there are moments when he himself advocates some liberal departure from the strict style of inherited Calvinist Congregationalism, and the idea of homeopathy is required if these recommendations of liberalization are to be distinguished from the general amnesia the book is written to oppose. Again, the assertion of liberalization within ordained limit – the point of excessive toxicity – is offered as a way to forestall the excessive extravagance of the times, as the infection artificially induced by inoculation forestalls the mortal infection by nature. In the "General Introduction," for example, Mather writes that certain rhetorical ornaments that exceed what the plain style would require "almost unavoidably [put] themselves into the Authors hand." For those who would deplore such elaborations as contaminations, Mather quotes from Lange's comments on Erasmus's style in *Florilegii*:[8] "*Sicuti sal modici cibis aspersus Condit, & gratium saporis addit, ita si paulum Antiquitatis adminiscueris, Oratio fit venustior.* (Just as salt discreetly spread on food seasons it, and increases its flavor, so to mix in a little of antiquity makes style more pleasing.)" (*MCA*, I:19). Plainly, this section anticipates the remarks on style in the *Manuductio ad Ministerium.* As in the later book, Mather justifies his inoculation of the plain style with pagan ornament by the unlikely assertion that, for certain "Modern *Criticks,*" the *Magnalia Christi Americana* will still tend too much toward a "Simple, Submiss, Humble Style" (*MCA*, I:18). He exculpates his innovation, in other words, by postulating the existence of overdose – of wild critics devoid of filiopiety – in contrast with whose stylistic preferences his tentative modernity would be a proper dose.

And this stylistic inoculation in the *Magnalia Christi Americana* is accompanied by an inoculation of historical technique. Deploring "*Panegyricks composed by Interested Hands,*" he promises to be an "*Impartial Historian,*" not by recording "bare *Matters of Fact, without all Reflection,*" but by resisting the impulse to bend all reflection to a confined point of view: "I have endeavoured, with all *good Conscience,* to decline this writing merely for a *Party*" (*MCA*, I:13). He anticipates the possibility that this broadening and pluralization of point of view might bear some resemblance to the forgetfulness that he is writing the book to remedy, and that, as a consequence, it may offend those who would prefer, for example, the univocality of a Winthrop or the stern prejudice against toleration, however eloquent, of a Nathaniel Ward: "There are some among us, who very strictly profess the *Congregational Church-Discipline,* but at the same time they have an unhappy Narrowness of Soul, by which they confine their value and Kindness too much unto their own Party; and unto those my *Church History* will be offensive" (*MCA*, I:33). But he cautiously couples this bold chiding with another reminder of the possibility of overdose, of the point of toxicity which his liberality does not reach and so remains medicinal: "there is also a number of eminently Godly Persons, who are for a Larger way, and unto these my Church-

[8] Kenneth Murdock reveals the source of this quotation in his edition of the first two books of the *Magnalia Christi Americana* (Cambridge, Mass.: Harvard University Press, 1977), p. 379.

History will give distast, by the things which it may happen to utter, in favour of that Church-Discipline on some few occasions . . ." (*MCA*, I:33). For all of his liberality, Mather argues, he is still of Winthrop's and Ward's party, not a defector.

In fact, posological deftness is the virtue most stressed in his biography of Winthrop in the second book of the *Magnalia Christi Americana*, which provides a sort of theoretical justification for Mather's cautious liberality in the composition of the book which contains it. Mather quotes from John Cotton's funeral oration for Winthrop near the end of the biography, where, among the many varieties of Winthrop's judiciousness, Cotton celebrates Winthrop's skill as a doctor: "(he) has been . . . (a) *Help for our Bodies by Physick*" (*MCA*, I:131). This statement is not a simple addendum to the list of Winthrop's abilities: metaphorical references to diseases, contagion, and distemper run through the biography. Political good governance is analogous to medical wisdom, an analogy Mather returns to in a quotation from Thucydides included in the biography of Winthrop's son: "*Magistratus est Civitatus Medicus* (the magistrate is the physician of the state)" (*MCA*, I:159).

Much of Winthrop, Sr.'s political medicine is inoculative, according to Mather's biography, with democracy being the equivalent to the small-pox bacillus. Having broadened participatory membership in the corporation beyond what was required or even suggested in English law, Mather's Winthrop finds himself constantly confronted by an *excessive* pluralization of outlook that threatens to overwhelm the community's essential unanimity. The circumscribed and limited dose of participatory plurality introduced by Winthrop is repeatedly challenged by overdoses which promise to divide, rather than invigorate, the body politic:

> And unto all these, the Addition of the *Distempers*, ever now and then raised in the *Country*, procured unto him a very singular share of Trouble; yea, so hard was the Measure which he found even among Pious Men, in the Temptations of a *Wilderness*, that when the *Thunder* and *Lightning* had smitten a *Wind-mill*, whereof he was Owner, some had *such things in their Heads*, as publickly to Reproach this *Charitablest of Men*, as if the Voice of the Almighty had rebuked, I know not what *Oppression*, which they judged him Guilty of. (*MCA*, I:129–30)

The voice of the almighty, Winthrop finds, does not enunciate clearly: though Winthrop might see the demise of his windmill as a providential reminder that he had been slack in pursuing uniformity – as witnessed in the "distempers" – these others, who resent all authority, see it as a reproof of his exercises of authority. Mather's announced liberality appears in this biography as Winthrop's "MODERATION," which does not extend to include the plurality that manifests itself in the resentful distortion of meaning in the episode of the windmill. An excess of democracy is to be deplored, Mather implies, not because it takes power away from the aristocratically deserving, but because it will fracture the whole, reducing a city to a wilderness of chaotic, conflicting selves.

Mather's apprehensions about democracy, therefore, are connected with his anxieties about creative self-design exerting its independence from pious conformity to inherited models of identity. The result of a widespread outbreak of such independence would be just the sort of collective forgetfulness Mather so often deprecates in his own society. He calls it, at various points in his biography of Winthrop, a "distemper," a "contagion," and an "enchantment." Though Winthrop liberalized government by broadening participation in the corporation, he nevertheless constantly sought to subdue the anarchy that would come from an overdose of liberality: "the *Magistrates*, as far as might be, should aforehand ripen their *Consultations*, to produce that *Unanimity* in their *Publick Votes*, which would make them liker the Voice of God" (*MCA*, I:121). So far as unanimity declines into the plurality of independent views, then, the community drifts from divine intentions; consequently, the "moderate" introduction of participation by Winthrop is not to be confused with the people's "touchy *Jealousie* . . . about their *Liberties*" (*MCA*, I:127) which would "run the whole Government into something too *Democratical*" (*MCA*, I:125). Winthrop's introduction of some provisional popular participation is an inoculation meant to exorcise, not indulge, the fevered overdose of anarchic plurality: to combat such an excess, Winthrop, like Christ, must cast out the demons of delirium: "The *Spell* that was upon the Eyes of the People being thus dissolved, their *distorted* and *enraged* notions of things all vanished . . ." (*MCA*, I:128). The similarity in kind between Winthrop's moderate liberality and the delirium of plurality resulting from independent, self-designing citizens resembles the similarity between a dose of the pox and an actual infection by the pox.

The idea of homeopathy, therefore, has a significative power for Mather that reaches beyond medical practice, includes stylistic and political liberalization, and, finally, can be seen as a crucial moment in his attempt to reconcile in a simple whole the conflicting attractions of historical piety and modernization. Sacvan Bercovitch has argued that Cotton Mather represents the best first instance of American meliorism, of a "wholesale inversion of traditional hermeneutics" that imputes an unprecedented significance to the American plantation. In the next chapter I will argue that Mather found being in a hermeneutical series at all, no matter if at the privileged moment of the series, a chafing experience; and if in this way Bercovitch makes Mather too conservative by overlooking his occasional resentment of hermeneutics per se, he also makes Mather's hermeneutics too liberal by emphasizing only their implicit meliorism. Bercovitch's argument is refreshing and illuminating after Perry Miller's vilifications of Cotton Mather, but his emphasis on eager meliorism does not prepare the reader to understand Mather's participation in the common Puritan distrust of innovation and his repetition of the assertion that the American experiment is an attempt to restore the purity of primitive Christianity. In the vanguard of a modern correction of our perception of Mather, Bercovitch has perhaps made him seem too much of the other party, an incipient Whitman. Inoculation, as a figure, allows Mather to contend that what may seem to be an innovative departure from the sacred way (poison) is in fact a restoration (medicine) that forestalls true poisoning and thereby invigorates the sacred. It allows Mather to circumvent what we can only assume would be a massive personal crisis resulting from the contradiction between inclinations: as one may make himself sick in a way that will save his life, so homeopathy – again, as a figure – allows for departures from dutiful memory of orthodoxy in the interest of orthodoxy. The idea of homeopathy is therefore generally useful for American Puritanism, divided as it was between the de facto innovative self-fashioning of the great separation from England and its church and the ostensive self-denying fidelity to primitive patterns. Whereas the theory of degeneration projected innovation outward as an adversary, allowing the Puritans to represent themselves as memorial preservers, homeopathy allows them to acknowledge some posologically supervised participation in innovation without compromising their claims to historical filiopiety. With Clement of Alexandria, the inoculist may assert that what seems to be a new song is in fact an aid to the logos, the most ancient cosmic music.[9]

Though inoculation was new in Mather's period, the recognition of homeopathic ambiguity was not: "Within the infant rind of this weak flower / Poison hath residence and medicine power . . ."[10] And the metaphoric potential of homeopathy was recognized, for example, in Milton's *Reason of Church Government*, where the danger prelacy poses to the health of piety leads the author to conclude that "she is not such a kind of evil as hath any good, or use in it, which many evils have, but a distill'd quintessence, a pure elixir of mischief, pestilent alike to all."[11] The toxicity of Anglicanism was without any potential for regeneration. The Puritans who came to Massachusetts, however, did find ways to cure the

[9] Sacvan Bercovitch, *The Puritan Origins of the American Self* (New Haven, Conn.: Yale University Press, 1975), p. 109; Clement of Alexandria, *Exhortation to the Greeks*, trans. G. W. Butterworth (New York: G. P. Putnam's Sons, Loeb Classical Library, 1919), p. 17.

[10] William Shakespeare, *Romeo and Juliet*, II, iii:23–4.

[11] John Milton, *The Reason of Church Government Urg'd against Prelaty*, ed. Harry Morgan Ayres, in *Anti-Prelatical Tracts*, *The Works of John Milton* (New York: Columbia University Press, 1931), vol. 3, p. 276.

body politic homeopathically, by permitting the introduction of measured doses of the innovative selfhood that, taken in excess, would poison the community's pious unanimity. In his account for 1628, for example, Bradford suggests that the circulation of wampum – an Indian
currency made from the lovely, rare shells found at Wampumkeag – might
remedy the dearth of available currency, but that, become the object of
enthusiasm, it might "prove a drug." The vexing dependence of the pilgrims' spiritual corporation on the financial corporation in England that
supports it requires Bradford to distinguish rigorously between them;
consequently, he finds it troublesome to have to give his assent to the
pilgrims' own desire for financial aggrandizement, since this interest seems
to blur the distinction he works constantly to keep clear. The solution is
homeopathy, supervised doses of economic opportunity that forestall the
infection and plague that are such frequent emblems in *Of Plymouth Plantation* for unbridled, theologically indifferent adventurism and the fragmentation of unanimity it inspires. Discussing the failure of the community to operate from a common store, for example, he writes:

> The experience that was had in this common course and condition,
> tried sundry years, and that amongst godly and sober men, may well
> evince the vanity of that conceit of Plato's and other ancients applauded
> by some of later times; that the taking away of property and bringing
> in community into a commonwealth would make them happy and
> flourishing; as if they were wiser than God. For this community (so far
> as it was) was found to breed much confusion and discontent and retard
> much employment that would have been to their benefit and comfort.

The decision to depart from the pure consensual sharing of goods and to
include a limited and circumscribed encouragement of economic self-
interest invigorates the flagging health of the colonial body:

> At length, after much debate of things, the Governor (with the advice
> of the chiefest amongst them) gave way that they should set corn every
> man for his own particular, and in that regard to trust to themselves; in
> all other things to go on in the general way as before. And so assigned
> to every family a parcel of land, according to the proportion of their
> number, for that end, only for present use (but made no division for
> inheritance) and ranged all boys and youth under some family. This had
> very good success, for it made all hands very industrious, so as much
> more corn was planted than otherwise would have been by any means
> the Governor or any could use, and saved him a great deal of trouble,
> and gave far better consent.

Plato's vain conceit – that a sort of spiritual communism that excludes
the impurity of independent self-interest is possible – is not repudiated
as enthusiastically as the former quotation suggests it should be. Bradford justifies the departure from the common course by identifying the

desire to go in a common course as a desire to be wiser than God, that is, a desire to identify and expel all inmixed impurity and to attain to a communally perfect, undarkened presence. Such a desire, Bradford knew, is Donatistic, an excessive belief in the human powers of identification and purification, a criticism that was directed repeatedly at his group of separatists by the same people who first labeled them "Puritans."

But disavowal of Donatism, though it may be an admirable act of humility, creates a problem: if the Puritan community is unable to purge itself of marring inmixture, how is it different from the not especially holy communities from which it attempts to differentiate itself? The solution lies in a homeopathic attitude, which allows the governor to inoculate the community with some measure of adventurism without therefore opening the door to a plague of theologically forgetful self-interest: Bradford seeks to stem the worst of such self-interest by subordinating socially loose young men under the consensus of family and by stipulating that property reverts to the community at the decease of the tenant so that labor dedicated to the future is dedicated to the future of the colony rather than to an exclusivistic attention to one's own progeny. Nevertheless, despite these precautions, the economic trajectory of the individual will henceforth point in a direction different from the sweet and anonymous consent that Bradford hopes will continue to pertain in devotional matters. So the governor supervises the introduction of the infection of self-interest into the body of the community as the inoculist would measure his injection.

Bradford's attempt to represent the decision as a resplendent repudiation of incipient Donatism is superimposed over his suspicion that the Elect have shown themselves to be different from the Reprobate only in degree, not in kind, and that a distinction based on degree – on dosage – is much more blurry and difficult than a distinction based on obvious difference in kind. Thinking they were "wiser than God," Plymouth's citizens had thought they could live completely free of the anticommunal motives that governed others; repudiating this ambition, they blur their spiritual superiority. The heightened possibility of a blurring of distinction between the Elect and surrounding groups lurks in Bradford's phrase "every man for his own particular," since "particular" is the most common label for disruptiveness in Of Plymouth Plantation. And it also lurks in Bradford's remark that it "would have been worse if they had been men of another condition." True enough: the human debility that has been allowed into the community in this episode is identical in kind with what prods Weston and Allerton to perpetrate their infamous frauds against the community, and with the general communal drift toward prosperity-seeking that enfeebles Plymouth's spiritual life and brings Of Plymouth Plantation to its tired, quiet conclusion, to its degeneration from history to annals.[12] Profit is a "benefit turned to their hurt," a "remedy proved worse than the disease."[13] Circumscribed, controlled, and supervised, the splitting-off of fiscal economy from the economy of faith may be an invigorating dose; but, not measured according to the doctor's meticulous prescription, it is a pandoric poison, a Circe's cup.

Bradford's homeopathy ends where, according to Derrida, Plato's does: the ambiguous simultaneity of poison and medicine in one entity proves unmasterable; the remediation cannot be permanently and effectively separated from the contamination; and opening the door at all already spells the end. This great risk of homeopathic innovation, and the magnitude of the risk, shows the magnitude of homeopathy's attractiveness, since a risk is rarely taken without a sense of proportionate possible gain. In the case of homeopathy, the possible gain is the filiopious Puritan's ability to indulge innovation without sacrificing himself to it, and thus to alleviate the tension between strong, assertive selfhood and the devout sacrifice of self to imperious transcendental mandates that do not ask for useful suggestions. Though we cannot argue sure causality, it is nonetheless no surprise that Cotton Mather's active analogical imagination should gravitate toward an interest in the smallpox inoculation.

The concept of declension, as I argued in the last chapter, masked innovation by projecting it outward as a superpersonal cosmic tendency to decay. Though this device provided a sense of personal significance by making young remembrancers necessary to the maintenance of tradition, the task of *repairing* did not permit the scion to express qualitatively transformative impulses; but by *forestalling* decay through homeopathy, the Puritan heir may *impersonate* the other, even if the eventual end is still the return to the same. Though with rueful results, Plymouth's homeopathic innovation released it from strict adherence to the letter of the model it had set for itself; and, though the end was the restoration of primitive New England piety, Cotton Mather's *moderate,* inoculative liberality released him from anti-innovative strictures without a massive hemorrhage in his sense of duty. In the next chapter, I will argue that in his biography of Sir William Phips in the *Magnalia Christi Americana* Mather seems to have allowed his inoculative modernity to bleed over into an outright and unabashed indifference to filiopiety that anticipates Franklin's *Autobiography.* This instance, however, is a fascinating exception to his general confinement of transformation to the pattern of homeopathy, an exception that confirms the rule, a moment of astonishing lapse. With

12 On the distinction between history and annals, see Hayden White, "The Value of Narrativity in the Representation of Reality," *Critical Inquiry,* vol. 7, no. 1 (Autumn 1980), pp. 5–28.

13 William Bradford, *Of Plymouth Plantation 1620–1647,* ed. Samuel Eliot Morison (New York, 1966), pp. 203, 120–1, 120, 121, 253, 254.

this exception, Mather's written works observe the point of excessive toxicity and remain content with the rhetorical opportunity provided by the idea of homeopathy, which allows a Puritan to suppose that he is separate from and free of the epidemical, contaminating influence of the other *and* to suggest that some of the other's methods might be adopted – carefully. Fortified by the idea of homeopathic technique, one may expect to be all the more healthy for having swallowed what poisoned others; though he appears to share their methods, this apparent doubling fails to obscure the fact that he is still separate and different in kind, still robust, more robust.

Jonathan Edwards, like Cotton Mather, interested, in incorporating the wisdom of the other party (in his case, Locke and eighteenth-century British psychology) without going over to it, died from smallpox inoculation. His death is not symbolic unless we choose to make it so. But the symbolic suggestiveness of homeopathy and inoculation continues to be exploited in those specimens of American literature where the attractiveness of contamination remains a source of anxiety. Homeopathy appears frequently in those American classics where a civilized son wishes to be both admitted to and saved from the fascinating peril of an alien *culture:* in Rappaccini's Paduan garden, where a plant may put the scarlet of either life or fever into the cheeks of depleted students, and where the difference between life and fever is obscure; in *Walden,* where Thoreau, seeking to keep faith with austerity, remarks that trips to town are homeopathic doses; in Emerson's contention that we are all "privy counsellors to that Hint which homeopathically doses the system," or when, reluctant to reprove Alcott's desire to convert the "Hint" into a foundation for Utopia at Fruitlands, he recommends that error be drunk to the lees because "this will be the best hellebore," the best forestalling of the dislocating force of imaginative social innovation that is condemned in "Politics" and "Demonology"; or even on the raffish Boulevard *Malesherbes,* where Strether finds his reclining Antony and wonders if it might not be best to stay just a little longer, though what he stays to see proves to be too much, an overdose. Though this brief survey is reductive, it testifies to the continuing symbolic usefulness of homeopathy for those writers who inherit Cotton Mather's desire to preserve purity *and* to meet the outside.

During the first heat of the controversy over inoculation, a grenade that failed to go off was thrown through Cotton Mather's window with this note attached: "Cotton Mather, you Dog; Dam you; I'l enoculate you with this, with a pox to you" (*D,* II:658). The fury in this gesture – which surpasses the satiric bombings that the Franklins were printing in the *New England Courant* – should not obscure its analogical cleverness: poison in the body is no more therapeutic than a bomb (or a demented wife) in the house, a conclusion with which Bradford or Edwards might belatedly agree. But a man such as the bomber-critic, Mather says, is a "blasphemer" eager to undermine obedience to the sixth commandment.[14] He is a "Child of the Wicked One," as Increase Mather wrote, a "fierce Enemy to Inoculation." The man of true virtue recognizes the excellence of a medical technique that allows health through submission, rather than succumbing at a later, unknown hour:

> Here the Man *makes himself Sick,* while he is well; and thinks that he is not *the whole who has no need of a Physician,* while he has the *Humours* in him which render him obnoxious to a *Deadly Sickness.* He won't think it his Duty to stay till God send the Sickness in *Another* way upon him; when it will be too late for him to seek relief; But he will give Thanks to GOD for teaching him, how to *make himself Sick,* in a way that will save his Life. He most properly takes GOD's Time to fall Sick: He does it seasonably, and in the *Time* when *God* has *commanded* him to do it.[15]

Mather's words are ripe to dropping with theological analogy: to suppose that health will last without the industrious assistance that the Lord commands is to invite retributive infection; he who ignores the physician is too proud; one must be diligently humble, that is, triumph through submission, rather than over it. In replacing quarantine, the seventeenth century's most effective prescription for preventing infection, the smearing of matter from one person's pustules across incisions made on the arm of another not only saved lives but signified, for Cotton Mather, a new apprehension of the permissible bearing of purity toward contamination. *Felix culpa* is made a matter of choice, and of medical practice. Perhaps the anonymous bomber was less insightful than shortsighted, failing, like some modern critics, to know that Cotton Mather's medical theory was meant to be a shot in the arm for received dogma.

[14] Mather, "Sentiments on the Small Pox Inoculated," p. 2.   [15] Ibid.

5

COTTON MATHER'S RENAISSANCE

Sine Christo omnis virtus est in vitie.

Cotton Mather, *Bonifacius*

The virtuous *example* of such an one, is almost enough to reform whole nations! It carries irresistible *charms* with it, by which *totus componitur orbis* [all the world is put in order]. A *prince* exemplary for piety, sheds the rays of Heaven, as the *sun shining* in his meridian *strength,* with a most penetrating force into the people, *rejoicing under his wings.* 'Tis now a rarity; but it will not be so, in the approaching age, when the *kings of the earth, shall bring their glory and honor* into the Holy City! A *little piety* in princes, makes a glaring show; the eyes of their subjects are dazzled, their minds ravished, with it: they *numinize* them. What would be done by a *degree of piety* in them, that should bear proportion to the *degree* of their *quality;* and if their *piety* were as much above that of other men, as their *station?* Roll about, O *age,* that shall bring on such admirable *spectacles!*

Cotton Mather, *Bonifacius*

Cotton Mather's self-expression is governed by a virtually constant tension between sacred pattern and the obstinate human material that is reluctant to submit to pattern. In his self-searchings, he described a tension between his duty to remembrance and his apostate self; when he left his introspection to pursue his work in the community, he located the tension between his blameless intentions and the various extravagances in which he sought to realize those intentions. Work offered relief, because it allowed him to project doubt outward as opposition to the host of antagonists set against his father's way. Consequently, when he argued for the importance of homeopathically impersonating the antagonists' allure, he was providing the self that had been projected outward with a guarded, provisional opportunity to speak, if only to be silenced again in the eventual moment of absorption.

In the *Magnalia Christi Americana,* the tension between pattern and material manifests itself as a tension between the compositional principles brought to bear on the historical facts and the facts themselves. To present exemplary lives and deeds for New England's future good, Mather must overlook or downplay aspects of the real lives and deeds that are irrelevant or opposed to the particular virtues he is attempting to exemplify, and he must foreground moments of Christian virtue that might be only of secondary importance in the actual lives and deeds. The project of exemplifying meticulously defined Christian virtues is therefore implicitly reductive, though Mather's piety would argue that the aspects of the lives and deeds that are left out are unimportant, and that their omission is thus no major loss.

However, piety is not Mather's sole motive. When the life or deed at hand is most conspicuous for the sort of achievement or magnificence championed in Renaissance theory, rather than for Congregationalist self-annihilating fealty, Mather's interior strife emerges as the stress of a double narrative intention, exemplification *and* secular admiration. In the first book of the *Magnalia Christi Americana,* he contends that the hand of God in the construction of the New England way showed in the simultaneity of three historical events – the discovery of America, the Reformation, and the "Resurrection of Literature," that is, the Renaissance and the invention of printing (*MCA,* I:42). Though Mather here calls this a congenial trio, it is not his uniform opinion. In the introduction, he acknowledged his debt to the resurrection of literature in his laudatory references to Herodotus, Livy, Tacitus, Plutarch, and other predecessor historians. In the works of these writers, however, and in the lives and deeds they chronicle, there is little precedent for specifically Christian exemplification, and Mather recognized that his admiration for these writers and their subjects was potentially conducive to the very amnesia he was writing the book to cure. Mather would have been reminded of this danger by a sermon his father preached at Harvard the year before the *Magnalia Christi Americana* was published. The impact of the sermon was sufficient to move Cotton Mather to transcribe it when he wrote his biography of his father in 1724:

> Let your Sermons be as full of a Christ as may be. Sermons full of *Self,* and made for the Ostentation of your own Learning; Are these the *Sacrifices, that* GOD *will be well-pleased with?* The *Sermons* of the Apostles were not such! No, they could say, *We preach not our selves* but CHRIST JESUS *the Lord* . . . Alas there are *Preachers* in the World who have little of a CHRIST in their *Sermons:* Nothing higher than what is to be met withal in a *Cicero,* a *Seneca,* an *Epictetus,* or a *Plutarch* is to be found in their *Sermons* . . . Have an Eye still on a CHRIST even when you are preaching on *other Subjects.*[1]

[1] Cotton Mather, *Parentator* (Boston, 1724), p. 174.

Increase Mather's jeremiad against Renaissance learning is built on a familiar conjunction of themes: self must be sacrificed to piety though the
sacrifice is as arduous as Christ's; only in this way can the writer be a son
in whom the father is well pleased; and the particular means of sacrifice
is the subjugation of secular scholarly pleasure to the higher pattern.
   To be the good son of Increase Mather, Cotton Mather knew that he
had to govern his admiration for the pagan historians, as he would later
constrain his admiration for the regular design of nature with his father's
science of the prodigious and inexplicable in *The Christian Philosopher*.
The son of Increase Mather could no more rest in his interest in the
classics than Milton could have concluded *Lycidas* at line eighty-four.
Accordingly, at the end of his survey of the pagan historians, Cotton
Mather's tone changes abruptly from approval to disdain:

> The achievements of one Paul particularly, which [Luke] hath embla-
> zoned, have more *true glory* in them, than all the acts of those execrable
> plunderers and murderers, and irresistible banditti of the world which
> have been dignified by the name of "conquerors." Tacitus counted *In-*
> *gentia bella, expugnationes urbium, fusos captosque reges* [great wars, sacked
> cities, kings in flight or chains], the rages of war, and the glorious vio-
> lences, whereof great warriors make a wretched ostentation, to be the
> *noblest matter* for an historian. But there is a nobler, I humbly conceive,
> in the planting and forming of Evangelical Churches, and the tempta-
> tions, the corruptions, the afflictions, which assault them, and their sal-
> vations from those assaults, and the exemplary lives of those that Heaven
> employs to be patterns of holiness and usefulness upon earth: and unto
> such it is, that I now invite my readers; things, in comparison whereof,
> the subjects of many other Histories are of as little weight as the ques-
> tions about *Z*, the last letter of our Alphabet, and whether *H* is to be
> pronounced with an aspiration, where about whole volumes have been
> written, and of no more account than the composure of Didymus. (*MCA*,
> I:29)

(In his notes to the Harvard edition of Books I and II of the *Magnalia
Christi Americana*, Kenneth Murdock reveals that Didymus was an Alexandrian grammarian reputed to have written four thousand volumes
investigating problems that, according to Seneca, "the answers to which
if found were forthwith to be forgotten.") Mather's dismissal of the historians he had admired shows his resolve to keep them as sauce rather
than food, to identify them as an incipient poison to be regulated. Unless
so governed, they could distract Mather from his major purpose, the
celebration of the advancement of the Gospel which was the "sole end"
of the Massachusetts plantation (*MCA*, I:45). The book was to be a
"Christiano-graphy" (*MCA*, I:42), "an *history* of some *feeble attempts* made
in the American hemisphere to anticipate the state of the New-Jerusalem,
as far as the unavoidable *vanity of human affairs* and *influence* of Satan upon
them would allow" (*MCA*, I:46). To this end, Mather felt obliged to

distinguish, as he had urged in *Unum Necessarium,* Christian rebirth from the speciously similar Renaissance.[2] He would celebrate piety, not excellent secular achievement, no matter how fascinating it might be. As he would write in *Bonifacius,* without Christ every virtue is a vice. Secular ability must be strictly subordinated to pious designs, to selfless adherence to paternal pattern.

In the majority of the biographies in the *Magnalia Christi Americana,* the subjugation of the attraction of the Renaissance poses no problem because the subjects of the biographies – ministers and the benefactors of Harvard – collectively developed the New England version of the idea of Christian rebirth, and they had recorded their conversions in diaries, autobiographies, and sermons. They were models of zeal, and so the model of zeal does not amount to a coercion of the facts of their lives. The tension between piety and the influence of the Renaissance comes to the fore, however, in Book II, which recounts the lives of the governors. As Mather contended in the passage from *Bonifacius* used as the second epigraph for this chapter, the conjunction of strenuous Christianity and able magistracy was still an unrealized ideal. The governors whose lives are recorded in Book II were church members, their conduct was generally reputable, and they labored to protect the coherence and independence of New England as a political entity. But conspicuous piety is not their outstanding attribute in all cases, and it is not the reason they are chosen for biographical treatment. Though they were "patterns of usefulness" in maintaining the harmony of the governments that enclosed holy churches, they themselves were not necessarily "patterns of holiness." The principle of inclusion is thus distinct from the principle of composition, since piety and magistracy can be unrelated or even at odds. In the last two biographies in Book II, those of John Winthrop, Jr., and Sir William Phips, the tension becomes a surprisingly open celebration of secular interest and self-design. In these biographies, as a result, the assertion of the subject's piety seems either forced or perfunctory, but in either case extrinsic to what Mather finds laudatory in the life.

This tension may explain why the book of the ministers follows immediately after the book of the governors: the ministerial biographies, displaying the pattern of Christian rebirth more clearly, can absorb the potential forgetfulness in Book II:

> I must so far consider, that it is an *ecclesiastical history* which I have undertaken, as to hasten unto a fuller and larger account of those persons who have been ministers of the gospel, that fed the "flocks in the wilderness"; and, indeed, New-England having been in some sort an ecclesiastical country above any in this world, those men that have here

---

[2] Cotton Mather, *Unum Necessarium* (Boston, 1693), p. 7.

appeared most considerable in an ecclesiastical capacity, may most reasonably challenge the most consideration in our history. (*MCA,* I:235)

This transitional remark becomes a moment of authorial self-discipline
akin to the castigation of the classic historians. The nonpious interest that
has attained to self-expression in the biographies of Winthrop, Jr., and
Phips must be reined in by a remembrance that is larger, fuller, and more
considerable. Mather's remark subordinates New England as secular *polis*
to New England as virtual *civitas dei;* it subordinates the capacities of the
governors to the holiness of the ministers, and it subordinates Cotton
Mather as creative secular self to Cotton Mather as filial remembrancer.
It is thus, like the second and fourth steps in *The Christian Philosopher,* a
dialectical containment of the danger of free, self-determining individuality. Consequently, if we listen to what will be contained before it is
contained, we will hear Cotton Mather's self.

The first biography in Book II, that of John Winthrop, Sr., is the most
convincing victory in Mather's attempt to assemble a hagiography of
governors. Winthrop reveals a subjugation of self so complete that divine
intention – a "sweet yoke," as Winthrop called it in his speech on liberty
and authority – is a constitutive, rather than an extrinsic and regulative,
law of his personal being. Edward Hopkins is a close second: though his
worldly work is conspicuous for its excellence, the argument for his
sanctity does not need to be based on works, since his "*Suffering* as well
as *Doing*" gives him the "Compleat Character of a Christian." Sanctity is
an extrinsic addition to, rather than an intrinsic attribute of, just magistracy: midway through life, Hopkins's wife, "*the Desire of his Eyes,*" proves
to be the victim of an "Incurable *Distraction*" (the same providential test
that would be sent to Cotton Mather thirteen years after the publication
of this biography of Hopkins); Hopkins's affliction, one of the "*Lord's
Rarities,*" teaches him to "*Die Daily*"; and, at his life's end, Hopkins is
horrified by the approaching darkness, but receives last-minute assurance. Hopkins's certainty and competence as governor are broken by the
affliction, and replaced by meeker, more contrite Christian assurance,
and this course of events suggests that able magistracy is not only alien
to sanctity but may even be opposed to it.

The events in Hopkins's life are conventional elements in chronicles of
conversion. William Bradford also fits the pattern: he loses his wife on
the threshold of the New World, and, in the last darkness, is "rapt up
unto the *Unutterable* Entertainments of *Paradise.*" These private events
may seem unrelated to Bradford's able career as governor. But for Mather
the spiritual experience supplements and legitimizes the public work, since
the work by itself is not evidence of holiness. Though Mather approves
of Bradford almost completely, he still balks at Bradford's Brownist

separatism, eighty years after the foundation of Plymouth. His hesitation could not be doctrinal: in point of practice, as Edmund Morgan and Larzer Ziff have demonstrated, the difference between "separating" and "nonseparating" Congregationalisms quickly became inconsequential in the American colonies;[3] and, the "nonseparating" English Puritans having won and lost a revolution in the meantime, Bradford's "separatism" would hardly have seemed radical. Even though Mather assents to Bradford's contention that his congregation was driven to separate, rather than choosing to do so out of ingrained "newfangledness," and even though Mather agrees that the motive for Bradford's separatism was to escape corruption so that he might live in peaceful accord with primitive Christian models, yet the lingering connotations of "separatism" still put a slight taint on Bradford's memory. Separatists, as Mather contends in Book III, acknowledge no father (*MCA*, I:480). The bare suggestion of independence from paternity, in this book where pattern's hold on its material is potentially slight, merits the author's suspicion, and leads him to rank Bradford behind Hopkins and Winthrop.

Winthrop, though, is an epitome without any admixture of nonsaintliness. And the record of Winthrop's life consequently provides Mather with his best example of secular virtue and ability proceeding from a morphologically precise conversion experience. Born to a substantial inheritance which did not include special spiritual prescriptions, Winthrop undergoes conversion and, at an early age, becomes more than a merely able magistrate. At the end of his life, he wrestles with doubt in a scene that is, again, a convention of hagiographical narrative:

> He took a *Cold* which turned into a *Feaver*, whereof he lay *Sick* about a month, and in that *Sickness*, as it hath been observed, that there was allowed unto the *Serpent* the *bruising of the Heel;* and accordingly at the *Heel* or *Close* of our Lives the *old Serpent* will be Nibbling more than ever in our Lives before; and when the Devil sees that we shall shortly be, *where the wicked cease from troubling,* that *wicked One* will *trouble* us more than ever; so this eminent Saint now underwent sharp Conflicts with the *Temper,* whose *Wrath* grew *Great,* as the *Time* to exert it grew *Short;* and he was Buffetted with the Disconsolate Thoughts of Black and Sore *Desertions,* wherein he could use that sad Representation of his own Condition. (*MCA*, I:130)

But he conquers doubt, and recovers shortly before he dies. This doubt might seem to discredit Winthrop's lifelong acquiescence in piety. But for Mather, complacent assurance of salvation would be a probable sign of having listened to Satan's sweet tongue. So Winthrop's deathbed buf-

---

[3] See Edmund Morgan, *Visible Saints: The History of a Puritan Idea* (Ithaca, N.Y.: Cornell University Press, 1965) and Larzer Ziff, *The Career of John Cotton* (Princeton, N.J.: Princeton University Press, 1962).

feting actually confirms his piety. His doubt signals not his enfeeblement but the devil's special hatred of spiritual magnificence.

Winthrop's good works as governor, then, proceed from his piety, and indicate it, but they are not said to cause, increase, or affect his holiness. Consequently, he exemplifies the relation of faith to achievement delineated in the maxim *"Sine Christo omnis virtus est in vitie,"* and he provides a happy, if not a necessary, anticipation of the Christian prince described in *Bonifacius.* He epitomizes a convergence between the criterion that dictates his inclusion in Book II – achievement – and the principle that shapes his biography – conversion. Winthrop's deathbed doubt shows that he did not mistake his worldly deeds for sufficient evidence of holiness. His works are the emanation and product of his Christian self-reform: "He was a very *Religious* Man; and as he strictly kept his *Heart,* so he kept his *House,* under the Laws of *Piety*" (*MCA,* I:120). His piety as householder proceeds from the economy of the converted heart. So too does his achievement as the paternal head of the house of the state: he was "a *Governour* in whom the Excellencies of *Christianity* made a most improving addition unto the *Virtues,* wherein even without *those* he would have made a *Parallel* for the Great Men of *Greece,* or of *Rome,* which the Pen of a *Plutarch* has eternized" (*MCA,* I:118).

The classical virtues of magistrates – patriotism, judiciousness, honesty – were brought to perfection in Greece and Rome; and, were Winthrop's virtue confined to classical virtue, he would still qualify for a Plutarchan parallel biography. But the addition of Christianity, as in the case of Hopkins, is less a simple addition than a contrite transcendence of the glory of works that lifts him above being a mere parallel. Winthrop allows Mather, the Christian American Plutarch, to show the classical virtues being matched and surpassed when they are capped with the wonder of conversion, without which the classical lawgivers were incomplete sketches of virtue. Mather here recapitulates the Christian hermeneutical absorption of the classical world. Classic virtues are prolepses of Christian service in the City of God. They foreshadow true virtue, but do not suffice in themselves. The reformed spirit must be added to them, and they must proceed from it, for the pattern to be complete. Without the reformed spirit, classical virtue is an admirable machine without a purpose; the reformed spirit is the *telos* of classic virtue, which is otherwise remiss.

Insufficiency poses a problem for Mather as biographer since the principle of inclusion in the book would automatically bring to the fore the classical virtues of the good governor, but would not necessarily entail the conversion experience which, though it might be a significant addition to good governorship, is nevertheless not intrinsic to good governorship. As Mather concedes, Christianity is an addition to classic virtue in the lives of the governors, rather than vice versa. It is not a necessary element. Though Mather always conscientiously praises the Christianity of the governors whom he celebrates, few of the subsequent governors show Winthrop's perfect display of inner holiness: they are significant for the most part because they contributed to the general communal well-being of New England Puritanism.

Most of Bradford's and Winthrop's successors are present only in the long lists of officeholders who testify, much like the genealogical recitations in Genesis, to the continuity of the New England tradition. But in the cases of those magistrates whose achievement is substantial enough to entitle them to a biography, the disjunction between the record of their achievement and the pattern of conversion Mather would like to find added to it compels him to liberalize his hermeneutical stringency. Winthrop's exact fidelity to holiness goes unduplicated in the subsequent biographies. As a result, Mather presents him as a sort of standard of measurement with which to appraise his successors' degree of distance from the model life. The repetition of adherence to pattern that generally holds in the book of ministers proves more difficult in the book of governors, so Mather employs instead a measurement of each governor's degree of proximity to Winthrop's example.

Consequently, Mather can celebrate figures notable for non-Christian virtue even though they do not display dramatic conversion. Edward Winslow serves New England with "Fidelity, Discretion, Vigour and Success," and is therefore a "Hercules" (*MCA*, I:115). Thomas Prince is a *"Mecaenas of Learning"* (*MCA*, I:115). Winslow and Prince qualify as Plutarchan parallels for classical epitomes, but they do not surpass. Thomas Dudley is capable with a sword, and careful in financial administration. John Endecott is celebrated for "Prudent and Equal Government" (*MCA*, I:137). Richard Bellingham shows a noble Greek's immunity to bribes. John Leverett is conspicuous for "Courage, Wisdom and Virtue" (*MCA*, I:137). To be sure, Mather never admits that these virtues do not proceed from reformed souls: "The Report may be truly made concerning the *Judges* of *New-England*, tho' they were not *Nobly Born*, yet they were generally *Well Born;* and by being *Eminently Exemplary for a Virtuous and a Sober Life*, gave demonstration that they were *New-Born*" (*MCA*, I:138). But the brevity of these biographies, the absence of any narrative of inward alteration, and the miscellaneous listing of virtues that might belong to Greeks or Anglicans as easily as to Puritans suggest that Mather's blanket assertion that they were all new born in the conversion experience is an attempt to disguise his resignation to the hermeneutic of more-or-less in place of the all-or-nothing expressed by "*Sine Christo omnis virtus est in vitie.*"

Mather's hermeneutic liberality, then, is an *inoculation* of the complete adherence to the pattern of sanctification prescribed in *Bonifacius*. Mather grafts historical achievement onto personal reformation, all the while aware that this is an insertion of otherness that may cure, but may also poison by drifting toward an Arminian emphasis on works and an indifference to the careful Puritan psychology of the devastated self. By adding the otherness of historical work onto the spectacular inward event of conversion, Mather is able to assert that these men were *probably* reformed. The danger in a recourse to probable evidence is the temptation to defer the question of conversion altogether by overlooking it in an enthusiastic celebration of able activity.

The tension between spirit and achievement in the lives of the governors is a manifestation of the general tension underlying the Puritan attempt to make a spiritual idea into a sociopolitical institution: pious state government extends the dominion of spirit, but the immediacy and intrigue of diurnal activity constantly threaten to reduce piety to religiosity, a perfunctory and token vestige. Government, then, is a *pharmakon* that, coming to extend and aid spirit, may also tend to betray. As aloes may be poison or remedy, so too may the urgencies of a governor's activity. In the biographies of Winthrop, Bradford, and Hopkins, the record of achievements is clearly subordinated to the narrative of soul trial and piety; but the later gubernatorial biographies show Mather's admiration for vigorous and independent achievement growing toward prominence and his celebrations of inwardly humble submission to pattern shrinking to pro forma vestigial appendages that are not organically bound to the development of the biography.

Mather relies on each governor's public record to provide a probable demonstration of his sanctification, all the while aware that such demonstrations, like all visible signs, were highly equivocal. This dilemma is most clear in Mather's comments on Sir Henry Vane, governor of Massachusetts from 1636 until his disgraced exit from the antinomian controversy in mid-1637. Vane's public record affords Mather no clear vision of his inward state:

> While some have counted him an Eminent *Christian,* and others have counted him almost an Heretick; some have counted him a Renowned *Patriot,* and others an Infamous *Traitor.* If *Barak* signifie both to Bless and to Curse; and Ευλογειν be of the same Significancy with βλασφε-μειν, in such Philology as that of *Suidas* and *Hesychias;* the Usage which the *Memory* of this Gentleman has met withal, seems to have been Accommodated unto that *Indifferency* of Signification in the Terms for such a Usage. (*MCA,* I:136)

By itself, the record of Vane's career, which included siding with Anne Hutchinson and intense partisanship for the specifically Congregational wing of English Protestantism during the Puritan Revolution, offers

Mather no clear evidence of Vane's inward state. His uncertainty is understandable: the history of Vane's lifelong political activity shows little ideological consistency, though he was always nominally in the Congregationalist wing of the English Puritan cause. Vane's most recent biographers have attempted to provide him with some consistency by postulating a secret Antinomianism, absorbed from Anne Hutchinson, that rarely emerged clearly, and was otherwise scrupulously and judiciously concealed.[4] Mather seems to recognize the difficulty in appraising Vane according to theological standards when he remarks on the "*Indifferency* of Signification" in the "*Memory*" of Vane's activity: a record of vigorous political life need not signify anything about the soul. Mather's explication of the word "Barak" – to bless and to curse – foreshadows his explication of the aloes – poison and remedy – and anticipates the general theme of inoculation, suggesting that a public career is at best loosely connected with Puritan virtue. It may supplement zealous virtue, but it may also distract.

The ambiguousness of Mather's sentiments concerning Vane is further revealed by the story of the man Barak told in the fourth chapter of Judges and recounted in the *Bay Psalm Book*. Called upon by the prophetess Deborah to deliver the Israelites from their bondage to the Canaanite king Jabin, Barak agrees, but on the condition that Deborah accompany him on the campaign. She replies: "I will certainly go with you, but you shall not gain the glory in the expedition on which you are setting out, for the LORD will have Sisera [Jabin's general] fall into the power of a woman." Barak's submission to Deborah, like Vane's to Hutchinson, inverts what Mather would have considered proper gender roles. But the mission is the deliverance of Israel from bondage, which makes the story of Deborah and Barak a confusing type for the story of Hutchinson and Vane – it intimates a connection between Winthrop and Jabin, and associates Massachusetts theocracy with pagan despotism. After his defeat, Sisera tries to hide in the tent of an ally's wife, but when he sleeps she drives a tent peg through his skull and delivers his body to Barak. Ed-

---

[4] J. H. Adamson and H. F. Folland, *Sir Harry Vane: His Life and Times (1613–1662)* (Boston: Gambit Inc., 1973), pp. 196–7: "Thus, because Vane could never make full disclosure of his ultimate purposes, he always found it necessary if not to dissimulate, at least to conceal something, and that constant concealment puzzled and disturbed hs contemporaries. Because of it they could never quite make out what he was after; and his changes of tactics, his readiness to use whatever effective means lay to hand, led to his being called weather-Vane and Sir Harry Weathercock, or as Anthony Wood put it, the Proteus of his time. Vane himself believed that he was not dissembling, but merely reserving full disclosure until the time was ripe for it, and that the end he sought, the Heavenly Jerusalem on earth, justified the means he was forced to use."

ward Johnson had already connected the Antinomian controversy with the story of Deborah, Barak, and Sisera, but he identified Hutchinson with Sisera, with evil, rather than with Deborah, commenting that, whereas the biblical Sisera was taken by a woman, the New England Sisera was a woman. This makes for a clumsy or confused typological figure, but it is an interesting confusion: was Winthrop the New England Deborah? Who was the New England Barak? Johnson's confusion is unraveled if we speculate that he initially identified Hutchinson with Deborah, an unusual female redeemer, but then swerved into awkwardness to avoid heterodox connotations. Johnson's treatment of Antinomianism, like Mather's, imperfectly hides a disquiet or uncertainty that glimmers in the figures after having been expurgated from the explicit discourse. The fourth chapter of Judges is permeated by sexual discomfort, and its typological adoption by Mather entails a convoluted amalgam of horror, disapproval, and unusual self-assertion. To seek to appraise the lives of the governors with a standard that is not innate to the gubernatorial experience is to risk either a coercion of historical fact, or, as in the commentary on Vane, a contortion or confusion of the values that memory is seeking to uphold. These risks express, or recapitulate, Mather's own sense that his life–alternatives were to submit personal desires to coercive authority or to adulterate the good with admixtures of the abominable.

The narrative tension that pervades Book II is an inevitable result of trying to comprehend the governors' lives by means of the pattern derived from the self-representations of ministers. During the period of his influence (1630–49), Winthrop dominated the political thought of Massachusetts with his contention that magistrates are God's chosen vessels and that popular election confirmed but did not cause their presence in office. According to this way of thought, governorship is similar to conversion: as sanctification is made manifest in but is not caused by good works, so magistracy is made manifest in but not caused by popular assent. Magistracy, Winthrop argued, is a theological activity with salient analogies to spiritual states. But, though most of the colony's governors during the first three decades gave nominal assent to Winthrop's principles, Cotton Mather is unable to demonstrate a general repetition of Winthrop's spiritual excellence. The independence of magistracy from piety prompted John Cotton to remark that, if the people chose to live like heathens, "a Heathen man or meerly civil worldly Politician, will be good enough to be their Magistrate."[5] And Thomas Hutchinson later

[5] John Cotton, "*A Discourse about Civil Government in a New Plantation Whose Design Is Religion* (Cambridge, Mass.; 1663), p. 17, quoted in T. H. Breen, *The Character of the Good Ruler: Puritan Political Ideas in New England, 1630–1730* (New Haven, Conn.: Yale University Press, 1970), p. 39.

noted that "sundry eminent gifts of wisdom, courage, justice, fit for government" were sometimes given to nonreligious men.[6] If the requirement that magistracy proceed from inward accord with the pattern of conversion was unevenly observed before 1670, when Mather was seven, it became increasingly irrelevant afterward: "By the mid-1670's it had become almost impossible for a ruler to emulate the mythical founders, while at the same time trying to solve the real problems of the rising generation."[7] In 1683 Edward Randolph arrived with a *Quo Warranto* "against the Charter and Government" of Massachusetts, beginning a series of royally appointed governors; and Cotton Mather's memories of the depredations of Randolph and Sir Edmund Andros, and his intimate acquaintance with the circumstances of Sir William Phips's appointment would have persuaded him that Winthropian piety was a problematic standard to apply to the governors.

Consequently, Mather's attempt to make the conversion experience the measure of the governors in the second book of the *Magnalia Christi Americana* seems doomed to frustration. He accepts compromise, the hermeneutic of more-or-less, but even that fails in the biographies that conclude the book, the lives of John Winthrop, Jr., and Sir William Phips, where Mather forces reluctant historical matter into almost completely irrelevant pattern, or even seems to abandon pattern. In both cases, Mather expatiates on historical figures who, if the conversion experience had been the sole standard of accomplishment, would have been consigned to the long lists of governors that merely mention their having held office. But Mather writes extensive biographies of both, despite the fact that they are clear cases of the disjunction between Puritan holiness and worldly accomplishment, and he is compelled to distort the historical record with a pattern it clearly does not support.

Or perhaps Mather writes extensive biographies of Winthrop, Jr., and Phips *because* they are clear cases of the disjunction between Puritan holiness and worldly accomplishment. In both cases, a richness of action, ambition, and invention is paired with a minimum of zeal; and this aggravated manifestation of the formal disjunction between the hagiographic, self-effacing saintliness of the conversion experience and the assertive modernity of Winthrop, Jr., and Phips provides a rhetorical opportunity for an allegorically autobiographical expression of the tension at the heart of Cotton Mather's self-conception. In the first and second chapters, I summarized Mather's belief that an inimical and hostile alterity doubled and dogged his filiopious attempts to return selflessly to

---

[6] Thomas Hutchinson, *The History of the Colony and Province of Massachusetts Bay,* ed. Lawrence S. Mayo (Boston, 1936), vol. 1, p. 413, quoted in Breen, *The Character of the Good Ruler,* p. 39.

[7] Breen, *The Character of the Good Ruler,* pp. 103–4.

the same: in the biographies of Winthrop, Jr., and Phips, however, the alterity that eludes and evades hagiographic patterning is neither a diabolical nor an amnesiac assault from some vague horrifying outside; rather, it is chosen, developed, presented, and even celebrated by Cotton Mather; and these two biographies, virtually alone among Mather's writings, allow us to speculate that Mather's *anatomies of the other* are evidence of the filiopious self in the act of circumscribing and disavowing those parts of the whole, rich character that are potentially discordant. Cotton Mather's presentations of an alterity that strays from domination by pattern, these biographies imply, may be read as allegories of his own desire to activate those parts of the creative imagination that the sense of duty seems to prohibit. And if Benjamin Franklin's self-design was an antithesis to Puritan traditional piety, we will find that antithetical position anticipated in these biographies, where Mather's horror of the other seems to dissolve into an unadmitted expression of candid desire for vigorous, imaginative modernity.

The analogy between the lives of Mather and Winthrop, Jr., is so striking as to make Mather's biography of Winthrop, Jr., a virtual autobiography. If Winthrop, Jr.'s indifference in matters of the soul makes the verisimilitude of the biography Mather writes of him somewhat dubious, his life's resemblance to Mather's life suggests that the motive for writing the biography may have been less to achieve another hagiographic demonstration than to explore verbally the pressure exerted against creativity by filiopiety. Winthrop, Jr., had a huge interest in nonreligious subjects, such as the development of an American iron industry. His life was spent in able public service: as a prominent figure in Connecticut politics from 1634 to his death in 1676, Winthrop, Jr., was a successful representative of Connecticut's interests at the English court; he helped expedite the acquisition of New York from the Dutch, and he was the motive force behind Connecticut's absorption of the New Haven colony. His attention was frequently taken up with medicine, which fascinated him as much or more than it did Cotton Mather. Like Cotton Mather, he read whatever he could find on the subject; but unlike Cotton Mather, he felt no special urge to theologize medicine, preferring actual practice, advising the sick and writing thousands of prescriptions. His frequent absences from controversial political discussions (among them discussions that involved theological disputes), though arguably sly avoidances of commitment, may also show that he shared Cotton Mather's anxious surveillance of his own body's dysfunctions.

Mather's admiration for Winthrop, Jr.'s medical interests is quite explicit:

> *Ne Habites in urbe caput urbis est Medicus:* But highly reasonable the Sentence of *Aristotle, Ubi praeses fuerit Philosophus, ibi Civitas erit Faelix;* and

this the rather for what is truly noted by *Thucydides, Magistratus est Civitatus Medicus*. Such an one was our WINTHROP, whose Genius and Faculty for *Experimental Philosophy*, was advanced in his *Travels* abroad, by his Acquaintance with many Learned *Virtuosi*. One Effect of this Disposition in him, was his being furnished with *Noble Medecines*, which he most Charitably and Generously gave away upon all Occasions; insomuch that where-ever he came, still the Diseased flocked about him, as if the Healing Angel of *Bethesda* had appeared in the place; and so many were the *Cures* which he wrought, and the *Lives* that he saved, that if *Scanderbeg* might boast of his having slain in his Time Two Thousand Men with his own Hands, this Worthy Person might have made a far more desireable Boast of his having in his Time *Healed* more than so many Thousands; in which Benificence to Mankind, there are of his Worthy Children, who to this Day do follow his Direction and Example. (*MCA,* I:159)

Whether or not Mather includes himself among those "Worthy Children" who follow Winthrop, Jr.'s example, his approval is nevertheless clear. Beginning with classical sentences on the idea of the governor as doctor of the state, Mather quickly abandons even this classical improvement in order to indulge undisguised admiration for Winthrop, Jr.'s active, inventive experimental spirit: Winthrop, Jr., travels, and meets the best modern minds, and his journeys may incite Mather's envy, since he never had traveled, though he tried to rectify this lack with English and other foreign correspondence; Winthrop, Jr., becomes a kind of secular Jesus to whom the diseased flock, but for medicine, not miracles; and Mather calls him an Angel of Bethesda, a term he will use as the title for his own book on medicine in the 1720s. But this Christian reference to the healing angel conceals, or attempts to conceal, the entirely nontheological nature of Mather's admiration, which nevertheless comes through in the word *Virtuosi,* a celebration of clever ability that is closer to Machiavelli's "virtù" than to the converted grace indicated in *"Sine Christo omnis virtus est in vitie."* Mather continues by chronicling Winthrop, Jr.'s acquaintance with Bacon, and his invitation to join the Royal Society, which Mather contends was designed to "advance the *Empire* of Man over the whole visible Creation." Mather himself was invited to join the Royal Society, this bold and not especially pious enterprise, in 1713, some fifteen years after this biography was written.

But if Mather associated himself with Winthrop, Jr.'s experimental spirit, and if the passages acclaiming that spirit describe a markedly nontheological virtuosity, this conjunction rouses a characteristic syllogism: if Mather associates his own experimental inventiveness with Winthrop, Jr.'s, and if Mather's inventiveness is constantly challenged and curbed by his filiopiety, what of Winthrop, Jr.'s filiopiety? This question provokes an abrupt turn in the biography toward the other great conjunction be-

tween the lives of Cotton Mather and John Winthrop, Jr., their theologically accomplished and massively authoritarian fathers: both of their names
signify their repetition of the past, not the singularity of their innovation.
Just when Mather's admiration for Winthrop, Jr.'s explorations reaches
its most enthusiastic point, he interrupts by quoting from a 1643 letter
that Winthrop, Sr., wrote to his son. The father tells the son that his
inheritance obliges him to extend the empire of *God* over the human
world, and reminds him that this responsibility

> was not *forced* from you by a Father's Power, but freely *resigned* by your
> self, out of a Loving and Filial Respect unto me, and your own readi-
> ness unto the Work it self. From whence, as I do often take Occasion
> to Bless the Lord for you, so do I also Commend you and yours to his
> *Fatherly Blessing,* for a plentiful Reward to be rendred unto you. (*MCA*,
> I:161)

Winthrop, Sr., calls himself noncoercive in this request for filiopietistic
cooperation, and he probably was not coercive in explicit or outright
demands; but the obvious affiliation of his paternal desire with the Lord's
"Fatherly Blessing" would associate the son's independence with apostasy;
and, when the alternative is posed in this way, the father's desire ampli-
fied into an entire structure of divinely approved rectitude, it is a disguised coercion. When the father transmits a complete, extant model for
a life that permits no qualitative amendment to the son, and associates
the transmitted model with the wishes of divinity, the son's desire for a
creative and independent modernity can only manifest itself as a heinous,
bastard perturbation in the order of things.

Later in the same letter, the father expresses his relief that, in his travels, the son has never contracted the foreign vice of licentiousness, "a
Mercy vouchsafed but unto few Young Gentlemen Travellers." Having
praised his son for this escape, the father proceeds to the more present
threat, the son's talent for experimental philosophy:

> Study well, my Son, the saying of the Apostle, *Knowledge puffeth up.* It
> is a *good Gift* of God, but when it lifts up the Mind above the *Cross of
> Christ,* it is the *Pride of Life,* and the *High-Way to Apostacy,* wherein
> many Men of great learning and Hopes have perished. – In all the Ex-
> ercise of your *Gifts,* and Improvement of your *Talents,* have an Eye to
> your *Master's End,* more than your *own.* (*MCA,* I:161)

Extending his provincial connection of geographical and sexual way-
wardness, the father puts learning with philandering: learning and sexuality are temptations that, indulged for themselves, will lead astray, but
that, subdued to the proper end, will supplement faith. Winthrop, Sr.'s
letter, quoted at length by Cotton Mather, begins with wayward sexuality, and then broadens the affective connotations proper to promiscuity
to include a number of nonsexual interests. Indulging learning for its

own sake is here called a violation of the Augustinian injunction to love the Creator before the creature: the unsubordinated love of the creature – curious investigation – is called the son's "own end" and the proper direction of learning – the memory of Christ's anguished acceptance of the duty of sonship – is called the "Master's End." The father no doubt means God when he writes "Master," but this is the same God he had associated with fatherhood and the exercise of authority shortly before. The father tells the son that the originality expressed in his inquiries must be subordinated to the holy, patterned, inherited (and freely accepted) life; and he justifies this demand by attaching God's authority to his own, thereby connecting the son's disobedience with moral flaw.

It is not difficult to imagine the pertinence Mather found in this letter, or the relief he sought in the enthusiastic conclusion that follows. He declares that Winthrop, Jr., is a "second Winthrop," entitled, unlike the degenerate son of Scipio Africanus (or his own Creasy), to wear his father's signet ring. The subjugation of worldly ability to the pattern of holiness which is the salient formal attribute of the second book of the *Magnalia Christi Americana* is, in the biography of Winthrop, Jr., condensed into the specific form of the tension between a son's incipiently wayward scientific curiosity – which the father likens to sexual promiscuity – and the father's noncoercive but God-backed demand for Christic self-sacrifice to devoutness. The dynastic tension present in all of Mather's discussions of the contradiction between inherited pattern and the allure of modernity here takes literal, explicit dynastic form. For Winthrop, Jr., as for Cotton Mather, pattern, paternal, and divinity are so analogous as to be synonymous. Because Mather himself is dominated by such a presentation of authority, and because he is also sympathetic to Winthrop, Jr., he is delighted to be able to conclude that Winthrop, Jr., successfully pursued his inquest into modernity *and* satisfied his father's requirements. His victorious fusion of the potentially contradictory directions of his character demonstrates a successful inoculation. The son is enticed by speculative inquiries, as if by exotic and available women, and the enticement is a potential poisoning, or forgetting, of his required repetition of holiness. But if they are circumscribed, subdued, and subordinated to the "Cross of Christ" – the most holy son's submission to the most holy father – these inquiries can be tolerable supplements that actually enhance holiness. Alien inquiry is permissible in supervised doses: the son may explore, and still repeat.

However, though Mather's portrait of Winthrop, Jr.'s scientific interests is largely correct, his contention that the son curbed those interests in order to duplicate his father's piety is not. In his youth, Winthrop, Jr., was enthusiastic in new interest, but indolent in committed application, and in his maturity he was politically deft, intellectually impressive, but theologically indifferent. He shows no signs of his father's zeal, and Robert C. Black III argues that the letter from which Mather quotes probably indicates the father's recognition of his son's indifference to piety:

> For all of their unfeigned and mutual esteem, he may have questioned the wisdom of establishing a fixed residence so close to his father. They were not genuinely compatible; their respective viewpoints lay an interplanetary distance apart. Even the elder Winthrop was aware of this, and there were times when he tried earnestly to reduce the gulf between them – by urging the younger man to change.

Black then quotes from the letter, and concludes that "even such Jacobean phrases availed him little; to mold this son into the Massachusetts pattern would have required no less than divine intervention. Failing this, a too constant and intimate association must have become an embarrassment to them both."[8] In the reference to Winthrop, Jr.'s entitlement to his father's signet ring, then, Mather either distorts facts or perpetuates a distortion of fact, perhaps even an employment of the story of Winthrop, Jr.'s life as an admonitory *exemplum* by Increase Mather. But that such a distortion should originate with Cotton Mather would not be surprising, since the biography of Winthrop, Jr., is veiled autobiography: Mather stresses that the son was divided between holy knowledge and secular inquiry, or devotion and apostasy; he contends that the son found a way to harmonize the two, inoculating his father's will with independent enterprises, leading a magnificent life that ended with his being "Honourably Interred in the same Tomb with his Honourable Father" (*MCA*, I:160); and Mather thereby reassures himself that there can be some compatability between self and obligation. If Mather's portrait of Winthrop, Jr., is historically inaccurate, it is nevertheless a true sight of Mather himself; and though Winthrop, Sr.'s letter to Winthrop, Jr., may have been a futile intervention into his son's life, Cotton Mather's act of quotation from Winthrop, Sr.'s letter is a successful (if abrupt and distortive) intervention of his sense of dynastic obligation into his nearly outright admiration for Winthrop, Jr's secular independence. It is a moment of sudden self-consciousness and restraint, like the condemnation of the pagan historians in the "General Introduction" and of the poets in the *Manuductio ad Ministerium*. When Mather asserts that Winthrop, Jr., reconciled goodness and genius, without demonstrating how he did it, he is indulging wish-fulfillment, celebrating the son's creativity while still maintaining that he is "*Non minor magnis Majoribus* [not inferior to the great elders of his name]."

Despite Mather's pious assertions, however, the biography of Win-

[8] Robert C. Black III, *The Younger John Winthrop* (New York: Columbia University Press, 1966), p. 133.

throp, Jr., points the way toward secularizing revisions of the two admirable traits Mather had attributed to the ministry, a universal power of address and a universal range of investigation. Like his father, according to Mather, Winthrop, Jr., was a fine magistrate because he had the art of going below the particularities that divided men in order to quicken the common interest. Mather carefully asserts that this common interest is holiness, and that Winthrop, Jr., acquired the art through preliminary self-annihilation:

> If one would therefore desire an exact picture of this worthy man, the description which the most sober and solid writers of the great *philosophick work* do give of those persons, who alone are qualified for the smiles of heaven upon their enterprizes, would have exactly fitted him. He was a *studious, humble, patient, reserved* and *mortified* person, and one in whom the love of *God* was fervent, the love of *man* sincere: and he had herewithal a certain *extension of soul*, which disposed him to a *generous behaviour* toward those who, by learning, breeding and virtue, deserve respects, though of a perswasion and profession in religion very different from *his own;* which was that of a reformed protestant, and a New-English Puritan. In sum, he was not more of an *adoptist* in those noble and secret *medicines,* which would reach the *roots* of the distempers that annoy humane bodies, and procure an *universal rest* unto the *archaeus* on all occasions of disturbance, than he was in those Christian qualities, which appear upon the cure of the distempers in the minds of men, by the effectual *grace* of our Lord Jesus Christ. (*MCA*, I:160)

Because he is self-mortified, having cured the disease within, Winthrop, Jr., has acquired an extension of soul, a grace that proceeds from Christ rather than from self: this freed soul allows him to address men who are not conspicuously reformed, therefore forestalling self's power to exacerbate social disunion; the "archaeus," self, pacified in Winthrop, Jr., is also subdued in those to whom his charisma beckons. The Winthrop, Jr., of this paragraph is a near epitome of Mather's version of representative personality.

But, though Winthrop, Jr., brings his various contemporaries to social agreement, Mather does not contend that he brings them to agreement in self-mortifying piety. According to Mather, many admired Winthrop, Jr., for his medical learning, and Charles II was fond of Winthrop, Jr., because Winthrop, Jr., gave the king a ring that Charles I had given to Adam Winthrop. At such moments, Winthrop, Jr., is shown appealing to his contemporaries' self-interest rather than instigating their self-sacrifice, and a wholly secular mode of universal harmony is being insinuated. The adoptist understands the self-interest in his social audience, and he is *ingenious* in his art of appeal. This process of secularizing the concepts of representative personality and consequent social harmony is implicit in the very word *ingenuity* as it appears in Mather's and Franklin's writings. During their period, *ingeniousness* was replacing its near-homophone *in-*

genuousness as the primary meaning of the word *ingenuity*. All three words resonate with a fourth that is important to the idea of representative personality, *genius*. As with the words *inoculation* and *virtuoso*, the etymological and phonological continuity provided a rhetorical opportunity to intimate a semantic continuity between what were in fact significantly disparate traits: *ingenuous* signifies candor and filiopiety: *ingenious* signifies cleverness, secular intelligence, even craftiness, and, implicitly, innovation. Therefore, as Mather realized, ingeniousness such as Winthrop, Jr.'s posed a threat to the ingenuousness his father demanded; and, as Franklin realized, ingeniousness sometimes required that ingenuousness be relegated to secondary importance. The etymological and phonological continuity between the two words, fortified by the fact that *ingenuity* could signify either of them during this period, permits different modes of genius to seem synonymous. Ingenuousness can slide toward ingeniousness despite the important reversals involved, and this slide can underwrite the secularization of representative personality that is intimated in the biography of Winthrop, Jr., and that is at the center of Franklin's *Autobiography*.

Winthrop, Jr.'s power of social appeal, as Mather hints, was more a product of ingeniousness than of Calvinist ingenuousness. According to Richard S. Dunn, Winthrop, Jr., "reflected almost every aspect of his burgeoning society," and he was "all things to all men, a highly receptive person, open to new ideas, adaptable to new situations." Mather's biography is correct in celebrating this versatility, but it is distortive in its assertion that Winthrop, Jr.'s versatility emanated from a piety to which it was subordinated. As Dunn argues, religion "framed his life, but he did not experience his father's crusading zeal."[9] Mather's unfounded assertion of Winthrop, Jr.'s piety is an alien intrusion into the real life, and its discordant intrusiveness reveals Mather's consternated attraction to the subtle declension of representative personality from a Calvinist to a Franklinian ideal. Released from bondage to the father, freed ingenuity is a universal factotum capable of eliciting acclaim from the many seasons of man without preliminary mortification in either the genius or the social audience. Winthrop, Jr., was not inextricably committed to any particular calling: governor, doctor, diplomat, and miner, he displays a Piconian freedom from particular intellectual commitment, and a consequent capacity for involvement in the full range of a society eager to shed the domination of religious ideals. His representativeness, therefore, doubles universal piety, but in such a way as to replace and discredit it.

From the point of view of Mather's dynastic commitment, conse-

---

[9] Richard S. Dunn, *Puritans and Yankees: The Winthrop Dynasty of New England, 1630–1717* (Princeton, N.J.: Princeton University Press, 1962), p. 59.

quently, ingenuity represents a diabolical simulacrum, a specious resemblance to rectitude designed to make men believe that they are adhering
to the good when they are actually poisoning the good. This suspicion
underlies Winthrop, Sr.'s assertion that "knowledge puffeth up," a quotation from 1 Corinthians 8, where Paul contends that knowledge is an
idolatry, akin to polytheism and eating unclean meats, that attempts to
substitute itself for Christian love. Mather displays his suspicion of this
false lord in *Bonifacius,* in the addresses to doctors and lawyers, where he
commends them on their learning but warns that wide-ranging interest
can divert from religion. In his biography of Thomas Hooker in the
Magnalia Christi Americana, Mather cites the case of Alexander Richardson, "who was a master of so much understanding, that, like the great
army of Gideon, he was too many to be employed in doing what was to
be done for the church of God" (*MCA,* I:336).

But from the point of view of secular ingenuity, Matherian piety might
seem like an unjust and reductive burden on a legitimate, productive
activity. Rather than being a corrosive simulacrum of piety, ingenuity
would be a reputable portion of human nature that had long been encumbered by a now-anachronistic religious onus. Mather's obvious interest
in Winthrop, Jr.'s secular versatility, together with his self-consciously
compensatory invocation of Winthrop, Sr.'s prestige, shows that he was
attracted to the kind of representative personality that Franklin would
epitomize, and that he was aware of the contradiction between the attraction and his dynastic legacy. In his vexed biography of Winthrop, Jr.,
Mather gives voice to both sides of the contention that Ernst Cassirer
calls the central project of the Enlightenment:

> The lust for knowledge, the *libido sciendi,* which theological dogmatism
> had outlawed and branded as intellectual pride, is now called a neces-
> sary quality of the soul as such and restored to its original rights. The
> defense, reinforcement, and consolidation of this way of thinking is the
> cardinal aim of eighteenth century culture; and in this mode of think-
> ing, not in the mere acquisition and extension of specific information,
> the century sees its major task.[10]

This ambition, recollecting Renaissance and prefiguring Enlightenment,
is not visible directly in the biography of Winthrop, Jr, but indirectly, in
the tension between Mather's inclination to Winthrop, Jr., and the consequently coercive imposition of the hagiographic pattern. The important point is not that the biography is distortive, and therefore inferior
history writing, but that its distortiveness is a lucid image of Mather's
interior division between duty and inclination.

[10] Ernst Cassirer, *The Philosophy of the Enlightenment,* trans. Fritz A. Koelln and
James P. Pettegrove (Boston: Beacon press, 1955), p. 14.

COTTON MATHER'S RENAISSANCE

The power of secular interests to lure one away from adherence to pattern into vigorous independence is again the issue in the next biography, Mather's life of Sir William Phips, which concludes the book of governors. There are two major differences between the biographies of Phips and Winthrop, Jr.: in the biography of Phips, the secular interests at hand are political, military, social, and economic self-advancement, rather than experimental science; and in the biography of Phips the presence of the hagiographical pattern seems not coercive, but vestigial and perfunctory. There is no convincing and sustained assertion that Phips's ingenious modernity is also pious; and the biography as a whole, consequently, emerges as a kind of personal renaissance for Cotton Mather, as Mather's single most frank and coherent confession of gravitation toward the ideal of a curious, modern, assertive life not bent to suit the pattern of conversion. At several points, Mather attempts to present Phips as a specimen of New England zeal, but this has been rightly called a halfhearted gesture at sanctifying the thoroughly secular man Hawthorne would depict, and at bringing a diverse, lively, and realistic narrative back within the pale of hagiography. Phips did join the Mathers' congregation after having tendered a conversion-narrative that Mather includes in the biography. The narrative is punctiliously correct, but its very punctiliousness suggests that it was more opportune than heartfelt, and David Levin notes that the prose is closer to Cotton Mather's than it is to Phips's. Whether sincere or not, though, the narrative is a single, discrete event: conversion and self-mortification do not run throughout Phips's life as they did through Mather's. There is too much expedition and completeness in Phips's conversion. Without prolongation and regular renewal, Phips's conversion makes piety seem like one of ingenuity's many devices, rather than its unyielding governor.

Phips was an ambitious man of common birth who propelled himself to prominence through wit, dedication, and some connivance; an adventurer who cleverly recovered sunken Spanish treasure and who, directing some of the treasure toward the crown, won a knighthood; a fat hedonist and, occasionally, a hothead who reduced argument to fistfight. Plainly, Mather's praise for Phips's saintliness is unconvincing, and the perfunctoriness of the praise leaves the biography less coercive, less compelled by the requirement of the hagiographic pattern than any of the others in the second book of the *Magnalia Christi Americana*. His praise might be attributed to Phips's partisan sympathy for the Mathers' political stances, or to the fact that the biography of Phips was written and published separately and only later included in the *Magnalia Christi Americana*. Though these factors are certainly pertinent, neither is a sufficient explanation for Mather's astonishingly candid admiration for Phips's life as a whole (rather than simply for his political choices), nor for the meditations on experience and pattern that are woven throughout. The *Magnalia Christi Americana* was conceived and designed as a coherent whole, a single vast demonstration, and a clearly divergent entry deserves (and has attracted) more conjecture than a simple notation of Mather's partisan interests or of the biography's publishing history. The biography of Phips is an explicit manifestation of the tension between pattern and experience that runs throughout the book of governors in which it is enclosed, rather than simply an accident of interest or publication. In fact, the history of publication becomes *more* significant, since the temporal priority of the biography of Phips allows us to read its characteristic tension into the biographies that precede it in the text of the *Magnalia Christi Americana*.

This disparity has been the topic of recent criticism. Jane Donahue Eberwein notes that "Mather opens himself to charges of character simplification or even distortion in his effort to coordinate Phips with the more typically Puritan subjects of the other Puritan lives."[11] Though she treats the other biographies as a homogeneous whole, lumping Vane and Winthrop, Jr., with the other "typically Puritan subjects," Eberwein does notice that the tension between pattern and fact is a key dimension of the biography:

> Naturally, Mather attempts to depict this new kind of life within the familiar conventions of his hagiographic style; but, when he salutes "a person as memorable for the wonderful changes which befel him, as imitable for his virtues and actions under those changes," the key word is changes rather than virtues or actions, and changes in content force changes in style, structure and tone.[12]

Phips's life is conspicuous for "changes" that cannot be understood in the context of the conversion experience, and this topic affects the form of the biography, as mere partisanship or temporal disparity in publication would not. Phillip Gura agrees:

> Rather than composing his *Life of Phips* in the manner of his other "lives" in which "the subject . . . was never glorified in and for himself but for the ulterior purpose of glorifying New England's primitive past," Mather was forced to create a new set of "virtues" to identify his subject, thus making the biography so much more engaging than the conventional, highly idealized lives of Bradford and Winthrop (later to appear in the *Magnalia* with the *Life of Phips*).[13]

The new virtues – patriotism, ingeniousness, self-design, perseverance, diversity – are closer to Winthrop, Jr.'s "virtuosity" than to the inward

[11] Jane Donahue Eberwein, "'In a Book, as in a Glass': Literary Sorcery in Mather's Life of Phips," *Early American Literature* 10 (1975 / 76), p. 293.

[12] Ibid., p. 289.

[13] Phillip F. Gura, "Cotton Mather's *Life of Phips*: A Vice with the Vizard of Virtue upon It," *New England Quarterly*, 50 (September 1977), p. 447.

virtue that without Christ is vice, and closer still to Benjamin Franklin's virtue, in which inheritance is subordinated to personal rational excellence. But Eberwein and Gura simply note that this biography departs from pattern. They do not consider that, viewed as a temporal predecessor to the lives of the governors in Book II of the *Magnalia Christi Americana*, the biography of Phips delineates a tension that pervades the whole book, or that it represents the conspicuous emergence of that tension into clear definition. Neglecting to describe what the biography of Phips tells us about Book II as a whole, Eberwein and Gura also fail to describe the allegorically autobiographical importance of the topic of liberalization, and they do not draw attention to Mather's treatment of the subject of hermeneutic looseness within the biography itself. As the book of the governors proceeds, Mather's desire for an independent modernity gains increasingly direct expression in the form of admiration. He uses the formal tension between pattern and experience that is innate to the book as a vehicle for his own characteristic affective tension; and his desire emerges fully articulate (though still in the form of admiration for another) in the biography of Phips, an emergence that is signaled by Mather's use of liberality as a central theme.

Mather's Phips is not simply cool to religion, as Eberwein and Gura suggest. Rather, he has a coherent and developed position on crucial theological questions. Early in Phips's life, for an example, an astrologer sends him a prospectus of his future. Point for point, the astrologer's prospectus accurately anticipates "the most material Passages that were to befall this our *Phips* in the remaining part of his Life" (*MCA*, I:222). Phips is tempted to believe that the prospectus will continue to be accurate, and to use it as a basis for planning and action. But he escapes this trap, and Mather reports his reason:

> Sir [he says to Mather], *I do believe that there might be a cursed snare of Satan in those Prophesies: I believe Satan might have leave to foretel many things, all of which might come to pass in the beginning, to lay me asleep about such things as are to follow, especially about the main Chance of all; I do not know but I am to die this Year; for my part, by the help of the Grace of God, I shall endeavour to live as if I were this Year to die.* (*MCA*, I:223)

Mather summarizes the doctrine in Phips's position:

> That albeit Almighty God may permit the *Devils* to *Predict,* and perhaps to *Perform* very many Particular things to Men, that shall by such a *Presumptuous and Unwarrantable Juggle* as *Astrology* (so Dr. Hall well calls it!) or any other *Divination,* consult them, yet the *devils* which *foretel* many *True* things, do commonly foretel some that are *False,* and it may be, propose by the things that are *True* to betray Men into some fatal Misbelief and Miscarriage about those that are *False.* (*MCA*, I:223)

The accuracy of the prospectus makes it likely that it will continue to be accurate, but Phips argues (taking the words right out of Mather's mouth) that probability is Satan's most sophisticated temptation. This argument seems like an isolated anecdote until it is remembered that Phips stopped the witch trials, at which probability of reprobation had been used as sufficient legal evidence.

The use of probability at the trials had a venerable history of precedent in Puritan thought, since it was a convenient device for providing a foundation for the just exercise of authority while still acknowledging the inaccessibility of divinity. In the second half of *Of Plymouth Plantation,* for example, Bradford lays great stress on the adamantly repetitious mischief of men such as Lyford and Oldham, and on the legal requirement that there be two witnesses to an abuse of order. Bradford knew that he was doctrinally forbidden to speak with certainty about the secrecy of his or others' souls; but, on the other hand, the socialization of spirituality in a community required that he proceed to action. So he proceeded from probability, which told him that signs were *clear enough,* as I contended in the first chapter, to provide a foundation for moral activity. In the later years of his history, however, Bradford's encounters with the manifold duplicity of the hypocrites and with the general drift of the community away from collective zeal left him impressed with the profound equivocality of things. As the book progresses, there is a resurgent sense of the unknown god, though there are moments of clarity, such as the conviction and execution of a boy for bestiality (he is compelled to watch the animals with which he copulated killed and burned before he is himself executed). But with such exceptions, Bradford's preoccupation with the unsearchable grows during the years recounted in the second half of *Of Plymouth Plantation:* experience had grown baffling, compelling him to remember the inscrutability of divine intentions; his reading of providential signs becomes looser, and sometimes he fails to improve an event that seems to require theological construction; hence his growing emphasis on probable conclusions.

Bradford's drift from clarity separates him from the mainstream of seventeenth-century American Puritanism, which persevered in the use of enthymemic probability as a sufficient device for separating the correct from the heinous, for admitting communicants and exiling heretics. The need to exercise social authority, and to justify that exercise as an expression of divine intention, led the Puritans, as Perry Miller argues, so strenuously to emphasize the clarity to which God submitted himself under the Covenant that occasional remembrances of the unknown god seem to be virtually token allusions to a doctrine that had been more useful in the repudiation of the authority of the Church of England than in the administration of the theocracy.[14] With few exceptions, such as Anne Bradstreet's brilliant writing from the periphery of power, or such ritual observances as *The Day of Doom*, the difference between the doctrinally correct assertion that judgment was based on likelihood and the assertion of simple certainty, such as informed *The Simple Cobler of Aggawam*, "Liberty and Authority," or the epistemological position of the judges in the witch trials, was minimal.

But the biography of Phips suggests a flaw in Miller's argument. According to Miller, the gradual commitment to certainty was the beginning of the end for American Puritanism, since it unwittingly sponsored the epistemological optimism of what he called the declension. However, the clarity that the theocrats claimed for themselves was entirely different from the rationalistic and commercial confidence of Enlightenment. The assertion of the unknown god, therefore, could serve the interest of Enlightenment, since it would strip theocracy of authority, as the Puritans had legitimated their own repudiation of Anglicanism with their remembrance of the divine mysteriousness that would not accept objectification in ritual, hierarchy, and surplice. This subversion is already manifest in the Antinomian crisis where, according to Larzer Ziff, the commercial interest sided with Hutchinson because her assertion of the divine mystery implicitly divested Winthrop's group of the divine right to impose such restrictions as the just price: "The relatively wealthy and well-positioned group behind Anne Hutchinson was attracted to her doctrine because free grace above the legalistic restrictions of the moral law meant freer enterprise beyond the specific regulations of the state."[15]

Phips's assertion of uncertainty in the repudiation of the astrological prospectus, therefore, is not necessarily a return to piety. For example, until long after the composition of the biography of Phips, Cotton Mather followed his father in believing that the especially pious are rewarded by God with specific intimations of the future: Mather's diary for 1707 even includes "Esquire Bickerstaff's Predictions for 1708," among them the death of the Dauphin on May 7 and twelve days of frosty weather in early September. It is impossible to say whether Mather was credulous or simply intrigued with this prospectus: but he is not denunciatory as the Phips of the biography Mather wrote fourteen years before had been.

Clearly, Phips's epistemological humility diverges from Mather's belief that vigorous self-mortification would bring prescience. Rather than a moment of piety, Phips's epistemological humility is a denial of the

[14] Perry Miller, "The Marrow of Puritan Divinity," in *Errand into the Wilderness* (Cambridge, Mass.: Harvard University Press, 1978), pp. 48–99.

[15] Larzer Ziff, *Puritanism in America* (New York: Viking Press, 1973), p. 75.

assertion that God clearly sponsors the use of authority to prescribe the
proper shape of life and to proscribe others: this denial cuts life loose
from divine pattern, so that if Mather's Phips cannot defend his manner
of life on the grounds of theological rectitude, he is on the other hand
immune to accusations made in God's name; the connection between the
divine paternity and the earthly fathers who had claimed to be its trustees
is severed without an atheistic assault on God himself. Franklin will develop this strategy in his *Articles of Belief and Religion* (1728): "More especially, since it is impossible for me to have any positive clear idea of
that which is infinite and incomprehensible, I cannot conceive otherwise
than that he *the infinite Father* expects or requires no Worship or Praise
from us, but he is even infinitely above it" (*P,* 1:102). This statement is
the birth of American pragmatism: if, as the Puritans had claimed, divinity transcends understanding completely, then it cannot enter human calculations: the self's proper course cannot be, *and need not be,* meticulously
governed by specific patterns of indubitable rectitude.

Consequently, the epistemological humility that is the regular theme
of the meditations Mather attributes to Phips is potentially subversive of
filiopiety and hagiography. After the wreck of an expedition he sent against
Canada, Phips tells the story of a hermit who was invited to travel with
an angel who would refute the hermit's skepticism by demonstration.
The first night, they stay at a kind man's house; the next morning, the
angel steals a valuable cup from the kind man and gives it to a wicked
man. The third night, they stay at the house of a loving, godly man; the
next morning, the angel throws the godly man's servant into the river,
where he drowns. The fourth night, they stay with another godly man,
whose child the angel drowns before morning. The hermit quite rightly
protests that these actions do not nourish his faith in a loving god. The
cup and the child, the angel replies, had grown to be objects of excessive
love, and so they were removed, so that the men would not lose their
devotion. The obvious rendering of these episodes would seem to be that
the Creator should be loved before the creature, a common Puritan lesson that may be found, for example, in Bradstreet's poem about the
burning of her house. But the drowning of the servant does not fit the
pattern. Phips's angel reveals that the servant had planned to murder
the master, and so was drowned to save him. Here, God's agent acts
practically, rather than pedagogically. Consequently, the homiletic requirement that the Creator be loved above the creature cannot be the
single lesson to be learned from *all three* stories: the story of the murderous servant disenfranchises the lesson strongly implied in the other two
stories, and it seems to surprise deliberately expectations that would have
accumulated after the hundreds of providential interpretations of affliction that any Puritan reader would have heard or read. The lesson, ac-

cording to Mather, is *not* that one's taste for the world should be chastened: "Thus General *Phips*, though he had been used unto *Diving* in his time, would say, *That the things which had befallen him in this Expedition, were too deep to be Dived into!*" (*MCA*, I:190). Phips's improvement of the parable veers from the predictable interpretation of the Canadian defeat as a didactic humiliation, instead concentrating on the assertion that failure to understand is no reason to disbelieve, because divine intentions, whatever they may be, are beyond the mind's reach; he incidentally suggests that adversity does not necessarily result from overinfatuation with the world, as it did not in the story of the murderous servant.

The latent meaning of Phips's parable, in other words, might have gratified Mather a great deal: God's frustration of human desire is not necessarily a result of a flaw in the nature of that desire; and to claim that it is is to aspire to a prohibited godliness of understanding. The lesson is not that pride will be humbled, but that human explication of the invisible divine is apt to be delusory, as it had been at Salem. In the anecdote of the astrologer and the parable of the hermit, we see Mather providing Phips with a coherent theological position: the imposition of humanly conceived theological patterns of understanding onto experience, even if accompanied by appropriate disclaimers about the patterns' probable reliability, is inappropriate and injudicious, the sign of an aberrant claim to divine understanding.

If divine intentions are unavailable, then all authoritative human prescriptions about the proper manner in which life is to be lived are inventions, no matter how admirably motivated, on a par with the astrologer's chart. Though this may resemble an Antinomian position, it is really more closely related to Franklin's pragmatism: God may have a plan for me, Mather's Phips reasons, I don't doubt that, life may follow an ordained pattern; but no human tradition may have detected and described it, and so gained the authority to stipulate proper attitudes and actions for me; even adversity cannot be said to prove I am following the wrong path; similarly, I will not anguish over that pattern, since I may not detect it either; so I must proceed as if there were no pattern, as if I were self-designing. Mather's Phips pragmatically proceeds to the conclusion that an unknown god cannot enter as a factor in the conduct of a reasonable and responsible life: sentiments of propriety and justice do not require divine assent, and cannot have it, but should not therefore be abandoned. Most importantly, the authority of past generations to stipulate the letter of acceptability in attitude and action is invalidated. The greatness of the past, for all its eminence, is a manufactured human construct without authority to command repetition. It is a resource to be judged for its contemporary utility, and self-design in accord with personal judgments and interests is appropriate and virtuous. Mather's biography of Phips is a sympathetic defense *from the inside* of the modern indifference to inherited pattern that he labels and deplores as the alterity of forgetfulness in most of the rest of his writing, including the *Magnalia Christi Americana* in which the biography is enclosed.

The biography of Phips, therefore, exists in the midst of the book as a kind of national park in which the usual subjugation of the desire for self-design to the requirements of filiopiety is waived, and this waiver accounts for the biography's obvious differences in form and tone. It is no coincidence that Mather goes to great lengths to celebrate Phips's reluctance to impose theological patterns of understanding onto his experience in this biography which most strays, thematically and formally, from the biographical pattern Mather usually seeks to impose on the recalcitrant lives of New England's governors. Phips's opinions are an internal theoretical justification for the biography's formal and thematic innovation and for the author's desire it conspicuously reveals.

If the biography of Winthrop, Jr., celebrates the son's independence from the patterned, predesigned life, only to recuperate that exuberant otherness with the improbable assertion that the son turned out to be his father reborn, the biography of Phips that follows it is Mather's most explicit protest against the stringencies of filiopiety. It is a chronicle of a life unredeemed by any father's remonstrations, internally bolstered against the charge of apostatic newfangledness. Phips's epistemological humility is a precondition for vigorous self-assertion, and becomes Mather's license to write a wish-fulfilling biography that is figurally and narratively independent of hagiography and that openly celebrates not especially Puritan virtues. Though Phips never denies that divinity planned his life, he does deny that the plan is available to himself, to the astrologer, or to any other man. Consequently, he is free to pursue its course without encumbering human prescription, as Mather is free to compose liberal narrative.

Parker H. Johnson has argued that the "basic metaphor of distilling then reconstituting" pervades the *Magnalia Christi Americana*.[16] This is quite true, since the breaking down of certainty and the emergence of Christic virtue is the essential structure of the conversion experience and of Mather's view of sacred history. Johnson begins by analyzing the metaphoric restoration of the plant from its salts which introduces the biography of Phips (see Chapter 2), and throughout his essay Johnson continues to draw examples of this kind of metaphor from the biography of Phips. Johnson's argument is convincing, though it misses one reflec-

---

[16] Parker H. Johnson, "Humiliation Followed by Deliverance: Metaphor and Plot in Cotton Mather's Magnalia," *Early American Literature* 15 (1980 / 81), p. 237.

tion: metaphors of distillation and reconstitution abound throughout the *Magnalia Christi Americana;* why does he find particular satisfaction in explicating such metaphors chosen primarily from the biography of Phips? Usually, when Mather finds a material or historical analogy for conversion or for reconstitution, he presents it, and thoroughly explicates it, often to tedium, leaving little doubt as to the tenor of the figure. But in the biography of Phips the connections are sometimes not made explicit. When Phips finds the Spanish treasure, for example, Mather writes:

> Thus did there once again come into the Light of the Sun, a Treasure which had been half an Hundred Years *groaning under the Waters:* And in this time there was grown upon the Plate a Crust like *Limestone,* to the thickness of several Inches; which Crust being broken open by Irons contrived for that purpose, they knockt out whole Bushels of rusty Pieces of Eight which were grown thereinto. (*MCA,* I:172)

This passage reminds the reader of the buried gold of Hindustan (see Chapter 1) as well as of the plant reconstituted from its salts. Mather's seasoned readers expect the improvement: the light of the sun, the waters, the crust, the irons, and the gold all signify: they might signify the recovery of the lost soul, the European or English Reformation, the recovery of New England's past in the *Magnalia Christi Americana,* or all of these. But the improvement does not come: Mather proceeds to itemize the treasure, and then resumes the narrative. Hagiographic expectations are aroused and disappointed. Hagiography remains in the background, so that Mather's admiration for Phips's individual excellence does not collapse into filiopietistic approval for Phips's convergence with a sempiternal type.

As Johnson argues, many of the events narrated in the biography of Phips fit the pattern of decimation and reconstitution, but Mather seems to decline outright explication: it remains for Johnson or the reader to supply the significance, and Johnson does so quite well. What he misses, however, is this: it is not significant that these episodes show the pattern of decimation and reconstitution, because this pattern is common to all Mather's writing; the uniqueness of the narration in these episodes lies in Mather's not having lifted narrative into typological significance. As readers whose taste has been affected by Emerson and Thoreau, we may find the pleasing suggestiveness of symbol rather than the mechanical specificity of allegory, but that is not to the point. Rather, we should notice that the allegorical, hagiographical, and typological devices that usually dissolve the immediacy of experience into the eternity of pattern and archetype are here kept in abeyance, so that the biography may be a realistic narrative where events retain an aura of actual phenomenality rather than being absorbed into eternal patterns. Mather's extraordinary interest in the biography of Phips leads him to abjure explicit analogical or typological improvement and commentary, which nonetheless remain in the background. Though realism and analogy are potentially incompatible modes, the life of Phips shows the Puritan figural imagination at work even when it has been dismissed as an outright worldview, as a kind of ghost in the narrative background. This double epistemology also occurs in several of Franklin's writings.

The epistemological humility that Mather attributes to Phips, therefore, licenses a kind of narrative that comes closer to Defoe's or Franklin's writing than anything else in Mather's *oeuvre*. The biography of Phips may explain why the conversion experience was gaining popularity in fictional forms during the same period that it was waning as an actual requirement for church admission in America: the Puritan elements that George A. Starr finds in the early novel might be seen less as a theologization of experience than as a secularization of theology, a fictional play with formal strictures that had previously bound religious practice.[17] The loose suppleness of Defoe's use of the conversion narrative might be the sort of creative appropriation and adaptation of intellectual inheritance that Mather usually felt that inheritance prohibited.

The secular realism of Mather's narration in the biography, in fact, advances to a point where Mather includes adventure narrative in which Phips plays no part, except insofar as his pronounced suspicion of imposed pattern licenses such realism. At one point in the biography, a brigantine carrying sixty men back from the Canadian defeat is wrecked on the "desolate and hideous Island of *Antecosta*." Their subsequent travails – including the threat of starvation, furious strife, regression to "*Pamphagous Fury*," and harrowing escape – do imply, as Johnson contends, the narrative of decimation and reconstitution. The Antecostan episode suggests a vivid emblem of the state of sin. But, again, Mather does not make this explicit, so the narrative acquires realism. The narrative in the biography of Phips shows a liberal application of Mather's usual techniques, or even their virtual absence, and this liberal application is legitimated in Phips's own warnings against the strict application of pattern.

If the biography of Phips indulges the wandering from the *pattern* of hagiographical demonstration that was circumscribed and controlled in the biography of Winthrop, Jr., it also indulges an indifference to the *paternal* that was correspondingly controlled in its predecessor. As the biography of Phips is not patterned by the conversion narrative that testifies to divine election, so the course of Phips's outward life is not charted

---

[17] George A. Starr, *Defoe and Spiritual Autobiography* (Princeton, N.J.: Princeton University Press, 1965).

and supervised by his father. Whereas the modernity of Winthrop, Jr., and Cotton Mather was constantly reduced to being an inoculative revival of the father, Phips was never subjected to such imposed prescription and, surprisingly, Mather approves: "Reader, enquire no further who was his *Father?* Though shalt anon see, that he was, as the *Italians* express it, a *Son to his own Labours!*" (*MCA,* I:167). Whereas others may have found their lives directed by an urgent sense of filiopiety, Phips is self-fathered, produced by "an Unaccountable *Impulse* upon his Mind . . . *That he was born to greater Matters*" than his paternal legacy would suggest. I find this to be the most startling moment in Mather's writing: if the remark on Winthrop, Jr., the son of Scipio Africanus, and the father's signet ring is a transparently autobiographical expression of the filiopiety that dominated Cotton Mather's self-conception, the remark about Phips being a son to his own labors, and the promise that this is what the biography will set out to demonstrate ("Thou shalt anon see . . ."), is an abruptly clear declaration of the desire he usually spent enormous energy concealing or disguising from himself. This remark slips past the purview of the dynastic imperative that shapes the entirety of his thought, and articulates an apostasy that Milton put in Satan's mouth: "self-begot, self-rais'd / By our own quick'ning power . . ." With Milton's Satan, Mather's Phips enjoys a denial of filiopious secondariness – of being shaped by paternity.

Like Benjamin Franklin after him, Phips is self-fathering, if self-fathering be taken to mean that he is antithetical to filiopiety, self-designing rather than acquiescent in the design given to him by dynastic predecessors. Sacvan Bercovitch explores this similarity between the biography of Phips and Franklin's *Autobiography:*

> The most prominent of Mather's success stories is also the longest biography he wrote, the "life of His Excellency Sir William Phips, Knt." Patriot, "inventor," and "enterprising genius," Phips' career – a model of *"one raised by God"* – unmistakeably prefigures Franklin's *Autobiography.* Born into a destitute family in a far border settlement, he becomes "a son to his own labors," the now-familiar poor provincial boy who makes good in the Big City. He leaves at the age of eighteen for Boston, the "place of the most business in those parts of the world, [because] he expected there more commodiously to pursue the *Spes Majorum et Meliorum* [aspirations toward greater and better things] – hopes which had inspired him." And the fulfillment of those hopes, his progress from apprentice ship-carpenter to bourgeois proprietor to governor of the colony, is marked, step by step, by the Franklinesque "virtues": "chastity," "prudence" and "resolution," "indefatigable patience, with proportionate *diligence,*" "*honesty* with *industry,*" and always, of course, humility and piety. Toward the end of the biography, Mather has his hero sum up the lessons of his life in an appeal which

traces his development from "meanness to greatness." As he sails one day in sight of Kennebeack, his birthplace, he summons his subordinates on deck and declares: "'Young men, it was upon that hill that I kept sheep a few years ago; and since you see that God has brought me to something, do you learn to fear God, and be honest, and mind your business, and you don't know what you may come to.'" About a hundred years later Benjamin Franklin's son received well-nigh identical "Inducements" to emulate his illustrious father who had, like Phips, "emerg'd from . . . Poverty and Obscurity" and "with the blessing of God, so well succeeded."[18]

As Bercovitch implies, the salient similarities between Phips and Franklin lie in their common revision of Puritan virtue – their independence from an inherited life, their definition of objectively apprehensible successes as sufficient evidence of virtue, and their conscious cultivation of virtues tooled to success in the actual world rather than virtues that would wrench them out of innovation in order to render them attentive to ancient inherited models. As Franklin rejects the various plans his father and brother have for him, so Phips, in transcending his humble beginnings on Maine's coast, resists any life written for him, be it paternal, astrological, or hagiographical.

In fact, Mather writes, there is no Old World typological predecessor for Phips – he is a historical novelty. Among New World heroes, Mather chooses Pizarro, a surprising choice, first, since Pizarro was the product of a Roman Catholic civilization and, second, since Pizarro was a "*Spurious Offspring,* exposed when a *Babe* in a Church-Porch . . ." (*MCA,* I:166) – a bastard. Phips's debt to Protestant dynastic origin, Mather is telling us, is so negligible that he may as well have been a bastard, an identity completely barred from definition by its origin, a loose self compelled to be self-designing if it is to be at all. If the reader will remember Mather's horror at the "harlot big with bastard" who "laid her belly" to his son Creasy, he will again observe, in this praise of Pizarro, the relief from normal discipline that Mather enjoys in his biography of Phips. Phips's metaphorical bastardy detaches him from the prescripts of identity that guide the rest of Mather's thought, leaving him free, like Franklin, to devise his own "Plan for a Life," and to make it work. Early on, Phips envisions knighthood and a "Fair *Brick-House* in the *Green-Lane* of North-Boston," and he gets them, foreshadowing Franklin's eventual access to the houses he sees and to the woman who stares down at him when he first enters Philadelphia in obvious poverty. And, free to choose an end, Phips is also free to choose the "right scene" in which to advance

[18] Sacvan Bercovitch, "'Delightful Examples of Surprising Prosperity': Cotton Mather and the American Success Story," *English Studies* 56 (1970), pp. 41–2.

COTTON MATHER'S RENAISSANCE   165

himself, thereby "improv(ing) opportunity to a vast advantage." Mather's biography of Phips is strikingly similar to Part One of the *Autobiography* in its unashamed celebration of the life loosed from inheritance and freed for self-design. The shape of Phips's life and the activity of shaping it do not lie outside the domain of Phips's intelligent imagination in the will of a predecessor, as they did for Cotton Mather and for Mather's Winthrop, Jr. The biography of Phips is a vicarious wish-fulfilling in which a usually disguised desire that hovers in a great deal of Mather's writing claims its legitimacy and its *voice*, coming, as it were, from beneath the subjugation of the stammer. Furthermore, the biography of Phips reveals that, if Franklin's carefully designed character is antithetical to Mather's, if they seem to us like completely different men, this antithesis is already present within Mather's self-conception. We perceive Cotton Mather most clearly when we see him not as a simple opposite to Franklinism but as a lifelong internal struggle to resist the appeal of Franklinism; and we perceive Benjamin Franklin most clearly when we see him not as a rejection of Matherism, but as a disarming neutralization of filiopiety that allows ingenious representative personality to reach its legitimacy and its voice. Mather's horror of the new, Franklin's example informs us, is not a product of the nature of the new, but of an over-literal fidelity to strict definitions of what is sane and permissible that do not allow creative modification.

Mather's biography of Phips is thus among the first American celebrations of the self-made or "rising man," and this label is banal only because frequent unreflective use of it has worn away our sense of the complexity and anxiety it involves. Self-making is self-fathering if we think of paternity, as Cotton Mather did, as an inclusive term for the authority that confers *secondariness,* that is, which restricts the individual's modernity to patterns of self-conception that were developed without his creative participation. Remember that Mather argued that the shape of the flower is contained in the seed, and that this is an allegory for human identity: though he conceded the plant some plasticity, he still asserted that the plant's whole virtue lay in its dutiful execution of a pattern that was entirely extant before the individual plant's inception; and his use of the generations of the plants as a field allegory for human dynasty reveals his arduous conviction that the pattern of a son's life is *fathered* into him with as much authority as his physical shape. The temporal priority of the father is identical with his authoritarian priority, as we see when John Winthrop associates his having sired Winthrop, Jr., with God's "Fatherly Blessing": the son enters a reified, complete world whose structure his birth does not affect, to which he must suit himself; to the history of this world, his life is a footnote, and his whole energy is devoted to maintenance. In this context, the son's originality would be at best nonexistent, at worst an apostate ingratitude that scratched away at the foundations of the holy.

When piety turns to its heirs and demands filiopiety, the heir must respond with self-effacement in both theory and practice, acknowledging that his birth represented no promised transformation of the holy or rectification of any flaw in the human order of things. He is barred from essential participation in the formation of life – including the shape of his own life – and instead he is a kind of footnote to history's crises. Any desire he might have to transform creatively the human order and the identity that that order confers on him could only be apostatic and aberrational. No wonder, then, that Cotton Mather spent so much time and intelligence demonstrating that inherited order was subject to degeneration and that it consequently required his earnest, if nontransformative, assistance, or contending that small injections of the unprecedented could actually invigorate the old rather than poisoning it, so long as the dose was supervised.

But the biography of Phips, in its expression of the desire for self-fathering, reveals Mather's discomfort with these strategies, both of which acquiesce in the filiopious dictum that the transformative self is at best nonexistent and at worst a world-wrecker. Self-fathering would separate the father's automatic temporal priority from the authoritarian priority that is propped upon it. In *Prodigals and Pilgrims: The American Revolution against Patriarchal Authority, 1750–1800*, Jay Fliegelman has demonstrated that the severance of the right to dominate the son's life from the fact of physical paternity is essential to the more characteristically American feeling that the human world is not complete but is instead barely begun: "Having left the British parent as a child, America miraculously becomes capable of its own nurturing: independence transforms the son into his own parent."[19] Mather's able leadership in the revolt against Andros indicates his participation in the spirit Fliegelman describes: but this participation is generally suppressed, emerging as the projected object of detestation – Satan, or forgetfulness – or, conditionally, in his use of the idea of inoculation. There is only one truly direct and explicit renaissance for self-fathering, the biography of Phips, where the father is a bare and negligible outline and the son makes himself in a world perceived less as a complete order than as a fresh and unsettled field of opportunity.

Franklin's *Autobiography*, with its outstanding resemblances to the biography of Phips, becomes the most open and persuasive development

---

[19] Jay Fliegelman, *Prodigals and Pilgrims: The American Revolution against Patriarchal Authority, 1750–1800* (Cambridge: Cambridge University Press, 1982), p. 224.

of the affirmative theme of self-fathering in American literature in the
years to come. One of the suppressed desires that is branded apostate and
diabolical in the majority of Mather's writing emerges in the *Autobiography* as a sane and useful plan for living, without any connotation of
Satanism or degenerative amnesia. But if Mather's celebration of Phips's
self-fathering is his most open anticipation of what would become the
common American self-conception, it is nevertheless an extremely rare
moment, an open wish for independence, which all of his acumen and
energy were spent concealing under or fitting to filiopiety.

In his *Puritan Origins of the American Self*, Sacvan Bercovitch argues
that the biography of Winthrop, Sr., is Mather's most striking insight
into topics that will later preoccupy Americans. Mather calls Winthrop
a "Nehemius Americanus," and Bercovitch concludes that, whereas traditional typology might make this connection to validate Winthrop pro-
spectively by likening him to Nehemiah, Mather is in fact retrospectively
validating Nehemiah by indicating his *prolepsis* of Winthrop's achievement. By making the glory of the American Christians into history's
telos, according to Bercovitch, Mather detaches authoritarian priority from
temporal priority, and even reverses them: the temporally prior figure is
an approximative prefiguration who is legitimated by the arrival of the
more magnificent figure he had foreshadowed. Bercovitch calls this a
"wholesale inversion of traditional hermeneutics," and he acknowledges
the affinity of his idea with what Harold Bloom calls *apophrades*: the
obvious achievement and excellence of insight in the successor's work
makes the predecessor's work seem like a faulty and imperfect adumbra-
tion.[20] Winthrop's excellence as governor and city-builder makes him the
father, in a sense, or pattern-setter, of his historical predecessor, Nehemiah, who is now seen as a kind of overture to a later achievement. As
Bercovitch points out, this interpretation is a familiar Christian hermeneutic based on the explication of the meaning of Christ: Christ, the
Logos, is the parent or original of the Old Testament luminaries that
precede him. The radicalism of Mather's biography of Winthrop, according to Bercovitch, lies in its relocation of the Christic transumption from
Jesus to America:

> As the eschatological focus thus shifted from memory to anticipation,
> the correspondence between the believer and the Bible narrative took
> on a radically historical significance. The *process* now, not the fact of
> fulfillment demanded elucidation. The source of personal identity was
> not the Jesus of the gospels but the ongoing works of Christ leading

[20] Harold Bloom, *The Anxiety of Influence* (New York: Oxford University Press,
1973), pp. 139–55; Sacvan Bercovitch, *The Puritan Origins of the American Self*
(New Haven, Conn.: Yale University Press, 1975), pp. 163–4.

towards the Messiah of the apocalypse. For historically considered, Jesus too was a *typus Christi*, a scriptural figure signifying greater things to come.[21]

But this attempt to escape the sense of supernumerary belatedness seems not to have satisfied Cotton Mather. The originality that it permits Winthrop and his fellow Americans was an originality of degree, not of kind. The impulse to a superior excellence spoke to Mather in the name of his father and of his son – Increase – and in his remark that sons contribute to their fathers' glory by outdoing them. Winthrop's historical importance derives from a vigorous holiness that, coupled with a continent opened by God as a setting for history's last act, will honor great predecessors by carrying their work to its most glorious conclusion. However, though this claim to splendor may go contrary to the assertion that the pattern of historical prefiguration was transumed in the person of Jesus Christ, it does not release the moderns from their obligation to observe ancient forms of personal piety. In fact, it requires the modern who wishes to surpass predecessors to submit to the hagiographic pattern still more completely than they did. An insistence on the son's historical period as a particularly crucial historical episode will magnify the sense of independence as aberration, and convince him he must find a way to do still better the work of predecessors. Though this insistence might ameliorate the anxious feeling that one was no more than an appendage to a sufficient tradition, the resulting egotism would nevertheless be that much more uneasy because the conditions for enjoying it would be the egotist's meticulous introjection of specific inherited patterns of piety and his unflagging extirpation of the desire for free and creative participation in the design of an open world. The egotism of the magnificent modern heir is anxiously poised above his sense that he must not only replicate the father but replicate still more strenuously. To be obliged to achieve a greater excellence at the same task is a deeper bondage to the past, not a liberation from it.

The novelty that Bercovitch describes in the biography of Winthrop is a novelty of degree, not of kind, a subservience to predecessors who demand that the scion repeat with even greater success. Whether Winthrop outdoes Nehemiah for perfection, or Nehemiah Winthrop, Winthrop is not self-fathering, since the essential contour of his life and his interest is not of his own choice or design. If we take the biography of Winthrop and place it in its context in the second book of the *Magnalia Christi Americana,* we observe that the most acute tension is not between Winthrop and Nehemiah, but between Winthrop on the one hand and Winthrop, Jr., and Phips on the other. The contest for excellence in degree

[21] Bercovitch, *The Puritan Origins of the American Self,* p. 60.

between Puritan moderns and Old Testament predecessors is, in the book as a whole, subordinate to the contest for qualitative originality between Winthrop, who fits the hagiographic pattern so well that he may even surpass Nehemiah, and Winthrop, Jr., and Phips, who seek to design their own patterns for living, as Franklin will. The more important tension is not between the ancient and the modern type, but between being a type (transumptive or not) and self-fathering. Though the assertion that Winthrop outdoes Nehemiah may violate the Augustinian dictum that sacred history concludes in the person of Jesus Christ, the assertion that self-fathering is a valid style of life would violate ingrained prejudices that were much more primordial to Cotton Mather's emotional self-conception than specific tenets of hagio-historiography.

In surveying the fate of the idea of self-design in the American Puritan experiment we should also indicate the difference between Winthrop's and Cotton Mather's positions. Mather, unlike Winthrop, received the legacy of holiness in a specifically dynastic form, whereas Winthrop was only metaphorically a son to his models. Though Winthrop may have proven to be different only in degree from distant typological fathers such as Nehemiah, he was different in kind from Adam Winthrop, the prosperous, not especially fervent, lord of Groton Manor. Like Phips and Franklin, Winthrop did not accept the world made for him by the circumstances of his birth: he designed his own life, or fathered himself, in accord with the wishes of a god alien to the life into which he was born, as did John Cotton, Richard Mather, and the other prominent members of the first generation of Massachusetts piety. Though the secular brilliance of Renaissance self-fashioning was part of the world these men repudiated, such repudiation was for them a kind of self-fashioning, albeit in ostensible conformity with historically distant Christian models.

But if the repudiation of self-fathering is a kind of self-fathering for the members of a first generation, it is not for their heirs, whose inherited task is to adhere, not to the brilliant and courageous self-designing spirit of their predecessors, but to the letter of their predecessors' impassioned repudiation of creative and independent modernity. Increase Mather seems to have circumvented this version of the "Puritan Dilemma" by emigrating to England in 1656, planning to settle, only to refuse a sinecure that would have required a compromise of piety in the years after the Restoration. He returned to Boston and rectitude in the early 1660s to assume the pulpit of the Second Church, to father Cotton Mather, to deplore the extravagances of the rising generation, and, in the late 1680s, to return to England to play the devout and self-possessed Puritan ambassador amid the spectacle of the court in the period after the Glorious Revolution. Increase Mather's two sojourns in England, then, allowed him to recapitulate in miniature his father's designing of self out of a loathing for an impure world. But for Cotton Mather there was to be no such difference between the constitutive laws of true piety and the regulative laws of social origin; to be different in kind from the inherited world was to deny rather than to excel in the legacy of holiness.

Surpassing the father, like defending, reviving, or inoculating him, may justify the son's presence on the historical stage, making him more than an extra, lending his part urgency. But he is still playing his father's part, still laboring for a return to the same, not self-fathering, not achieving some qualitative difference from the already achieved. Though the scion may surpass his predecessor, and thereby clasp pattern to himself more successfully than ever before, the predecessor's insuperable temporal priority is still authoritarian; though the predecessor is surpassed, the context for the surpassing is still, and always will be, the predecessor's choice. Phips, a self-fatherer, however, is uniquely himself, a contention Mather seems to advance when he provides a portrait of Phips's physique, a visualization of the particular man that is rare in the biographies:

> Know then, that for his *Exterior*, he was one *Tall*, beyond the common Set of Men, and *Thick* as well as *Tall*, and *Strong* as well as *Thick*: He was, in all respects, exceedingly *Robust*, and able to Conquer such difficulties of *Diet* and *Travel*, as would have kill'd most Men alive: Nor did the *Fat*, whereinto he grew very much in his later Years, take away the Vigour of his Motions. (*MCA*, I:217)

Phips's gross bulk, a near-spurious offspring, like the organic monstrosities spun in the womb of Antinomianism, resists reduction to epitome, to a physical rectitude that could provide the model for a moral propriety; but, unlike Hutchinson's products, Phips's bulk is no source of horror. There is just too much admirable, natural man to convert into type, and Mather's centrifugal admiration of Phips's self-designed life pulls his biography of Phips away from its orbit around the hagiographical model of piety. Mather's remark that Phips was a son to his own labors and his implication that Phips was a bastard loose from traditional determinations speak volumes: they are admissions of the desire that he began suppressing when he "cured" his stutter, and that he dedicated himself to subduing, in himself and (in projected versions) in the world, at massive personal cost, until he died, in February 1728. This was one year and some few months after the twenty-six-year-old Benjamin Franklin had returned to Philadelphia from England to begin the life he had designed for himself during the voyage back, and it was exactly one year after Franklin had suffered from a near-mortal pleurisy. It was also four and a half years after Increase Mather died in his faithful son's arms.

6

BENJAMIN FRANKLIN'S NATURE

> The People have a saying, that God almighty is himself a Mechanic, the greatest in the Univers; and he is respected and admired more for the Variety, Ingenuity, and Utility of his Handyworks, than for the Antiquity of his Family.
>
> Benjamin Franklin, *Information for Removal to America*

Like Cotton Mather, Benjamin Franklin did not simply accept or seek a prominent public role as circumstances allowed. He also theorized concerning the psychological and social context that permitted prominence to occur, and he designed himself accordingly. In his writings as well as in his dealings with his contemporaries, his personal being is in the largest sense *rhetorical,* an evocation and cultivation of characteristics he felt were in accord with what the age demanded, and a discouragement or concealment of those he felt were not. As his lifelong reliance on clever personae suggests, he was aware of and able at the art of presenting a face. Observing the diversity of the surrounding social world, he postulated a common essence, a human nature: and he advertised himself as one in whom that nature was a pure presence without admixture, rather than as one in whom that nature was one element among many in an amalgam of passions. Consequently, Franklin's self-representation continually emphasizes his inclination to detachment from complete immersion in the circumstances at hand and his capacity for widely diverse interests, since these traits would testify to the pure presence of nature within him by demonstrating his freedom from the particularizing passions that blur or darken the efficacy of nature in others.

Like Cotton Mather, he aspires to representative personal universality. At early points in their lives, Mather and Franklin arrived at explicit conceptions of the nature of human nature, and, for the rest of their lives, they attempted to *be* that nature. There are important vicissitudes and mutations in Mather's and Franklin's careers, but these tend to be responses to others' failures to be true to the nature within them, rather than reconsiderations of their own acts of self-design. Confronting "declension," in Mather's case, or, in Franklin's, such manifest unreason as the fury of the Paxton boys, the group egotism of the English Parliament, or the sectarian squabbling at the Constitutional Convention, Mather and Franklin did on occasion doubt whether their examples would have the desired effect, and this doubt led to bitter or cynical statements on the obstinacy of man. It did not, however, lead to any profound reconsideration of the central project of self-design in either case. Their lives were dominated, from adolescence or earlier until death, by unwavering purpose. The consequent achievement is always astonishing, and frequently admirable: both men were widely learned and original thinkers, and their productivity was enormous; and their belief that they had devoted themselves to living in accord with human nature yielded political courage when they encountered forms of government and authority they felt were at odds with that nature. In both cases, the persistent central determination made them bold and acute critics of what they saw as unnatural. But in neither case was the project itself, or the conception of nature upon which it was based, subjected to criticism; nor was there any consistent sense that the right path can be obscure, to be discovered gradually, perhaps even at odds with the chosen path, and that thought and feeling should be accordingly ready and plastic. As men of achievement, Mather and Franklin merit acclaim; but as models for self-conception, they merit scrutiny.

In neither case is there a perfect match between the man each aimed to be and the man he was. In the previous chapters, I contended that at several points in Mather's writing we may detect a muted protest against piety that escapes from beneath its authority. Correspondingly, Franklin's personality as it emerges in his writings is larger and more diverse than the man he aimed to project. He is more vulgar, playful, sarcastic, courageous, petty, magnanimous, outrageous, libidinous, and resentful than his dedication to calculating moderation, or "serious cheerfulness" to use his term, would seem to allow. This is not surprising, since full personality is rarely identical with self-conception. The issue here, however, is not what Mather and Franklin were, but what they aimed to be, and the remarkable extent to which disciplined self-conception dominated other motivations.

Franklin differs from Mather in that, though at moments full personality escapes from the selfhood he wished to project, few of these moments can be taken as protests against the self-imposed discipline. It is consequently tempting to call Franklin's self-design no discipline at all, but instead a mild and humorous equanimity in sharp contrast to Mather's incessant anxiousness, and to leave it at that. But, since Franklin repeatedly contends that it is useful to seem relaxed and agreeable, we should not rest with the thought that he simply was. To accept the contrast between Mather's anxiousness and Franklin's harmony is to take Franklin at his word, an unwise choice with one so attentive to and accomplished at the art of useful semblance. We should suspect what seems to be a patent and sufficient personality type so that we may inquire into how the trait of emotional harmoniousness would be a useful element in a coherent rhetorical enterprise – especially since Franklin was concerned to contrast himself with what Mather epitomized.

Franklin's projected face has proved so successfully appealing that criticism has in the main substituted emotional acceptance for analysis: this acceptance has confined criticism to itemizing Franklin's achievements and opinions, as if the enclosing personal context needed no examining, and it has resulted in regular and near-ritual derision of dissenters such as D. H. Lawrence and Max Weber. I will cite several exceptions in the coming pages, but Franklin criticism has in general failed to achieve the level of intellectual reappraisal to be found in recent works on Mather: Franklin is still treated largely as a benign and open sensibility rather than as a coherent and deliberate rhetorical project. I do not mean that we should begin to think of him as villain or as dissembler rather than as our friend (though I will assume that the chronicling of his achievements is an accomplished task). I do propose that, in contrasting Mather and Franklin, we should begin with the assumption that their different conceptions of the nature of human nature resulted in different techniques of rhetorical self-projection, rather than with the assumption that they are outstanding specimens of completely disjoint modes of human sensibility.

This concentration on their notions of nature would locate the difference between them in the major philosophical contest of their period. According to Arthur O. Lovejoy, *nature* is at once the "most sacred and the most protean" word in the vocabulary of the seventeenth and eighteenth centuries. Lovejoy's implicit thesis is that there is a competition for possession of the word during this period, and that it would be naive to assume agreement between two thinkers who make use of it:

> For "nature" has, of course, been the chief and most pregnant word in the terminology of all the normative provinces of thought in the West; and the multiplicity of its meanings has made it easy, and common, to slip more or less insensibly from one connotation to another, and thus in the end to pass from one ethical or aesthetic standard to its very antithesis, while nominally professing the same principles.[1]

[1] Arthur O. Lovejoy, "'Nature' as Aesthetic Norm," in *Essays in the History of Ideas* (Baltimore: Johns Hopkins University Press, 1948), pp. 69–77, quotation from p. 69.

The use of the word *nature,* with its connotations of essence and its power to discredit alternatives, is a device for self-legitimation. Its common use by diverse thinkers, therefore, is potentially confusing; but, on the other hand, uncovering the different meanings beneath two thinkers' common use of the term can bring us to the heart of the difference between them, since they use it to sanction their most cherished notions of propriety.

For Mather, nature was a transcendental order in the midst of which the self or *I* was an area of darkness and decline; through ruthless self-annihilation, consciousness could struggle free to an assent as perfect as the automatic conformity that abounds among the other creatures, or more perfect, for the victory. Unlike Winthrop, Mather did not consider self a natural liberty: it was not a corrupt nature, but a corruption of nature. Self-annihilation brought a man into accord with his nature, as Mather contended in *Reasonable Religion:* "Either become a sincere Servant of the Lord Jesus Christ, or else pretend not unto the Name of MAN."[2] Consequently, the relation of nature to the interests, habits, and enjoyments of the self was a relation of devastation, of tense contradiction, the more continuous the better. If nature did not interrupt and interrogate the self, self was refusing divinity; and if the explosion of its pretensions in the activity of wanting and working seemed to self to be unjust, this reaction only measured self's epistemological and moral turpitude.

Though Franklin will make use of many of Mather's sacred words, such as God, Christianity, virtue, and so on, he will not accept the doctrine of correct nature as an intrusion into the self's automatic course. Since Franklin frequently contended that it is useful to seem to believe in God when one is living among others who do believe, it is impossible to judge the sincerity of his professions of belief. Whether they are sincere or not, however, his professions all affirm a divinity that approves of the self that holds to its own standards of orderliness, consistency, and innocence:

> I believe he is pleas'd and delights in the Happiness of those he has created . . . And since he has created many Things, which seem purely Design'd for the Delight of Man, I believe he is not offended, when he sees his Children solace themselves in any manner of pleasant exercises and Innocent Delights; and I think no Pleasure innocent, that is to Man hurtful. (*P,* 1:103)

This affirmation is a discipline, rather than a ticket to license, but it is a discipline that resides within self and its understanding. Once self has assured itself that it is not injuring another, it may proceed: the activity of evaluation and the standards of evaluation are native to the self, and God is a kind of ancillary onlooker.

[2] Cotton Mather, *Reasonable Religion* (Boston, 1700), p. 4.

This morality is equivalent to the first and third steps of the meditation in Mather's *Christian Philosopher:* nature is available for human consumption and comprehension, both of which are legitimate activities. However, Franklin does not go on to accept Mather's insistence on the negation of these faculties by a transcendental paternal authority. To reply to the Puritan conception of the negation of the self by higher law, Franklin turns the question to the social function, rather than the truth, of religion. In individuals or societies where the reasonable orderliness of self has only a slight purchase on inclination, religion is a useful assertion, since its harsh threat proves more cogent to those furious passions that will not respond to the kinder blandishments of reasonableness. It opposes their obstinacy with the obstinacy of an imperative, rather than with the subtleties of persuasion. Where the rational self is not developed, morality by absolute fiat must hold the place of reason until reason reaches its majority.

In his two famous speeches to the Constitutional Convention, Franklin recommended that the delegates reach accord by praying and by observing the principles of the general rational interest. The first recommendation may be seen as a cynical version of the second, as a product of Franklin's having concluded that the bickering delegates were so far from being a consensus of rational selves that only a sense of transcendental obligation could unite them. In 1786, one year before his speech on prayer to the convention, Franklin wrote to an unnamed correspondent (perhaps Thomas Paine) concerning a manuscript in which the idea of a particular Providence was criticized. Franklin replies by contending that, though the manuscript may be correct, it would injure the useful role played among the unreasonable by religion:

> You yourself may find it easy to live a virtuous Life, without the Assistance afforded by Religion; you having a clear Perception of the Advantages of Virtue, and the Disadvantages of Vice, and possessing a Strength of Resolution sufficient to enable you to resist Common Temptations. But think how great a Proportion of Mankind consists of weak and ignorant Men and Women and of inexperienc'd, and inconsiderate Youth of both Sexes, who have need of the Motives of Religion to restrain them from Vice, to support their Virtue, and retain them in the Practice of it till it becomes *habitual,* which is the great Point for its Security. (*W,* X:282)

According to Franklin, the sequence of attitudes in *The Christian Philosopher* is reversed: the religion of harsh and absolute negation is necessary for the society or the individual in which the rational faculty is still weak, but it should make way for a government that lies within the self when that government is ready to take its rightful place.

Should it refuse to make way, it can retard the maturation of reason by seeking to restrain development, thereby degenerating from protector to despot. In *The Levee,* for example, Franklin's gloss on the book of Job, he notes that Job led a blameless life in accord with standards of decency, and he concludes that Job's sufferings are tokens of an unjust sovereign whose ear is too easily bent by unctuous courtiers such as Satan:

> What then is the instruction to be gathered from this supposed trans-action?
>
> Trust not a single person with the government of your state. For if the Deity himself, being the monarch, may for a time give way to cal-umny, and suffer it to operate the destruction of the best of subjects; what mischief may you not expect from such power in a mere man, though the best of men, from whom the truth is often industriously hidden, and to whom falsehood is often presented in its place, by artful, interested and malicious courtiers?
>
> And be cautious in trusting him even with limited powers, lest sooner or later he sap and destroy those limits, and render himself absolute. (*W,* II:165–6)

Such satire of divinity would have been unthinkable for Mather, who asserted that divinity must seem arbitrary and capricious to the self's norms because self is so distant from the divine nature. By shifting from the truth of religion to the social function of religion, Franklin is able to contend that Mather's attitude is an attempt to retain an obsolete author-ity. Men should have government within themselves, rather than over them, and they should recognize that rectitude is distinct from even the most eminent figures of authority.

In a society of rational selves, transcendental religion seemed to Frank-lin to be an able sophism meant to maintain and exploit the credulous-ness of those who could be made to succumb. In "To the Editor of a Newsletter," written in 1765, Franklin pretends to decry suspicion and offers instead the modest proposal of a greater credulousness:

> And yet all this is as certainly true, as the Account said to be from Quebec, in all the Papers of last Week, that the Inhabitants of Canada are making Preparations for a Cod and Whale Fishery this "Summer in the upper Lakes." Ignorant People may object that the upper Lakes are fresh, and that Cod and Whale are Salt Water Fish: But let them know, Sir, that Cod, like any other Fish when attack'd by their Enemies, fly into any Water where they can be safest; that Whales, when they have a mind to eat Cod, pursue them wherever they fly; and that the grand Leap of the Whale in that Chase up the Fall of Niagara is esteemed, by all who have seen it, as one of the finest Spectacles in Nature. Really, Sir, the World is grown too incredulous. It is like the Pendulum ever swinging from one Extream to another. Formerly every thing printed was believed. Now Things seem to be disbelieved for just the very same Reason. Wise Men wonder at the present Growth of Infidelity. They should have consider'd, when they taught People to doubt the Author-

ity of Newspapers and the Truth of Predictions in Almanacks, that the next Step might be a Disbelief in the well vouch'd Accts of Ghosts Witches, and Doubts even of the Truths of the Creed! (*P,* 12:132–5)

Poor Richard had already testified to the rigor of almanac-predicting:

The Stargazer . . . spies perhaps VIRGO (or the Virgin); she turns her Head round as it were to see if any body observ'd her; then crouching down gently, with her Hands on her Knees, she looks wistfully for a while right forward. He judges rightly what she's about: And having calculated the Distance and allow'd Time for its Falling, finds that the next Spring we shall have a fine *April* shower. What can be more natural and easy than this? (*P,* 2:217–8)

If you'll believe this, Franklin implies, you'll believe anything, even a divinity hostile to the faculties he puts into you; if you believe this, you're ready prey for the vultures of piety. The tonic is government that resides within self, or, more properly, self as functional, developed government. The authority that for Mather resides across a chasm from self for Franklin crosses the chasm and reappears as self.

Self is human nature, rather than an enemy to nature. Nature is the order of causes among physical things, and human nature is the activity of discerning those causes, without appeal to holy allegory or invisible agency, in the interest of shaping to human use – to minimizing pain of all kinds. Like Tillotson, Franklin believed that severe Protestantism increased psychic pain, and that the emphasis on prodigious monitions and arbitrary divine sovereignty led to a distended theology, one meant to lure men away from the judgment God had given them, at which point they could be gulled. Franklin's god does not assault the self during its activity of devising and executing useful works.

Consequently, there is no need to be anxious over the transcendental and omniscient scrutiny of secret intentions. In America, "people do not inquire concerning a Stranger, *What is he?* but, *What can he do?*" (*W,* II:469). As lightning and the whirlwind can be explained without thaumatographical premises, so too the self can be apprehended sufficiently from what it causes – works – without any spelunking exploration for recessed fidelity. Theological searching for the secret quality of the man is a kind of exactitude that only interferes with what needs to be done. Rather than the divine eye searching out the secret man behind the fair-seeming works, only the public eye testifies that the works have reduced pain in either its physical or social varieties. The displacement from the eye of God to the eye of the community was already at work in Mather's thought, but for Mather public acclaim was an inferior surrogate for divine reassurance. It always fell short: at the height of reputation, the thought of the more perspicacious divine insight could demolish accumulating satisfaction. For Franklin, however, the thought of the omniscient eye was a manufactured construct useful, perhaps, for those who lacked rational interior government, but obstructive for those who have it. The question of the secret man behind the work in accord with or violation of an evergreen body of absolute principle is waived in favor of a capacious versatility not tied to particular ends. The acclaim of the human community *as a whole,* in its present moment, is sufficient reassurance, the only reassurance: but Franklin's entitlement of acclaim is not a situational morality, since it must come from the whole community if it is to be an expression of abstract human nature rather than of some special interest whose cause has been served by Franklin's work.

Though Franklin recognized that men did dissemble, for good and bad reasons, he rejected the Puritan metaphysical psychology of the man behind the mask, of the fidelity or turpitude behind the good-working self. The self is entirely extant in the body of its works as they are on view in the common public light, and the only thing that lies behind the works is the free and versatile ability to do them. Consequently, Franklin's writing is determinedly exterior in its avoidance of the question of the truth of the man. Neither the physical world nor the speaking self is a well with its secret at bottom, and, though Franklin's reader may chuckle, learn, admire, and approve, he will not experience the intrigue described by Georges Poulet:

> This feeling [books] give me – I sometimes have it with other objects. I have it, for example, with vases and statues. It would never occur to me to walk around a sewing machine or to look at the under side of a plate. I am quite satisfied with the face they present to me. But statues make me want to circle around them, vases make me want to turn them in my hands. I wonder why. Isn't it because they give me an illusion that there is something in them which, from a different angle, I might be able to see? Neither vase nor statue seems fully revealed by the unbroken perimeter of its surfaces. In addition to its surfaces it must have an interior. What this interior might be, that is what intrigues me and makes me circle around them, as though looking for an entrance to a secret chamber.[3]

But Franklin's writing is meant to strike us in the manner of the plate or the sewing machine, as an unbroken perimeter of surface suitable for immediate use. Franklin's unremitting stylistic lucidity is partly a product of his practiced acquaintance with English prose, but it is also a result of his resolute ideological avoidance of mystery – everything that counts, for Franklin, is in the open, at least for those readers whose reasonableness is sufficiently advanced. There is consequently much to annotate in

[3] Georges Poulet, "Criticism and the Experience of Interiority," in *The Languages of Criticism and the Sciences of Man,* eds. Richard Macksey and Eugenio Donato (Baltimore: Johns Hopkins University Press, 1970), pp. 56–7.

Franklin's writing, but relatively little to *explicate*. This is not to say that as a writer he was shallow or vacuous, at least in the modern pejorative senses of those words, but that if the reader desires the sort of intrigue Poulet describes (and Leopold Bloom manifests), he does not find it in Franklin. Franklin does not cooperate: insofar as the reader demands, expects, or desires the interiority that characterizes theological and romantic writing, Franklin replies with an obstinate blankness, though he might choose the words *neutrality* or *mediocrity*. This blankness is not so much a property of Franklin's texts as it is a product of the encounter between a reader's desire for interiority and Franklin's refusal to gratify the desire. For his part, Franklin would wish the reader to dispense with such desire in order to admire the work chronicled in the writing and the work of the writing, and to look for nothing behind the versatile capacity to do the work.

This determination is not primarily an aesthetic choice, nor is it a pure stylistic expression of an irreducible sensibility. Rather, it is an integral part of Franklin's revision of Cotton Mather's Puritanism. Franklin received the concept of psychological interiority in the form of Puritan examination and introspection, and he correctly perceived that Puritan introspection amounted to an incessant diversion of consciousness away from the secular occupations of the self. Consequently, his determination to legitimate secular life led him to class introspection (and the personal interior it presumes) with the whales that leap the falls and with such searches for occult pattern as astrology or demonology. Introspection was an abuse of nature, an undue interference in nature's smooth operation.

Franklin's definition of nature therefore entails a denial of the piety Mather called remembrance, and of the absolute authority of those predecessors to whom Mather's remembrance was faithful. For Mather, the external authority of such fathers was interiorized as a chastising voice always in harsh dialogue with the self; for Franklin, government is also an interior voice, but it is the self or *I*, rather than a counterweight to self. Once self has assumed the role of governing, the concept of a separate and opposed part of consciousness that has a "tendency of return" to ancient patterns becomes for Franklin an anachronism. He sees no need for a detached appraiser that governs self's innovativeness and that testifies to the father that it is an exact recovery of primitive piety. This reasoning in turn leads him to disregard the authority claims of those persons who would insist that there be such a government opposed to the self. The stylistic and psychological decision against the interiority of remembrance is also a social rebellion against the supposedly unchallengeable right of those persons whose authority had been interiorized as remembrance.

Like Mather (and, according to Jay Fliegelman, like eighteenth-century American thinkers in general),[4] Franklin viewed forms of authority as forms of paternity. In the *Autobigraphy*, for example, as Hugh J. Dawson contends, those who acquire authority over the young Franklin are properly viewed as father-surrogates,[5] though father-analogies might be a better term. Franklin makes the association of authority and paternity explicit in his *Proposals Relating to the Education of Youth in Pensilvania* (1749), where he urges the members of the corporation founding the academy and the teachers to view the students "as in some sort their Children." Franklin's adherence to Mather's connection of authority and paternity, however, underscores the difference. The trustee-parents do not intervene against the self of the student-son: rather, they are technical advisers, showing the self the most expeditious course to its own ends, and reducing the number of false starts (or errata). They correct mistakes (rather than profound wrongs) that the son would have corrected on his own, as Franklin did: they prevent the waste of time. They teach by incentive, showing the son the utility of learning, but they do not impose standards for what the learning is to be useful for: they incite him to recognize the relevance of learning to his own desires. They are resources or catalysts, but not authorities. The student judges the learning useful, rather than accepting the *fiat* of a paternal word that judges him: "When the Minds of Youth are struck with Admiration at this, then is the Time to give them the Principles of that Art, which they will study with Taste and Application" (*P*, 3:397–422). Natural paternity observes a standard, rather than claiming to be an unquestionable standard: it receives its legitimacy from its respect for the natural legitimacy of the son. Unlike the god of the book of Job, it does not presume to decry the son's self and to substitute the mandate of precise remembrance. Should it attempt to banish the son for a failure of fidelity, it will itself be banished from the clarity and correctness of nature; it will be exposed as arbitrary power acquired in the accident of circumstance, rather than as right power instilled by the clarity and force of nature.

Franklin thus participates in the widespread rethinking of filial relations that Fliegelman has described, a rethinking that, as Fliegelman contends, has analogical repercussions in all considerations of authority, rather than just in actual family relations. In his *Observations on the Increase of Mankind*, for example, Franklin argues that the good governor will, after the manner of Bolingbroke's Patriot King, observe the form of paternity outlined in the *Proposals Relating to the Education of Youth in Pensilvania* by

[4] Jay Fliegelman, *Prodigals and Pilgrims: The American Revolution against Patriarchal Authority, 1750–1800* (Cambridge: Cambridge University Press, 1982).
[5] Hugh J. Dawson, "Fathers and Sons: Franklin's *Memoirs* as Myth and Metaphor," *Early American Literature*, vol. 14, no. 3 (Winter 1979 / 80), pp. 269–92.

encouraging the natural development of his subjects' social and economic capacities:

> Hence the Prince that acquires new Territory, if he finds it vacant, or removes the Natives to give his own People Room; the Legislator that makes effectual laws for the promoting of Trade, increasing Employment, improving Land by more or better Tillage, providing more Food by Fisheries; securing Property, &c. and the Man that invents new Trades, Arts, or Manufactures, or new Improvements in Husbandry, may properly be called *Fathers* of their Nation, as they are the Cause of the Generation of Multitudes, by the Encouragement they afford to Marriage. (*P,* 4:231)

He deplores the form of paternity championed in "the old acts of Parliament restraining the trade or cramping the manufactures of the colonies" (*P,* 5:449) and in the rodomontade of the English people: "Every Man in England seems to consider himself as a Piece of a Sovereign over America; seems to jostle himself into the Throne with the King, and talks of OUR *subjects in the Colonies*" (P, 14:65). To contrast just government with such despotism, Franklin occasionally employs *maternal* images, to emphasize nurture and protection rather than constraint and regulation: "Therefore *Britain* should not too much restrain Manufactures in her Colonies. A wise and good Mother will not do it. To distress, is to weaken, and weakening the Children weakens the whole Family." (*P,* 4:229). To seek to define or design or constrain the future by shaping one's sons is to weaken the future, rather than to guard against error or abomination. Franklin's political struggles, whether with the Pennsylvania proprietors or the English Parliament, return repeatedly to the issue of proper natural paternity, showing his formal retention in general of the Puritan association of paternity with authority, but a reversal of many of Puritanism's assumptions about duty: the son-self is a proper nature to be advised and encouraged by the father, but the son's innate propriety entitles him to decide when the father has advanced from counseling into domination.

These issues are in the fore in a letter Franklin wrote to his actual parents in 1738. Fifteen years after having left his father's Boston, and one year after having been appointed the Philadelphia postmaster, the thirty-two-year-old son received a letter questioning the quality of his remembrance of the religion of the fathers. In reply, he writes to both parents, though the first draft of the letter was addressed only to his father: "Honour'd Father and Mother, I have your Favour of the 21st of March in which you both seem concern'd lest I have imbib'd some erroneous Opinions." He responds firmly, not by defending his opinions, but by disputing the importance of doctrinal exactitude:

> Doubtless I have my Share, and when the natural Weakness and Imperfection of Human Understanding is considered, with the unavoidable

Influences of Education, Custom, Books and Company, upon our Ways of thinking, I imagine a Man must have a good deal of Vanity who believes, and a good deal of Boldness who affirms, that all the Doctrines he holds, are true; and all he rejects, are false. And perhaps the same may be justly said of every Sect, Church and Society of men when they assume to themselves that Infallibility which they deny to the Popes and Councils.

Like Mather's Phips, Franklin evokes the doctrine of human fallibility to imply that those who act with certainty of divine support are guilty of pride. Franklin's assertion here is a restatement of his position in the Hemphill controversy, which may have occasioned the inquisitorial letter from his parents in the first place. He took the same stance in the *New England Courant* and in his *Articles of Belief and Religion,* suggesting, again, that the evocation of transcendent divinity proved useful to those who wished to divest Puritan norms of their absolute authority. If divinity is truly transcendent, the son will have to live without ontological justification, but the human father's authority is also diminished. The son, in fact, is closer to the right, because he admits the potential dubiousness of his opinions, and he does not claim god-sponsored authority to assert his over another's. Such undue assumption of godliness as a prop for domination is a theological aberration, and Franklin subtly implies that Josiah Franklin's Puritan assurance may have been one of the "unavoidable influences" that led the son into *wrong* opinions.

The important concern is not the man's interior state, as Josiah Franklin's religion insisted, but instead the general goodness of works: "I think Opinions should be judg'd of by their Influences and Effects; and if a Man holds none that tend to make him less Virtuous or more vicious, it may be concluded that he holds none that are dangerous; which I hope is the Case with me." Having denied the authority of sure moral standards, Franklin is here confronted with a problem: who is to judge the work for its dangerousness or productiveness? He avoids the question with passive constructions: "should be judg'd of," "it may be concluded that." He is substituting a general human consensus for the judging divinity embodied in the father, but the act of substitution is glossed over grammatically. Goodness will be founded on the community's acclaim rather than on the father's assent, but this assertion is foregone in the interest of another criticism of the father's claim to certainty. Franklin begins humbly, with the assertion that he is unfortunately stuck with opinions he cannot change at will, but moves on to assert that such humorous self-skepticism should lead to a general toleration, a toleration his parental accusers seem to lack:

I am sorry you should have any Uneasiness on my Account, and if it were a thing possible for one to alter his Opinions in order to please others, I know none whom I ought more willingly to oblige in that respect than your selves: But since it is no more in a Man's Power *to think* than *to look* like another, methinks all that should be expected from me is to keep my Mind open to Conviction, to hear patiently and examine attentively whatever is offered me for that end; and if after all I continue in the same Errors, I believe your usual Charity will induce you to pity and excuse than blame me.

In 1771, in the first part of the *Autobiography,* Franklin will contend that in England in 1729 he had given up deism because, though "it might be true, it was not very useful" (*A,*114), implying that nine years before he wrote this letter he had found that it was possible "to alter his opinions to please another," *to look as if he thinks like* another. But he does not do so in this letter, perhaps from respect, perhaps because he concluded it would not convince his parents, or perhaps because his willingness to consider his opinions as errors and the consequent open-mindedness are being offered to them as a model: he will not judge others with the self-certainty they have brought to bear on him, a self-certainty he has already linked with papal pride (*P,* 2:202–4). An incomplete draft for a letter to his father that Franklin wrote a month later reveals that his mother was satisfied with his reply to their doubts (*P,* 2:206).

Franklin's parents might have expected their son to extricate himself from exact filiopiety. In the *New England Courant,* he had shown himself to be an able satirist of Puritan remembrance and of Mather's rhetoric in particular. In the eighty-eighth issue he brilliantly mimed the rhetoric of declension, the lamentation of the present divergence from the example of the past:

> The Increase and Progress of Vice, Immorality and Prophaneness, together with a visible Decay of Godliness, in the Life and Power of it, among us, is a Matter of Grief and Sorrow to every serious Christian, whose Soul *trembles for the Art of God,* in this Day of Darkness and General Apostacy.
>
> Certainly, it must be acknowledg'd by every observing Christian, that Iniquity *does abound* among us, and the love of many to Religion, and the serious Professors of it waxeth exceedingly cold; that there is a universal Degeneracy and Declension from the good Ways of God, which our Fore-fathers walked in. They, indeed, were a chosen Generation of Men; they were planted a *Noble Vine,* and wholly a right Seed; but we are a Generation risen up, *who know not the God of our Fathers,* but are become like the *degenerate plant of a Strange Vine,* Jer. VIII. 8. *Why is this People of Jerusalem slidden back, by a perpetual backsliding? they hold fast deceit, they refuse to return.*[6]

---

[6] *The New England Courant: A Selection of Certain Issues Containing Writings of Benjamin Franklin* (Boston: American Academy of Arts and Sciences, 1956), n.p. after introduction.

It is not clear whether this missive to the *"ancient and venerable Doctor*
JANUS" is actual or a pastiche, though the pleonasm ("Why is this People
of Jerusalem slidden back, by a perpetual backsliding?") suggests pastiche, a bemused and ironic observation that conservative authority will
deride change as decline. Franklin, who was seventeen years old, stepped
from behind his irony in the one hundred and tenth issue, which clearly
demonstrates his adolescent disagreement with the ideology that governed Cotton Mather's self-conception:

> So great is the Power and Influence of Custom and Education on Hu-
> mane Nature, that men are commonly more tenacious by far of *Errors,*
> handed down to them by their Ancestors, than they are willing to re-
> ceive and embrace *Truth,* when offered to them by their Contempora-
> ries, tho' with the clearest Evidence and Demonstration.

Human nature gives way too easily to credulous ancestor worship:

> Hence it is that Truth and Error promiscuously, are transmitted from
> one Generation to another, while unthinking Men do greedily imbibe
> both one and the other, and can give no other Reason of their Faith and
> Practice, than, *That their Forefathers were always of that Perswasion and
> acted accordingly.* Every Age (to the cruel Reproach of Mankind) has
> afforded Pregnant Instances of this Truth, which might easily be pro-
> duced, did not our own sad Experience render the Task needless; for
> how obvious is it to every curious Observer, that the multitudes of men
> suck in the Opinions and Tenets of their Predecessors, and then put
> them off to their Children for current, without the least Scrutiny or
> Examination whether they are true or False.

This is not a quarrel between the ancients and the moderns, but a contention between filiopiety, here reduced to an "unthinking" appetite
("imbibe," "suck"), and self-government, which treats the past as a potential resource to be evaluated for its contemporary utility.

History-revering, Franklin argues, is a particularly acute problem in
New England:

> Every one is sensible, with what veneration the Principles and Practices
> of our Fore-fathers here in *New-England,* relating to Church Order and
> Discipline, have been entertain'd; For the sake of these it was that they
> left a goodly pleasant Land, and ventured themselves over a dreadful
> Ocean, into this howling Wilderness, where they suffered Hardships &
> Miseries inexpressible; These their Posterity have all along been ex-
> horted to contend earnestly for, and Invariably adhear to. And hence it
> is that the very name of a Bishop sounds formidable to our Honest
> plain-hearted People; the bare mention of Forms and Liturgies, strikes
> Terror into their minds, and they desire to dwell at the utmost Distance
> from them.

The reference to Catholicism here plays the same role as the reference to
the pope in Franklin's letter to his parents: he is delineating the paradox

of the American Puritan heir, born to the double legacy of righteous revolt against imposed authority and submission to theocratic authority. He is recalling the Puritan objection to Anglican practice, and expanding that objection into a thoroughgoing objection to all ecclesiastical authority. This strategy allows him to contend that Mather's sort of filiopious remembrance is actually a forgetting of the vigor that brought the godly across the sea:

> Now, I would not be understood to blame the People of this Land, for adhering to their Fore-Fathers principles, provided they were right, yet I apprehend them worthy of Censure, for receiving those principles merely because they were their Father's, without inquiring how far they are agreeable to Truth and Scripture; For it is evident, that there are multitudes among us, who are *zealous for the Traditions of the Fathers,* but yet are in a great measure ignorant of those Principles upon which our Ancestors settled in this Wilderness.[7]

The neglected principle is Congregationalism pushed to the point of Antinomianism: no authority over the individual judgment. Franklin is wrong to call this the foundation of New England Calvinism, because it pushes separation to an extremity to which the first generation would not go, and which it punished in Anne Hutchinson. But this argument is a polemic, and Franklin's historical inaccuracy is less interesting than his revisionism. He is rhetorically exploiting the dilemma at the heart of American Puritanism, stressing the anti-ecclesiastical element in Puritan thought that proved so vexing to the members of the first generation. This reasoning allows him to assert that the social codification of religion in the form of theocracy (and the attendant filiopious psychology) is in fact an anamnesis rather than a remembrance of the genius of the fathers, and that the individualist innovations that men of Mather's persuasion called declension were in fact recommencements, rather than betrayals, of the spirit of the great migration.

In recalling the period of youthful rebellion in his *Autobiography,* Franklin chose to depict it with a chronicle of practical action rather than through intellectual debate. More powerful than any abstract assertion, the story of his flight from indentured service under his brother's despotism made him a spokesman for the idea of a free life. In leaving Puritan Boston and the indenture, of which his father approved, Franklin signified his rejection of the most concrete manifestation of filiopiety – the father's dominance in the son's vocational choice. John Cotton had argued that particular talents adapted to a particular calling had been built into each man by God, and it was a commonplace assumption that the discovery of these talents was the father's rather than the son's task. Before Cotton Mather had reached the age of ten, his father had unabashedly noted that

[7] Ibid.

he had "designed" his son for the ministry,[8] and, according to Edmund
Morgan, Increase Mather was not exceptional in his assumption of the
right to strict vocational guidance:

> The choice of a calling therefore was a solemn affair. It was not so much
> a choice as a discerning of what occupation God called one to, for since
> the days of immediate revelation had passed, God did not call directly
> by an inward voice . . . Since a boy normally had to decide upon his
> lifework by the age of fourteen, he was seldom competent to make the
> decision by himself. He could not understand where his best abilities
> lay nor could he be trusted to choose an occupation useful to society. It
> was therefore incumbent upon his parents to guide the choice. Their
> guidance must in many cases have amounted to an absolute determi-
> nation.[9]

James Axtell quotes Samuel Willard's contention that parents "ought to
have an over-ruling influence in this Affair," and he accepts Morgan's
conclusion: "It seems that choosing a calling for New English children
was regarded with some scrupulosity as the prerogative of the child's
natural parents." Franklin's contracted indenture to his brother did not
replace mandatory filial subservience, since his father approved of the
contract and since the "stated terms of the indenture established the edu-
cational nature of apprenticeship as familial, as Englishmen, and especially Puritans, understood that word in its fullest sense. According to
Puritan casuistry the duties of masters were synonymous with those of
natural fathers."[10] Though Franklin would represent his exodus to Philadelphia as a reprise of the great migration, it was in fact a direct rejection
of Puritanism as it manifested itself in the economic lives of young men
in the early years of the eighteenth century.

Subsequent history may have blurred our sense of the magnitude of
what Franklin was defending in the chronicle of his migration in the
Autobiography. He was attempting to establish legitimacy for the "head-
long dashes for freedom" that were becoming increasingly common and
that were leading to the "declension" of patriarchal authority in the matter of vocational choice: "In spite of the ministers' preference, however,
parental authority over the choice of calling eroded with the gradual
recession of patriarchalism in the wake of, among other things, the eco-

---

[8] Increase Mather, *Autobiography*, p. 301, as quoted in David Levin, *Cotton Mather:
The Young Life of the Lord's Remembrancer* (Cambridge, Mass.: Harvard University Press, 1978), p. 14.

[9] Edmund Morgan, *The Puritan Family: Religion and Domestic Relations in Seventeenth-Century New England* (New York: Harper & Row, 1966), pp. 71, 72–3.

[10] James Axtell, *The School upon a Hill: Education and Society in Colonial New
England* (New Haven, Conn.: Yale University Press, 1974), pp. 104, 107, 116.

nomic conditions of the New World."[11] Franklin was not simply an example of this restlessness; he was a spokesman, and his revision of the
Puritan conception of nature is an attempt to provide his generation with
its own justification. He did this, in the *New England Courant* and in all
his subsequent critiques of real or analogical paternity, by denying that
the father automatically has a knowledge of the son's nature superior to
the son's own, and by asserting that natural paternity assists and advises
the son in the son's own self-aware progress to maturity.

A premonition of Franklin's position appears in Mather's *A Christian
at His Calling: or Two Brief Discourses, One Directing a Christian in His
General Calling; Another Directing Him in His Particular Calling* (1701).
This pamphlet is largely a restatement of Mather's and Willard's position
on vocational acceptance: Mather urges the reader to be content with his
situation and calling (even if they are of low degree), he cautions against
leaving or changing positions, and he deplores the desire of young men
to escape confinement by going to sea. (This pamphlet was published
twenty-three years before Creasy's maritime demise, and approximately
twenty-two years before Josiah Franklin persuaded his son not to go to
sea.) In such recommendations, Mather expresses his acceptance of the
role for which his father "designed" him, and he recapitulates Cotton's
conservative emphasis on the obligation to submit and to be content.
Mather makes this view clear in a parable about a saint who devotes all
his time to meditation and devotion: the saint goes in search of a truly
holy man; God brings him to Alexandria, and shows him a shoemaker.[12]

But, midway through the pamphlet, Mather cautions parents not to
foist irksome vocations onto their children, but to seek instead an agreeable calling. He distinguishes, in other words, between an attentive discovery of the child's inclination and a simple imposition of career, thereby
shifting the parent away from absolute authority and toward the sort of
expediting adviser described in Franklin's *Proposals for the Education of
Youth in Pensilvania*. Mather postulates the child's full individuality preceding the parent's act of design, which should be adequate and conforming. It is a brief remark, and Mather does not deduce Franklinian consequences, such as that the son burdened with a despotic parent has the
right to resist. But the remark is nonetheless the germ of Franklin's theory
of education.

Franklin did not leave his brother's shop, however, simply to choose
another profession or to work at the same profession under his own employ. If self is capable of surveying the range of possible vocations and

[11] James Axtell, *The School upon a Hill*, pp. 131, 108.
[12] Cotton Mather, *A Christian at His Calling* (Boston, 1701). The passages referred to here and below are on pp. 1–14, 32–4, and 60–5.

comprehending the merits of each, then self is distinct from both the vocation that might have been pushed upon it and from any subsequent vocational choice. Though Franklin did demonstrate his social utility by working diligently at his subsequent choice, the subsequent choice did not absorb this undetermined, self-fathering capacity, a fact demonstrated when he gave up complete involvement in his printing business. The pages of the *Autobiography* that follow the narrative of the flight from Boston, by chronicling the *series* of Franklin's widely diverse occupations, demonstrate that the escape was not simply from one form of particular life, but from indissociable attachment to particularized life per se. In the midst of any occupation, the undetermined capacity – *self* – remains vital, mindful of later detachment from the matter at hand, and thus it is not completely ensconced in the present form it has allowed its life to take. The selves of the students at the Pennsylvania Academy envisioned by Franklin will "come out of this School fitted for learning any Business, Calling, or Profession, except such wherein Languages are required," and they will therefore be able to "pass thro' and execute the several Offices of civil Life, with Advantage and Reputation to themselves and Country" (*P*, 4:108). Their education, that is, has not fitted them to single callings, but readied them to fit themselves to virtually any important secular calling; and they will retain this readiness, using it to pass through a number of particular offices.

Franklin thus preserves the ambition of personal universality extant in Mather's thought: the pure capaciousness of the students at Franklin's Academy recalls the cultivated multifacetedness of the young ministers addressed in the *Manuductio ad Ministerium*. But the personal universality advocated by Franklin is a de-sublimated version of Mather's: it *is* the self, rather than the result of sacrificing the self to a larger plan that stipulates the self's unquestionable locale in the order of the whole; such self-annihilation, in fact, would for Franklin be an adulteration of self, a confinement of capacity to piety, which, as was argued in the *New England Courant*, is only one of the seasons of man. Franklin's universal self is the troublesome simulacrum that Mather had chastised in his addresses to doctors and lawyers in *Bonifacius* and in his remark on Alexander Richardson in the biography of Hooker in the *Magnalia Christi Americana*, and that he had more or less secretly envied in his biographies of Winthrop, Jr., and Phips. But, whereas Mather would call Franklin's universality a simulacrum or distemper of true universality, Franklin would see in Mather a capacious ingenuity impeded by the piety it carries on its back.

Franklin's universality is closer to the virtuoso performance of Winthrop, Jr., than it is to the self-annihilation demanded in the injunction *Sine Christo omnis virtus est in vitie*. Campbell Tatham contends that, as a

reader of *Bonifacius*, Franklin must have ignored the early pages in which
this injunction is developed.[13] However, Franklin's virtue is a revision
rather than a plain rejection of Mather's. For Mather, the virtuous man
was always distinct from his works, a proposition that Franklin alters to
the assertion that the virtuous self is not determined by its works: as the
Puritan was to be in the world but not of it, always aware of the Creator
behind the creature, the Franklinian self is in its occupations but not of
them, always mindful of the pure dexterity behind the specific application in the moment at hand. In both cases the danger is captivation by
present circumstances: and the response is a careful detection and government of personal inclinations that would result in such captivation, an
unyielding detachment from the matter of the moment in the interest of
a more abstract commitment. Though neither Mather nor Franklin would
tolerate a withdrawal from worldly activity, in both cases the relation of
consciousness to present activity was to be negational. In *A Christian at
His Calling*, for example, Mather contends that, though the Christian
must labor at his particular calling, he must not lose sight of his general
calling by letting his occupation become an end in itself. He must live
each day as if it were his last: such a constant remembrance of death will
loosen him from complete attachment to the particular calling. Franklin
also practices such a detachment, and like Mather he developed specific
techniques for maintaining it: but his is a detachment of self from its
endeavors, rather than detachment of filiopious remembrance from self.
In both cases, close government yields an emancipated universality: but
for Franklin discipline is in service to self, rather than to the god of the
fathers.

   This cultivated detachment is manifest in Franklin's lifelong inclination
to the use of personae in his writing. Some of Franklin's personae – such
as the voices in "An Edict by the King of Prussia" and the "Rules for
Reducing a Great Empire to a Small One" – are ironic in the way the
voice in "A Modest Proposal" is ironic: the writer intends the reader to
conclude the opposite of what the persona is urging as right. But many
of Franklin's personae – such as Silence Dogood, Janus, The Busy-Body,
Patience, Poor Richard, and the Gout – do not fit this pattern. In these
cases, the voice expresses opinions of which we assume the writer approves, but the writer is nevertheless distinct from the voice: the writer
is capable of and congenial to the persona's argument, but the voice is
not a complete embodiment of the writer's capacity; the capacity hovers
above its current articulation, not in ironic disagreement, but in a preservation of its pure boundlessness from complete identification with the

---

[13] Campbell Tatham, "Benjamin Franklin, Cotton Mather, and the Outward
State," *Early American Literature* 6 (1971), p. 226.

present assertion. These verbal devices therefore typify Franklin's self-presentation as a whole: self takes on occupations, but in such a way as to make it clear that no one or group of occupations is an adequate expression of its potentiality. In *Israel Potter,* Melville suggested that Franklin's detached elusiveness revealed some undetected subterfuge. The perception of Franklin's detachment is correct, but Melville's assumption that there *must be* some real intent behind the appearances misses the point: it is a question not of the self's hidden commitments, but of a self that never converges entirely with any particular commitment. The only thing behind the execution of ingenious works is the resourcefulness capable of doing them: but the line between ingenuity and its works must always be clear, so that ingenuity will not seem to be a subordinate assistant to a particular purpose, but will instead appear in its unmixed independent purity, rising from forms of life that interest but do not define it. Hence the difficulty in finding a morality based on a positive standard in Franklin's writings, because such a positive morality might turn out to be a confinement of ingenuity to only one of the seasons of man. Franklin's morality proceeds instead from a pragmatic negativism: any personal position that can injure another is obviously a particular position, so the self that maintains its detachment from particular positions *must be* operative in service to human nature in the abstract. This is not to say that Franklin was immoral according to any standard we might devise, but that his morality cannot be shown to emanate from a coherent positive standard.

Hence, Franklin's occasional comments on the moral faculty, the soul, are remarkably similar to his descriptions of self. Like self, soul is a capacity, rather than an affective allegiance:

> All our Ideas are first admitted by the Senses and imprinted on the Brain, increasing in Number by Observation and Experience; there they become the Subjects of the Soul's Action. The Soul is a mere Power or Faculty of *contemplating* on, and *comparing* those Ideas when it has them; hence springs Reason; But as it can *think* on nothing but Ideas, it must have them before it can *think* at all . . . Now upon *Death,* and the Destruction of the Body, the Ideas contain'd in the Brain, (which are alone the Subjects of the Soul's Action) being then likewise necessarily destroy'd, the Soul, tho' incapable of Destruction itself, must then necessarily *cease to think* or *act,* having nothing left to think or act upon. It is reduc'd to its first unconscious State before it receiv'd any Ideas. And to cease to *think* is but little different from *ceasing to be.*
>
> Nevertheless, 'tis not impossible that this same *Faculty* of contemplating Ideas may be hereafter united to a new Body, and receive a new Set of Ideas; but that will no way concern us who are now living; for the Identity will be lost, it is no longer that same *Self* but a new Being. (*P,* I:69–70)

The jejune Lockeanism of the nineteen-year-old Franklin's *Dissertation on Liberty and Necessity, Pleasure and Pain* (1725) was intended as a definitive repudiation of his Puritan background, in which the soul was a "tendency to return" to the emotional states of primitive Christianity. In Franklin's treatise, however, the soul is little different from the power of intellection, and hence it poses no threat or contradiction to the secular self. Franklin would never again devote so much time to faculty-psychology, but his description of the soul is a draft for the conception of the self to which he would adhere for the rest of his life. Like the soul in the passage above, the self was a pure capacity which assumed the specific characteristics of the circumstances in which it was involved. But those characteristics never became defining properties of the soul or self: in passing from one embodiment to another, soul or self left behind the peculiar properties intrinsic to the earlier embodiment. The transfer from one occupation to the next revealed the emigrant's unalloyed qualitative neutrality, its entirely abstract readiness. The self passing from calling to calling in the *Autobiography*, like the soul passing from body to body, shows its ability to enter into specific identity *and* its unrelinquished independence from complete identification. Its occupations are personae.

The Franklinian self is a secularized version of the soul described in the *Dissertation on Liberty and Necessity, Pleasure and Pain,* which is a sort of transition between Puritan piety and the self as Franklin would define it. Three years later, in his "Apology for Printers," the transition is almost complete. Responding to those who might be angry with what he has printed in the *Pennsylvania Gazette,* Franklin contends that printing is a public particular calling: a proper newspaper includes the full spectrum of opinion that exists among its readership, so that readers who can respect only their own factious commitments will inevitably be offended. Such an unyielding attachment to particular cause, however, shows an unfortunate narrowness, a failure of nature: "it is as unreasonable in any one Man or set of Men to expect to be pleas'd with every thing that is printed, as to think that nobody ought to be pleas'd but themselves." Printers, however, are "educated" away from such illiberality: they believe that all positions should be heard, and they consequently develop a "vast Unconcernedness" in the midst of controversy, a habitual "Calmness and Indifference." The printer, therefore, should not be blamed, because he believes only that what has been printed should have been printed, not that it is true. The printer's self is no more identical with the arguments he prints than the soul is identical with the body it inhabits: his paper is a pure receptacle or vessel not conditioned to any interest, and he differs from his fellow citizens not in his adherence to one congenial or controversial position among the others, as his accusers have implied, but in his calm and indifferent unconcernedness. He is the agent, representative, or *prosopopeia* of the superfactional human truth he hopes will emerge from the controversy. He stands for man, rather than for any of the seasons of man, and the "Apology for Printers" is written to define and defend this universality by denying his attachment to any segments of the spectrum (*P*, 1:194–9): like the vessel in Franklin's "Meditation on a Quart Mugg" (1733), the natural self is distinct from its contents. It is human nature in its pure state. In the years to come Franklin will refine this position: his complete dissociation from particular stances will be replaced with the assertion that other men's positions are mixtures of nonrational commitment and natural ingenuity. Franklin's role will be to detach the ingenious from the obtuse, acting as the agent of universal humanity embodied: the contrast between himself and others will be a contrast between universality embodied and a weak or partial universality embroiled in unsubdued passions, rather than between pure universality and pure factious particularity.

This encouragement of the other's unfledged ingenuity is more involved than the simple process outlined in Franklin's "Proposals Relating to the Education of Youth," and the fact that such complex education is required reveals that Franklin's able "unconcernedness" is not a purely spontaneous sensibility, but a result of work. In 1760, writing to Lord Kames concerning his *Art of Virtue* now contained in Part Two of the *Autobiography*, Franklin contended that his innovation lay not in a new definition of virtue but in having written a usable manual:

> Many people lead bad lives that would gladly lead good ones, but know not *how* to make the change. They have frequently *resolved* and *endeavoured* it; but in vain, because their endeavours have not been properly conducted. To expect people to be good, to be just, to be temperate, &c., without *shewing* them how they should *become* so, seems like the ineffectual charity mentioned by the Apostle, which consisted in saying to the hungry, the cold, and the naked, "Be ye fed, be ye warmed, be ye clothed," without showing them how they should get food, fire, or clothing. (*P*, 9:104–5)

The acquisition of virtue, like other forms of acquisition, is work, more or less intelligence and energy directed toward a goal, and against a context of resistance. In the work of virtuous self-design, the resistance comes from the obstinate persistence of impulses contrary to the self being constructed. Unconcernedness requires techniques for becoming aware of, for evaluating, and for governing the resisting elements of consciousness. Because Franklin's virtue is work, therefore, it involves, like Mather's, contradiction within consciousness: determined discipline is a contrary element within the amalgam of the whole that meets with resistance from the remainder.

But, whereas Mather's ethic of discipline emphasized the contradiction between determination and resistant material in the form of the drama of holy conversion, Franklin's ethic suppresses awareness of contradiction. The source of Franklin's nature's rhetorical appeal is its seeming easy expression of common thought and emotion: the natural self is presented as a harmony, as an equipoise of thoughts and emotions that is without vexation, turbulence, or inner imbalance. Franklin's example seems to offer the goods – reliable orderliness of thought and emotion – without the Matherian price – the anguish and anxiety of self-contradiction. To advertise this bargain, Franklin must demonstrate that service to self is not onerous in the way that service to the father is. He does so by contrasting his discipline with Puritan discipline, in which the governing authority is admittedly external to and in contradiction with self, and by regularly circumventing the question of whether self as he designs it is an authority external to the remainder of consciousness, which it governs. By evoking the example of Puritan discipline for contrast, Franklin can imply that enlightened virtue is a *happy work* in which the materials upon which determination operates are eager volunteers.

A virtuous education is dramatized in the "Dialogue between Philocles and Horatio, Meeting Accidentally in the Fields, Concerning Virtue and Pleasure," printed in the *Pennsylvania Gazette* in 1730. In 1949, A. O. Aldridge discovered that Franklin did not write this dialogue and its sequel, but only borrowed them from the *London Journal* from the previous year. Aldridge speculates that the true author might be Lord Ashley Shaftesbury, Francis Hutcheson, or Bishop Benjamin Hoadly. However, the mistaken attribution of authorship to Franklin is easily understood, since the manner and matter of the dialogue are consonant with Franklin's. As Aldridge writes, the "conclusions concerning Franklin's intellectual development drawn by critics under the assumption that the dialogues were Franklin's are equally valid when we know that the works originally appeared elsewhere."[14]

After some preliminaries, the virtuous Philocles wishes he could help Horatio to be a reasonable creature, and he tells Horatio that he loves him better than Horatio loves himself. Horatio replies that he loves himself a great deal, but Philocles cautions that "he only loves himself well, who rightly and judiciously loves himself." Philocles here distinguishes between two sorts of self-love: self-indulgence, and an aloof appraisal that is disinterested, unconcerned, right, and judicious. Loving well, according to Philocles, requires an observing eye that transcends self in order to measure it. This transcending appraiser, which Horatio lacks, abstains from enjoyment in order to calculate the eventual outcome of enjoyment. According to Philocles, indulgence can be "the Ruin and De-

[14] A. O. Aldridge, "Franklin's 'Shaftesburian' Dialogues Not Franklin's: A Revision of the Franklin Canon," *American Literature* 21 (May 1949), pp. 151–9.

194   COTTON MATHER AND BENJAMIN FRANKLIN

struction of that very Self which he loves so well! That Man alone loves
himself rightly, who procures the greatest possible Good to himself thro'
the whole of his Existence; and so pursues Pleasure as not to give for it
more than 'tis worth." An important shift has occurred. Philocles had
begun by accepting Horatio's definition of self as the complete body of
personal affections, desires, and interests in the things of the world. Then,
he posited the appraiser, who transcends self in order to evaluate those
attractions. Finally, in the passage above, that appraiser, detached from
immediate life, and always conscious of the long range of its design, is
self. Self is now the appraiser, abstaining from the eloquent personality
of impulse in order to treat impulses as quanta, costing so much, yielding
so much, and thereby orienting itself to a temporally distant goal. The
artful Philocles has introduced a new concept of self, but he has not acknowledged the transition, so he will be able to persuade Horatio that
self-denial is not self-denial.

This factor will be important, because Horatio does not like discipline.
In accord with Franklin's *Articles of Belief and Religion,* Horatio is "sure
the wise and good Author of Nature would never make us to plague us."
If he disapproves of these impulses that Horatio calls *self,* why, Horatio
asks, did he put them in me? Why must I dissever my integrity in order
to observe a discipline that is contrary to my nature?

> He could never give us Passions, on purpose to subdue and conquer
> 'em; nor produce this Self of mine, or any other self, only that it may
> be denied; for that is denying the Works of the great Creator himself.
> Self-denial, then, which is what I suppose you mean by Prudence, seems
> to me not only absurd, but very dishonourable to that Supreme Wis-
> dom and Goodness, which is supposed to make so ridiculous and Con-
> tradictious a Creature, that must always be fighting with himself in
> order to be at rest, and undergo voluntary Hardships in order to be
> happy: Are we created sick, only to be commanded to be Sound?

Like Mather, Horatio conceives of *self* as all of personal consciousness.
But, unlike Mather, he eloquently protests the vexation piety demands.

According to Philocles, however, calculating reason is a government
that is not "contradictious." Philocles takes one component of the apostate continuum that Horatio and Mather call *self* and sets it in regulatory
opposition to the rest of what Horatio and Mather call *self.* This dissociated governing part will now be called the whole of *self,* and the rest
will be called *passion.* This transition, however, this dissociation of one
element from the whole and its enthronement as governor of the whole,
goes unacknowledged, so that Philocles may promote a self-government
that is not contradictious. Since the calculating reason that Philocles calls
self was one part of what Mather and Horatio called *self,* and since the
disparity between the two senses in which the word is being used is hid-

den, Philocles is able to come up with a happy formula: "This, my dear Horatio, I have to say; that which you find Fault with and clamour against, as the most terrible Evil in the World, Self-denial; is really the greatest Good, and the highest Self-gratification." But the happy conundrum unravels when we realize that it depends upon hiding the disparity between the two definitions of self: the denial of self as Horatio defines it is the gratification of self as Philocles defines it.

Philocles' rhetorical prestidigitation is designed to persuade Horatio that he can have discipline and self too. But Philocles is disguising the fact that what he calls *self* is affectively closer to Puritan piety than it is to what Horatio calls *self*: Philocles' *self is* a discipline. It requires that one part of feeling be put apart from the rest, that its interests be observed before the inclinations of the whole. As Puritan piety was in the world but not of it, always mindful of the Creator behind the creature, so the Philoclean self is in the moments of its life but not of them, always mindful of its larger project; as Puritan piety detached itself from the self's enjoyments in order to assess them, so the self is detached from its passions in order to measure their amount of contribution to or detraction from the transcending purpose. It is work directed toward a goal and against a resistance, but, since Philocles allows both the work and the resistance to be called *self,* the work can be made to seem a contradiction-free harmony.

The only remaining step is to reduce desire, affection, and interest to a kind of extrinsic irritation at play on the perimeter of self: "All intelligent, rational Agents find in themselves a Power of judging what kind of Beings they are; what Actions are proper to preserve 'em, and what Consequences will generally attend them, what Pleasures they are form'd for, and to what Degree their Natures are capable of receiving them." The Philoclean self is human nature: it is what a man is formed for, it is his life to be preserved, his single legitimate pleasure. The other inclinations, therefore, are non-nature, obstinate quanta to be measured rather than listened to:

> All we have to do then, *Horatio,* is to consider, when we are surpriz'd with a new Object, and passionately desire to enjoy it, whether the gratifying that Passion be consistent with the gratifying other Passions and Appetites, equal if more necessary to us. And whether it consists with our Happiness To-morrow, next Week, or next Year; for, as we all wish to live, we are obliged by Reason to take as much care for our future, as our present Happiness, and not build one upon the Ruins of t'other.

At the beginning of its career, self is to envision in concrete terms its eventual goal. This plan is its life ("as we all wish to live"), and all potential distractions are mortal dangers, rather than sources of amendment or transformation. New objects will present themselves with the force of scintillating novelty, with the appearance of unparalleled and unanticipated uniqueness, but this appearance must be punctured: the new object must be seen in a context of commensurability with other objects. The model for this transcendent context of commensurability is *number*, a mode of representation that permits pure comparability:

> But, if thro' the Strength and Power of a present Passion, and thro' want of attending to Consequences, we have err'd and exceeded the Bounds which Nature or Reason have set us; we are, then, for our own Sakes, to refrain, or deny ourselves a present momentary Pleasure for a future, constant, and durable one: So that this Philosophical Self-denial is only refusing to do an Action which you strongly desire; because 'tis inconsistent with your Health, Fortunes, or Circumstances in the World; or, in other Words, because 'twould cost you more than 'twas worth. (*W*, II:46–51)

The author does not mean that the injury desire does to resolve can be calculated with the exactitude of the price of corn, but he uses the model of economy to signify an appraisal of impulse that is maximally abstracted from what it appraises. From this altitude, the apparent incommensurability of the present – its power of surprise – is dispersed, the bounds that determination has set to personal life are natural, and the appeal of the here and now is only error, rather than recall or petition. Like Mather's piety, Philocles' self is a regulated detachment from the force of the world at hand and a perfect continuity in which alteration is degeneration. The discipline, however, is "for our own Sakes," rather than for the glory of the god of the fathers.

At their reunion, "A Second Dialogue Between Philocles and Horatio, Concerning Virtue and Pleasure," Horatio tells Philocles that he is now a convert, and he recites the happy conundrum: "You shewed me, that Self-denial, which above all things I abhorred, was really the greatest Good, and the highest Self-gratification, and absolutely necessary to produce even my own darling sole Good, Pleasure." "Self-denial," he now sees, is, "in Truth, Self-recognising, Self-acknowledging, or Self-owning." Now, Horatio says, "I can, without a Sigh, leave other Pleasures for those of Philosophy; I can hear the word *Reason* mentioned, and Virtue praised, without Laughing. Didn't I bid fair for Conversion, think you?" Horatio's irony (or sarcasm) here is meant to mark the revisionary difference between the self-annihilation required in conversion and the self-enhancement that is rational education – but, again, without taking notice of the two senses in which the word *self* is being employed: Horatio might reply that in both cases *self* is simply *me*, but this tautology would only further disguise the quiet revolution that has occurred within the signification of *I*. Philocles congratulates him, adding that in all creatures, "their Happiness or chief Good consists in acting up to their chief Faculty," and "the chief Faculty in Man is his Reason; and consequently his chief Good; or that which may be justly called his Good, consists not merely in Action, but in reasonable Action." Abstracted calculation is human nature, and the self at one with it has made nature the constitutive rule of his individual being: "Look, *Horatio,* into the sacred Book of Nature; read your own Nature, and view the Relation which other Men stand in to you, and you to them; and you'll immediately see what constitutes human Happiness, and consequently what is Right" (*W,* II:51–7). Though Philocles' cheerful philosophy requires him to observe a discipline with affinities with Puritan discipline, Horatio seems not to dislike the new regime, because it brings him into accord with his own ends. His sense of what his own ends are, however, has undergone substantial rearrangement.

Philocles' major precepts are echoed in many of Franklin's writings. Five years after the dialogues between Philocles and Horatio, for example, Franklin himself wrote a dialogue on virtue between Socrates and Crito (after the manner of Xenophon, rather than Plato) for the *Pennsylvania Gazette.* Socrates tells Crito that the character of a man of sense derives from his unflagging attention to his one "*true Interest.*" When a man of sense lapses from this vigilance, "he loses the *Favour* of God and Man, and brings upon himself many Inconveniences, the least of which is capable of marring and demolishing his Happiness." Straying from the self-assigned course, the calculating self reduces its efficacy, allowing itself to be blurred and injured by false interests that overcome discipline. These "waste his Time and Substance." Waste is expenditure without sufficient return: the very use of the word therefore implies an ascent to a plane of abstraction where the calculating self is as diverse from the inclinations it surveys as number is from the things it represents. The analogy between virtue and number is made explicit shortly afterward:

> There seems to be no necessity that to be a Man of Sense, he should never make a Slip in the Path of Virtue, or in Point of Morality; provided he is sensible of his Failing and diligently applys himself to rectify what is done amiss, and to prevent the like for the future. The best Arithmetician may err in casting up a long Account; but having found that Error, he *knows how* to mend it, and immediately does so; and is notwithstanding that Error, an Arithmetician; But he who *always* blunders, and cannot correct his Faults in Accounting, is no Arithmetician; nor is the habitually-vicious Man a *Man of Sense.* (*P,* 2:15–19)

If the man of sense slips from discipline, his slips are errata, they have no content. They do not reveal a private longing concealed by the discipline. In an essay printed a week later, Franklin contended that "SELF-DENIAL *is not the* ESSENCE OF VIRTUE" because, for the man of sense, self is virtue, and there are no apprehensible countervailing parts of consciousness: "And Self-denial is neither good nor bad, but as 'tis apply'd: He that denies a Vicious Inclination is Virtuous in proportion to his Resolution, but the most perfect Virtue is above all Temptation, such as the Virtue of the Saints in Heaven" (P, 2:19–21). Like Mather, Franklin holds that virtue is a perfect accord between consciousness and abstracted discipline that leaves no obstinate resistance; but, unlike Mather's, Franklin's discipline is the self, rather than the result of the annihilation of the self.

The recommendation that one be so detached from inclination that he can measure impulses as more or less facilitation of an abstract end reappears as the famous moral or prudential algebra:

> To get over [uncertainty in decision-making], my Way is, to divide half a Sheet of Paper by a Line into two Columns; writing over the one *Pro,* and over the other *Con.* Then during three or four Days Consideration, I put down under the different Heads short Hints of the different Motives, that at different Times occur to me, *for* or *against* the Measure. When I have thus got them all together in one View, I endeavour to estimate their respective Weights; and where I find two, one on each side, that seem equal, I strike them both out. If I find a Reason *pro* equal to some two Reasons *con,* I strike out the three. If I judge some two Reasons *con,* equal to some three Reasons *pro,* I strike out the five; and thus proceeding I find at length where the Ballance lies; and if after a Day or two of farther Consideration, nothing new that is of Importance occurs on either Side, I come to a Determination accordingly. And, tho' the Weight of Reasons cannot be taken with the Precision of Algebraic Quantities, yet, when each is thus considered, separately and comparatively, and the whole lies before me, I think I can judge better, and am less liable to make a rash Step; and in fact I have found great Advantage from this kind of Equation, in what may be called *Moral* or *Prudential Algebra.* (P, 19:299–300)

This balancing is one of the techniques of virtue, and, as in the case of the story of Franklin's flight from Boston, its familiarity may disguise what is involved. All motives – desire, love, interest, appetite – are to be reduced to quantities. When Franklin concedes that perhaps he cannot measure with precision, he implies that the emphasis on quantity may be somewhat metaphorical, but that is the point: *number* is the most abstracted mode of representation, completely separated from the individuated qualities of the thing; its transcendence of quality, its reduction of things down to units, is what permits a pure comparability. At this level of abstraction, the whole lies before him, he has everything in one view.

But the self that lives at this plane of abstraction has competitors. Franklin notes repeatedly that the act of appraisal must span several days: "during three or four days consideration," "that at different times occur to me," "after a day or two of farther consideration." In the intensity of the mo-

ment, consciousness is appreciating the qualities of the individual motives, and thus perhaps over- or underestimating their just "Weights."
Momentary thought and feeling stray or sink from the plane of abstract
calculation: the present configuration of the fronting world can lure this
algebraic Ulysses from abstraction into immersion, and the long view
spanning several days is a way of tying him to the mast of reason.

Immersion then, and qualitative representation, are silent presences,
or ghosts, in the machine of moral algebra. They do not become a voice
in competition with abstraction, as self and piety speak in competition
in Mather's texts, but they are nonetheless *there*, as the mute and obstinate inclination to the "rash Step." The government of rashness is what
makes chess a "moral" game:

> We learn by Chess the habit of not being discouraged by present ap-
> pearances in the state of our affairs, the habit of hoping for a favourable
> Change, and that of persevering in the search of resources . . . And
> whoever considers, what in Chess he often sees instances of that success
> is apt to produce Presumption, & its consequent Inattention, by which
> more is afterwards lost than was fain'd by the preceding Advantage,
> while misfortunes produce more care and attention, by which the loss
> may be recovered, will learn not to be too much discouraged by any
> present success of his Adversary, nor to despair of final good fortune
> upon every little Check he receives in the pursuit of it. (*W,* II:189)

Such abstention from the feeling of the moment is of course an indis-
pensable component of thought: it is the condition for any decision, because decision requires the commensurability of the choices. But it is
only one of thought's seasons; aesthetic attention, for example, is quite
contrary to it. For Franklin, however, it *is* self, and those other seasons
are rashness; they are examples of thought lapsing from its nature. Detached calculation is a life *habit,* a near-mechanistic persistence in techniques that keep self separate from contamination by its emotional fellow
travelers. This celebration of habit is what separates Franklin's discipline
from Stoicism, though Franklin often adopts the rhetoric of Stoic virtue:
in the writings of Seneca and Marcus Aurelius, reflective detachment is
an arduous victory, a relief from the surrounding madness that permits
remembrance of the order of things, rather than a governance of impulse
that furthers ambition. In the Stoic writings, ambition is itself subjected
to reflection, so that a moment of beauty or surprise can instigate abstraction from self, rather than simply self's abstraction from other inclination. For Franklin, however, such accession to rarity and such profound reevaluation of life purpose are unthinking responses to the allure
of rashness. Despite his vaunted secularity, Franklin shares Mather's conclusion that the present and the immediate represent a power of decay or
decline, rather than a source of amendment, to be divested of their elo-

quence: his realism is not an act of adequation to consciousness immured
in what is actual, but a rhetorical revision of Puritanism's emphatic insistence on allegiance to the invisible world.

As D. H. Lawrence contended, Franklin's project is the restriction of
self or *I* to one part of consciousness.[15] If the remainder of thought and
feeling can be subjugated to the habits of calculation, the result will be
liberty, in the sense of a univocal accord with self's law; and this liberty
will be more appealing than Mather's Christian liberty if the subjugation
of inclination it involves can be hidden.

> By Liberty is sometimes understood the Absence of Opposition; and in
> this Sense, indeed, all our Actions may be said to be the Effects of our
> Liberty: But it is a Liberty of the same Nature with the Fall of a heavy
> Body to the Ground; it has Liberty to fall, that is, it meets with nothing
> to hinder its Fall, but at the same Time it is necessitated to fall, and has
> no Power or Liberty to remain suspended. (*P*, I:62)

The liberty of Franklin's selfhood is not a relaxation of incessant and
unaltering determination, but, like Mather's, an overcoming of all passional personal components at odds with determination.

Franklin's project thus has the trappings of Christian goodness: denial
of impulse in the interest of a detached calculation and fidelity to distant
ends. The Franklinian self, in its moments of occupation but not of them,
is a pure fealty to its project, a fealty so complete that it is a liberty. But
is the higher law that self poses to consciousness a goodness? The two
Shaftesburian dialogues reprinted in the *Pennsylvania Gazette* promise to
delineate virtue, but they are silent on what the self's "good" is, and their
promise that self-discipline will bring self into an immediate intuition of
the order of humanity is just a promise: the habits of clearheaded calculation and self-maintenance that Philocles outlines would be as useful to
a determined malefactor as they would be to a determined philanthro-
pist. They might restrain Falstaff; but they might assist Iago. No doubt,
Philocles' decision aginst presenting a code of precepts or of prescribed
attitudes is pragmatic: self is the end of the process, and to tie self to a
definition of virtue would be to subject it to the sort of transcendental
restraint Horatio finds so irksome. But this means that the "virtue" in
the title is actually virtú, virtuosity – ingenuity.

Philocles, therefore, cannot be taken as a complete spokesman for
Franklin. The detachment he urges on Horatio becomes a virtue, rather
than simply a technique for personal efficacy, only when it is added that
the self Franklin aimed to secure was a universal self: it was to be a digest
of human nature, adroitness embodied rather than an adroit pursuit of a

---

[15] D. H. Lawrence, *Studies in Classic American Literature* (New York: Viking Press,
1923), p. 9.

particular end. Any vicious (that is to say, hurtful) action would be a particular preference for one segment of the human whole, to the injury of another, and it would therefore be rejected by a detached, calculating self *bent on projecting its universality*. The art of virtue described in the dialogues can be represented as a goodness only if it is shown to be dedicated to building a self that is a pure epitome of man. Its success will be certified not by a demonstrable accord with any specific principle, but by acclaim that leaps from the human community to the universal self, in whom it is well pleased. Reputation, then, on the condition that it is a reputation common in all parts of the human group, is the guarantor of the goodness of the nonmoral self-design delineated in the dialogues. Where Mather sought relief from the eye of God in the pursuit of acclaim, a relief that never became sufficient, Franklin depends upon acclaim absolutely if his self-construction is to be more than the ingenious gratification of one personal drive that has gained power over the others.

7

THE SPARK AND THE DOLLAR: FRANKLIN'S PUBLIC CAREER

There seems to me at present to be great Occasion for raising an united Party for Virtue, by forming the Virtuous and good Men of all Nations into a regular Body, to be govern'd by suitable good and wise Rules, which good and wise Men may probably be more unanimous in their Obedience to, than common People are to common Laws.

Franklin (*A:*162–3)

It is on this account that the communication of pure insight is comparable to a silent expansion or to the *diffusion,* say, of a perfume in the unresisting atmosphere. It is a penetrating infection which does not make itself noticeable beforehand as something opposed to the indifferent element into which it insinuates itself, and therefore cannot be warded off.

Hegel, "The Struggle of the Enlightenment with Superstition," *The Phenomenology of Spirit* (trans. A. V. Miller)

Franklin's self-design is allied with his social theory: as self replaced its former opponent, transcendental divinity, as the agent of personal order, so too citizens were entitled to government that purely expressed the secular lives of their selves, rather than imposing a will that was diverse from them. The relation between Franklin's constructed self and good government was to be causal: in the *Pennsylvania Gazette* for May 7, 1738, Franklin quoted Confucius's declaration that if "the Understanding of a Prince is well enlighten'd, . . . his Family being arriv'd at this Perfection, 'twill serve as an Example to all Subjects of the particular Kingdoms, and the Members of the particular Kingdoms to all those that compose the Body of the Empire. Thus the whole Empire will be well-govern'd."[1] The diffusion of the philosopher's reputation throughout the population

[1] Quoted in A. Owen Aldridge, *Benjamin Franklin and Nature's God* (Durham, N.C.: Duke University Press, 1967), p. 121.

was the perfume that lured them to virtue. By offering an exemplary demonstration of the benefits of calculating self-government (and of the practical techniques that made it generally available), Franklin hoped to excite the human nature latent in his fellow men, leading them from the divisive passions of particular interest toward unanimous admiration for reason. This ideal of unanimous fusion with law was already conceived in Mather's social theory, but with the condition of self-annihilation. For Franklin, however, government would not be an interfering correction, but instead a benign (or even vestigial) manager or adviser, like the trustees of the Pennsylvania Academy, or like the god who helps those who help themselves. Franklin's government, to use Hegel's formulation, would not make itself known as something opposed to the element in which it works, and so it would not irritate a nation of Horatios unpersuaded by the requirement of self-suspicion. In 1755 Franklin wrote to Catherine Ray that "I must confess (but don't you be jealous), that many more people love me now than ever did before; for since I saw you I have been enabled to do some general services to the country, and to the army, for which both have thanked and praised me, and say they love me" (*P*, 6:182). He adds that he will probably not benefit from this acclaim personally, since these people are unlikely to return favors. But Franklin believed that his *general services* did have an appreciable benefit: by applauding Franklin, the American Horatios would be applauding what he had taught them to call their selves, thereby tending toward the unanimity of virtue.

Franklin's exemplary pedagogy, moreover, would be a two-way process: truly general acclaim would be an accreditation of Franklin, a certification that he was a partisan for the cause of man, rather than simply an ingenious man in effective pursuit of private ends. In the letter to Catherine Ray, he notes that, though his reputation may not bring him specific benefits, "it pleases my humour." As he wrote in "The Busy-Body" in 1729, "Almost every Man has a strong natural Desire of being valu'd and esteem'd by the rest of his Species, but I am concern'd and griev'd to see how few fall into the Right and only infallible Method of becoming so." The right way is a universal friendship that avoids close commitment to any specific portion of the human spectrum. This friendship is a "known Impartiality" that makes the man "the Arbitrator and Decider of all Differences"; it is a "mixture of Innocence and Wisdom," of detachment from particular ends and of long-sighted abstract calculation. Once achieved, the "long habits of Virtue have a sensible effect on the Countenance," showing a central undaunted calm that does not vary with its circumstances. (*P*, 1:118–21). By cultivating a visible independence from particular commitment, the man of sense is speeded to a reputation that certifies the virtue that causes it. As Carl Becker contends,

[to] be esteemed a "man of virtue" was both sufficient and efficacious, and likely to give one, without any painful searchings of the heart, the assurance of being in a state of social justification, or even, if the esteem were general enough, of complete sanctification. I suppose that Hume and Franklin, when they were in France, for example, must have had this assurance as fully as any saint of the church ever did.

Reputation, therefore, replaces the discerning eye of Mather's god, a metamorphosis that Becker calls characteristic of the Enlightenment at large: "In this enterprise posterity played an important role: it replaced God as judge and justifier of those virtuous and enlightened ones who were not of this world."[2] Franklin was concerned with immediate as well as distant posterity: his contemporary reputation would testify to his validity, enabling him to waive Puritan introspection, as he did in the letter to his father and mother. His reputation, however, would have to spread through the whole community of man: a good name among one group of men, or several, even if they were a majority, would not suffice, since it might demonstrate only a particular service that could turn out to be injurious to another segment of man. The certification of Franklin's calculating detachment as a sufficient virtue, therefore, mandated an incessant pursuit of reputation that could end only when the universal self had earned a universal acclaim. At that point Franklin would have proved himself, and man would have discovered himself.

In a letter to Jared Ingersoll written in 1762, Franklin contrasted harsh with congenial means of unifying man:

> I should be glad to know what it is that distinguishes Connecticut religion from common religion. Communicate, if you please, some of these particulars that you think will amuse me as a virtuoso. When I travelled in Flanders, I thought of your excessively strict observation of Sunday; and that a man could hardly travel on that day among you upon his lawful occasions without hazard of punishment; while, where I was, every one travelled, if he pleased, or diverted himself in any other way; and in the afternoon both high and low went to the play or the opera, where there was plenty of singing, fiddling and dancing. I looked around for God's judgements, but saw no signs of them. The cities were well built and full of inhabitants, the markets filled with plenty, the people well favoured and well clothed, the fields well tilled, the cattle fat and strong, the fences, houses, and windows all in repair, and no Old Tenor anywhere in the country; which would almost make one suspect that the Deity is not so angry at that offence as a New England Judge. (*P*, 10:175–6)

---

[2] Carl Becker, *The Heavenly City of the Eighteenth Century Philosophers* (New Haven, Conn.: Yale University Press, 1932), pp. 49, 140–1.

The Sunday enjoyments of the citizens of Flanders are as orderly and regular as their weekly employments: the sabbath festiveness, Franklin implies, is a satisfying form of glorifying God, who does not disapprove. Divine law, therefore, is more in accord with what Franklin calls his "lawful occasions" than it is with the harsh and imposed moralism of the New England judge: it is an expression of, rather than an adversary to, ordinary life.

Connecticut and Flanders may be taken as surrogates for the end-points of Franklin's adolescent exodus, Massachussetts and Pennsylvania. Cotton Mather's complaints about Massachusetts' "declension," about innovations that betrayed the faith of the fathers, must be taken in the context of his insistence on *exact* preservation. In fact, the Massachusetts of the first half of the eighteenth century maintained what E. Digby Baltzell calls its "hierarchical communalism." Though there were theological revisions, the possession of political power, and concomitant conservative assumptions about the proper use of power in maintaining a specific decorum, remained largely static, as Franklin learned when his brother was imprisoned for the contents of the *New England Courant*. This continuity was encouraged by the fact that the population of Massachusetts was stable throughout this period, and that relatively low levels of immigration kept it mostly English and permitted the consolidation of power in the hands of men such as William Shirley and Thomas Hutchinson.[3]

Pennsylvania, on the other hand, according to Richard Hofstadter, was as "complex ethnically as New England was simple." Greater economic opportunity, together with the reputation for toleration which was Penn's legacy, contributed to a population growth from 51,000 in 1730 to 240,000 by 1770. Ethnically, Pennsylvania's population was roughly divided in three by the English, Scotch-Irish, and Germans, though there were also Dutch, Swedes, and Welsh. Its religions included the Quakers, Presbyterians, Episcopalians, Catholics, Lutherans, Mennonites, Dunkers, Schwenkfelders, Moravians, smaller sects such as the Brethren of the River, and invented individual religions such as those of Franklin's employer Samuel Keimer or of the patriarch in Charles Brockden Brown's *Wieland*.[4] This diversity ensured that in Pennsylvania the controversy over the Great Awakening would be especially acute and vehement.

Philadelphia was the economic and cultural crown to Pennsylvanian diversity. According to Hofstadter, Philadelphia grew because of the

---

[3] E. Digby Baltzell, *Puritan Boston and Quaker Philadelphia* (Boston: Beacon Press, 1979), pp. 115, 124, 150.

[4] Richard Hofstadter, *America at 1750* (New York: Knopf, 1971), pp. 5, 135–6.

richness of the interior it served, "coming into existence during one man's lifetime." By 1750, it had twenty thousand inhabitants, making it one of the premier cities of the empire, since in 1750 only fourteen cities in England contained more than ten thousand. Even before the Revolution, as Carl and Jessica Bridenbaugh have shown, Philadelphia was culturally modern, numbering among its luminaries innovators in medicine, literature, political theory, and philanthropy. Whereas, according to Baltzell, Boston remained a "provincial and essentially Puritan town," Philadelphia was the point at which the "values of the French Enlightenment came to America." In 1744 Franklin predicted that "*Philadelphia* shall become the Seat of the *American* Muses" (*P,* 2:405), a role it had clearly assumed by the time it became the national capital.[5]

Because of Pennsylvania's abundant diversity, its politics were an "amiable anarchy," according to Baltzell. William S. Hanna goes further, contending that the fragmentation of Pennsylvanian life made its politics "distinctively violent." The only consensus that could be assumed was negative – that government should not speak for a single interest, and that its interference in the conduct of daily business should be minimal. This resentment of sectarian opportunism was vigorous in proportion to the domination of Pennsylvania politics by sectarian opportunism. The German interest was scarcely represented in the Pennsylvania Assembly, the eastern counties were disproportionately overrepresented, and the Quakers, who had transformed themselves from old light enthusiasts into an effective political machine, regularly imposed their standards of decency onto the whole. In fact, according to Hanna, the general population might have felt that their rights were more satisfactorily represented by the royal proprietor, Thomas Penn, who consolidated his power in 1746, than they were by the Assembly.[6]

Baltzell contends that Franklin's talent thrived in this "mobile, anarchical" world, an assertion that accords with the major thesis of Carl Van Doren's biography. According to Van Doren, Franklin was himself "a harmonious human multitude," a "federation of purposes working harmoniously together," and he was therefore uniquely suited to represent the whole of Pennsylvanian diversity, rather than merely one of its seg-

---

[5] Ibid., pp. 8, 135–6; W. A. Speck, *Stability and Strife: England, 1714–1760* (Cambridge, Mass.: Harvard University Press, 1979), pp. 62–6; Carl and Jessica Bridenbaugh, *Rebels and Gentlemen* (New York: Oxford University Press, 1943); Baltzell, *Puritan Boston and Quaker Philadelphia,* p. 143; Van Wyck Brooks, "Philadelphia in 1800," in *The World of Washington Irving* (New York: Dutton, 1944), pp. 1–20.

[6] Baltzell, *Puritan Boston and Quaker Philadelphia,* p. 118; William S. Hanna, *Benjamin Franklin and Pennsylvania Politics* (Stanford, Calif.: Stanford University Press, 1964), pp. 1–2, 8, 15–7.

ments: "Pennsylvania, with its mixture of races and its rapid growth and its irregular development, seemed to him disorderly. In that confusion he thought in forms – in forms which life might take."[7] Franklin spoke for life taking its due form, rather than for any particular form imposed on life by a special interest. Consequently, according to Hanna, Franklin constantly operated as an independent: though he affiliated himself at various times with both the Assembly and the proprietorial causes, these were expeditious alliances, and he broke from them when he felt coerced to be of that party as well as in it.[8] Though some, especially Thomas Penn, felt that this independence showed a sharp-dealing self-service, Franklin himself believed it was service to man: as long as a particular faction was serving the general interest, he could coordinate himself with it, but when the faction showed itself to be distinct from the general interest, he dissociated himself from it.

It seems a moot point whether Franklin personally summed up the general interest. His continuing popularity in a radically divided political milieu may suggest that he made himself into an adequate representation of the whole. However, his discussions of techniques of self-presentation seldom explain how to detect what man, or even Pennsylvanian man, is: instead, they teach the art of avoiding appearances that, appealing to some, might irritate others, and of demonstrating that the roles that are assumed are avocations and not expressions of an inherent particular interest or inclination. As Hanna argues, the eighteenth-century Pennsylvanians had a strong sense of what human nature was not – factional aggrandizement – rather than of what human nature is. In responding to his political scene, therefore, Franklin developed an adept rhetoric that distinguished him from particular causes and that demonstrated that he was essentially distinct from the tasks he took on. Regardless of what Franklin was, that is, the face he presented to the public eye was most conspicuous for its "unconcernedness," "neutrality," disinterestedness," or "mediocrity" – all negative terms emphasizing what he was not. Despite what biographers may contend was the truth of Franklin, his public persona was a blank capacity in no way confined to special cause or faction or passion. His self-presentation was primarily negational, a demonstration of the commitments from which he abstained, rather than of the commitment to man to which he held. In public life, Franklin's humanism operated by process of elimination: since he eventually demonstrated that he was free from indissociable commitment to any of the seasons of man, in but not of them, he *must have been* man in the pure

---

[7] Carl Van Doren, *Benjamin Franklin* (New York: Viking Press, 1938), pp. 129, 189, 782.
[8] This thesis runs throughout Hanna's book.

state. But, though tact and humanism are not necessarily opposed, neither are they necessarily synonymous.

Franklin's lifelong struggle against the abuses of privilege, therefore,
does not prove his claim that he was the virtue of human nature embodied, only that he was not tied to any interest that was in his period widely
perceived to be contrary to human nature. This disjunction between his
strategy and his claim to universality does not reduce the importance of
his political mediations, but it does mean that his humanist-metaphysical
claims for self should be separated from his historical feats. His persona
was a shrewd, personally and socially efficacious invention. In Franklin's
representations of his persona, however, it is more – the force of human
nature come into its own, liberated from the various sorts of obtuseness
that had formerly contaminated it. This advancement of historical strategy into metaphysics has two effects worthy of attention: it elevates opinions that were generally held in Franklin's period – such as that the poor
were poor because they fell short of the ingenuity and industriousness of
human nature (P, 15:104) – into superhistorical verities; and it demotes
uncalculating modes of thought and feeling – whether aesthetic, curious,
political, affectionate, or erotic – to the category of waste, of obstructive
non-nature, whence they will be rescued by Emerson, Thoreau, and
Whitman, as Franklin had rescued ingenuity from Mather's category of
the abominable.

Franklin naturalized his social strategy by analogically associating the
"unconcerned" self with other natural phenomena, a type of legitimation
already at work in Mather's connection of correct theology with the rectitude of the well-formed torso or of historical remembrance with the
continuity in the generations of the flowers. In a letter written to John
Perkins in 1753, Franklin showed his familiarity with Cotton Mather's
method of joining physical with spiritual phenomena (P, 4:439). Though
his purpose was to dispute with Mather, to show that unusual phenomena could be explained without appeal to spiritual agency and consequent
annulment of the rational capacity, Franklin's explorations of physical
reality nevertheless have figural reference to the natural self. Though
Franklin adhered to rational causal explanation, his choices of what phenomena to explore (and of what traits of those phenomena to explore)
frequently retain the analogical method extensively employed by Cotton
Mather in the sermons he preached during the period of Franklin's boy-
hood. Nature is an array of handy lessons. The whirlwind, an invisible
vortex that takes on the sensible properties of the surroundings it pulls
into itself; the small bit of oil that can disperse itself across the surface of
the water and calm it; the gulf stream, a nearly invisible current in the
midst of the other water that can speed or impede progress depending
on whether or not one conforms: in all of these cases, Franklin is both

exercising the rational self and figuratively delineating it. At various points in his career, Franklin wondered whether the several organizing forces in nature such as magnetism, electricity, and light were species of a single universal vibration in the cosmic medium; and his objections to Mesmerism in the mid-1780s had less to do with Mesmer's contention that animal magnetism was one version of a universal force than they did with the hysterical crises and the uncritical belief in miracle cures that were requisite at Mesmer's performances.[9] Mesmer's sessions would have seemed too much like a faintly disguised ecstatic religion requiring vocal paroxysms of conversion and abject submission to an alien will. But, for Franklin, if the universal self was analogous with (or even a species of) natural force in general, it would have to be orderly and obedient to its own law. Franklin's interest in Mesmerism suggests that his objections may have been on the order of refuting a simulacrum rather than of simply dismissing nonsense. Rational exemplary instruction, unlike hypnotic influence, would speak to a corresponding reason in those upon whom it acted, rather than requiring the surrender of self to another. In this, it would be analogous with electricity and money, both of which were pure and independent manifestations of a force latent in the particular things with which they interacted.

Franklin's interest in electricity should be held in the context of the Puritan use of thunder and lightning as symptoms of the voice of God. This *topos,* self-consciously and somewhat ironically revived in *The Waste Land,* was quite common in seventeenth-century Massachusetts literature. In Michael Wigglesworth's *God's Controversy with New England,* thunder is the voice of God breaking into men's declension: "The Air became tempestuous; / The wilderness gan quake: / And from above with awfull voice / Th' Almighty thundring spake." The image reappears in *The Day of Doom,* the first American bestseller:

> For at midnight brake forth a Light,
>   which turn'd the night to day,
> And speedily an hideous cry
>   did all the world dismay.
> Sinners awake, their hearts do ake,
>   trembling their loynes surprizeth;
> Amaz'd with fear, by what they hear,
>   each one of them ariseth.

John Josselyn used the image in his *Account of Two Voyages:*

> And Heaven to Seas descended: no star shown;
> Blind night in darkness, tempests, and her own
> Dread terrours lost; yet this dire lightning turns

[9] Van Doren, *Benjamin Franklin,* pp. 713–7.

To more fear'd light; the Sea with lightning Burns.
The Pilot knew not what to chuse or fly,
Art stood amaz'd in Ambiguity.[10]

The use of lightning as a suitable figure for divinity intruding in the night of self was common in sermons, such as Cotton Mather's *Une Grande Voix du ciel à la France*, or his "Brontologia Sacra," included in the *Magnalia Christi Americana*, which was preached extemporaneously upon the occasion of a thunderstorm in September 1694 (Mather was interrupted in the middle of his discourse to be told his house had been struck). Acknowledging the "Cartesian account," which holds that lightning and thunder are produced by "the common laws of matter and motion," Mather contends that the "*tonitruous* disposition and generation with which the air is impregnated" is nevertheless a sign from the God who made matter and motion. It reminds the faithful of Moses' reception of the law and of the turmoil of the Last Judgment; it humbles the self:

> Methinks there is that song of Hannah in the thunder (1 Sam ii. 3, 10), "Talk no more so exceedingly proudly; let not arrogancy come out of your mouth. For the adversaries of the Lord shall be broken to pieces; out of heaven shall be thunder upon them." The omnipotent God in the thunder speaks to those hardy Typhons, that are found fighting against him; and says, "Oh do not harden yourself against such a God; you are not stronger than he!" (*MCA*, II:368)

The association of lightning with humiliation recurs in Jonathan Edwards's *Personal Narrative*:

> Before, I used to be uncommonly terrified with thunder, and to be struck with terror when I saw a thunder storm rising; but now, on the contrary, it rejoiced me. I felt God, so to speak, at the first appearance of a thunder storm; and used to take the opportunity to fix myself in order to view the clouds, and see the lightnings play, and hear the majestic and awful voice of God's thunder, which oftentimes was exceedingly entertaining, leading me to sweet contemplations of my great and glorious God.[11]

In Puritan symbolism, lightning is associated with what Mather called the "self-annihilating stroke," the violent intervention of divine wrath into the complacent and secular self of the first and third steps in *The Christian Philosopher* – a terror that could be overcome only by giving over the self and ascending to perfect conformity with the sweet yoke of alien and superrational law.

Franklin's electrical experiments, therefore, take place in a rich sym-

---

[10] Harrison T. Messerole, ed., *Seventeenth Century American Poetry* (New York: New York University Press, 1968), pp. 46, 56, 404.

[11] Jonathan Edwards, *Works* (New York: G. & C. & H. Carvill, 1830), vol. 1, p. 62.

bolical context, and it seems safe to assume that he knew his researches
had connotations beyond their empirical theses. When he demonstrated
that the rod could make the lightning detour the house, that lightning
actually leaped from earth to sky, that the "electrical fluid" was a passive
component of the commonest things, or that electricity could be brought
to earth and bottled by the device of a key on the string of a kite, he was
recording observed fact *and* signifying the modern period – the appropriation of divine virtues by the earthbound secular self. This Prome-
thean symbolism – treated explicitly in the writings of Kant, Byron, and
Sainte-Beuve – was an important part of Franklin's renown during his
own time; so important, in fact, that, during the Revolution, George III
declared that his lightning rods would have round tops, rather than points,
as Franklin's had. Franklin's electrical experiments were both examples
of Enlightenment inquiry and images of the Enlightenment's act of lay-
ing claim to the virtues man had previously beheld from afar in the divinity that demanded self-annihilation. Self had become godly: Franklin
reported that the ingenious electrician could make artificial spiders dance
(*P,* 3:133) and that he might be able to alleviate or even cure paralysis (*P,*
7:298–300). In a 1784 letter Franklin notes that Mesmer's patients are too
eager to deceive themselves, but he adds that "maladies caused by ob-
structions may be treated by electricity with advantage" (*W,* X:75–6).

It is therefore appropriate that Franklin should call electrical lumines-
cence a "virtue" (*P,* 5:68) and that his writings on the relation of electricity to the "common Matter" into which it enters should echo his discussions of the relation between the representative self and its surrounding
society: "The Electrical Matter consists of Particles extremely subtile,
since it can permeate common Matter, even the densest Mettals, with
such Ease and Freedom as not to receive any perceptible Resistance" (*P,*
4:10). Franklin is not simply intrigued with electricity here: he *admires* it,
and *personifies* it with attributes such as subtlety, ease, and freedom, though
this is perhaps less an ornamental personification than a detection of actual analogy between two natural forces – electricity and self. Franklin
emphasized this permeating subtlety on several subsequent occasions in
similar terms: "Your Conception of the Electric Fluid, that it is incom-
parably more subtil than Air, is undoubtedly just. It pervades dense Matter with the greatest ease" (*P,* 4:298); "this matter of lightning, or of
electricity, is an extremely subtle fluid, penetrating other bodies, and
subsisting in them, equally diffused" (*P,* 14:261). As exemplary reason
can enter all men, despite their array of differences, so electricity enters
all matter – with ease and freedom, without sore disruption. Though
Franklin did recognize the danger posed by electricity in the form of
lightning, the brunt of many of his experiments was that the motion of
the fluid *need not* be violent.

As electricity enters its various containers, it is essentially continous: its nature does not vary, only the vessels. Like fire, it is in its vessels, but not of them.

> And yet the fire when produced, though in different bodies it may differ in circumstances, as in colour, vehemence, &c., yet in the same bodies is generally the same. Does this not seem to indicate that the fire existed in the body, though in a quiescent state, before it was by any of these means excited, disengaged, and brought forth to action and to view? (P, 10:49)

The same is true of electricity, he goes on to argue, but electricity does not consume its vessel in emerging, a difference that reprises the difference between piety and reason. The particular manifestations of electricity are properties of its circumstances, not of the electricity itself, and those circumstances do not essentially affect it: rather, it returns to its indeterminate, versatile purity when it is released or "set . . . at liberty to act" (P, 10:49). Like the ingenious self, electricity enters and leaves its temporary homes, always returning to itself unaltered. This essential sameness of electricity beneath its diverse appearances was what the experiment with the kite was designed to demonstrate: "At this Key the Phial may be charg'd; and from the Electric Fire thus obtain'd, Spirits may be kindled, and all the other Electric Experiments be perform'd, which are usually done by the Help of a rubbed Glass Globe or Tube; and thereby the *Sameness* of the Electric Matter with that of Lightning compleatly demonstrated" (P, 4:367). A month or so before the experiment with the kite, Franklin had written that "I think the Electric Fluid is always the same." He added that "I find the weaker and stronger Sparks differ in Apparent Colour, some white, blue, purple, red; the strongest white, weak ones red" (P, 4:300). The *appearance* of qualitative variation disguises a qualitative constancy varying only in quantitative intensity. Such appearances of variety can also be generated by the medium in which electricity is performing: the air does not conduct electricity readily, so water in the air accounts for electricity manifesting itself as the leap of lightning; the degree of the air's dryness affects the quality of the thunderclap; and sulfurous vapors rising from stacks of moist hay, corn, or other vegetables can make the lightning seem to have an odor (P, 3:365–76). Color, noise, and odor are not qualitatively particular properties of the electricity itself, but instead products of its entrance into qualitatively particular things. Like the soul in the *Dissertation on Liberty and Necessity, Pleasure and Pain*, electricity is distinct from the properties it takes on. Like that soul, or the self in the *Autobiography*, it is only apprehensible in its moments of transfer from form to form, in its freedom from the particularities it enters: "For the Electrical Fire is never visible but when in Motion, and leaping from Body to Body; or from Particle to Particle thro' the Air . . . in passing along a Chain, it becomes visible as it leaps from Link to Link" (*P,* 3:372–3); a chain, perhaps, that is like the diverse series of occupations detailed in the *Autobiography.* Electricity, with its permeating subtlety, is analogous with the rational character Franklin designed for address to the dense and various populations of Pennsylvania. Embarking on these electrical experiments in his mid-forties, having resigned from single-minded dedication to business, Franklin is emulating electricity, showing that self is distinct from its vessel. Or perhaps he is meditating on the subtlety he had developed as a businessman during the previous decades. During this period, he had managed to make himself so entirely useful and inoffensive that he had been well received in virtually all quarters to which he had applied himself; and they were many, since as printer and editor of the *Pennsylvania Gazette* he had attempted to be a "UNIVERSAL INSTRUCTOR," to speak to the experience of Pennsylvanians in general. The electrical experiments represent a kind of meditative pause between the editor-businessman's diplomacy that had preceded them, and the political diplomacy that interrupted them. In 1784, contending that, though factions differed on procedure, their friction would bring out the fact that they were all concerned with the general good, Franklin wrote that parties "will exist wherever there is liberty; perhaps they help to preserve it. By the collision of different sentiments, sparks of truth are set out, and political light is obtained" (*W,* II:465). The spark contained in the common matter is like the rational ground of consensus contained within the human particularities of interest. For fifty-three years, he had been considering himself the spokesman for that general interest – the spark leaped free from its vessel, into its pure state.

In itself without qualitative variation, electricity varies only in quantity. Franklin's greatest contributions to the theory of electricity, according to I. Bernard Cohen, were his development of the law of the conservation of charge, which stipulated that there was no quantitative degradation or enhancement of electricity as a result of its entrance into a body, and his insight into positive and negative charge, plus or minus, *amount.*[12] Strictly speaking, variation in amount was therefore not a property of the electricity per se, which stayed constant, but instead a means of apprehending the things that electricity charged. It was a mode of representing the world of matter: the electrician could ignore, or transcend, the uniquenesses of things, and see them instead in a scheme of pure commensurability, as so much measurable presence or absence of electricity. As a mode of symbolization, the electrician's view enjoys the perfect clarity of number, giving him a godlike purchase on the nature

[12] I. Bernard Cohen, *Benjamin Franklin: Scientist and Statesman* (New York: Scribner, 1975), pp. 49–56.

of the physical universe: "[God is] *notoriously the greatest mechanic in the universe;* having, as the Scripture testifies, made all things, and that by *weight* and *measure*."[13] He is not, however, the only such mechanic. The electrician can also ascend to an epistemological height where the seemingly complex quiddities of things are reduced to number:

> The knocking down of the six men was performed with two of my large jarrs not fully charged. I laid one end of my discharging rod upon the head of the first; he laid his hand on the head of the second; the second his hand on the head of the third, and so to the last, who held, in his hand, the chain that was connected with the outside of the jarrs. When they were thus placed, I applied the other end of my rod to the prime-conductor, and they all dropt together . . . A person so struck, sinks down doubled, or folded together as it were, the joints losing their strength and stiffness at once, so that he that drops on the spot where he stood, instantly, and there is no previous staggering, nor does he ever fall lengthwise. Too great a charge might, indeed, kill a man, but I have not yet seen any hurt done by it. It would certainly, as you observe, be the easiest of all deaths. (*P,* 5:525)

In this episode, the six men are reduced to so much quantitative readiness to receive, and they are qualitatively identical. Franklin's mode of representing human life rarely reached this level of cold abstraction, where the moral question of murder is less interesting than the question of tolerable magnitude of charge: but the tendency toward a pure and untroubled mode of symbolization is constantly present, in his demographic writings, for example, so that this experiment represents a kind of limit-case, rather than a simple exception.

As the experiment with the six men suggests, the circulation of electricity could furnish an analogy for pedagogy – for the easing of a student's stiff commitment to unreason – as well as for rational symbolization: in 1773 Franklin wondered whether electricity could be used for tenderizing meat, but reluctantly concluded it would only toughen the meat (*W,* V:456–8). Though the total amount of electricity remained constant, the "electrical kiss" could elicit the electricity latent in things and thus swell the amount of freed electricity: "There are no Bounds (but what Expence and Labour give) to the Force man may raise and use in the Electric Way: For Bottle may be added to Bottle *in infinitum,* and all united and discharg'd together as One, the Force and Effect proportioned to their Number and Size" (*P,* 4:202). The experiment with the six men showed that such a conversion into oneness, and consequent enhancement of the total, could even operate with human bodies, though Franklin's discharging rod was not always required:

[13] Quoted in Aldridge, *Benjamin Franklin and Nature's God,* p. 41.

We electrise a Person 20 or more Times running, with the Touch of the Finger on the Wire, thus; He stands on Wax; give him the electrised Bottle in his Hand; touch the Wire with your Finger, and then touch his Hand or Face, there are Sparks every Time. We encrease the Force of the Electrical Kiss vastly, thus; Let A and B stand on Wax; give one of them the electrised Vial in hand; let the other take hold of the Wire; there will be a small Spark; but when their Lips approach, they will be struck and shockt. (*P*, 3:132–3)

The initial charging of the vial is done by the electrician. To generate "American Electricity" (*P*, 3:132), "we rub our Tubes with Buck Skin, and observe always to keep the same Side to the Tube, and never to sully the Tube by handling . . . This I mention, because the European Papers on Electricity frequently speak of rubbing the Tube as a fatiguing Exercise" (*P*, 3:134). The circulation of electricity can engender an attraction among the matter of man as well as among other matter. It is thus an analogy for rational pedagogy, which taught Horatio that self-cultivation could be his greatest pleasure.

The traits Franklin discerned in the movement of the electrical fluid – subtlety, power of permeation, freedom from qualitative distinctiveness, abstract symbolization, the power to elicit a corresponding element from the particularity of its surroundings, and accumulation through unification – reappear in his discussions of money. In *A Modest Enquiry into the Nature and Necessity of a Paper Currency* (1729), Franklin observed that the diverse kinds of Pennsylvanian productive activity were without sufficient cash to encourage them and to organize them into a well-functioning whole, and he argued vigorously for a paper currency originating in the colony. He was rewarded with the printing contract for several issues of bills, and he devised ingenious techniques for preventing counterfeiting.[14] He was thoroughly involved with money – personally (in his business), technically (in his printing of currency), and theoretically (in his speculations on the *nature* of money).

More than a few of Franklin's apologists have exonerated Franklin from the implicit contention of Max Weber's *The Protestant Ethic and the Spirit of Capitalism*, that he was a spokesman for the single-minded dedication of life to moneymaking. They have pointed out that Franklin gave up

[14] Eric P. Newman, "Franklin Making Money More Plentiful," *Proceedings of the American Philosophical Society*, vol. 115, no. 4 (August 20, 1971), pp. 341–9; John R. Aiken, "Benjamin Franklin, Karl Marx, and the Labor Theory of Value," *The Pennsylvania Magazine of History and Biography*, vol. 90, no. 3 (July 1966), pp. 278–84; W. A. Wetzel, "Benjamin Franklin as Economist," *Johns Hopkins University Studies in Historical and Political Science*, 13th ser., no. 9 (September 1895), pp. 7–58.

complete absorption in swelling his personal capital when he embarked on his electrical experiments, to the point where he faced several fiscal crises in his later life. Franklin's career as a whole is therefore too varied and multiple to be reduced to Weber's portrait. However, they do not consider that versatile efficaciousness was the attribute that Franklin emphasized most in his descriptions of the nature of money, and therefore they fail to consider the analogy between the self and money itself. Giving up moneymaking as its sole occupation, the self would be more like money. In *The Way to Wealth,* written ten years after Franklin had withdrawn from active participation in his printing business, Poor Richard hears his maxims recited at length by another, the sententious Father Abraham, and he watches Father Abraham's auditors wander off and start buying as if they had heard nothing, but only listened politely, as if to a sermon. The confinement of self to the manufacture of pecuniary wisdom, Richard may have realized, could reduce his power to earn the acclaim of his contemporaries.

Therefore, in the *Autobiography,* in which Franklin demonstrates that moneymaking is just one manifestation of the factotum-self's abstract capacity, he analogically associates self with money at several points. Near the end of Part One, remarking that the wealthy had opposed paper currency, Franklin remembers himself walking about the streets of Philadelphia in 1729, observing that, whereas before there had been houses with *to let* notices on their doors, there are now old houses inhabited and new ones built. He attributes this prosperity to the increase in trade employment that came about as a result of a 1723 issue of paper money. In addition, he carefully notes that the streets on which he was strolling are the same ones he walked when he first entered Philadelphia, "eating my Roll": as the paper money has overcome initial skepticism, earned a reputation for itself, and thus become able to vitalize the life of Pennsylvanian society, so too has Franklin's self in the time since he first walked into town (*A:*124). In Part Three, Franklin contends that George Whitefield allowed certain "unguarded expressions" into his writings that reduced his reputation after his death, and in the next paragraph follows that observation with the assertion that money is "prolific" and can reproduce itself *in infinitum* (*A:*180–1). And in Part Four, in the last paragraph of the book as it stands, the Pennsylvania Assembly, observing the success of the paper money, votes acclaim to Franklin, who first recommended the bills (*A:*266).

The third reminiscence, like many of the papers on electricity, operates on two rhetorical levels. On the causal level, Franklin's advocacy of paper money, like the majority of his ingenious innovations, proves to have been useful, and so fuses the population into a consensus of acclaim that certifies the identity of his self with human nature. On the analogical level, paper money is itself dependent on a general social acceptance that acknowledges its validity, and so, unlike the bifocals or the stove, it is *like* self, as well as being testimony to self's ingenuity. As in the papers on electricity, this reminiscence closing the *Autobiography* both shows the self's deftness in action and analogically represents that deftness.

In *A Modest Enquiry into the Nature and Necessity of a Paper Currency,* Franklin contended that the source of value is labor, thus anticipating Adam Smith, though perhaps borrowing heavily, to the point of including slightly paraphrased sentences, from Sir William Petty. He may also have encountered a rudimentary labor theory of value in an anonymous pamphlet (attributed to Cotton Mather in T. J. Holmes's bibliography) where the association of money and metal is criticized as a kind of secular idolatry that mistakes an arbitrary sign for an essence. According to the pamphleteer, the *"Nature of Money"* is its symbolic function as a *"Counter or Measure* of mens Proprieties and Instituted *mean* of permutation."[15] Though in *The Christian Philosopher* Mather would rebuke those who felt that gold has a soul and who worshiped gold as a god (*CP*:119–22), the 1691 pamphlet chastises those who confuse gold with the permutative power of productive man, rather than with creative divinity. Franklin mounts a similar demystification of gold, contending that it had proved a useful symbol of labor because it is portable, divisible, and rare. But herein lay the problem: as Georg Simmel argues, gold must be rare above a certain minimum necessary supply;[16] but in Pennsylvania, as in many colonies, the amount of coin often fell below that minimum, in part because money necessarily flows from a producer of raw materials to a producer of finished goods. Franklin proposes that, since gold is only a symbol, another symbol will do, and he advocates a paper currency. But he realizes that this is a controversial proposition. Through long association, gold has been taken to *be* value, rather than a symbol of value, whereas paper money is obviously a symbol and so seems less trustworthy. Consequently Franklin stresses that labor is the source of value: if the Pennsylvanians' reason is sufficient to understand, they will realize that all forms of money are symbolical, and they will choose the most efficacious form. The use of paper currency will raise their economy up from barter, and encourage investment development. In a sense, paper money is the *most* rational money, since the relative valuelessness of the paper and ink calls attention to the material vehicle's function as symbol, as persona, rather than embodiment, of value. For those

15 Wetzel, "Benjamin Franklin as Economist," pp. 30–1; *Some Considerations on the Bills of Credit Now passing in New-England* (Boston, 1691), p. 2.
16 Georg Simmel, *The Philosophy of Money,* trans. Tom Bottomore and David Frisby (Boston: Routledge & Kegan Paul, 1978).

whose skepticism remains and for whom the symbol of value must have value itself, Franklin proposes a land bank, not because land is value, but because Pennsylvania has more land than gold. But this proposal is only a concession to residual unreason. The most rational money is not one that poses as an embodiment of value, but one that is known as a society's general consensual symbolization of its collective productivity. Money is not valid because it is a particular embodiment, but because in accepting it, in acclaiming it as effective symbol, a society collectively and consciously perceives that value is not an exterior thing, such as gold, but instead the human nature that runs throughout it. Like self, money teaches men what their nature is; and their consequent acclaim validates it.

This human nature is labor in the abstract, divested of its particular characteristics and refined down to its common denominator, intelligence and energy (or ingenuity and industry, to use Franklin's terms) directed toward a goal and against the resistance of the materials. Hence Franklin's association of money and self: if money is a symbol of human nature, and if Franklin's self is a pure epitome of human nature, then money can also signify self. Money's field of action, like the rational self's, is the diversity of the total human community:

> As Providence has so ordered it, that not only different Countries, but even different Parts of the same Country, have their peculiar most suitable Productions; and likewise that different Men have Geniuses adapted to Variety of different Arts and Manufactures, Therefore *Commerce,* or the Exchange of one Commodity or Manufacture for Another, is highly convenient and Beneficial to Mankind. As for instance, A may be skilful in the Art of making Cloth, and B understands the raising of Corn; A wants corn, and B Cloth; upon which they make an Exchange with each other for as much as each has Occasion, to the mutual Advantage and Satisfaction of both. (*P,* 1:148)

Despite A's and B's diversity of particular genius, their work has a common element, because their products can be exchanged; despite the obvious physical differences of the commodities, they are numerically commensurable based on the amount of the common element each contains. Discovering this element common to both of their labors in the practical act of exchanging, the producers reach agreement, "the mutual Advantage and Satisfaction of both."

Abstract labor is the common element, and money is the symbol of it:

> But as it would be very tedious, if there were no other way of general Dealing, but by an immediate Exchange of Commodities; because a Man that has Corn to dispose of, and wanted Cloth for it, might perhaps, in his search for a Chapman to deal with, meet with Twenty People that had Cloth to dispose of, but wanted no Corn; and with Twenty others that wanted his Corn, but had no cloth to suit him; to

remedy such Inconveniences, and facilitate Exchange, Men have invented MONEY, properly called a *Medium of Exchange*, because through
or by its Means Labour is exchanged for Labour, or one Commodity
for another. (*P*, 1:148)

Mediating between particular forms of productive activity, money signifies labor in the abstract, separated from its particular vessels, in them,
but not of them. Though Franklin begins with qualitative diversity,
therefore, the tendency of his reasoning is away from it, toward a purely
quantitative and transcendental appraisal of human economic life: as the
electrician sees the various common matters in terms of the amount of a
single subtle, universally pervasive element they contain, the economist
sees instances of human productivity reduced to the sums of value they
contain. Because it is the representation of human labor purged of all
qualitative distinctness, money can symbolize (or *buy*) all things insofar
as they are containers of abstract labor:

> And whatever particular Thing Men have agreed to make this Medium
> of, whether Gold, Silver, Copper, or Tobacco, it is, to those who pos-
> sess it (if they want any Thing), that very Thing which they want,
> because it will immediately procure it for them. It is Cloth to him that
> wants Cloth, and Corn to those that want Corn; and so of all other
> Necessaries, it *is* whatever it will procure. (P, 1:148)

Like the electrician, the economist is concerned with a universal substance that gives him a godly outlook on the surrounding world from
which he can view all things in undisturbed numerical comparison; the
obscurity of uniqueness and apparent qualitative incommensurability lies
behind him.[17]

The circulation of money, like the circulation of electricity, can serve
as a model for pedagogical influence. When it is used for investment,
money converts the disparity of products into the qualitative uniformity
of an accumulating sum, at least from the perspective of the investor.
Though in the passages quoted above Franklin is making his pitch to
those Pennsylvanians who wish to sell their products in order to buy
others, the bulk of the pamphlet is directed to those who wish to invest.

---

[17] My argument throughout this chapter, but especially here, is informed by the
brilliant speculations on money's psychological significance in Simmel's *Philosophy of Money*, Weber's *The Protestant Ethic and the Spirit of Capitalism*, and
Marx's *A Contribution to a Critique of Political Economy*, *Grundrisse*, and *Capital*,
vol. 1. I have abstained from quoting extensively from this group of books
simply because Simmel, Weber, and Marx are so frequently to the point that
I could not find a few brief relevant remarks. Any of my readers who wish to
pursue the topic of bourgeois capital as a form of metaphysics, rather than as
a practical opponent to metaphysics, should begin with the works listed above.

When money is in short supply, Franklin argues, those who wish to use money to get money will tend to use it in the safe way of usury. But, if money is more plentiful, the group of borrowers will be smaller, and the former usurers will "venture their money at sea" or invest in land. Investment will "double the supply of running Cash," a term that also appears in Mather's *Some Considerations on the Bills of Credit Now passing in New-England* in connection with paper money's electrifying effect on economy. Usury is criticized for its timidity, not for its chrematistic motive. The pamphlet is addressed primarily to those who are accumulating sums of money, not to those who are looking to buy luxuries or necessities to consume. Though Franklin is departing from his earlier appeal to producers wanting others' products, he does not acknowledge this difference within his audience. And the appeal to investors is a logical culmination to his theory of money, as well as a pragmatic appeal to those with true influence: quantitative appraisal is perfected in investment, where purchase is motivated not by need or want, but by the calculation of potential yield; and, though money can represent all things, any given sum of money cannot buy all things, so any expenditure other than investment would extinguish the money's vitality, returning it to the merely particular, whereas investment would keep the money alive, incrementally projecting it toward absolute wealth. The abstinence from uncalculating enjoyment that Franklin recommends in his "Advice to a Young Tradesman," *Way to Wealth,* and the *Autobiography* keeps the calculating self free from adulteration, as Philocles recommended, and it also keeps the young man's money ready for the growth which is its natural life:

> Remember that Money is of a prolific generating Nature. Money can beget Money, and its Offspring can beget more, and so on. Five Shillings turn'd, is *Six:* Turn'd again, 'tis Seven and Three Pence; and so on 'til it becomes an Hundred Pounds. The more there is of it, the more it produces every Turning, so that the Profits rise quicker and quicker. He that kills a breeding Sow, destroys all her Offspring to the thousandth Generation. He that murders a Crown, destroys all it might have produc'd, even Scores of Pounds. (*P,* 3:303)

Franklin's vocabulary – "prolific," "beget," "murder" – makes the growth of money a natural and procreative process. If no unreasonable despotism obstructs it, money, like Polly Baker's progeny or like the generations of Americans that double every twenty years, will grow freely ad infinitum, along an arithmetical progression which can make the minuscule huge in a relatively short time. As the "Advice to a Young Tradesman" is careful to point out, the arithmetical progression of the five shillings toward a fortune is analogous with the progression of the young man's character toward an extensive and admirable reputation. Public activity, as Franklin may have learned from Mather's *Bonifacius,* is an investment, a small practical expression of good intention that can convert large numbers into consensual conformity with it.

But Franklin's appeals to monetary investors are incongruous with his assertion that money is a symbol of human nature, rather than an embodiment. When the euphoria that the economist derives from his transcendental vantage on human society turns him into a moneymaker who thinks he can possess human nature in compact form, he has confused the vehicle with the tenor. And he has betrayed self: though the investor resists spending money on particular things to consume, he heedlessly spends self on a single preoccupation, moneymaking, and so removes self from free circulation; though the moneymaker may become renowned for his fortune and for his avarice, he will not be seen as human nature in the abstract. As in *Bonifacius,* actual moneymaking can distract a man from the activity that the circulation of money had been made to signify, in Mather's case, self-annihilating piety, in Franklin's, self-disciplined exemplification of rational human nature. Franklin continues to encourage investment, because it invigorates society, but he realizes that by confusing the sign with what it signifies the moneymaker succumbs to a particular passion and ends up obscuring the analogy between self and money. So Franklin withdraws from active participation in his own business to embark on electrical experiments and public service, thereby demonstrating a nonspecific ingenuity analogous to the money he had analyzed in *A Modest Enquiry into the Nature and Necessity of a Paper Currency.*

Something of this motive may also lie behind his conversion to French physiocracy in the late 1760s. His physiocratic writings do not challenge his basic contention that labor is the source of value, but they do lay special stress on agricultural labor as a source of value. According to Carl Van Doren, the emphasis on agriculture was a way of distancing the American economy from the British economy, of exempting America from what Franklin had been observing in England.[18] In his major physiocratic statement, *Positions to Be Examined, Concerning National Wealth* (1769), Franklin argued that there were three ways for a nation to increase its wealth: war, commerce, and agriculture. War was robbery. Commerce, Franklin remarks, is "generally *cheating.*" This remark may seem curious, but it follows from *A Modest Enquiry into the Nature and Necessity of a Paper Currency:* if exchange is properly exchange of equal values, then only improper exchange or speculative investment can yield a profit. Once

[18] Van Doren, *Benjamin Franklin,* pp. 371–2.

a land is stably settled, like England, and once its merchants have learned not to be sharped, exchange will settle into exchange of equals. In that case, agriculture will be revealed as the true source of wealth, because it regularly produces what the physiocrats called a *produit net,* a product worth more than the farmer's maintenance requires.

The interesting thing about *Positions to Be Examined, Concerning National Wealth* is that Franklin does not discuss industry, in which there is also a *produit net* – surplus value, the disparity between what a worker requires to maintain himself and what he produces. This omission must be deliberate: in *On the Labouring Poor,* written in the previous year, Franklin allowed that "there are middle men, who make a profit, and even get estates, by purchasing the labour of the poor, and selling it at advanced prices to the rich" (*P,* 15:106). Franklin is plainly dismayed by the English poor in this pamphlet, and he offers one consolation, that the rich will spend their money and so the poor will get it back again, an odd and unpersuasive remark coming from a theorist of accumulation such as Franklin. Franklin's remark that commerce is generally cheating shows he had reached Marx's conclusion that "circulation . . . begets no value":[19] he had begun to consider that in a rationalized market the growth of wealth would have to come from a commodity that produced more than it cost – labor power. Investment capital would therefore tend of its own innate motion to transform a nation of free entrepreneurs into a nation of wage-laborers, subordinated to masters, pressed into particular niches in an ingenious division of labor. Franklin's English sojourn showed him a nightmare American future, and this led him to celebrate the virtues of American agriculture, where one retained his own *produit net,* and where his "innocent life and virtuous industry" were not pressed into service to another or confined by that master to a specific and delimited performance (*P,* 16:107–9).

The free farmer would retain the virtue Franklin had praised in Dupont de Nemours, one of the fathers of physiocracy, "freedom from local and national prejudices and partialities, so much benevolence to mankind in general" (*P,* 15:181). By being exempted from the sort of capital combinations already common in England, the American farmer would be more like money.

I am not proposing that analogy in Franklin's writings on electricity and money introduces a hidden agenda that annuls them as rational inquiry, nor that his theories of electricity and money are in every aspect intentionally symbolical. Rather, I claim that at many points a double

---

[19] Karl Marx, *Capital,* trans. Samuel Moore and Edward Aveling (New York: International Publishers, 1967), vol. 1, p. 163.

purpose is at work – rational inquiry, and the development of recurrent formal themes – and that the rhetorical purpose of this recurrence is to naturalize by analogy (and so to legitimate) self-design and the pursuit of reputation as Franklin conceived them. Franklin's virtue, unlike Mather's, is deliberately nonspecific, so that the self's ingenuity will not be tied to a standard outside of itself, as money is not to be tied to gold. Without a sure standard of validation, however, Franklin must seek legitimation in the human community's universal recognition, and/or in the demonstration of analogy between self's socially efficacious tact and the behavior of natural entities such as electricity or paraprocreative money. Self-design is authorized by its resemblance to unrestricted, spontaneous nature.

Franklin's writings on electricity and money contain two recurring themes. First, Franklin celebrates the emergent independent purity of a natural substance that can pervade all things because it is free from their particularities. This pervasion enables a sufficient transcendental symbolization of the things pervaded based on their reduction to lucid commensurability, to the presence or absence of quantities of the natural substance. Second, Franklin describes the substance's additive power to reproduce itself endlessly by soliciting the latent nature within the things pervaded, bringing additional specimens of nature into the clearing and joining them in a uniform whole. The common aspect of both themes is abstraction: the natural substance's subtlety is based on its blank "unconcernedness," its freedom from common qualitative characteristic; consequently, its history, or life story, can only be the monotony of quantitative diminution or accumulation, since qualitative transformation would be the beginning of a different history, the melancholy tale of electricity trapped or money spent.

These themes reappear in what Paul W. Conner describes as the two major concerns of the political theory Franklin derived from his observation of Pennsylvanian life. First, Franklin looked consistently for "'happy mediocrity'" or "cultural homogeneity," the common denominator subtending the ethnic, religious, and economic disparities of the Pennsylvanians. Second, he described this mediocrity not by tying it to an explicit definition, but by celebrating its power to grow. According to Conner, Franklin's idea of a society "was a dynamic one, for Franklin's conception of the Virtuous Order was rooted in the American continent. Here the ideal society would increase numerically, expand geographically, and rise culturally." "The vision of a people at work animated his social thought," Conner contends, "infusing it with purpose and meaning. The Virtuous Order was never at rest; with its constant achieving, producing, and growing, it strikes the modern reader as rather exhausting." In his "desire for an expanding material output," Franklin was "implacable": "there was something about human life – especially in quantity – that set him to scholarship, and energized his politics."[20]

In America, the particular commodity noble birth has no value: "people do not inquire concerning a Stranger, *What is he?* but, *What can he do?*" The careful qualitative definition of nature (human or otherwise) is less important than the celebration of its power to grow:

> There is, in short, no Bound to the prolific Nature of Plants or Animals, but what is made by their crowding and interfering with each other's means of Subsistence . . . In fine, a Nation well regulated is like a Polypus; take away a Limb, its place is soon supply'd; cut it in two, and each deficient Part shall speedily grow out of the Part remaining. Thus if you have Room and Subsistence enough, as you may by dividing, make ten Polypes out of one, you may of one make ten Nations, equally populous and powerful; or rather increase a Nation ten fold in Numbers and Strength. (*P*, 4:233–4)

A. Owen Aldridge calls this idea Franklin's "philoprogenitiveness," "the vindication of maximum procreation,"[21] and notes its presence in "The Speech of Polly Baker":

> Take into your wise Consideration, the great and growing Number of Batchelors in the Country, many of whom from the mean Fear of the Expences of a Family, have never sincerely and honourably courted a Woman in their Lives; and by their Manner of Living have left unproduced (which is little better than Murder) Hundreds of their Posterity to the Thousandth Generation. (*P*, 3:125)

This enthusiasm for arithmetic progression will reappear as the nation-polyp and the shilling-breeding-sow, and in Franklin's preface to Heberdeen's pamphlet on smallpox inoculation, in which the criticisms printed in the *New England Courant* have been succeeded by numerical rapture:

> On the whole, if the chance were only as *two to one* in favour of the practice among children, would it not be sufficient to induce a tender parent to lay hold of the advantage? But when it is so much greater, as it appears to be by these accounts (in some even as *thirty to one*) surely parents will no longer refuse to accept and thankfully use a discovery GOD in his mercy has been pleased to bless mankind with; whereby some check now may be put to the ravages that cruel disease has been accustomed to make, and the human species be again suffered to increase as it did before the small-pox made its appearance. This increase has indeed been more obstructed by that distemper than is usually

[20] Paul W. Conner, *Poor Richard's Politics: Benjamin Franklin and His New American Order* (New York: Oxford University Press, 1965), pp. x, 16, 40, 46, 69, 75, 88.
[21] Aldridge, *Benjamin Franklin and Nature's God*, p. 133.

imagined: For the loss of one in ten thereby is not merely the loss of so many persons, but the accumulated loss of all the children and childrens children the deceased might have had, multiplied by successive generations. (*P*, 8:286)

Beginning with the passion of a parent's love, Franklin moves quickly to the abstraction of seeing each child as a child-producing unit. Though "The Speech of Polly Baker" may be, as Aldridge contends, a vindication *of* maximum growth, Franklin's more frequent strategy vindicates *by* the description of maximum growth. The polyp doubles itself asexually, and its progeny are not different beings, really, but essential continuations of itself; spontaneous multiplication, so horrifying in Mather's image of the Antinomian hydra, is for Franklin deeply satisfying, because it is orderly self-fathering, rather than a proliferating menace to government.

The Franklinian self plays an instrumental part in this burgeoning of the free nation: its blank "unconcernedness" epitomizes the general "mediocrity," and its consequent accumulating reputation catalyzes a simultaneously accumulating consensus among those who admire him. In Franklin's *Autobiography*, his account of self and its fame, the two themes from his writings on electricity and money, appear as self-construction (and that self's power to apprehend its world), the topic of Part One, and as education, or influence, the topic of Parts Two, Three, and Four. Franklin's aim in reviving both themes in the *Autobiography* is to inspire the reader to follow his example. The *Autobiography* is Franklin's most sustained pedagogical tract, an attempt to prolong the accumulation of reputation narrated in Parts Two, Three, and Four by inciting the reader to imitate the procedure narrated in Part One. Though the text terminates abruptly, in another sense it is unended: so long as there are admiring readers, the polyp is still dividing, and that first breeding-sow lives in her contemporary progeny.

In his *Autobiography*, Franklin abjures the rhetorical resources of Mather's jeremiads; he cannot conjure obligation, guilt, or shame in any direct way, because these would contradict nature rather than obey nature. They would repel Horatio. Consequently, incentive is his major resource, and it guides his revival of the two themes from his electrical and monetary inquiries: in Parts Two, Three, and Four he shows that the reward for self-design is potentially great, and in Part One he shows that the cost of self-design is not terrible. As Philocles contended, this discipline is in service to self, and thus it is not a sacrifice. The thesis of the *Autobiography* is that self-design is not a duty but a bargain: consequently, Franklin will not publicly deliberate over whether self is, like its predecessor, a harsh master to the whole of conscious life, or whether the incessant pursuit of accumulating quantities of reputation might be less than the good life. Instead, he will show the easy exit of the gist from its accidental vehicles, and the clarity and reward that the exit instigates.

The deepest allure of Franklin's example, perhaps, is not the fame and fortune, but the clarity, or, better, the clarification that such a self achieves. From the vantage of nature, the Franklinian self, like the electrician and the economist, views the things and persons of its world as abstract quanta, as vessels that contain or lack amounts of the substance that the self epitomizes perfectly. This calculus occurs within consciousness, when self surveys personal inclinations in order to assess the degree to which they advance or impede the life-project – to evaluate them as investments. The abstraction this process involves is apparent in Franklin's judgment that nonproductive impulses are a waste of time, a judgment that reduces a desire or interest to its minimally descriptive attribute, the fact that it has duration. At the most elemental level of will, the project rejects the vitality of traits and inclinations that cannot be classified in its evaluative category. The calculus also occurs between self and the members of its world, when self observes its contemporaries (such as Collins, Ralph, or Keimer in the *Autobiography*) in order to assess whether the ingenuity within them is sufficient to overcome what are made to seem their quirky, inexplicable passions. Franklin's pragmatism advertises itself as realistic by contrasting itself with Puritan attention to abstract truth that transcends secular circumstances. However, this pragmatism's resolute attachment to the calculus of benefit against loss is itself a way of being distanced from the actual through the reduction of the actual to quanta: it is itself as much in contradiction with the invitation of life as its predecessor was; but, unlike the Puritan Father, the Pragmatic Son conceals his reductive discipline, rather than emphasizing it.

Following this procedure of clarification, the Franklinian self acquires a godlike vantage on the interior and exterior human worlds. The Puritan god's primary activity toward man was assessment: to him, individual men were not unique or precious complexes, but vessels full or empty of piety. Congregational authority assumed the power of godlike assessment in the institution of the conversion requirement for church membership. But in the finest and most eloquent Puritan literature, the distance between harsh Winthropian clarification and an affection for the particularity of something cherished is emphasized, made into a precautionary focal concern: in the writings of Mary White Rowlandson and Anne Bradstreet, for example, or in Edwards's *Personal Narrative,* where the trip from the way of the heart to reconciliation with assessing divinity is arduous, and filled with regrets and rebellions. The insistence on contradiction between the personal and the transcendental view recurs in the pained affirmations of the great elegiac statements of the American Renaissance, such as "Threnody," "When Lilacs Last in the Dooryard

Bloom'd," or the conclusion of *Walden;* in each case the writer learns to treat the lost object of love as merely one of nature's myriad commensurables, but the teaching is devastating. The literature of American Puritanism, revised by Franklinism, and the literature of the American Renaissance, a revision of Franklinism, are most specifically connected not by their transcendental impulses, but by their emphatic acknowledgment that only a respect for the independent life those impulses contradict, and the resultant humble receptiveness to amendment, can advance the desire for transcendence into wisdom.

For Franklin, however, the concept of contradiction is an obsolete heritage, and the self can be continually and habitually free and clear. According to Marx, Franklin's resistance to the concept of contradiction between transcendental representation and the represented object is the source of his monetary theory's insufficiency. In Franklin's pamphlet, Marx contends, the "transformation of actual products into exchange-values is taken for granted." Quoting Franklin's assertion that "trade in general being nothing but the Exchange of Labour for Labour, the Value of all Things is, as I have said before, most justly measured by Labour," Marx writes:

> If in this sentence the term labour is replaced by concrete (that is, particular) labour, it is at once obvious that labour in one form is being confused with labour in another form. Because trade may, for example, consist in the exchange of the labour of a shoemaker, miner, spinner, painter and so on, is therefore the labour of the painter the best measure of the value of the shoes? Franklin, on the contrary, considers that the value of shoes, minerals, yarn, paintings, etc. is determined by abstract labour which has no particular quality and can thus be measured only in terms of quantity.[22]

For Marx, a commodity and the labor behind it are both a contradictory unity of their usable particularity and their commercial commensurability: to represent them quantitatively is to blank out one aspect that is as essential as the other. According to Marx, Franklin fails to acknowledge the reductiveness of this blanking-out. But Marx is wrong to imply that Franklin's omission is a sign of confusion: rather, it is deliberate. For Franklin, quantitative representation is "just measurement" that does not contradict significant features of what it represents, an assertion Franklin maintains, as Marx realizes, by using the single word *labor* in diverse senses – as he had used the word *self* in diverse senses: as self-denial is self-fulfillment, so too monetary representation is a fair summary of human work because both are labor.

[22] Karl Marx, *A Contribution to a Critique of Political Economy* (Moscow: Progress Publishers, 1970), p. 56.

In the *Autobiography*, Franklin's resistance to the concept of contradiction between representation and object manifests itself as the identity between the narrator and the young man whose life is described. According to John Griffith, there is no gradual evolution or sudden reversal between the man Franklin was and the narrator he is: "These conversions never become organically connected; they form no logical progression leading by steps from a state of ignorance to a state of enlightenment, or from vice to virtue, or even from poverty to affluence." Acclimated to autobiographies that do delineate such dialectical progressions, Griffith assumes that there *must have been* such turmoil, and that the narrator *must be* distinct from the young man. Consequently, according to Griffith, the two figures, narrator and character, are discrete, or "neatly distinguishable," because no narrative of development through contradiction spans the distance between them.[23] However, Griffith's familiarity with the genre of autobiography has closed his eyes to Franklin's strategy. Objecting to the Puritan form of Augustinian autobiography, Franklin omits the "organic turmoil" of "conversion" during which the particular man is transformed into the universally acceptable, qualitatively blank voice so that readers such as Horatio will not object to the necessary trauma. Rather than suggesting a difference between the young man and the narrator, the absence of reformative turmoil implies their continuity. Unlike Augustine or Proust, Franklin needs undergo no harrowing as preparation for writing: the young man who is described is represented as being substantially identical with the older man who describes. Though the older man has discovered more efficacious devices and become more adept at farsighted assessment, the important ambitions, intentions, inclinations, and talents are in place from the first. The points of divergence between the narrator and the young man are only errata, insignificant mistakes in calculation; the young man is "neatly distinguishable" from the errors that might otherwise make him different from the narrator; and the narrator is not wiser, but only smarter. In the *Autobiography*, as in the monetary theory as Marx analyzes it, the abstract symbolization is made to seem a just and adequate summation of its object that leaves nothing of importance out.

This mode of transcendentalism was for Max Weber the essence of Franklin's contribution to the economic thought and practice of the Enlightenment:

> The important fact is always that a calculation of capital in terms of money is made, whether by modern book-keeping methods or in any other way, however primitive or crude. Everything is done in terms of

[23] John Griffith, "The Rhetoric of Franklin's *Autobiography*," *Criticism*, vol. 13, no. 1 (Winter 1971), p. 91.

balances: at the beginning of the exercise, an initial balance, before every individual decision a calculation to ascertain its probable profitableness, and at the end a final balance to ascertain how much profit has been made.[24]

As his letter to Joseph Priestley concerning moral and prudential algebra reveals, Franklin endorsed the ideal of extending such assessment to extra-economic areas of human conduct. In this, he participates in what Louis I. Bredvold calls the Enlightenment's "hope of a millenium," "a complete mathematical philosophy of the universe, including human life and personality," "a complete and final understanding of the nature of man." Bredvold chronicles the development of this ambition from its origin in Descartes's thought (Husserl chose Galileo) through Hobbes and Leibniz to Frances Hutcheson and Jeremy Bentham. Of these thinkers, Hutcheson is probably the most direct influence on Franklin, though demonstrating direct influence is not especially important when dealing with such a widespread cultural ambition. In his *Inquiry into the Original of Our Ideas of Beauty and Virtue* (1725), Hutcheson proposed equations such as the following: "The *moral Importance* of any *Agent,* or the *Quantity of publick Good* produc'd by him, is in a *compound Ratio* of his *Benevolence* and Abilitys: or (by substituting the initial Letters for the Words, as M= *Moment of Good,* and μ= *Moment of Evil*) M= B × A."[25] The great difficulty of Hutcheson's scheme is the unexamined assumption that human realities are subject to quantification in the first place. In his letter to Priestley, Franklin regretted that "the Weight of Reasons cannot be taken with the Precision of Algebraic Quantities," but he contended that his "estimates" were sufficient to lift him out of the confusions of quality, where "various Purposes or Inclinations . . . alternately prevail and . . . Uncertainty . . . perplexes us." Eight years later, Franklin wrote to Priestley commending him on his contributions to the progress of natural science, and wishing for a similar detached clarity for viewing man: "O that moral science were in as fair a way of Improvement, that men would cease to be Wolves to one another, and that human beings would at length learn what they now improperly call Humanity!" (*W,* VIII:418). The rational gaze, adumbrated in exemplary artifacts such as the *Autobiography,* would provide the basis for concord and common clarity.

Number per se is not the important thing, but instead the development of a kind of symbolization that is detached from affective participation in the objects it represents, and that thereby lifts the scientist out of the

[24] Max Weber, *The Protestant Ethic and the Spirit of Capitalism,* trans. Talcott Parsons (New York: Scribner, 1958), p. 18.
[25] Louis I. Bredwold, "The Invention of the Ethical Calculus," in *The Seventeenth Century* (Stanford, Calif.: Stanford University Press, 1951), pp. 165–80.

sphere of perplexed uncertainty, crossed inclinations, and complicity. Following from Weber, Theodor Adorno and Max Horkheimer detect this transcendental desire in the impulse to mathematicization: "Bacon's postulate of *una scientia universalis*, whatever the number of fields of research, is as inimical to the unassignable as Leibniz's *mathesis universalis* is to discontinuity. The multiplicity of forms is reduced to position and arrangement, history to fact, things to matter." In pursuit of such "demythologizing," "number becomes the canon of the Enlightenment." Making the "dissimilar comparable by reducing it to abstract quantities," clarity asserts "total interchangeability," and extricates self from the confusion of participation: "The abstract self, which justifies record-making and systematization, has nothing set over against it but the abstract material which possesses no other quality than to be a substrate of such possession."[26] Franklin differs from Leibniz or Hutcheson with respect to this ideal by practically embodying it, as representative man, rather than by merely stating or proposing it. Such is the great promise of Franklin's example: an alluring (and, should it develop from observation to enforcement, abusive) dream of a human world freed from its obscurity and from its murkiness, of a life in the light.

[26] Theodor Adorno and Max Horkheimer, *Dialectic of Enlightenment,* trans. John Cumming (New York: Seabury Press, 1972), pp. 7, 10, 12–13, 26.

8

THE DEMONSTRATION
OF CHARACTER

Thence it comes my name receives a brand,
And almost thence my nature is subdued
To what it works in, like the dyer's hand.

Shakespeare, Sonnet 111

In the 1760s, as Franklin's political responsibilities multiplied with the worsening crisis, his writing became more occasional, more tailored to the urgent exigencies at hand. His writings during this period, though they are samples of the rational self at work, do not frequently represent the self, either directly or figurally. There are exceptions, and the *Autobiography* is the greatest of these. Begun on vacation at Twyford in August 1771, during "a week's uninterrupted leisure" (which stretched to two weeks), continued in snatched periods of free time at Passy in 1784 and at Philadelphia in 1788 and 1789, the *Autobiography* was a diversion of Franklin's attention from his obligations, both in its circumstances of composition and in its rhetorical purpose.

Franklin stepped back from the self at work in order to represent the selfhood that spanned the distance between adolescent rebellion and imperial brinksmanship. Perhaps he found some emotional satisfaction in being able to delineate the continuity beneath the whirl of changes that had brought the apprentice to Parliament. The pedagogical tone that dominates from the first page, however, suggests that Franklin's primary aim was not self-discovery, but instead self-preservation for the benefit of posterity. He was sixty-five when he began, and the thought of death led him to autobiography as a means of perpetuating the accumulation of acclaim past the demise of the self's mortal vehicle. Though he may have been confident that he would be remembered, he wrote the *Autobiography* to intervene into how he would be remembered: supervised by the *Autobiography*, Franklin's reputation would not depend on the fanciful vicissitudes of others' remembrances of the great man. Demonstrating, in Part One, the art of distinguishing the virtuous self from various botched simulacra, and, in Parts Two, Three, and Four, the habitual maintenance and the consequent successes of the virtuous self, Franklin is not reflectively reconsidering his lifelong self-design, but definitively instituting it in a durable textual body that will continue to win over young Horatios with its reasonable blandishments. The difference between Franklin the historical actor and Franklin the autobiographer is primarily a difference between more immediate and more abstract calculations of self-promotion, between short-term and long-term investments, rather than between ambition and confession. The narrator of the *Autobiography* is therefore essentially continuous with the young self he recalls, and he differs from the self of the earlier writings only in his being more completely and meticulously articulated.

This narrating self is difficult to define. Definition usually proceeds from a qualitative discrimination between the thing being defined and related things to a discovery of the thing's unique positivity. But Franklin's self differs from the identities of others in its resolute independence from qualitative particularity. His strategic tact leads him to distinguish himself from modes of identity that would confine personal universality, warning against allowing self to be associated with any positive commitment. Consequently, the first movement of definition – negative contrast – will in Franklin's case not lead to the second – the statement of unique positive quality.

This difficulty inevitably crops up in the best discussions of Franklin's character. For example, Robert F. Sayre, noting that "Franklin's life was a plastic and unformed substance that could be pushed and prodded into whatever mold he chose to put it in," concludes that the *Autobiography* is "as shapeless as he was protean." Sayre observes the absence of a clear and positive particular identity tying together Franklin's diverse occupations:

> The problem Franklin unconsciously illustrated was the problem of the man whose life and character was one of discontinuity. He was, as he delighted in telling, the Philadelphia printer who had dined with kings. There are certain fundamentals of his character which were always the same, but they are by no means as prominent as the fundamental facts about Augustine's character, though his life had witnessed many turnings too.

But discontinuity was neither a problem for Franklin, nor was he unconscious of it. The continuous fundamentals permitting a universal variety of employment – ingenuity and industry – were for Franklin maintained by avoiding the sort of positive "prominence" that tied other men to particular parts of the human whole. Franklin's disciplined maintenance of an "unconcerned" or blank capacity was the condition for self's suc-

cessful passage from printer to royalty's dinner guest. In calling this tactful austerity a "discontinuity," Sayre is unconsciously recoiling from the
fundamental strangeness of the *Autobiography*'s narrator – a traitless capacity that is the self, rather than a device at the disposal of a more familiar sort of character with quirks, preferences, desires, biases, and affections. Sayre flees from this strangeness by postulating that Franklin
did have a more familiar sort of character, but that he kept it behind the
scenes: "Carl Becker observed that Franklin was never thoroughly submerged in anything he undertook. Everything he did he gave his best to,
and most everything he did he did well, but behind the gestures and
routines of his participation was always a reserve, a certain ironic sense
which took amusement as well as satisfaction from experience."[1]
    It seems to me that, though one may or may not choose to believe in
a "reserved" Franklin, the existence of a secret man can neither be demonstrated nor argued with any hope of progress. We can observe, however, that Sayre's speculation concerning the hidden Franklin shifts the
focus from the narrator of the *Autobiography* to what Sayre considers to
have been the truth about the man Benjamin Franklin. Sayre's argument
is therefore similar to Melville's in *Israel Potter;* Franklin's unremitting
impersonal serenity is made to seem ominous, and to seem to conceal a
devious purpose. As John Griffith contends, one "reads his collected
writings from end to end without seeing a trace of serious self-doubt,
self-loathing, self-anger or any other form of intrapsychic conflict and
anxiety." This absence is strange, and intriguing: "I believe that for many
readers there is at the heart of Franklin's works a mystery, as enigmatic
in its way as Thoreau's sensual asceticism is, or Faulkner's despairing
exuberance. To read Franklin at length and with real attention is to have
one's imagination stirred by the sense of something unique and not wholly
explicable going on between and behind the lines." Consequently, "the
myth of the man behind the masks is a permanent part of the discussion
of Franklin and his writings." But the premise of the secret man may be
a function of the reader's desire, rather than of his observation of the text:
"Some Franklin commentators, of course, see his supposed tranquility
as an affectation. They see his almost unbroken introspective silence as a
void, and are tempted to fill it in."[2] But Franklin's self, beginning in
reaction against the pressure of Puritan introspection, against the obligation to search out the true man behind the works, *is* this "void": behind
the masks is the universal capacity to take on masks. In America, we do

[1] Robert F. Sayre, *The Examined Self: Benjamin Franklin, Henry Adams, Henry James* (Princeton, N.J.: Princeton University Press, 1964), pp. 16, 20, 22, 25.
[2] John Griffith, "Franklin's Sanity and the Man Behind the Masks," in *The Oldest Revolutionary*, ed. J. A. Leo Lemay (Philadelphia: University of Pennsylvania Press, 1976), pp. 124, 127, 131, 134.

not ask what a man is, but what he can do. Whether or not there was a private Franklin, the self Franklin aimed to project in his writings, preeminently in the *Autobiography,* was an industrious ingenuity unrestrained by particular prominences, and uninhibited by demands for positive self-definition.

Franklin's own self-definition in the *Autobiography* is resolutely negative and contrastive, a repeated evocation of "roads not taken" that defines the road that was taken by the process of elimination that tact uses to advertise itself as humanism. Franklin clues his reader to this rhetorical device in his portrait of William Keith, the governor of Pennsylvania from 1717 to 1726, who died in 1749 while imprisoned for his debts. Keith met and admired the young Franklin in Philadelphia, and in 1724 offered to set Franklin up in business. Franklin sailed to London to buy the necessary types and other printer's equipment, only to find on arrival that the letters of credit supposedly in the ship's mail pouch did not exist. Remembering this betrayal in the *Autobiography,* Franklin reacts not with anger or disgust, but with calculating appraisal: "He wish'd to please every body; and having little to give, he gave Expectations. He was otherwise an ingenious sensible Man, a pretty good Writer, and a good Governor for the People, tho' not for his Constituents the Proprietaries, whose Instructions he sometimes disregarded. Several of our best Laws were of his Planning, and pass'd during his Administration" (*A:*95). As a representative man, ingenious, attentive to the needs of the people at large, Keith is a potential role model for Franklin. But Franklin learns from Keith's example that a universal self cannot *be* all the particular things that a diverse constituency might desire. Instead, he must abstain from close attachment to any part of the whole, as Keith did when he failed to obey the special interests of the proprietors. The pressing task for self-definition is the demonstration of things self can do but is not.

This use of dissociation complicates praise for Franklin's realism. A. Owen Aldridge, for example, has likened the *Autobiography* to the memoirs of Carlo Goldoni, Giovanni Casanova, and Carlo Gozzi in its attention to "intimate details," "anecdotes and philosophical reflections," "the simple affairs of his daily life, his ordinary concerns and intimate thoughts." Aldridge rightly contends that his inclusive realism was "something novel and refreshing in literature," a contribution to the loosening secularization of literature already at work in Mather's "Life of Phips." But he errs when he contends that Franklin's realistic representation of his world is meant to delineate his character *directly* by detailing "the inherent relationship between the author and his times."[3] Franklin always intends

---

[3] A. Owen Aldridge, "Form and Substance in Franklin's Autobiography," in *Essays on American Literature in Honor of Jay B. Hubbell,* ed. Clarence Gohdes (Durham, N.C.: Duke University Press, 1967), p. 57.

his reader to see a *contrast* between his own blank universal ability and the motley, particular vitality of the surrounding world. The careful, realistic sketching of episode and of the characters of others accentuates the undetermined boundlessness that moves through their midst. He carefully develops the sharp particularity of situation and acquaintance so that he can surpass it and reveal what cannot be shown in itself, the aloof and capacious blankness of a character that does not succumb to being defined by the diverse situations it engages and masters. Like electricity moving among the denser matters or money moving among commodities, Franklin's character moves through the departments of a secular world but it is not essentially defined or modified in any of the stages of its motion. Franklin's self is negatively related to the specific seasons of man so that it can seem to be directly related to human nature in the abstract. His expository presentation of character requires the realistic delineation of concrete character options that are clearly and carefully avoided, precisely because the Franklinian self is not susceptible to direct positive description.

The acts of self-definition in the early pages of the *Autobiography* can be divided into two categories – Franklin's avoidance of the sort of character that submits to the despotic authority of another, or allows itself to be shaped by another, and thus is at least vestigially filiopious, and his avoidance of the kind of character that relaxes its vigilant maintenance of calculation, allowing itself to settle into some defining partial inclination. Franklin will present himself to the reader as one who neither allows himself to be determined by another nor fails to protect his own rigorous and immanent self-government. In this double negation, Franklin is rebuffing the Puritan binarism that, in the works of Winthrop, Cotton, and the Mathers, saw the Prodigal Son as the only alternative to filiopious remembrance. Franklin proposes a third option that combines the independence of the prodigal with the orderliness of the remembrancer – self-fathering.

Double negation is also the hallmark of his political theory. According to Paul Conner, Franklin's idea of social order was based on a search for an indigenous stability natural to society's activity: "A society whose virtue sprang from the moral, racial and intellectual qualities of its people would appear to have little need of a supervisory power to ensure political harmony." On the other hand, Franklin believed that internal regulation must be separated from turmoil: "The antithesis of Franklin's political ideal was disorder, and its incarnation was the mob. Mobs flit in and out of Franklin's writings like specters. They serve as haunting reminders of the fate that lurked in the shadows, waiting to seize the society which turned aside from the virtuous quest." Franklin's political theory departs from Winthrop's by adding the idea of immanent self-regulation as a mediating possibility between conformity to extrinsic regulation and

chaos. Society can free itself of heteronomous domination *and* resist anarchic fragmentation into its constituent particular interests. As Conner
writes:

> Franklin thought the cardinal fault of lesser systems lay in imbalance
> between the principle of individualist egalitarianism on the one hand,
> and the cohesive principle of unified authority on the other. The one
> degenerated into anarchy, the other into tyranny. His solution lay in the
> simultaneous emphasis on both equality and cohesion, fortified by what
> might be termed a "strategy of humility." This meant the use of con-
> ciliation and seeming neutrality to advance the positive cause of vir-
> tuous social evolution.[4]

Representative humility, mediating between the undesirable extremes of
Puritan binarism, extracts, or detaches, the ingenious component in each
of them, and, offering itself to society as an *exemplum,* catalyzes the sort
of regular and incessant growth that validates it in place of a careful definition of what it is. Presenting himself as neither the submissive nor the
prodigal son, Franklin avoids saying what he is, and instead focuses our
attention on what he and his society can grow to.

Franklin's wit is a handy aid in this enterprise. To contend theoretically
with either the concept of transcendental authority or with modes of
feeling other than abstract calculation, Franklin would have to take a concrete argumentative position. But if he can present the tin despot and the
self-enslaved prodigal as ludicrous modes of personality, as the sort of
automata that Bergson called the essential butt of humor, his satire will
implicitly assert his own rational vitality and suffice in place of a statement of position. If late-Puritan zeal can be reduced to the zestless piety
of Polly Baker's judges, to the supercilious self-aggrandizement that Silence Dogood finds rampant at Harvard, to the machinelike sententious-
ness of the Cotton Mather characterized in the *New England Courant,* or
to the churchgoers whom Canassatego overhears conspiring to lower the
price of pelts, then a noncommittal wit will do in place of a position
taken against what Miller called "the marrow of Puritan divinity." If, on
the other hand, sentiment and desire that do not constantly appraise their
own utility in some larger scheme can be reduced to John Collins's
drunkenness, James Ralph's nonstop bad versifying, or Titan Leeds's foot-
heavy sputterings, then Franklin's wit will do in place of a position taken
against the sort of eloquent feeling expressed in Bradstreet's poems.
Franklin's satires thus cover over his two most controversial propositions:
that self *as Franklin defines it,* though it can criticize those in whom ingenuity is absent or only partially realized, need not itself be submitted

---

[4] Paul W. Conner, *Poor Richard's Politicks: Benjamin Franklin and His New American Order* (New York: Oxford University Press, 1965), pp. xi, 111, 136.

to any higher standard, since it is nature; and that self as Franklin defines it, unlike Matherian piety, is not a regimenting domination that contradicts the whole body of human feeling, because it *is* self. His wit, therefore, is the perfect contrastive device, since it differentiates the narrator from comic butts, while using the shared chuckle to avoid a statement of what he is.

But Franklin knew that for many eighteenth-century Americans piety was more than credulous obtuseness, and that, consequently, if he relied on satire as his sole controversial device, his range of influence would be severely diminished. In his comprehensive survey of Franklin's religion-related activity, A. Owen Aldridge contends that Franklin avoided "militant deism," and managed to make himself appealing to virtually all sects: "As John Adams remarked in great disgust, 'The Catholics thought him almost Catholic. The Church of England claimed him as one of them. The Presbyterians thought him half a Presbyterian, and the Friends believed him a wet Quaker.'" Franklin accomplished this, according to Aldridge, by making good use of "occasional conformity," by a tactful evasion of an outright statement of sectarian disagreement, such as when he took an oath subscribing to the Athanasian Creed required for entrants to crown offices in the colonies.[5] In his *Articles of Belief and Religion*, Franklin contended that, beneath the sectarian specificities of all religions was a common rational germ, a contention that no doubt enabled a tactful avoidance of open violation of any one sect, which would repel its members, and of full participation, which would repel the members of the other sects. Once again, tact was the practical representative of the universal humanism postulated in the *Articles of Belief and Religion*.

This tact, rather than open satire, informs the early pages of the *Autobiography*, where Puritan forms of self-conception and personal narrative are observed, but in such a way as to assert subtly the Franklinian difference. Franklin begins by presenting God as the determining author of his life's progress toward felicity, though he mentions that he made use of the conducing means. He implies that his life was designed by an exterior will, and that as author of the narrative he will only recount a story composed by another: "That Felicity, when I reflected on it, has induc'd me sometimes to say, that were it Offer'd to my Choice, I should have no Objection to a Repetition of the same Life from its Beginning, only asking the Advantage Authors have in a second Edition to correct some of the Faults of the First" (*A:43*). Franklin here introduces a theme that will recur regularly, that in the course of his life he made regrettable mistakes: but, though he here implies that these are an author's faults –

---

[5] A. Owen Aldridge, *Benjamin Franklin and Nature's God* (Durham, N.C.: Duke University Press, 1967), pp. 8, 189–91.

suggesting that his participation in them was large and intense – he will later call them errata, a compositor's slips of the hand, a metaphor that will greatly reduce the implication of any intense participation of the self in the commission of the mistakes. For the moment, however, he implies that the divine author of his felicity left some room for his will, whether to exploit the conducing means or to commit the errors. In the large, in other words, he is implying that his life's story was written by a superior will that graciously allowed his designing self some small room to move.

Though Franklin is indifferent to Puritan piety, he knows that he lives in a late Puritan world and that an open and obvious repudiation would make him seem impious. In Part One of the *Autobiography*, consequently, Franklin will posture in Puritan attitudes because he wishes to avoid the appearance of prodigality. Two pages later, for example, the earlier mention of his faults leads him to contend contritely that God has generously waived the punishment they deserve:

> My belief of [God's kind Providence] induces me to *hope, tho'* I must not *presume,* that the same Goodness will still be exercis'd towards me in continuing that Happiness, or in enabling me to bear a Fatal Reverse, which I may experience as others have done, the Complexion of my future Fortune being known to him only; and in whose Power it is to bless us even our Afflictions. (*A*:45)

In these passages, Puritan dogma is completely observed: with what small freedom God has permitted the self, it has gone awry; the error may deserve the correcting influence of a fatal reverse; but the consequence will not be unequivocally asserted, because the ways of God are beyond human understanding; the only certainty about God is that He directs the course of the self's experience, and the freedom permitted the self is mostly illusive, or at least paltry. Downplaying the significance of both the self-fathering will and its ally the understanding, Franklin is demonstrating not his fealty to the Calvinist god but his unwillingness to begin by flouting the conventions of Puritan autobiography. He pays homage to the unknown god, he downplays the significance of will and intelligence, and he acknowledges his participation in error and the rectitude of punishment.

Franklin's true intentions, however, show through at several points. The remark on exploiting the conducing means, for example, recapitulating Poor Richard's observation that God helps those who help themselves, emphasizes the independent will as an acceptable self-determining force, shaping its own life with divine approval. This theme, briefly introduced here, becomes clear later, in 1726, when Franklin reveals that he wrote out in advance the story of his own life, and stuck to it:

> We sail'd from Gravesend on the 23d of July 1726. For the Incidents of the Voyage, I refer you to my Journal, where you will find them all

minutely related. Perhaps the most important Part of that Journal is the *Plan* to be found in it which I formed at Sea, for regulating my future Conduct in Life. It is the more remarkable, as being form'd when I was so young, and yet being pretty faithfully adhered to quite thro' old Age. (*A*:106)

Franklin here presents himself as the author of his life while it was being lived as well as as the author of the life in recollection. Though God may approve, he does not define or compose. This job belongs to the self. Correspondingly, as the *Autobiography* progresses, Franklin's faults are downgraded from author's to printer's errors, and so are expelled from the self. They are faults insofar as they go contrary to Franklin's plan for himself, not to divine moral strictures. The piety and the contrition of the early pages of the *Autobiography* are a rhetorical ruse meant to placate residual Puritan prejudices in the minds of his readers. As Part One progresses, Franklin abandons the unknown god-author and the confession of the erroneous self by demonstrating that will and intelligence are combined in successful self-design and that any errors he may have committed were inconsequential, easily remedied interferences with his own plan. Franklin's self is more godlike than godly.

This unannounced discarding of Puritan conventions is already implied in the first paragraph, where Franklin asserts that the self is not bound to its circumstances of origin or to any particular determination and that the self is best known in terms of what it can achieve rather than what it is. This assertion goes contrary to the economic wing of Puritan filiopiety, which held that each soul was essentially shaped to a particular calling and that the circumstances of origin and the will of the father provided each son with this particular calling. Franklin's inoffensive posturing to the unknown god and to the confessional form in these early pages is contrary to the explosive definition of self as a blank, departicularized capacity that must shake off the will of anyone who would attempt to confine it to particularity. Neither a human father nor a divine father will shape the course of the self. This independence is what Franklin feels makes his life worthy of emulation by posterity, not his cautious attention to a superior will.

Consequently, on the second page, Franklin celebrates vanity as a useful attribute and a gift from the sort of god who helps those who help themselves:

> Most People dislike Vanity in others whatever Share they have of it themselves, but I give it fair Quarter wherever I meet with it, being persuaded that it is often productive of Good to the Possessor and to others that are within his Sphere of Action: And therefore in many Cases it would not be quite Absurd if a Man were to thank God for his Vanity among the other Comforts of Life. (*A*:44)

Vanity, as Fielding writes in his preface to *Joseph Andrews,* "puts us on affecting false characters, in order to purchase applause." Fielding assumes that each person has a true character and that to affect another deserves correction by ridicule. But Franklin's monetary self is departicularized, so there is no true particular self, only willingly assumed nondetermining roles. Franklinian vanity would be the self's perpetual refusal to believe that it is essentially determined by the circumstances in which it happens to be situated at any given moment of its life. Franklinian vanity is another name for the self – the determined refusal to believe that one has an innate particular character which condemns all other employments to being affectations. Franklin would hear in Fielding's conservative pronouncement on the folly of vanity a distant echo of the Puritan denunciation of satanic pride, the demonic belief that one is not confined to a particular place but is instead free to be self-fathering. Consequently, the celebration of vanity, together with the remark on the exploitation of conducing means and the assertion of the self as a potential for quantitative growth that is not bound to its circumstances of origin, shows that the Puritan allusions in the early pages are a kind of rhetorical surface meant to disarm the accusation of impiety without concealing completely the depiction of self-fathering that will become the book's major, post-Puritan tenor.

In fact, Puritanism proves to be the strongest obstacle to the emergence of his free character as it is chronicled in the pages that follow. Franklin's first opponent will be filiopiety in its economic form – the determination of self by the social and familial circumstances of origin and the authority of fathers to assign lives to their sons.

But before telling the story of his famous refusal of filiopious authority – his departure from Boston – Franklin gives us a brief rehearsal of his family's past. In part, this rehearsal is still another gesture toward filiopiety, a rooting of self in family history. However, it goes beyond that, because Franklin's history of "any little Anecdotes of my Ancestors" is carefully structured around an opposition between two traits: on the one hand, the family has a tradition of determining careers – and life stories – for its incipient prodigals; on the other hand, the ancestors who are singled out for special attention display a resolution that lifts them out of the traditionalistic particular life and allows them the boundlessness of wide, various application. Franklin names this resolution "ingenuity," a word that (if we also count "ingenious" and "genius") occurs at least twelve times in Part One and seems to be Franklin's preferred way of labeling what he approves of in himself and others. It is an interesting choice: Franklin here celebrates a personal efficacy that was for Mather subordinate to piety, except, perhaps, in the biographies of Winthrop, Jr., and Phips, but he is doing so with a word that bears residual connotations of piety. He is exploiting the usurpation of "ingenuousness" by "ingeniousness" as the meaning of "ingenuity," a semantic transformation whose ambiguity Franklin was familiar with: in a 1755 letter, Franklin had urged John Lining to claim credit for an invention, because if he did not he would not only "lose the credit of being in that instance *ingenious*," but he would also "suffer the disgrace of not being *ingenuous*" (*P,* 5:527). In the early pages of the *Autobiography,* Franklin does not openly distinguish these near-homophones that were competing for possession of the one word *ingenuity* because permitting the confusion will allow self-assertion while retaining the connotative aura of fideistic piety. This bargain makes *ingenuity,* together with *vanity,* one of the key words Franklin is using to defend the validity of the calculating self. The opposition between ingenuity and traditionalism in the history of Franklin's family, therefore, lifts that history out of Puritan rehearsals of genealogy. In Franklin's account, the significant trend will be the ascendancy of ingenuity which discards the determination of its nature by another. Franklin's account will describe the success of a kind of personality that is not shaped by the history or will of its family. Therefore, though Franklin's family chronicle may pose as homage to Puritan dynasticism, it is in fact a rebuttal of the Puritan traditionalism that assigns a crucial role in the shaping of the son to the collective will of his fathers.

The first obstacle to ingenuity's self-realization is the filiopietistic subjugation of the entire self to a supervening extrinsic authority. Franklin's uncle Benjamin's notes on the family reveal that its members

> had liv'd in the same Village, Ecton in Northhamptonshire, for 300 years, and how much longer he knew not . . . on a freehold of about 30 acres, aided by the Smith's Business which had continu'd in the Family till his Time, the eldest Son being always bred to the Business. A Custom which he and my Father both followed as to their eldest Sons (*A:*45–6)

This assigning of life station by tradition continues, though accident may change the specific position: "John was bred a Dyer, I believe of Woolens. Benjamin was bred a Silk Dyer, serving an Apprenticeship in London" (*A:*48). The use of the verb *to breed to* to signify the determination of a son's economic life gained currency in England during the early Puritan period and survived in common use until the middle of the nineteenth century, when it would have seemed absurd to think that a young man's eventual career was a virtually genetic component of his selfhood. Though the use of *to breed to* was hardly archaic in Franklin's period, the frequency with which he uses the construction in these early pages is significant: Franklin repeats the term enough to call attention to it, to show us that in his family's variety of traditionalism, which was quite typical, the determination of the son's eventual career was considered to have been *fa-*

thered into him as inescapably as his physiological shape. In brief, he refers us to the attitude we saw in John Cotton – that God, as interpreted by the human father, equips each son with the innate particularity of talents suited to a specific task – and in Cotton Mather – that the predetermined shape of a son's obligatory life is as innate as the rectitude of his own body. In his word-choice and in his citation of the family history, Franklin is delineating the force of prejudice which will contrast with ingenuity.

The tension between the two is present in the remark that expresses Franklin's father's resolve to continue the tradition: "My elder Brothers were all put Apprentices to different Trades. I was put to the Grammar School at Eight Years of Age, my Father intending to devote me as the Tithe of his Sons to the Service of the Church" (*A:*52). The tension is established in Franklin's mildly sarcastic choice of the word *tithe,* which not only mocks his father's ritual piety but also suggests that the son is *money* that the father is determined to withdraw from free circulation. This first mention of the son as money sets the stage for the rest of his father's and his brother's attempts to put him into a particular shape; such determination of his selfhood will always be like the "murder" of a crown kept from its quantitative destiny. The word *tithe,* which associates the self with money's nondeterminate purity, contrasts with the verb *to breed to,* which implies that the self is innately particular.

Abandoning his intention to spend his son on the church, Franklin's father still maintains his dominance: "At Ten Years old, I was taken Home to assist my Father in his Business, which was that of a Tallow Chandler and Sope-Boiler" (*A:*53). And, at twelve years, "there was all Appearance that I was destin'd to supply his Place and be a Tallow Chandler" (*A:*57). Franklin's ten-page account of his family is intended to demonstrate the traditionalism with which he was confronted.

The "Poverty and Obscurity in which [he] was born and bred," therefore, contrasts not simply with the success he eventually achieves, but, more fundamentally, with the type of character he would have us believe he was from the beginning. The traditionalism of breeding in these early pages is in constant counterpoise with the *ingenuity* shown by various family members: "[My uncle Benjamin] was an ingenious Man, I remember him well, for when I was a Boy he came to see my Father in Boston" (*A:*48). Franklin's remark that his uncle Benjamin was ingenious follows immediately after his remark that the uncle was bred a silk dyer, and the contrast becomes clear in the variety of the uncle's applications: he wrote two quarto volumes of poetry, several political pamphlets, and invented a shorthand. Ingenuity, consequently, is opposed to traditionalism in a special way: it incites its possessor to transcend not only the career chosen for him but also confinement in any one particular career.

Ingenuity is restless. It resents confinement, even self-chosen confinement, and Franklin's celebration of his uncle's variety of application indicates that the escape from the career to which one is bred is the first,
perhaps the most difficult, but certainly not the only escape from the trap
of particularity that the self will have to make if it is to realize its boundless dexterity. This restlessness is clear in Franklin's account of another
uncle, Thomas:

> Thomas was bred a Smith under his Father, but being ingenious, and
> encourag'd in Learning (as all his Brothers like wise were) by an Esquire
> Palmer then the principal Gentleman in the Parish, he qualify'd for the
> Business of Scrivener, became a considerable Man in the County affairs,
> was a chief Mover of all Publick Spirited Undertakings, for the County,
> or town of Northhampton and his own Village, of which many In-
> stances were told us at Ecton and he was much taken Notice of and
> patroniz'd by the then Lord Halifax. (A:47)

Ingenuity led Thomas to substitute scrivener for smith, but then to transcend even the self-chosen particular life, becoming versatile and earning
the acclaim of all segments of the local population, as true money can
buy everything by virtue of its blankness.

Plainly, Franklin is emphasizing the ingenuity of these uncles in order
to foreshadow himself. He even calls his father ingenious (A:54) and
suggests that the versatility of his father's character makes him a successful "Arbitrator between contending Parties" (A:55) because he is not constrained by the particular interests of any of the contending parties – thus
foreshadowing Franklin's own adept application of blankness to diplomacy. Franklin wishes to assuage the reader's suspicions: this chronicle
of the family's past is used as a preparation for the story of Franklin's
disobedience; it allows him to imply that, in disobeying the traditionalistic will of father and older brother, he is breaking one family tradition
in order to observe another that has existed but gone unacknowledged.
Suspecting filiopietistic prejudices against self-determination in the reader,
Franklin's chronicle of ancestors proposes that, in disobeying the will of
his father and brother, he is in fact being a faithful heir. The chronicle of
ancestors, therefore, along with the references to inscrutable providence
and fatal reverses in the first pages, is an attempt to preserve the narrator's acceptability in the mind of the reader by not establishing the particularity of prodigality.

Ingenuity, then, rather than courage or principle, according to Franklin, is the hallmark of his family's early-Yankee resistance to heteronomous authority:

> This obscure Family of ours was early in the Reformation, and con-
> tinu'd Protestants thro' the Reign of Queen Mary, when they were
> sometimes in Danger of Trouble on Account of their Zeal against Pop-

ery. They had got an English Bible, and to conceal it and secure it, it was fastned open with Tapes under and within the Frame of a Joint Stool. When my Great Great Grandfather read it to his Family, he turn'd up the Joint Stool upon his Knees, turning over the Leaves then under the Tapes. One of the Children stood at the Door to give Notice if he saw an Apparitor coming, who was an Officer of the Spiritual Court. (A:50)

The details of the Protestant argument with Marian suppression and the intensity of zeal that risks persecution are unimportant here: cleverness is the lesson, and the detachability of ingenuity from the piety that happens to accompany it is the tenor of this passage. Though some might be inclined to call this passage *reductive*, it displays a reductiveness that Franklin deliberately allows us to see – to demonstrate that talent is not essentially bound to motives that happen to attach themselves to it.

Franklin's account of his ancestors, chronicling the fugitive presence of ingenuity as a kind of counter-tradition briefly visible through the predominant traditionalism, resembles in form Protestant accounts of the development of the English Reformation such as in the first pages of Bradford's *Of Plymouth Plantation* or in Milton's *Of the Reformation in England*. As in those works, an underground element opposed to the prevailing orthodoxy shows itself in rare moments, gathers its strength, and bursts onto the scene as a full-fledged opponent. The purpose of the chronicle, therefore, in the *Autobiography* as in the Protestant tracts, is to provide the emergent antithesis with a history, and to assure the reader that it is not a spurious, unfounded, and anarchic innovation. The chronicle of ancestors, that is, is intended to defuse late-Puritan suspicions of innovation just as Bradford's and Milton's tracts include histories of the English Reformation in order to exonerate themselves of the charge of innovation.

But, though Franklin's chronicle of ancestors thus resembles Bradford's and Milton's histories in form and rhetorical purpose, the specific antithesis it defends – ingenuity – differs from the subject of Bradford's and Milton's histories – devotion. This difference is clear in the passage on the hiding of the English Bible, where Franklin shows the separability of faith and inventiveness and thus the absence of any necessary connection. But they are opposed as well as separable, since the predominant orthodoxy against which ingenuity struggles is the traditionalism of Puritan economy, not Anglican ritualization of faith. Franklin adopts the form of the Puritan history in order to use it against Puritan dogma, turning the energy of first-generation Puritan separation against the coercive ideology of later theocratic Puritanism in order to complete the detachment of self-fathering from filiopiety begun in Mather's "Life of Phips."

But his purpose for including the history of ancestors is the same as Bradford's and Milton's – to provide a public conflict with an underground history in order to supply the antithetical position with some venerability. The chronicle of the ancestors prepares the reader for Franklin's confrontation with his brother, using Franklin's great-great-grandfather and his uncles Thomas and Benjamin as a justifying foundation for his position in his argument with his brother's statement of the family's traditionalism. What had been unrealized contradiction within the generations of the Franklin family now develops into an open confrontation between two positions – the pure ingenuity of Benjamin, and the pure, obstinate, tyrannical traditionalism of James's insistence. The conflict between Benjamin and James, in other words, brings into the open a tension that had existed for generations, and this crisis will be the moment when ingenuity shrugs off the particularizing traditionalism with which it had been so long mingled. The ingenuity that had showed itself in company with various purposes – such as piety – emerges in the crisis as ingenuity per se, aware that it is not bound to those purposes.

In his conflict with his brother James over his indentures, Franklin was opposed by his father, who sided with James. Franklin mentions this fact once, but only briefly. Otherwise, he represents the crisis as a conflict between brother and brother, thereby eluding a rhetorically dangerous presentation of conflict between father and son. By leaving the elder Josiah out of the conflict, Franklin abstains from a situation in which he would have to challenge his father's "sound Understanding, and Judgement in prudential Matters" at the same time that he divests his antagonist of rectitude by making him a figure of excessive usurped authority. James exceeds fraternal right, and this justifies Franklin's revolt without imputing to him the prodigality that a father–son conflict would necessarily entail. A footnote at this point in the text indicates how useful Franklin found the disarming of authority to be: "I fancy this harsh and tyrannical treatment of me, might be a means of impressing me with that Aversion to arbitrary Power that has stuck with me thro' my Life" (A:69n.). The use of the term "*arbitrary* Power" is robbed of all potential rebelliousness in advance because it describes a usurped and irrationally domineering power, so that Franklin does not particularize himself as rebellious or resentful. This strategy is important, because the footnote is almost certainly an allusion to the English Parliament, with which Franklin had been negotiating when he wrote it. The footnote implies that Parliament is an elder brother to the American assemblies, the king being the common father; and the Parliament's overweening interference, like James Franklin's exploitation of his brother's apprenticeship papers, exceeds and therefore violates a proper fraternal benignity. Franklin establishes the rectitude of self-fathering without a direct assault on paternal authority: "Tho' a Brother, he considered himself as my Master, and me as his Apprentice; and accordingly expected the same Services from me as he would from another; while I thought he demean'd me too much in some he requir'd of me, who from a Brother expected more Indulgence" (A:68). He concedes that he may have been so treated because he had been vain about the success of his contributions to the *New England Courant* and so roused his brother's jealous resentment, but this confession really reflects more on his brother's touchiness than on Franklin's vanity. The more serious issue is the dubious legality of Franklin's violation of his apprentice agreement. However, he avoids this issue, concentrating on the ethics of relations between brothers because this emphasis allows him to represent himself as correcting an unnatural abuse of power rather than as rebelling against natural authority.

Franklin exculpates himself in this episode not only by making his brother, rather than his father, the onerous authority, but also by portraying the feisty James Franklin who outraged Cotton Mather as a pure autocrat of the printing shop who envies his brother's wit. Throughout the *Autobiography*, Franklin will defuse his conflicts with authority by reducing the antagonist to a hopeless victim of his own unreason. When he begins himself in Philadelphia, for example, Franklin goes to work for Samuel Keimer, whom he uses as the next father-surrogate to fill the rhetorical place left by his brother James. Once again Franklin is bullied by a figure of authority who threatens to compel his boundlessness to accept a determinate shape, and once again this compulsion is represented as being completely without legitimacy. The contrast between Franklin and Keimer is enhanced by Franklin's lavish depiction of Keimer's weirdness, which both heightens our perception of Franklin's sane rightness and makes sure that Keimer's eventual opposition to Franklin will not earn the reader's sympathy:

> But however serviceable I might be, I found that my Services became every Day of less Importance, as the other Hands improv'd in the Business. And when Keimer paid my second Quarter's Wages, he let me know he felt them too heavy, and thought I should make an Abatement. He grew by degrees less civil, put on more of the Master, frequently found Fault, was captious and seemed ready for an Out-breaking. I went on nevertheless with a good Deal of Patience, thinking that his incumber'd Circumstances were partly the Cause. At length a Trifle snapt our Connexion. For a great Noise happening near the Courthouse, I put my Head out of the Window to see what was the Matter. Keimer being in the Street looked up and saw me, call'd out to me in a loud Voice and angry Tone to mind my Business, adding some reproachful Words, that nettled me more for their Publicity, all the Neighbours who were looking out on the same Occassion being Witnesses how I was treated. He came up immediately into the Printing-

House, continu'd the Quarrel, high Words passed on both Sides, he gave me the Quarter's Warning we had stipulated, expressing a Wish that he had not been oblig'd to so long a Warning: I told him his Wish was unnecessary for I would leave that Instant; and so taking my Hat walk'd out of Doors. (*A:*110–1)

A perennial failure because of his personal quirkiness, a devotee of a strange, obscure religious sect who went on to compose a personal religion, Keimer is a Dickensian grotesque in whom any ingenuity that may have been has been strangled by the force of pecadilloes. We see him first neglecting business by using up all his available types for a bad elegy for Andrew Bradford's late apprentice, the lamented Aquila Rose, himself a poet of no discernible talent. As we appreciate Franklin's accumulating satire of Keimer, we should realize that he is pushing Keimer's peculiarity to a point of extremity where Keimer's opposition to Franklin can have no credibility but can only contrast with and so reveal Franklin. The remarkable thing about the episode above is that Franklin *does* show a particular emotion – anger – and so enters the realm of positively discernible character. This confession is a rare moment in the *Autobiography,* but remember the occasion: Keimer has ridiculed Franklin in the public eye, imputing a particular characteristic to him while others are watching. The only thing that rouses Franklin to show the particular characteristic of anger, it seems, is an irrational attempt to interfere with the public's acclaim for his boundlessness. But the anger is short-lived, and the equanimity is resumed as Franklin later recounts that Keimer failed in business.

The impatience and anger that Franklin shows at several points in Part One render him real. But in each encounter, Franklin's personality ends up justified, and so he returns to unaltered equanimity. The momentary perturbation does not intimate a critical reflection on his own nature, only a contrastive unreason *so* stubborn even he cannot be content to laugh at it. These encounters are not dramatic conflicts between two personalities so much as they are contrasts between a blank and blameless character and a bundle of fractious prejudices that only occasionally prods humor into anger, and even the confession of anger may be included to forestall the reader's disbelief in the seeming infinity of Franklin's patience. Confessions of rare anger prevent the reader from protesting the improbability of endless even-temperedness.

Franklin's anger is a response to Keimer's attempt to embarrass him by imputing a particular character to him and so to reduce his power of free circulation. However, this power is never seriously damaged by any of Franklin's encounters, and none of them threatens to change him beyond making him temporarily angry. Still, he depends on opponents to give episodes, and, consequently, his character, shape, a shape that is always the ingenious and resolute opposite of their motley brands of obtuseness. Each encounter shows us Franklin in reaction: "and so taking my Hat walk'd out of Doors." The characterization of the opponent is carefully developed to *show* Franklin when he differentiates himself from that character-option. As money is not any one commodity, so the Franklin of Part One is the series of his refusals, the compendium of his avoidances of all the odd habits, intolerable demands, and curious stupidities of the others who reveal but do not profoundly challenge him. In Part One, we see Franklin at his projects, but we do not *know* him as we know James or Keimer: what we know of his individuality, we know negatively, that is, that he learns to avoid the kinds of particularity that would inhibit the success of his project. The carefully developed unreasonableness of the other party suffices in place of a direct development of his own particularity; and the careful development of the other party's ridiculousness allows him to circumvent the particular position that argument would require.

He represents himself as reacting to irrational authority rather than as rebelling against just authority. He does this to disarm any suspicions about rebellion that the reader might have. To this end, he concedes that implications of criminality did follow him after he left his brother's shop. His friend Collins aids his escape: "He agreed with the Captain of a New York Sloop for my Passage, under the Notion of my being a young Acquaintance of his that had got a naughty Girl with Child, whose Friends would compel me to marry her, and therefore I could not appear or come away publickly" (*A:*71). In Perth Amboy, "I cut so miserable a Figure too, that I found by the Questions asked me that I was suspected to be some runaway Servant, and in Danger of being taken up on that Suspicion" (*A:*73). And in Philadelphia, "several sly Questions were ask'd me, as it seem'd to be suspected from my youth and Appearance, that I might be some Runaway" (*A:*77). To those who do not consider self-determination a viable possibility, Franklin's social looseness suggests hidden turpitude. These suspicions and innuendoes acquire a certain ominousness, like the sailors' suspicions of Job in Father Mapple's sermon in *Moby Dick* or like the vague guiltiness that afflicts Pip in *Great Expectations*. A more immediate parallel might be the signs of disfavor that begin to appear in Robinson Crusoe's life almost as soon as he decides to live his life his way. But Franklin allows this growing ominousness to dissipate: it never coalesces into a critical, coherent position with respect to his character. Rather, he introduces it only to anticipate the traditionalistic narrow-mindedness that would identify self-determination with prodigality. These imputations of criminality are introduced, that is, not to offer a critical purchase on Franklin's production of character, but to furnish a kind of obtuseness that will highlight by contrast the excellence of what he did become: "I have been the more particular in this Description of my Journey, and shall be so of my first Entry into that City, that you may in your Mind compare such unlikely Beginnings with the Figure I have since made there" (*A:*75). We are to compare our expectations about the likely outcome of such beginnings with their true outcome, and so apprehend the difference between what he became and what our filiopiety led us to expect.

These accusations are not misguided. Though innocent of any dalliance at this time, Franklin did father William, to whom the book is addressed, before he married Deborah Read. And he was at this time a runaway from legal apprenticeship. Franklin acknowledges such suspicions without acquiescing in the conclusion that he is blameworthy. Rather, he acknowledges them to show that he is neither one who succumbs to arbitrary power nor one whose revolt is a symptom of the dissipation of a prodigal son. Having extricated himself from the particular life into which father and father-surrogates would coerce him, he has to show his simultaneous avoidance of the kind of particularity that is widely perceived to be the only alternative to filiopiety. Mentioning the suspicions about his nature and about the likely outcome of such unlikely beginnings, Franklin is setting the stage for the introduction of several friends who do succumb to prodigality, so that he may in turn differentiate himself from them, like Hal from Falstaff. Having preserved his resourcefulness from the coercion of traditionalism, he must now defend it against the charge of dissipation, and to do so he again has to contrast himself with the unreasonable particularity of others, though the particularity is now dissipation rather than despotism.

Leaving Boston, he plunges into the eighteenth-century urban world of cranks, sharps, chiselers, prevaricators, philanderers, and hack poets, all of whom share his rebellion against inheritance, only to separate himself out from their midst. He is the "neither A nor B" in what had been thought to be a binary system, different both from what his father, James, and Keimer had sought to make him be and from the self-squandering extravagance of John Collins and James Ralph.

Collins and Ralph are first brought to the reader's attention because, like Franklin, they have resisted traditional authority and chosen their own way: "The others rather more lax in their Principles of Religion, particularly Ralph, who as well as Collins had been unsettled by me, for which they both made me suffer" (*A:*89–90). Like Franklin, these two are literally as well as figuratively unsettled, that is, departed from the assigned course. This sentence augurs, however, the difference that emerges within that similarity, a difference that grows until these chums make him suffer for the similarity. Franklin befriends them because they are free-living and freethinking: he leaves them because their freedom is dissipation rather than self-fathering. The narrative development of Franklin's nondefinite virtue in the *Autobiography* requires that he first join them and then abandon them to their irresolute dissolution, borrowing the positivity of their independence in order to contrast himself with traditionalism only to contrast himself with them in turn. He *is* neither *this* – the man his father, brother, or Keimer intended him to be – nor *that* – one who loses himself in license: his diligently developed rejections of these two personal options, in other words, are made to suffice in place of a direct development of a character that is not susceptible to direct development.

Similarity of circumstance originally draws Franklin to Collins: "At New York I found my Friend Collins, who had arriv'd there some Time before me. We had been intimate from Children, and had read the same Books together, but he had the Advantage of more Time for reading, and studying and a wonderful Genius for Mathematical Learning in which he far outstript me" (*A*:84). Despite Collins's greater leisure and ability in mathematics, he and Franklin are doubles, fellow members of a nascent, independently minded, potentially rising generation of young Americans who have declared that the place and circumstances of their origin are inconsequential to life's eventual outcome.

But the other side of Collins's genius soon shows itself in the riot that unconstrained living permits:

> While I liv'd in Boston most of my Hours of Leisure for Conversation were spent with him, and he continu'd a sober as well as an industrious Lad; was much respected for his Learning by several of the Clergy and other Gentlemen, and seem'd to promise making a good Figure in life; but during my Absence he had acquired a Habit of Sotting with Brandy; and I found by his own Account and what I heard from others, that he had been drunk every day since his Arrival at New York, and behav'd very oddly. He had gam'd too and lost his Money, so that I was oblig'd to discharge his Lodgings, and defray his Expences to and at Philadelphia: Which prov'd extreamly inconvenient to me. (*A*:84–5)

Collins's gesture of independence from external authority is not succeeded by the development of an internal regime, so his freedom degenerates into the petty rebelliousness and wasteful uncooperativeness of alcoholism. This sort of personal development, which Franklin finds useless as a model, proves extremely useful as a contrast to reveal the blank calculation of *his* life-method: personal resources are a kind of capital; time in Boston with Collins yields a return; Collins away from Boston is a low-yield friend. Here we have Weber's balance-book made into what Franklin called "moral algebra," an accounting of the return on affection. Such calculation is clearly presented in this section of Part One because it is exactly what Collins ignores. Franklin's appraisal of his friendship with Collins, that is, is presented to us as the negation of Collins's failure to make such calculations with personal resources: Franklin's ability to calculate is a consequence of his independence from that which is the subject of calculation – Collins's dissipation. This ability is the hallmark of Franklin's clarity: essential participation in what is to be understood must be avoided before understanding can begin, as money abstains from the particularity of commodities so that it may render them quantitatively commensurable. This is not to say that Franklin should have become an alcoholic, but that his choice of examples to illustrate the supremacy of clarity is such that we are not invited to think it might be otherwise. As in his representations of authority, Franklin is exaggerating the personal position he is rejecting so that the rejection is not controversial.

The economy of friendliness inevitably demands a break from Collins:

> His Drinking continu'd about which we sometimes quarrel'd, for when a little intoxicated he was very fractious. Once in a boat on the Delaware with some other young Men, he refused to row in his Turn: I will be row'd home, says he. We will not row you, says I. You must or stay all Night on the Water, says he, just as you please. The others said, Let us row: what signifies it? But my Mind being soured with his other Conduct, I continu'd to refuse. So he swore he would make me row, or throw me overboard; and coming along stepping on the Thwarts toward me, when he came up and struck at me I clapt my hand under hs Crutch, and rising pitch'd him head-foremost into the River. I knew he was a good Swimmer, and so was under little Concern about him; but before he could get round to lay hold of the Boat, we had with a few Strokes pull'd her out of his reach. And ever when he drew near the Boat, we ask'd if he would row, striking a few Strokes to slide her away from him. He was ready to die with Vexation, and obstinately would not promise to row; however seeing him at last beginning to tire, we lifted him in; and brought him home dripping wet in the Evening. We hardly exchang'd a civil Word afterwards. (A:85–6)

The unrewarding expenditure of self on friend proves to be too much: Franklin's humor – his "ironic reserve" – stretches and breaks; pitching Collins from the boat, he is also pitching him out of his life, which will progress more evenly without Collins; and his last gesture to Collins is educative, teaching him that refusing to hang together means hanging separately.

This outing that turned ugly, the surfacing of an animosity that reserve could no longer contain, shows Franklin's limit, and his difference from Collins. Or rather, it shows Franklin showing his limit, showing the reader not to confuse his blankness with stupid patience; but it must be noted that, though Franklin allows us to see him in his particularity, he is careful to maneuver it so that by the end of the story Collins's frustration has become the center of satiric attention and Franklin's irritation has faded into the background. Franklin's admission of his anger occurs under controlled circumstances, and is quickly put away so that by the end Collins's unreason is highlighted and Franklin – who has blended back into the "we" – is clear by contrast with him. At the moment of breaking from Collins, Franklin's individuality is visible, like the electric spark leaping free from common matter, only to return shortly to its calm and blank repose. Even at this moment, however, Franklin's only revealed individuality is refusal – irritation and anger – and it tells us no more about his particular sentiment than the vehemence of his desire not to be seen as one motivated by particular sentiments.

The other freethinking friend is James Ralph. He and Franklin versify together, but again as with Collins there is a latent difference: "I approv'd the amusing one's self with Poetry now and then, so far as to improve one's Language, but no farther" (*A:*90). In this, Franklin is a clear heir to the *Manuductio ad Ministerium,* but in a different key. For Mather, poetry can enhance the argument of the sermon, but it may also deflect meaning toward the devil's simulacra; but for Franklin its good lies in its power to improve one's language for any number of morally indifferent tasks, and its danger is wasted time and energy, not demonism. Stripping poetry's danger of cosmic dimension, Franklin can perfect the quantitative impulse already at play in Mather's idea of measured doses: poetry rhymes, and so to write it requires one to enhance one's vocabulary; such effort is worth the time, but carried further, poetry is a waste of self.

Lewis Thomas has called poetry and music "redundant, elegant sound that is unaccountable as part of the working day."[6] Poetry's distinguishing mark, according to Thomas, is its celebration of order per se and its abstention from calculations of use, gain, and worthwhile investment. Some might argue with this, but Franklin would not, and the failure to calculate in the attraction to poetry is what drives him from Ralph and his versifying. Ralph, unlike Franklin but like Collins, does not think in controlled doses. His interest in poetry is too great: but Franklin, not Ralph, does the measuring, as he did in his appraisal of the value of the friendship with Collins, and, in measuring Ralph, Franklin is also measuring the wisdom of his own involvement with someone who does not measure. As with Collins, he is able to survey the friend by his avoidance of the friend's quirk, and illustrates his clarity by contrast. The story of Franklin's association with Ralph communicates what Franklin is by showing his avoidance of Ralph-ism. Thus, as with Collins, the description of the early affinity – Franklin was attracted to versification in his

[6] Lewis Thomas, *The Lives of a Cell: Notes of a Biology Watcher* (New York: Bantam Books, 1975), p. 25.

younger years – sets the stage for the break that follows: "One of Young's Satires was just then publish'd. I copy'd and sent him a great Part of it, which set in a strong Light the Folly of pursuing the Muses with any Hope of Advancement by them. All was in vain. Sheets of [Ralph's] Poems continu'd to come by every Post" (*A*:98–9). All was in vain: Franklin recognizes the futility of his involvement with Ralph, a realization that is based on and revealed by contrast with Ralph's failure to recognize the futility of his involvement with poetry. In fact, Ralph's poetry is bad, but aesthetic appraisal is not the center of Franklin's critique.

In his descriptions of Collins and Ralph, Franklin measures what return may be expected from friends who do not measure returns. The young Franklin's eventual break from his friend is foreshadowed from the first by the narrator's appraising attitude: had the young Franklin tarried in uncalculating affection, the narrator's clarity would have been inhibited. "All was in vain": this sentence digests the difference between Franklin and Ralph. Ralph persists with poetry despite its lack of payment as Collins persists with alcohol despite its injury to his fortunes; Franklin abandons his friendships with Ralph and Collins because of their lack of payment, of useful return for time spent. This juxtaposition of Ralph's and Collins's prodigality with Franklin's measuring caution shows Franklin's character at work, displaying his own blankness as the surpassing negation of their self-waste. Avoiding their error, he can measure it; measuring it, he reveals himself to the reader, as one who avoids their error. The circularity of this contrastive self-display would degenerate into tautological sterility were it not constantly fed with new objects of measurement.

Part One thus demonstrates Franklin's detachment from filiopiety not only as a coercive authority in his life but as a worldview in the mind of his reader. Franklin realistically delineates the two alternatives admitted in the filiopietistic scheme – submission and riot – in order to differentiate himself from both of them. This demonstrative refutation of Puritan binarism is the specific purpose of Part One. But it also establishes the method of the *Autobiography* as a whole. We might expect that after Franklin has separated himself from both of the extant alternatives in the reader's mind he will go on to show what he *is*; but this does not occur, because his self-presentation never abandons the technique of showing himself by creating for the reader selves he might have become but did not. Franklin's character always remains itself – blank and unaltered – and refuses to accept essential definition from the human neighborhood in which it operates. Submission and prodigality are only the grosser forms of the particularity that threatens him in subtler forms in the subsequent parts. In Part Two Franklin demonstrates his independence from habits of slovenliness and so on, treating them as extrinsic irritations that affect him but are alien to his conscious selfhood, like internal Collinses and Ralphs that vex but do not alter him. In Part Three Franklin demonstrates his independence from any number of specific roles, such as civic benefactor, which are not innately objectionable like submission and prodigality, but only become objectionable if they absorb and define self, and which therefore require not rejection but only confinement to the level of worthwhile but nondefining occupations of his time. In Parts Two and Three Franklin shows how he protected and extended the range of the freedom he achieved in Part One. But the greater subtlety of temptation in the later parts should not disguise the continuity of technique: Franklin first realistically develops a character option, then identifies it as a potential captivation of his free mobility, then avoids it, and defines his character by contrast with it. As the list of these roads not taken grows longer, the reader's expectation of a definition of what Franklin's character *is* diminishes, and the apprehension of its purely negative blankness is incrementally advanced.

At the end of Part One, the boundless blankness of self has been defined as the avoidance of the two alternatives represented as the only alternatives in Puritan thought. More importantly, he not only avoids them, but does so without any record of terrible inner trauma. Because he does not concede that he feels the eloquence of either devout acquiescence or hearty license as a pressing factor in his calculations, there is no psychomachy, no sense that the success of pure purpose is achieved at the price of suppressing other elements of the whole consciousness. In Franklin's writings, the aberrant remains humorous or at most irritating: the divergence of *is* from *ought* never assumes the proportion of the truly monstrous, as it does for Mather, because Franklin presents himself as being completely aloof from the aberrant and so he is not drawn to it; Franklin's reaction to what he would consider wrong shows none of the secret affinity that is betrayed in the ferment of fascination and extreme revulsion with which Mather watched aberration. In transcending submission and prodigality, Franklin seems to be not so much waging war on parts of himself as simply shrugging off ineffectual and not very tempting roles. There is no disquiet in Franklin's resolution, no surface turbulence indicating submerged protest.

Near the end of Part Three Franklin presents an episode that is an allegory of the double avoidance described in Part One. Chosen by the Pennsylvania Assembly to represent the Assembly's quarrel with the royal proprietors to the Parliament, Franklin reserves passage on a packet leaving from New York. He is to travel with Lord Loudon, who repeatedly uses his privilege to delay the packet's departure: "One would imagine that I was now on the Point of Departing for Europe. I thought so; but I was not then so well acquainted with his Lordship's Character, of which

Indecision was one of the strongest features" (*A:250*). Once again, Franklin's free progress is restrained by the whim of one who abuses authority, a situation that recalls his relations with his brother and with Keimer and anticipates the encounter between America and Parliament that by the time this was written had resulted in revolution. Loudon's delays grow increasingly irritating, keeping Franklin and the other passengers waiting from early April till the end of June.

Finally, the packet sails, but its progress is initially sluggish:

> Our Captain of the Pacquet had boasted much before we sail'd, of the Swiftness of his Ship. Unfortunately when we came to Sea, she proved the dullest of 96 Sail, to his no small Mortification. After many Conjectures respecting the cause, when we were near another Ship almost as dull as ours, which however gain'd upon us, the Captain order'd all Hands to come aft and stand as near the Ensign Staff as possible. We were, Passengers included, about Forty Persons. While we stood there the Ship mended her Pace, and soon left our Neighbour far behind, which prov'd clearly what our Captain suspected, that she was loaded too much by the Head. The Casks of Water it seems had all been plac'd forward. These he therefore order'd to be remov'd father aft; on which the Ship recovered her Character, and prov'd the best Sailor in the Fleet. (*A:255–6*)

Traveling toward England and the activity that will bring him to the height of his career, having entirely emerged from the circumstances in which he was born and bred and having avoided the traps along the way, Franklin finds himself in a situation that is rendered in the *Autobiography* as an allegory of how he got to where he is. He has escaped the irrational constraint of arbitrary authority, Loudon, who had restrained him from free progress toward his future; and, like the ship, he has trimmed his ballast, purging himself of any specially prominent particularity that would slow his progress. Finally embarked on his life, he has avoided anything that would keep him from his destiny: like the ship, he has "recovered his Character" and "prov'd the best Sailor in the Fleet," because he has escaped the particularity of origin, of submission to heteronomous authority, and he has avoided the particularity of self-expenditure in a single permanent form.

The episode of the packet thus exemplifies the double freedom Franklin demonstrated in Part One, from the Scylla of external constraint and the Charybdis of dissipation, or self-waste. This double freedom, though, is also a single freedom, from the binaristic understanding of selfhood advanced in Puritan social theory. Taken as a whole, Part One of the *Autobiography* is Franklin's cautious, inoffensive self-extrication from the polarity that vexed Mather and left his life a fervent, agonized contradiction between worldly interest and the obligations of self-transcendence.

By demonstrating a form of self that is neither submissive nor prodigal, Franklin separates self-fathering from both submission and riot, and thereby divests the relation between boundless universality and worldly interest of its contradiction. Franklin's self-differentiation from the likes of Collins and Ralph shows that his brand of worldly interest does not require a sacrifice of universality; his self-differentiation from submission to father, brother, and Keimer shows that universality does not require a complete sacrifice of self to an alien will. By legitimating a secular universality that is self-chosen and self-regulated, Franklin proposes a way out of the contradiction that is the salient mark of Cotton Mather's life.

Franklin thus offers himself as a happy, noncontradictory combination of boundlessness and self-direction. But this mediation of Puritan contradiction has no conceptual foundation. He merely shows that he was *free from* both options, and that, consequently, there is a third. But the third is defined only as the negation of the other two. The domination of life by untransforming purpose is as clear in Franklin's life as it was in Mather's: but the negative force of purpose is for Franklin a practical avoidance of positive commitment rather than a principled critique of the individual from the point of view of a transcendent standard.

Describing the sect he envisioned for the promulgation of virtue, Franklin writes in Part Three that he contemplated naming it "the Society of the *Free and Easy;* Free, as being by the general Practice and Habit of the Virtues, free from the Domination of Vice, and particularly by the Practice of Industry and Frugality, free from Debt, which exposes a Man to Confinement and a Species of Slavery to his Creditors" (*A:*163). Vice is to be avoided not for its moral content but for its power to subject the self to domination, confinement, slavery. The intensity of Franklin's vision of the disagreeability of confinement is not matched by an equally intense vision of virtue as a state of personal being; rather, virtue is a *habit,* a cultivated automatism of behavior that – because it is automatic – does not define or possess the self. Franklin's freedom, therefore, is purely negative, a determined, claustrophobic avoidance of particularity that is not accompanied by an equally determined desire for a positive state. His desire for *freedom from,* in other words, does not commit him to a corresponding desire for *freedom to,* however much his rhetoric implies that his free tact is a humanism. This abstinence commits his life story to an incessant (and mono-tonous) series of self-separations and a search for an acclaim from the full human community that will certify his virtue in lieu of the satisfaction of having reached a positively defined goal. Without a destination, such a self can only be a productive and distinguished restlessness, like money.

In the later parts of the *Autobiography,* Franklin confronts forms of external coercion subtler than the despotism of his brother or the prodigality of Collins and Ralph. The early, objectionable forms of particularity are succeeded by potential forms of selfhood that are objectionable to Franklin simply because they are particular. As the *Autobiography* progresses, Franklin's contrasting of self with unacceptable varieties of particular life develops into his contrasting of self with the unacceptability of particular life per se. For example, Franklin declines, in his political career, to be the voice of a faction. Similarly, in his professional life, he declines to be tied to printing, stove design, and so on. He does not reject these activities because they represent untenable forms of personal positivity but because they represent the untenability *of* personal positivity.

Part One already contains the germ of this more subtle transcendence. Franklin writes that he cultivated inoffensiveness by avoiding committing himself to particular stances, and he associates this rhetorical strategy with Socrates: "And soon after I procur'd Xenophon's Memorable Things of Socrates, wherein there are many Instances of the same Method. I was charm'd with it, dropt my abrupt Contradiction, and positive Argumentation, and put on the humble Enquirer and Doubter" (*A*:64). Franklin is learning to avoid committing himself to *any* positive position rather than simply to flawed positive positions. He reports that he later gave up much of this method – doubting and subtle inquiry can be offensive too – but retained the avoidance of self-assertive "positivity" in order to escape the prominent particularity that such positivity would commit him to:

> I continu'd this Method some few Years, but gradually left it, retaining only the Habit of expressing myself in Terms of Modest Diffidence, never using when I advance any thing that may possibly be disputed, the Words, *Certainly, undoubtedly,* or any others that give the Air of Positiveness to an Opinion . . . I wish wellmeaning sensible Men would not lessen their Power of Doing Good by a Positive assuming Manner that seldom fails to disgust, tends to create Opposition, and to defeat every one of those Purposes for which Speech was given to us, to wit, giving or receiving Information, or Pleasure: For if you would *inform,* a positive dogmatical Manner in advancing your Sentiments, may provoke Contradiction and prevent a candid Attention. (*A*:65)

Franklin reaches this conclusion *before* he leaves his brother's employ and before he rejects Collins and Ralph, and it sets the stage for those rejections, indicating that the specific objectionability of the particular formation of self in which they would involve him is less offensive than the objectionability of particularity itself. To be perceived to be committed to a particular positive shape is to lessen the mobility of self throughout the diversity of society and so to be incarcerated.

This is not really a Socratic position. For Franklin, positivity and dogma are to be avoided not because the subtle daimon of irony senses the distance of truth from inherently shallow verbal formulations but because they would expose and make prominent the particular opinions of the speaker, and so diminish the quantitative range of his effect. Deliberating over Franklin's *impersonality*, Carl Becker postulates a Franklinian irony:

> Was there not then, on that placid countenance, even at the signing of the great Declaration, the bland smile which seems to say: This is an interesting, alas even a necessary, game; and we are playing it well, according to all the rules; but men being what they are it is perhaps best not to inquire too curiously what its ultimate significance may be.

Franklin, Becker surmises, brought his blankness, his disengagement, even to this most positive of assertions, the Declaration of Independence. Becker detects the absence of a fully present and committed personality; and he recoils from the possibility that this blankness *is* what Franklin has designed himself to be by postulating a reserved, recessed, ironic Franklin. This alienation becomes clearer when Becker remarks on the particular traits one *never finds* expressed in Franklin's performances – "inhibitions and repressions and *spiritual malaise.*" But even here Becker confines his indication of the absence of particular traits to psychological disorders, thereby once again swerving from a hard look at Franklin's special laconism. He observes the blank where there might otherwise be a prominent, involved personal presence, but he backs away from his own intuition by postulating a Franklin at an ironic distance and by reducing the signs of a visible presence to emotional dysfunctions. I would respond to Becker by contending that Franklin's self-presentation lacks not only "inhibitions and repressions and *spiritual malaise*" but *all* signs of actual particular character and that bland placidity at a moment of urgent commitment indicates a self-maintenance that views all commitments as confinements rather than a genial ironic contempt for human frailties.

Franklin's blankness should not be connected with irony since irony involves a relation between a superior particular commitment and an inferior one. It is a mode of argument, and so requires at least provisional positivity from one who employs it. Becker's assertion of Franklin's irony is akin to Nick Carraway's resisting fascination with Gatsby's nonsignifying smile and with his need to define the *real* Gatsby in opposition to all the false accounts that circulate at the parties. But the blank and negative Franklin is *all there is.*

And this construction of self as an abstract blankness is accompanied by a corollary reduction of the world to calculability. We have already seen one example in the episode of the English Bible taped to the bottom of the stool, where the courageousness of Protestant fervor goes unre-

---

[7] Carl Becker, "Benjamin Franklin," in *The Dictionary of American Biography*, ed. Allen Johnson and Dumas Malone (New York: Scribner, 1931), vol. 6, p. 597.

marked in the interest of cultivating admiration for the device of the Bible and the stool. Franklin does not disguise his reductiveness in this passage – since he himself provides the information about Protestantism and Marian persecution – but what we might see as reduction he intends as a demonstration of the easy detachability of ingenuity from the motives that enlist its aid.

He offers a similar demonstration when he offhandedly remarks in the *Autobiography* that Poor Richard's proverbs "contained the Wisdom of many Ages and Nations" (*A:*164). No doubt several of the maxims do originate in previous philosophy, but this remark makes a larger claim: the brunt of Franklin's assertion here, as in his contention that his *Articles of Belief and Religion* are a sufficient digest of the variety of human worship, is that such ingenious culling is not a violation of the source-text, that what is left behind is only a chaff with which ingenuity happened to be mixed. Because what remains is chaff, therefore, rational extraction comes up with a product that is a just and adequate representation of the original whole. This is a version of Philocles' reformation of Horatio's self: as Philocles took one element from what Horatio and Mather called self, and called this extracted calculation self, so Richard's summation of wisdom distills an element of philosophy and calls it a fair digest of the whole. The resulting aphorism, in its insular independence from surrounding expository or literary context, in its adaptive transferability to a virtually unlimited variety of rhetorical contexts, from almanac to letter to public address, and in its unself-critical criticism of an unreason it makes seem so easy to abjure (and so absurd not to abjure), is the perfect formal vehicle for the Franklinian self. But to succeed, such distillation must silence what remains behind, representing that residue as chaff, rather than allowing it any proper eloquence, which would expose the hermeneutic violence at work and defeat the illusion of spontaneous harmony.

We may observe this process in Franklin's proposal for the simplification of scripture. In his "Parable against Persecution" and "Parable on Brotherly Love," Franklin demonstrated his familiarity with the diction of the King James Bible: "And God called unto Abraham, saying, Abraham, where is the stranger? And Abraham answered and said, Lord, he would not worship thee, neither would he call upon thy name; therefore have I driven him out from before my face into the wilderness" (*W,* II:122). Franklin's pastiche of biblical language depends most heavily on pleonasm ("answered and said"), and his repetition of this device through the length of the two pamphlets is just slightly excessive, slightly overstated, and thus probably parodic, making the parables into satires of scriptural expression as well as of intolerance. In his proposal for the revision of scripture, Franklin implicitly contends that such eloquence is really only an encumbering disguise of what true ingenuity the Bible does contain.

He quotes, for example, this verse from Job: "And the Lord said unto Satan, Whence comest thou? Then Satan answered the Lord, and said, From going to and fro in the earth, and walking up and down in it." Franklin suggests this revision: "And God said to Satan, You have been some time absent; where were you? And Satan answered I have been at my country-seat, and in different places visiting my friends" (*W,* II:167). Again, Franklin is not disguising his reductiveness, but instead promoting it as a demonstration of the detachability of the useful from its accidental form. The revision of the verse from Job may itself be somewhat tongue-in-cheek, though this seems to me unlikely; and, even if it were, such slight facetiousness would not jeopardize the central proposition, that complex diction and feeling should be reappraised as wasteful redundancy, and exchanged for utilitarian simplicity, which would not be a significant sacrifice. The same proposal underlies Franklin's plans for revising the Lord's Prayer and the Book of Common Prayer. Sainte-Beuve thought that this determination showed Franklin to be a spiritual illiterate. But Franklin was not unaware of the deep wells of human emotion: rather, he proposed that they be boarded over, after the man had been hoisted out, so that the enlightened man could live in the open and common day.

In England during the sojourn described in Part One, Franklin encounters another of the richly particular characters who serve as contrastive foils to his blankness:

> In a Garret of [my landlady's] House there lived a Maiden Lady of 70 in the most retired Manner, of whom the Landlady gave me this Account, that she was a Roman Catholic, had been sent abroad when young, and lodg'd in a Nunnery with an Intent of becoming a Nun: but the Country not agreeing with her, she return'd to England, where there being no Nunnery, she had vow'd to lead the life of a Nun as near as might be done in those Circumstances: Accordingly she had given all of her Estate to charitable Uses, reserving only Twelve Pounds a year to live on, and out of this Sum she still gave a great deal to Charity, living herself on Water-Gruel only, and using no Fire but to boil it. She have lived many Years in that Garret, being permitted to remain there Gratis by successive Catholic Tenants of the House Below, as they deem'd it a Blessing to have her there. A Priest visited her, to confess her every day. I have ask'd her, says my Landlady, how she, as she liv'd, could possibly find so much Employment for a Confessor? O, says she, it is impossible to avoid *vain Thoughts.* I was permitted once to visit her: she was chearful and polite, and convers'd pleasantly. The Room was clean, but had no other Furniture than a Matras, a Table with a Crucifix and Book, a Stool, which she gave me to sit on, and a Picture over the Chimney of St. Veronica, displaying her Handkerchief with the miraculous Figure of Christ's bleeding Face on it, which she explain'd to me with great Seriousness.

Franklin abstains from commenting on her peculiarity – the keeping of self from free circulation, the keeping of little icons, and so on. But the conclusion of the episode is anticipated in the things he does notice – the inoffensiveness of her conversation, the cleanliness of the apartment, the frugality of its furnishings. Franklin's approval of these things is enabled by his indifference to her passion: where she might regard such little ingenuities as incidental and minor attributes of the passion, for Franklin they are the detachable gist to be taken away from the visit: "She look'd pale, but was never sick, and I give it as another Instance on how small an Income Life and Health may be supported (*A:* 102–3). In his dive into this woman's deep, Franklin swims past the pearls, the cross, and the skulls, and surfaces clutching the account book; ignoring the passion, he improves the visit by coming away with a Poor Richard maxim. His improvement is more conspicuous for what it leaves than for what it takes. Her imagination's peopled mansion, built word by word to the confessor with intensely grasped Catholic symbolism as a rough blue-print, registers less with Franklin than the frugality that is one small part of the whole passion. But again we must notice that our sense of all that is left out of the concluding improvement is permitted by the preceding account: we are not discovering anything we were not meant to discover when we see that the conclusion excludes much of the whole; we are, however, calling Franklin's demonstration of detachability a reduction.

The self that lifts itself out of the welter of the whole consciousness detaches itself from all the other components in order to identify com-pletely with the domination of calculating ingenuity, and therefore re-quires a similar event in its world. The significant note here is that the surpassed and then dominated parts of self and world are completely divested of their *voice:* they are a kind of dead chaff from which ingenuity is winnowed; they persist only in the mute form of being talked about by the ingenuity that has abandoned their neighborhood and then has returned to administrate it. Though they are empirically present, in other words, they do not have the vitality of being able to affect the resolute deliberation of the surveying narrative intelligence, whether through rea-son, plea, or threat.

Without a countervailing voice to qualify, deepen, or terminate the predominant resolution, the *Autobiography* will not be brought to clo-sure. Franklin picks it up three more times, extending but failing to fin-ish it. Rather than coming to a close, it expands quantitatively, register-ing numbers of successes and amounts of acclaim, becoming more a list than a narrative – infinitely, like the progeny of the breeding-sow and the polyp. The romance of numbers dictates the shape of the progress of the self that emerges in Part One, because that self has demonstrated its pu-rity and because it is not opposed by any voice that can challenge or alter it qualitatively. It can only grow. Franklin will of course die, but his death

will terminate the act of writing the *Autobiography*, rather than concluding the story it tells. He began to write it when he began to consider his
death and the best way to keep the self's reputation alive and circulating.
The act of writing the *Autobiography* is the last member of the long series
of self-investments chronicled in the *Autobiography;* like capital, the produced self disengages from the commodity that was its temporary vehicle, in this case, the body, and emigrates to a new body, the text, from
where it can seek out new vessels – the future Horatios who will emulate
the narrator. The history of the emulative readings of the *Autobiography*, in other words, is the *Autobiography*'s last, longest, still-unfinished
chapter.

9

THE DEATH, SHAME, AND RENOWN OF BENJAMIN FRANKLIN

Th'expense of spirit in a waste of shame
Is lust in action
                                        Shakespeare, Sonnet 129

He speaks of himself as he would have spoken of another.
                                        La Rochefoucauld, on Franklin

A Person is confin'd in a House which appears to be in imminent danger of Falling, this, as soon as perceiv'd, creates a violent *Uneasiness,*
and that instantly produces an equally strong *Desire,* the *End* of which
is *freedom from the Uneasiness,* and the *Manner* or Way propos'd to gain
this *End,* is to *get out of the House.*
                    Franklin, *A Dissertation on Liberty and Necessity, Pleasure and Pain*

In Part One of the *Autobiography,* some few pages after informing the
reader that it can be expeditious to avoid a "positive assuming manner,"
the narrator suggests that several lines from Pope might be improved to
better effect, but adds, "This however I leave to better judgements" (*A:*66).
Between Parts One and Two he includes two letters from friends who
have read Part One and have written to urge him to find time for continuing the work, for the public's good: the inclusion of these letters is
consonant with his advice, presented fifty pages later, that one should
never seem to want public acclaim. In Part Two, having resolved "to
imitate Jesus and Socrates," the narrator seems to confess having failed at
humility: "I cannot boast of much Success in acquiring the *Reality* of this
Virtue; but I had a good deal with regard to the *Appearance* of it" (*A:*159).
In this deft sentence, Franklin is both instructing the reader in a social art
in which the appearance is all that matters, and being humble ("I cannot
boast") about his success in attaining humility.
    At moments like these, the social art which is explained to the reader
throughout the book is also practiced on him. The second of these func-

tions is rhetorically prior: having won over the reader with his inoffensiveness, his unconcernedness, his humor, and his constant sanity, Franklin shows that these are not unique traits from which the reader is barred,
but instead the results of concrete, generally available techniques of self-
construction. Readings of the *Autobiography* are therefore to be sequels
to it, or continuations of it, and the readers are to be members of the
burgeoning consensus of admiring Horatios who populate the account
of Franklin's growing renown in Parts Two, Three, and Four.

I will not examine this story of the growth of Franklin's fame at length
because it adheres to a simple repeating pattern clearly present, for example, in the account of the formation of the Pennsylvania Academy
which Franklin had outlined in his "Proposals Relating to the Education
of Youth in Pensilvania." To ensure that the board of trustees for the
building of the physical plant is not biased, the planners appoint members of Pennsylvania's various sects – the Anglicans, the Presbyterians,
the Baptists, the Moravians, and so on. The Moravian dies roundly dis-
liked, and Franklin is appointed to his place, but not because he represents a particular interest: "At length one mention'd me, with the Observation that I was merely an honest Man, and of no Sect at all; which
prevail'd with them to chuse me" (*A:*194). He does so well in this post
that he is chosen to go between the trustees for the physical plant and the
trustees for curriculum design. The pattern, again, is simple: Franklin
enters the task and prevails because he has no particular stake or special
interest; he exits renowned for his disinterestedness, but *more* renowned.
The embodiment does not alter his reputation except quantitatively. If he
remains clearly unconcerned, unattached to visible partial cause, his activity is like money invested in a commodity: it is the same, but larger,
at the end. Once Franklin has demonstrated the emergence of self from
its circumstances of origin, this pattern becomes the repeated structural
unit of narrative.

The *Autobiography* becomes not protean, as Sayre contends, but mo-
notonous: this is the monotony, however, of careful pedagogy, showing
the growth of a Philadelphian, then a Pennsylvanian, then an American,
and then an imperial fame. Each of these stages in the progress of renown
is also a stage in the formation of human consensus: in Part Three, Franklin
remarks that, had his Albany Plan been adopted, the empire would be
intact, and British man would be that much closer to universal man.
"But such Mistakes are not new: History is full of the Errors of States
and Princes" (*A:*211). From small beginnings come great things if there
is no despotic interference with free and innate growth. Franklin's renown would mime the progress of the polyp, whose fissions duplicate it
infinitely, but retain the "native strictness and fastness" of the original.
Franklin describes such arithmetical progression in his account of the

success of the Junto. The group has grown famous enough that more young Horatios wish to join the original twelve (the apostles minus Christ?). Franklin opposes new members, recommending instead that each original member form a subordinate club with the same rules and the same queries required for entry. Franklin does not calculate the numerical results of such dodecafurcation, but he does envision "the Promotion of our particular Interests in Business by more extensive Recommendations; and the Increase of our Influence in public Affairs and our Power of doing Good by spreading thro' the several Clubs the Sentiments of the Junto" (*A:*170–1).

But the success of the fission is only modest: five or six clubs succeed for a while, but there appears to have been no second-generation division, perhaps because of the distance from Franklin's exemplary influence. Distance is not a problem with the *Autobiography;* Franklin contrives to be eloquently present to all ephebes, and thus extends his potential reach to an audience vaster than the population of the eighteenth-century British Empire – the Americans of the future, who, as he contended in his *Observations on the Increase of Mankind,* would double in number every twenty years. The reader is the "son" addressed on the first page, not Franklin's bastard son William, who in 1771 was the forty-year-old governor of New Jersey, and thus not in need of advice on how to avoid the temptations of youth and to get ahead. The *Autobiography* is an attempt to found a fraternal dynasty, in which conforming remembrance of the father can be self-interested rather than self-annihilating. Franklin's physical death, then, was not necessarily an interruption of the story of his life; his figural death – the transmigration of self from its mortal to its textual body – would be a fulfillment rather than an overthrow of the life's central ambition; and this figural death would differ from the series of self-detachments it caps only in being *more* ingenious, in shaping the universal self for acclaim from a universal audience.

The appropriation of death's secret as a figure for psychological transformation is frequent in Cotton Mather's writing. The essence of practical Christianity, according to Mather, is learning to die daily. This is a strong and apt figure for the emotional trauma self had to undergo to become pious. It is also, however, an ironic figure that plays on an ambiguity between opposed notions of life. The life of the self is the death of the filiopious soul, and vice versa. On the one hand, self rightly sees the harsh discipline of piety as an extinction of its independence and of its enjoyments, and so it contemplates its duty to God with fear and trembling. But, on the other hand, the soul in the process of conversionbirthing looks back at its predecessor, self, and at its former life, and despairs over the many years during which the bit of godliness was murdered by self's unhampered idolatries: it asks, does enough survive?

Conversion, therefore, was a transition from the first to the second notion of life: after the trauma of awakening humiliation, there is the moment when the self's fear becomes the soul's despair, the moment when
the Christian notion of vitality replaces its corrupt predecessor. The piety
that had seemed to be life-killing turns out to be life-preserving.

This conundrum is echoed in Philocles' assertion that self-denial is
really self-fulfillment. But, whereas Mather emphasizes that opposed
conceptions of life underlie his conundrum, Philocles does not admit that
he is using disparate conceptions of self. The calculating self, according
to Philocles, can arise spontaneously, purely, and easily from actual worldly
consciousness, without any harrowing by contradiction: the continuity
is what makes it so attractive to Horatio. When, in his later years, Franklin began to consider the death of his body, he followed Mather in using
this event as a figure for inner reformation; but he also concluded, like
Philocles and unlike Mather, that the survivor could be essentially continuous with its predecessor.

Like Mather, Franklin transferred properties from his figural understanding of death back to his literal understanding of death: as there is a
survivor in emotional reformations that are like death, so death itself is a
kind of reformation, or rearrangement, rather than a termination. Louis
Otto gave the following account of Franklin's death:

> Dr. Franklin, after patiently supporting the weight of 85 years, succes-
> sively passed in philosophic meditations and the whirlwind of affairs,
> has just finished his career with the serenity of a sage, who yearns after
> repose. A few moments before his dissolution he repeated these words
> that he had made for himself, *that a man is perfectly born only after his
> death.*

The moment when consciousness detached from body was consistent
with the philosophical detachment that governed the life. A. Owen Aldridge considers this the most believable account of Franklin's death, since
the last words are a nearly exact quotation from a letter of consolation
he had written to the stepdaughter of his brother John's widow in 1756.[1]

But God helps those who help themselves, and, as Becker suggests,
Franklin may have found reputation to be the most credible afterlife: one
could shape, or at least influence, one's afterlife by being an autobiographer, and the survivor would in that case be essentially continuous with
the living man. In a letter written to the Reverend John Lathrop two
years before his own death, Franklin remarked on the "growing felicity
of mankind, from the improvements in philosophy, morals, politics, and

---

[1] A. Owen Aldridge, *Benjamin Franklin and Nature's God* (Durham, N.C.: Duke
University Press, 1967), pp. 267–8. Aldridge translates and includes Otto's
account of Franklin's death.

even the conveniences of common living," and he wished it had been his lot to have been born two or three centuries later, because "invention and improvement are prolific, and beget more of their kind" (*W,* X:348). This letter was written during the same period that Franklin was composing the third and fourth parts of the *Autobiography,* a "convenience of common living" that would in some measure allow "Franklin" to continue to participate in the arithmetical increase of the general felicity he had been so dedicated to instigating. The textual "soul" that survived, designed by self, would therefore be fundamentally identical with self, since for Franklin self was defined as an abstract power to earn acclaim and to generate social agreement. If the voice of the narrator could do this, then it would be a perpetuation of the Franklinian self, since the particular circumstances in which self happened to have been "born and bred" were forms that self took on, but not self itself. The things left behind in the transition from Benjamin Franklin the man to Franklin the narrator were not necessary parts of the Franklinian self to begin with. The transition of the "unconcerned," fame-earning, consensus-inspiring self from its physical to its more durable textual body would not be a Matherian trauma: the self's emigration, like the jump of the spark between common matters or of the dollar between investments, would not alter it substantially, because, even while the physical body lived, self had been a disembodied capacity without permanent commitment. The major difference between this transition and others, such as that from moneymaker to electrician or politician, would be that it was the most ingenious of them all. The text would be the most efficacious vehicle for accomplishing the purpose which is self because it would have a theoretically limitless social, geographical, and temporal access to young Horatios.

It is impossible to say how much death was on Franklin's mind as he wrote the *Autobiography.* He was sixty-five when he began, and in reasonably good health. His wife died three years later. When he took it up again in Passy, his health was bad, and he was wondering whether he would survive a trip back to America. He did survive the trip, and Parts Three and Four were written in Philadelphia virtually until the day he died after profound suffering from stone and gout. Though we cannot know his thoughts, we can observe that he began to discuss death in his letters, and that his reports on the state of his health are sometimes accompanied by considerations of preservation. In a 1773 letter to Barbeu Dubourg, for example, Franklin expresses interest in Dubourg's speculation that those who appear to have been killed by lightning can sometimes be revived, and he offers other evidences of life in the apparently dead: "A toad buried in sand will live, it is said, till the sand becomes petrified; and then, being enclosed in the stone, it may still live for we know not how many ages." The secret of greater durability is a properly preserving medium or enclosure. Death comes when the nourishment needed for perspiration and exercise is not available; but when such bodily activity is minimized, life can be prolonged. Torpid animals, scaled animals, and plants buried in quicksilver can survive past their normal term. He recounts his own experience with three flies that were drowned in a bottle of Virginian wine that was opened in London; upon being taken out and set in the sun, two of the three flies got up, dried themselves off, and flew away. These speculations concerning greater durability bring Franklin to his own desire to see the future:

> I wish it were possible, from this instance, to invent a method of embalming drowned persons, in such a manner that they may be recalled to life at any period, however distant; for having a very ardent desire to see and observe the state of America a hundred years hence, I should prefer to any ordinary death, the being immersed in a cask of Medeira wine, with a few friends, till that time, to be then recalled to life by the solar warmth of my dear country! (*P*, 20:189–90, trans. *W*, VI:381-3)

But, failing such a means of complete preservation, Franklin had already begun to construct a medium for preserving self, the *Autobiography*, which would in some sense allow him to continue to supervise the progress of America.

The representation of the *Autobiography* as a device for securing immortality is clear in a letter Franklin wrote to George Whately in 1785. Franklin ponders the idea that the parsimonious forbearance from wasteful expenditures of self and money that he had maintained during his life might also enter into God's calculations:

> And when I observe that there is a great frugality as well as wisdom in his works, since he has been evidently sparing both of labors and materials, for the various inventions of propagation he has provided for the continual peopling his world with plants and animals, without being at the trouble of repeated new creations; and by the natural reduction of compound substances to their original elements, capable of being employed in new compositions, he has prevented the necessity of creating new matter; so that the earth, water, air and perhaps fire, which, being compounded from wood, do, when the wood is dissolved, return, and again become air, earth, fire and water; – I say that when I see nothing annihilated, and not even a drop of water wasted, I cannot suspect the annihilation of souls, or believe that he will suffer the daily waste of millions of minds made that now exist, and put himself to the continual trouble of making new ones. (*W*, X:174)

As specific commodities are reduced to their homogeneous substratum, money, which survives, and as the production of character reduces the whole complexity of consciousness to its homogeneous substratum, ingenuity, so death distills the essential element from its accidental particular form. Lucretius, and after him Whitman, doubted that the preservation of atoms could offer an easy consolation to consciousness: the undifferentiated state to which all things go seemed to them inimical to human integrity per se. In Franklin's speculations, however, there is no suggestion that the return of particular complex formations to their primary compositional elements is terrifying. Rather, Franklin considers such reduction with approval. As Marx said of Franklin's money theory, the conversion of particular things to the undifferentiated homogeneity of their universal element is taken for granted, that is, there is no violence of contradiction along the way. As an emergence of essential component elements from the accidental particular vessels in which they happen to have occurred, death might be an analogy to or even an extension of Franklin's lifelong project. As self emerges from the circumstances of humble origin, so death extracts self from body: God does not waste self by spending it once and for all, but instead invests it. So Franklin may proceed to speculate for Whately that the preservation of matter intimates a corresponding preservation of self. This argument suggests that the preserved self is no more essentially related to the particular man than are the original elements to the living compositions that are comprised of them.

But the next sentence of the letter suggests that Franklin is not willing to trust God's frugality completely but will instead do the preserving himself: "Thus finding myself to exist in the world, I believe I shall, in some shape or other, always exist; and, with all of the inconveniences human life is liable to, I shall not object to a new edition of mine; hoping, however, that the errata of the last may be corrected" (*W,* X:174). Whately had probably not read the manuscript of Part One, so he would not have recognized that the metaphors Franklin was using to describe God's preservation of character – second edition and corrected errata – had been used to describe his own preservation of character in the act of autobiographical writing (*A:*43). Franklin's first use of these metaphors seems to have been in the epitaph he wrote for himself in 1728:

> The Body of
> B. Franklin,
> Printer;
> Like the Cover of an old Book,
> Its contents torn out,
> And stript of its Lettering and Gilding,
> Lies here, Food for Worms,
> But the Work shall not be wholly lost:
> For it will, as he believ'd, appear once more
> In a new & more perfect Edition,
> Corrected and amended
> By the Author.
> He was born Jan. 6. 1706.
> Died   17   (*A:*44n.)

Franklin uses the metaphors of second editions and corrected errata, in other words, to describe both death's extraction of self from body and his own extraction of the blankness of character from the accidental, nondetermining circumstances of its origin. The epitaph, though explicitly anticipating Franklin's death, implicitly describes the process of divesting himself of particularity in which he was already engaged. Death and self-production are analogous and perhaps even allied, since both extricate an essential universal element from its vessel, which does not define what it carries. A book, after all, should not be judged by its cover.

Franklin did not invent the metaphor of the second edition. It appears, for example, in John Woodbridge's epitaph for John Cotton, quoted in the *Magnalia Christi Americana:* "O, what a monument of glorious worth, / When, in a new edition, he comes forth, / Without erratas, may we think he'll be / In *leaves* and *covers* of eternity!" (*MCA*, II:284). The Franklinian second edition, however, unlike the Matherian, is not an abrupt termination of self: rather, if God preserves self, or if the author preserves it in autobiographical writing, death is a refinement or perfection of the *I* that guided the life. The character lives on in the person of the emulating reader, and it gains a wider circulation than it otherwise would have. As Franklin wrote to Collinson, about electricity, "if they touch while Electrising, the Equality is never destroyed, the Fire only circulating."

B. Franklin, the walking man, falls out of circulation: "Franklin," the self-produced persona that continues to make itself, now lifted from proper to common noun, is freed to greater circulation. Franklin's *Autobiography* shows that, like his frugal god, Franklin has "inventions for propagation," for the preservation of self in the emulating acclaim of future generations. The analogy between death and self-production as it is implicitly developed in the epitaph and the letter to Whately suggests that the produced self has no more intrinsic a relation to the formations in which it involves itself than pure elements such as fire and water have to the bodies they enter: the distance between contemplating a living thing for its particularity and for the elements that compose it is equal to the distance between contemplating Franklin for his particular occupations and for his unconcerned self.

Like his money, therefore, Franklin does survive his death, if we distinguish between "Franklin" as a kind of abstract noun and as the material man that happened to carry it. Much of Franklin's money was left to his biological heirs, the group of legitimate, semilegitimate, and illegitimate products of his actual inseminations. But the will he wrote in 1788, while postponing work on the *Autobiography*, stipulated that a thousand pounds each were to go to Boston and to Philadelphia to care for Horatios attentive to his example. Portions of these sums were to be loaned to "such young married artificers, under the age of twenty-five years, as have served an apprenticeship in the said town, and faithfully fulfilled the duties required in their indentures, so as to obtain a good moral character from at least two respectable citizens who are willing to become their sureties." The money is to be loaned, that is, to young men who dupli-cate Franklin's example. The money, then, would find its way to those who, like Franklin, have demonstrated their ingenuity, avoided the prod-igality of rebelliousness and philandering, and earned the acclaim of prominent citizens, and it would aid them in continuing to do so. The recipients were to pay only 5 percent interest, and a tenth of the principal each year,

> which sums of principal and interest, so paid in, shall be again let out
> to fresh borrowers . . . And, as it is presumed that there will always be
> found in Boston virtuous and benevolent citizens, willing to bestow a
> part of their time in doing good to the rising generation, by superin-
> tending and managing this institution gratis, it is hoped that no part of
> the money will be at any time dead, or be diverted to other purposes,
> but be continually augmenting by the interest.

Disinterested Franklins who have achieved prominence will assist inge-nious Franklins who are rising: in this way. "Franklin," the abstract noun, will surpass the temporal limit of B. Franklin, and live by remaining in circulation, by permeating the future and consolidating it into a fraternal organization.

The money, too, will continue to grow, and here again the happy co-incidence of distinct interests comes into play. As the young men repay the principal and the modest interest, the sum grows alongside the sum total of young Franklins: "If this plan is executed, and succeeds as pro-jected without interruption for one hundred years, the sum will then be one hundred and thirty one thousand pounds." At this point, one hundred thousand was to be spent on public works and the rest offered to young tradesmen in the same way for another hundred years: "At the end of this second term, if no unfortunate accident has prevented the operation, the sum will be four millions and sixty-one thousand pounds to the dispo-sition of the inhabitants of the town of Boston [or Philadelphia] and three millions to the disposition of the government of the state, not presuming to carry my views further."[2] Van Doren notes that very few Americans had accumulated even one million pounds in this period, and Franklin probably died with no more than two hundred thousand; so the end product of Franklin's enraptured calculation of his money's future would have seemed a fair equivalent for the universal quantitative wealth that is

---

[2] Benjamin Franklin, *Autobiographical Writings,* ed. Carl Van Doren (New York: Viking Press, 1945), pp. 694–6.

the only complete satisfaction for pure investment. And, whereas most investors die or quit before reaching such a goal, "Franklin" grows alongside his money, in the swelling quantity of emulators in which his blank self is invested. Like "Whitman," the abstract cosmic principle that differs from W. Whitman, the man who took out the copyright, "Franklin" extends beyond the spatial and temporal limits of the lifespan and body of B. Franklin, permeating and enclosing the future, approaching absolute size. This codicil to the will reveals that for Franklin the exemplary self and money are analogous: their lives are not tied to the biological man in which they originate; they "live" insofar as they continue to circulate, that is, insofar as they do not settle permanently into any particular form. The death of one vessel, therefore, is no death at all, but a return of the universal substratum to its pure state in preparation for reinvestment; and both are aimed at a virtual quantitative infinity that is the only satisfactory destination for the blank, qualitative boundlessness that is the secret of their successes and their excellence.

The will is therefore another approach to exciting the sort of emulating fraternal-dynastic extension of the produced self that the *Autobiography* was written to provoke. At several points in the *Autobiography*, Franklin seems to have been interested in how one may live on after one's death. In one section, he refers to his unlikely admiration for the revivalist George Whitefield. The incongruity becomes clear once the reader realizes that Franklin's admiration derives less from Whitefield's fervent Protestant imagination than from the number and variety of people that his powerful voice can affect:

> He had a loud and clear Voice, and articulated his Words and Sentences so perfectly that he might be heard and understood at a great Distance, especially as his Auditories, however numerous, observ'd the most exact Silence. He preach'd one Evening from the top of the Court House Steps, which are in the Middle of Market Street, and on the West Side of Second Street which crosses it at right angles. Both Streets were fill'd with his Hearers to a considerable Distance. Being among the hindmost in Market Street, I had the Curiosity to learn how far he could be heard, by retiring backwards down the Street towards the River, and I found his Voice distinct till I came near Front-Street, when some Noise in that Street, obscur'd it. Imagining then a Semi-Circle, of which my Distance should be the Radius, and that it were fill'd with Auditors, to each of whom I allow'd two square feet, I computed that he might well be heard by more than Thirty-Thousand. (A:179)

With respect to the content of Whitefield's oration, Franklin might indeed be among the hindmost: however, even Franklin was so affected by an earlier Whitefield sermon that, though at first he planned to give nothing when the plate was passed, he eventually softened and decided to

give his coppers, then his silver dollars, finally weakening to the point
where his gold pistoles went in too. But in the episode quoted above,
Franklin's opinion of the content of Whitefield's sermon is waived in favor of appreciative quantitative calculation of the potential range of
Whitefield's voice.

But writing can reach even further than Whitefield's voice. In Whitefield's case, however, the advantage of greater reach is wasted, because
Whitefield loaded his writings with obstructive particular characteristics
that led some readers to object. He missed his chance by not purging
himself of the quirky singularity that slows the circulation of personal
capital:

> His Writing and Printing from Time to Time gave great Advantage to
> his Enemies. Unguarded Expressions and even Erroneous Opinions
> del[iver]ed in Preaching might have been afterwards explain'd, or qual-
> ify'd by supposing others that might have accompany'd them; or they
> might have been deni'd; but *litera scripta manet*. Critics attack'd his Writ-
> ings violently, and with so much Appearance of Reason as to diminish
> the Number of his Votaries, and prevent their Encrease. So that I am of
> Opinion, if he had never written anything he would have left behind
> him a much more numerous and important Sect. And his Reputation
> might in that case have been still growing, even after his Death; as there
> being nothing of his Writing on which to found a Censure; and give
> him a lower Character, his Proselites would be left at liberty to feign
> for him as great a Variety of Excellencies, as their enthusiastic Admi-
> ration might wish him to have possessed. (*A:*180)

In transferring the communication of self from voice to pen, Whitefield
loses what Franklin had most admired about his voice, its range. As Socrates argued in *Phaedrus,* writing extinguishes the vitality of voice by
reducing it to repetitive permanence, exiling the vitality of spontaneous
amendment, dialogue, revision, and retraction.

The permanence of writing appealed to Cotton Mather, since it reduced the possibility of monstrous linguistic vagary and promiscuity.
Franklin, too, was drawn to writing in preference to voice, but not to
avoid gross deformation. Rather, his preference was based on writing's
greater spatial and temporal range. No matter how many auditors, each
taking two square feet, a speaker can impress, the limitations of the body
ensure that voice would never circulate as widely as writing. Franklin's
critique of Whitefield's writing assumes that, when properly executed,
writing is the best tool for enhancing the number of votaries and for
promoting the growth of reputation. It is a more practical investment
than voice.

But Whitefield failed because he encumbered his writing with particular characteristics, giving himself a lower character and so diminishing

the reader's perception of the variety of his excellence. In Part Three, Franklin describes a meeting with Michael Wohlfahrt, one of the founders of the Dunkers. Franklin proposes that the Dunkers might refute some unfounded vituperations by publishing their Articles of Belief and the Rules of Their Discipline. But Wohlfahrt contends that such a move would commit them to a particular stance and so repel descendants who may have made further progress toward the truth (*A*:190–1). Though I imagine that Franklin had little sympathy for the specifics of Dunkerism, he clearly approves of the strategy of avoiding any statement of particular position or disposition that might reduce one's appeal to posterity. Particularity may be solved by not writing, as the Dunkers do not and as Whitefield should not have, but it might also be solved by writing an account of self that scrupulously avoids commitment to any particularity whatsoever and so remains proof against alienating *any* posterity.

Concerned with the opinion of the most abstract imaginable audience, the future, the narrator of the *Autobiography* is the maximal development of the unconcernedness Franklin practiced throughout his life. The remarks on Whitefield's writings and on the Dunkers thus seem transparent remarks on the nature of the memoirs that enclose them: *litera scripta manet,* a predicament if one commits particularities to writing, but an asset to ingenuity if the self put to writing observes the self-producing divestiture of particularity that had been Franklin's lifelong project. A self that, like money, signifies human nature refined from its particularities, is, therefore, the logical and appropriate content for written autobiography, as written autobiography is logically and appropriately such a self's best device. It is no coincidence, therefore, that the paragraph following the one describing Whitefield's failure to augment his character in his writings should concern the growth of Franklin's business and conclude by quoting the advice to a young tradesman he had written forty-three years earlier: "I experienc'd the Truth of the Observation, that *after getting the first hundred Pound, it is more easy to get the second:* Money itself being of a prolific Nature" (*A*:180–1).

The "Nature" or life of self and money lies in their free circulation, though in some ways this definition of life turns out to be opposite to the common one: on the one hand, there is the living man terminated by his own death; on the other, there is the self that, like the crown, dies or is murdered if it allows itself to be essentially identified with any particular formation. If, while he lived, Franklin had settled for the particular life his father and brother had tried to press on him or allowed himself to lapse into the obstructive particularity that disqualified Ralph, Collins, Keimer, Loudon, or Whitefield, he would have murdered his boundless ingenuity. Extracting himself from that, writing, and dying, he emerges most entirely from the existential limitation of the circumstances in which

he was born and bred into the free, entirely negational life of a full
boundlessness aimed at a quantitative infinity. The gravestone, the will,
the *Autobiography*: these all mark the passage of a universal, abstract, and
elemental social gist out of its confinement. With his money, Franklin
survives prolifically because, like his money and unlike Whitefield, he
has produced himself by expurgating the particularity that can kill – that
is, that can restrain free circulation. His death, therefore, is not the "fatal
reverse" mentioned on the third page of the *Autobiography*. Instead, it is
a conducing means to greater success.

The *Autobiography* can immortalize Franklin, however, only if it successfully earns the acclaim of readers. In his *Dissertation on Liberty and
Necessity, Pleasure and Pain,* the young Franklin had argued that the avoidance of pain was the prime human motive. The rhetoric of the *Autobiography*, as in so much of Franklin's writings, observes that maxim by a
close portrayal of the particular life as a kind of pain of which the reader
may not yet be aware, and by representing virtuous discipline as a relief,
as freedom from that pain. Of the two sorts of death, the first, the murder of the self's potential by restraining desires, affections, and interests,
must seem profoundly uncomfortable, so that the second, the extinction
of such noncalculation, can seem to be a kind of freedom – even though
it is based on rigid and unyielding self-surveillance and self-control.

The pain Franklin considers in the *Autobiography* is, however, more
abstract than the types of pain, such as hunger, that he discusses in the
Dissertation on Liberty and Necessity, Pleasure and Pain. It is shame, the
moment of chagrin when one becomes aware of having been unaware of
oneself. When it is gripped and manipulated by pure affection, the Franklinian self is a shilling murdered, withdrawn from circulation. It is so
intensely absorbed in its fascination that it forgets appraisal. Hedonism,
Franklin contends in *The Way to Wealth*, is a species of slavery, because
self is completely dominated by the avarice of consumption. And such
wanting ends in debt, Franklin claims, because indifference to the proper
expense of self is accompanied by indifference to the proper expense of
one's money. If we object that there are modes of feeling that can be
balanced against calculating appraisal that are not necessarily the ruin of
self and savings account, we will begin to appreciate Franklin's hidden
but strong sense of the extreme danger posed by enjoyment, a circum-
spection as powerful in its way as Mather's fear of the monstrous. To be
caught in the gaze of the other at such a moment of pure wanting, as
Franklin illustrated in "The Whistle," is to discover shame, to know oneself as a Collins or a Ralph who is less than whole, as one who has
incarcerated himself in a single aspect of a blighted or forgotten potentiality. The solution is Franklinian discipline, which anticipates the gaze
by making sure that all personal impulses are scrutinized and evaluated

in advance, and thus forestalls shame; to be observed in the act of wanting – for example, in seeking public office, or in pursuing private ends – is to be known, and shamed. The primitive matrix of self-discipline is a strong consciousness of the shamefulness of consciousness caught by wanting or needing – of that moment when one is so coerced by want that the lack of reason is abundantly clear to any observer. The more powerful the apprehension of being fixated, the more resolute, meticulous, and lifelong discipline will be – the more committed to demonstrating a free and unconcerned versatility that is never murdered in the chaos of the allure of the moment at hand.

But even if the discipline does succeed, one still encounters those who will impute particular motives to him, or refuse to respect his unconcernedness. At such moments, when the disciplined self is refused the recognition it deserves, as in the climactic encounters with his brother James, with Keimer, or with Collins, Franklin's equanimity gives way to anger, a more forcible (if less subtle) assertion of the resplendence of the self's discipline, and of its innocence of anything that might be called shameful. Such anger was barely concealed, or even came to the fore, at several points in Franklin's political career, when proper acknowledgment was withheld, and when he was accused of a mode of political self-service he would have found shameful, had it been true.

The sorest test of Franklin's discipline was probably his ordeal in the Cockpit at the hands of Alexander Wedderburn. Accused of having improperly made public certain letters exchanged by Thomas Hutchinson and Andrew Oliver, that requested or predicted "an abridgement of what are called English liberties," Franklin was summoned to appear before his Majesty's Privy Council for Plantation Affairs in the Cockpit in 1774 and roundly abused by Wedderburn, the solicitor general.

In the crowded room, he was very much in the public eye, accused of the particular desire of pursuing his own ends and of violating confidences. Franklin may have been painfully exercised by this, but he remained silent, playing Bartleby, his refusal to respond indicating his reluctance to emerge into argument. His nonresponse to those vituperations is a classic moment in his lifelong personal strategy. The worsening situation of English-colonial relations had exacerbated the division of opinion to the point where even Franklin's healing and unifying subtlety had become ineffective – to the point where he who had worked hardest for reconciliation was accused of division. In his account of the interrogation, he accentuates Wedderburn's irrational excesses:

> The solicitor-general then went into what he called a history of the province for the last ten years, and bestowed plenty of abuse upon it, mingled with encomium on the governors: But the favorite part of his discourse was levelled at your agent, who stood there the butt of his

invective and ribaldry for nearly an hour, not a single lord adverting to
the impropriety and indecency of treating a public messenger in so ig-
nominious a manner, who was present only as the person delivering
your petition, with the consideration of which no part of *his* conduct
had any concern . . . This part of the speech was thought so good, that
they have since printed it in order to defame me every where, and particularly to destroy my reputation on your side of the water, but the
grosser parts of the abuse are omitted, appearing, I suppose in their
own eyes, too foul to be seen on paper; so that the speech, compared
to what it was, is now perfectly decent. (*P,* 21:92–93)

This ordeal is as close to crucifixion as Franklin came: particular motives
are imputed to him, he seems to stand revealed in the public eye, his
reputation is damaged. His strategy is twofold: he emphasizes the degeneration of Wedderburn's rhetoric, a progression into unreason that highlights by contrast his own equanimity; and, even in this letter to Thomas
Cushing, he attempts to disavow particular sentiment by emphasizing
that this abuse of Franklin followed abuse of the colonies, that as agent
he was actually receiving an anger directed at those he represented rather
than at himself. And, he claims, he is angry only as a representative, not
as a single person:

It may be supposed that I am very angry on this occasion, and therefore
I did purpose to add no reflections of mine on the treatment the assembly and their agent have received, lest they should be thought the
effects of resentment and a desire of exasperating. But indeed what I
feel on my own account is half lost in what I feel for the publick. (*P,*
21:93)

Franklin pursues his way judiciously in this letter: Wedderburn's fractiousness is emphasized in order to show Franklin's calmness; Franklin
denies having done anything to attract this ire, even if it is unreasonable,
by suggesting it is really directed at the colonies; and he denies anger
except insofar as it is anger on the part of those he represents. The strategic reticence he maintained in the Cockpit, in other words, is also at
work in the composition of this letter.

But, unlike the letter, the session in the Cockpit was a Hobson's Choice
between arguing – and the concomitant commitment to a position – and
allowing his blankness to become conspicuous in the form of silence. He
chose the latter as the lesser evil, and the produced blank self was put on
display. The more severe danger, Franklin perceives, would lie in replying, which would lower him into the circulation of abuse and expose
him and his personal feelings, no matter that they might be just. So he
replies by not replying, by preserving unconcernedness, thereby hoping
to highlight not only the injustices in Wedderburn's accusation but also
the frenetic particularity of Wedderburn's descent into fury: "Splashes of

Dirt thrown upon my Character, I suffered while fresh to remain: I did not chuse to spread by endeavouring to remove them, but rely'd on the vulgar Adage *that they would all rub off when they were dry*" (*P*, 21:415–16). To reply, even to vindicate himself, is unacceptable, because it would expose particular motive – self-righteousness or susceptibility to insult – and therefore spread rather than cleaning the spot. The spot, therefore, is not primarily the individual kind of particularity imputed to him, but particularity *as such*.

Rather than defending himself, he will wait for public opinion to reach a correct perception with time. Wedderburn's unreason – like Milton's Satan's moral ugliness – will become obvious, and, by contrast, acclaim for Franklin's resolute reasonable blankness will swell. Having established himself as a "mere pipe" through which moves his constituents' will, Franklin is delighted to see that they respond appropriately (Franklin is referred to as "he" in this quotation though the editors of the *Papers* believe him to be the author):

> Being, however, satisfied within, the Doctor stood the Abuse extremely well, and felt the Advantage of a good Conscience, which wonderfully supports a Man on such Occasions, beyond what could be imagined without Trial; and he has the Satisfaction to find, that he has lost no Friends by this Attempt to disgrace him; his house has ever since been filled with Visitants, who come purposely to show their Regard for him, and express their Indignation at the unworthy Treatment he received. Some, who could not come, have written him Letters to the same Purpose. (*P*, 21:114)

Franklin's stalwart cultivation of an absence of discernible motive has paid off with the dividend of acclaim, once more represented as a quantity – a full house, and letters too.

Franklin's encounter with Wedderburn was not the first occasion on which his reserve was tested by political division, and he had not always maintained it with such rigor. When Franklin first entered Pennsylvania politics, as William Hanna argues, he attempted to exploit the neutrality and general congeniality that had served him so well in business and that he had commemorated in his approval of electricity. At first, he was successful, managing to appeal to both the proprietors and the Assembly, a difficult task because there was little agreement between them. If anything, he leaned toward the proprietors, and his appointment as Pennsylvania's postmaster was probably a token of this. Unfortunately, the proprietors soon expected him to signify his gratitude by coming out as one of their spokesmen. He responded to this pressure to ally himself with special interest by attaching himself to the Assembly's cause. By so doing, he did attach himself to a special interest, since the Assembly was by no means a representative body: the important point, however, is not

that he was affiliated with the Assembly, but that he was affiliated with
them because he was intensely and perhaps even excessively repelled by
the proprietor's demand that he declare himself their man. The intrinsic
merit of the Assembly's cause seems to have been less important than his
repudiation of the proprietors.[3]

During the 1750s, Franklin discovered that in periods of aggravated
political division ingenious appeals to the rational common interest of
the whole were futile. The situation compelled him to choose a side, and
he took the side opposite those who seemed to have forced him to the
decision. As a result of his decision, his reputation suffered. Proprietorial
remarks about him became and remained vituperative. As late as 1769,
Governor Penn refused membership in the American Philosophical Society because, as he declared, "I shall never be a patron of a Society that
has for its President such a ———— as Franklin."[4] While Franklin was in
England representing the Assembly's interests in the 1750s, Lord Loudon, formerly a Franklin partisan, revealed that Franklin "was not to be
trusted, was overly ambitious, and was known to have been drunk on
the crossing to England," the same crossing that had been delayed by
Loudon and the poor packing of the cargo. On the other side, Franklin's
remarks about the proprietors were uncharacteristically strident: he even
called Penn a "low jockey," though he later regretted the candor. Clearly,
Franklin departed from the equanimity he contends in the *Autobiography*
had guided him throughout his life (as he did not in the later episode
with Wedderburn), and his partisanship damaged his reputation for years
to follow.[5]

But this candor is not just a wandering from the path of blank neutrality. Rather, it is a token of the severe irritation Franklin could feel
when political division impeded a clear response to neutral ingenuity, an
irritation similar to his reaction to the obstinate drunken Collins. It is
also evidence of the unwavering disciplined rigidity that underlies his
humor and his equanimity. Until his break from the proprietors, he had
maintained his neutrality, "bestow(ing) his interests and friendships equally
among the competing factions with no apparent regard for the irrecon-
cilable differences that embittered not only politics but personal relation-
ships." To those embroiled in these divisions, "Franklin's behavior seemed
inscrutable, vacillating, and suggestive of some hidden, possibly sinister
motives." Only with the proprietorial demand for allegiance did Franklin

[3] William S. Hanna, *Benjamin Franklin and Pennsylvania Politics* (Stanford, Calif.:
Stanford University Press, 1964), pp. 54–149.
[4] Quoted in Carl and Jessica Bridenbaugh, *Rebels and Gentlemen: Philadelphia in
the Age of Franklin* (New York: Oxford University Press, 1962), p. 339.
[5] Hanna, *Benjamin Franklin and Pennsylvania Politics*, pp. 123, 127.

depart from noncommitment, and if his behavior after that point shows that he was "obsessed with a hatred for Penn that was far greater than the Assembly's grievances warranted," this intense feeling may be seen as a strong or even vengeful strike against a world that had rejected blank ingenuity rather than as a sudden libertarian decision in favor of the Assembly's cause.[6]

Even in the most vituperative remarks made about Franklin during this period, there is a kind of ineptness. Some, like Loudon's remark about his drinking, seem slanderous, improbable, or irrelevant. In other cases, as Hanna suggests, there is a wild speculativeness that reveals real puzzlement over "the nature of his ambition."[7] Though Franklin was during this period of his political life clearly committed to a special interest with an offense-giving ardor, he seems still to have remained essentially blank. This resolve was maintained in Paris during the Revolution, where, even in the midst of profound political division, John Adams observed that "he loves his ease, hates to offend, and seldom gives an opinion until obliged to do it . . . Although he has as determined a soul as any man, yet it is his constant policy never to say yes or no decidedly but when he cannot avoid it."[8] Though he felt that imputations of particular motive were an offensive and unjust response to his public work, Franklin rarely gave in to anger, and he did not reconsider his project of becoming an apprehensibly embodied human universality: to rub the spot is to spread it; better to let it wear off in time, as posterity discovers his true character, with the aid of the *Autobiography*.

But Franklin must accompany his revelation that particularity is a kind of sore pain with a corresponding demonstration that detachment from it is not. In the 1756 letter that Aldridge contends anticipates Otto's account of Franklin's last words, Franklin tells Miss E. Hubbard that mortal bodies must be laid aside "when the soul is to enter real life." Embodiment is thus an "embryo state": "A man is not completely born until he be dead." As long as the body is a commodious vehicle, the soul may occupy it, but when it becomes an "incumbrance" rather than an aid, the soul moves on: "Death is that way." But death can be anticipated, and practiced, during life:

> We ourselves, in some cases, prudently choose a partial death. A mangled limb, which cannot be restored, we willingly cut off. He who plucks out a tooth, parts with it freely, since the pain goes with it; and he, who quits the whole body, parts at once with all pains and possibil-

[6] Ibid., pp. 81, 131.   [7] Ibid., p. 115.
[8] John Adams, quoted in Carl Van Doren, *Benjamin Franklin* (New York: Viking Press, 1938), p. 600.

ities of pains and diseases which it was liable to, or capable or making him suffer. (*P,* 6:406–7)

Embodiment is thus an economy: the soul stays with a leg, a tooth, a body as long as each of these is an aid; but when they become an encumbrance, they must be discarded, like Collins, or a bad investment.

Amputation, therefore, is pedagogical: it teaches the soul that it is distinct from the particular form in which it is instanced, though the soul may have been confused enough to think that its body was an intrinsic participant in its rich complexity. The heart of Franklin's rhetoric here is his choice of kinds of death and amputation in which the body has become a source of pain and with respect to which, consequently, dissociation can be represented as no more than relief from pain: the soul is happy to get rid of those parts. Though Franklin's aim in this letter is to console, his thesis is only a variation on his usual representation of the desirability of detached calculation, which relies on a silencing of affection for what is given up as a bad investment. In the *Autobiography,* when Franklin chronicles the *petits morts* of the desires, interests, and attractions that would have interfered with his design, he quiets them, reducing them to obstinate irritations that do not enter or essentially affect the narrating voice. Though they may have impinged on the young Franklin's design, or even competed with it, they turn out not to have dislodged or transformed the design, and by the time of the narration they are unvoiced and submissive: the narrator speaks for them, as their adequate representative. There is no murmur of protest, as there is throughout Mather's writing, and so the reader will conclude that clarity, humor, and even-temperedness can be got for a bargain.

This silencing is most clearly outlined in the Project of Arriving at Moral Perfection. Progressing from Part One to Part Two, Franklin no longer relies on the negative examples of other lives, but instead discusses himself and his inner life. This discussion may, at first, seem to gratify our sense that, having shown what he is not, the time has come to show what he is. However, a revelation does not occur. Interior tempters such as sloth and venery replace exterior tempters such as Collins and Ralph, but the method is otherwise the same. As Franklin's various bosses and companions were reduced to grotesques so that the positions they represented would not be taken seriously, so sloth, venery, and the others are represented as nonrational drives accidentally inhabiting Franklin but not participating in the selfhood that designs the life and narrates the *Autobiography.* They enter the prose as defining contrasts to self, but they do not affect it. The prose remains serene and aloof: as La Rochefoucauld remarked of Franklin, "he speaks of himself as if he were speaking of another," though I would change this comment to, he speaks of the drives that oppose the aims of self as if they were not a part of him. They are exiled from the speaking voice of resolve. Like Mather, Franklin severs the part of his consciousness that fits the sense of ought and then denies the rest the power of legitimate self-representation. For Mather, however, the "rest" that did not converge with ought insisted on speaking, and insinuated itself into his discourse in a way that was alluring and repellent. For Franklin, however, the self *is* "ought," rather than the un-cooperative remainder, and that remainder is the self's mildly vexing but mute companion: it remains silent, to be spoken about, calculated and charted, and to illustrate the self's excellence by contrast.

In Part Two Franklin's exposition of self continues to be based on descriptions of what he stops himself from becoming. One leaves a house, to recall the epigraph to this chapter, because to remain threatens rather than because of what lies outside. By the time he wrote Part Two, he had found it expeditious to substitute the more traditional opposition between virtue and vice for the freethinking opposition between pleasure and pain, but this substitution of terms does not alter his assertion that the positive term – pleasure, virtue, or freedom – is to be apprehended as the absence of the negative term – pain, vice, or slavery. The negative term is a judgment passed on the particularizing impulses of consciousness by the monetary self that, by so judging them, expresses its transcendence of their neighborhood: the blankness of the ego, detached from the particularizing impulses of the rest of the whole consciousness, can treat them as an otherness, label them as pain, vice, or slavery, and clearly calculate the threat they pose to the achievement of its project – the earning of infinite emulative acclaim. Consequently the positive term – pleasure, virtue, or freedom – must be an avoidance of one of the negative terms and must have no definition of its own, since to be susceptible to definition is to have apprehensible particularity; this is also why the particularizing impulses that the calculating self collects under the negative judgment remain useful to it – they provide a defining contrast in lieu of the impossible direct definition. The impulses collected under the label pain or vice or slavery are not intrinsically, innately, or morally offensive in their nature: they are offensive in their power to restrain the free self and to contaminate the disembodied calculation it enjoys when it expresses its difference from them by passing judgment on them.

In the same period, Jonathan Edwards was writing his *Nature of True Virtue,* an eloquent tract which defines virtue as a selfless and passional "benevolence toward being." Because Edwards's virtue has an emotive certainty and positivity that breathe throughout his writings, he does not require the constant citation of vice to focus or sharpen by negation the reader's sense of virtue. In fact, vice is rarely mentioned, and the reader must conclude that for Edwards as for Augustine vice has no positivity – it is merely the awfulness of absent virtue. Franklin's virtue, however, resists positivity, since to identify the self with any particularity, even with Edwards's beatitude, would specify and therefore constrain it. Consequently, the Project of Arriving at Moral Perfection has two outstanding attributes: first, it presents virtue by evoking images of self-expenditures to be avoided; and, second, it demonstrates the result of such avoidance in its calculating ability to silence the supplications of the excluded parts of the whole consciousness by reducing them to so many check marks on a graph that records their diminishing numerical occurrence. The graph, in other words, not only records the success, but also demonstrates it: the vice whose diminishment it records is called a vice because of its power to obstruct the disembodied clarity that records.

A quick survey of Franklin's virtues:

> Eat not to Dulness, Drink not to Elevation. Speak not but what may benefit others or yourself. Avoid trifling Conversation. Make no expence but to do good to others or yourself: i.e. Waste nothing. Lose no time. Be always employ'd in something useful. Cut off all unncecessary Actions. Use no harmful Deceit. Think innocently and justly; and, if you speak, speak accordingly. Wrong none, by doing Injuries or omitting the Benefits that are your Duty. Avoid Extreams. Forbear resenting Injuries so much as you think they deserve. Tolerate no Incleanness in Body, Cloaths or Habitation. Be not disturbed at Trifles, or at Accidents common or unavoidable. Rarely use Venery but for health or Offspring; Never to Dulness, Weakness, or the Injury of your own or another's Peace or Reputation. (A:149–50)

Individually, most of these recommendations are sound and capable of improving the quality of life. Collectively, however, they are more than a miscellany of useful habits. First, the positive terms – "benefit," "useful," "innocently," "justly," "peace" – are so vaguely abstract as to lack true appeal, and so must be viewed as perfunctory inclusions, whereas the cautions *against* uncleanness, venery, and so on are specific enough to provide the true motivating force. The positive terms, in other words, do not attract by themselves, but only acquire force when converted to proscriptions. And second, the proscribed vices share a common characteristic – they represent an immersion in a present pleasure or interest that would damage the self's power to calculate the effect of such an immersion on its life-project. Virtue, in other words, is the avoidance of vividly presented involvements or interests that would compromise the clearheadedness that calculates whether any given expense of time is a wise investment. The list of proscriptions delineates the liability not of sin but of personal commitments that would reveal some particularity –

intoxication, exuberant loquaciousness, eagerness, involvement, desire, lassitude and reverie, resentment and anger, comfort, intensity, and passion.

There are three positive prescriptions in the list of thirteen: "Let all things have their Places. Let each Part of your Business have its Time. Resolve to perform what you ought. Perform without fail what you resolve. Imitate Jesus and Socrates" (A:149–50). But this positivity is tepid and deceiving. The insistence on order pays no heed to what the business to be done is, and the insistence on resolution does not disturb the purely formal "ought." Jesus and Socrates are to be imitated not for their attention to virtue, but for their humility, a preliminary to vision rather than vision itself. In fact, Franklin's humility has no more to do with Christian humility than his purity has to do with Christian purity, and it has no more to do with Socratic humility than his abstention from positive assertion has to do with Socratic irony. In the letter Franklin wrote to Samuel Mather in 1784, he remembers that Cotton Mather advised him on humility. As Franklin is shown out of the house, Mather, who is walking behind him, tells him to stoop. Not comprehending, Franklin bangs his head on a low beam. Mather, who "never missed any occasion of giving instruction," improves the episode: "*You are young, and have the world before you; STOOP as you go through it, and you will miss many hard thumps.*" Franklin tells Samuel Mather that this advice, "thus beat in my head," proved very useful: "I often think of it, when I see pride mortified, and misfortunes brought upon people by carrying their heads too high" (W, X:83–4). Franklin's remark, alluding to mortification and providential affliction, suggests the Puritan requirement that self be submitted to higher will. As such, it conceals the true Franklinian gloss on Mather's advice: an assertive bearing that calls attention to oneself and one's wishes will attract the suspicion, envy, and resentment of his fellow citizens. Franklin's brand of humility emerges not from the content of this letter, but from his willingness to assume a persona that Samuel Mather will not find in the least repellent.

When Franklin humbly concedes the insignificance of one of his occupations, he is distancing himself as narrating consciousness from one of the ways he invested that consciousness. When we join the narrator in laughing at the Franklin who circuitously reasoned his way out of vegetarianism – fish are eaten by fish that will be eaten by fish so why shouldn't these be eaten by Franklin? – we are not laughing at the narrator so much as congratulating him on his freedom from the sort of intense resolution and the tortuous justifying logic that would render him particular. The fact that laughter is directed at the young Ben in such episodes rather than at Keimer or Collins does not override the common purpose – to demonstrate the superior purity of the narrating consciousness freed from any dense individuality that might smear its blankness. If "vanity" is for Franklin a useful habit of thinking that self is not tied to any set of circumstances, then "humility" – the purposive satirization of earlier protocommitments that were intentionally discarded – is its tool and companion. Vanity asserts the self's blankness, humility expels interests before they escalate into defining particularities. The force in the three positive prescriptions, in other words, is still proscriptive: do not let things get out of their places because you are immersed in the matter at hand; do not lose sight of your larger plan in the pursuit of present temptations; do not give into visible pride, because it will commit you to particularity in the eyes of others and perhaps even in your own.

The virtues may be digested into three related statements: never succumb to a complete immersion in immediate present circumstances – do not waste words, time, sperm, or any other resource; never lose sight of the importance of any moment's expenditure of self in the development of a larger plan – invest; avoid waste, calculate investment, and you will acquire a cool head. As Weber contended, the clarity of the balance-book is facilitated by its transcendence of the use-values that it surveys and renders commensurable. So for Franklin the graph of days and mistakes which reduces the opponent parts of the self to dots on the grid demonstrates the virtue that enables disembodied clarity.

Franklin's virtues are strongly reminiscent of Puritan ethics stripped of theology. The Puritan, in the world but not of it, his entire selfhood sacrificed to the evergreen truths it might otherwise obscure, is God's investment of grace in the mundane sphere, the commitment of a seed of regeneration to the soil of the mundane precarious media in which it may grow or be lost in deformation. Immediate involvement, or love of the creature, is to be subordinated to the maintained wish to make contributions to the glory of the Creator as he is perceived in the persons of the dynastic predecessors. Never "of" the world, the Puritan is to avoid becoming completely and snugly ensconced, to retain that germ of remove which is his fidelity to larger concerns. Franklin revises this. Full immediate involvement is sacrificed to the self's plan for itself, rather than to the dynastic god's plan for it, so that its maintenance of investments is an attention to the continuity of the self. And the end has become the legitimating assent of popular acclaim rather than the approval of a jealous god. Temptations are to be avoided because they would dull the man's blank luster, rendering him specific and visible, lowering his efficacy as a specie, rather than because they would turn his attention away from divine patterns.

Having overcome temptations, Franklin attains to the habit of avoidance and then to clearheaded appraising. In the encounters with Collins and Ralph, this clearheadedness took the form of the ability to calculate expenditure against return and to judge the wisdom of continuing the friendship. He is appraising, in other words, his own receptiveness to the shamelessly noncalculating monitions of affection, and demonstrating the abstraction that is required in order to see what one puts into a friendship as qualitatively identical with what one receives from it and to be able, consequently, to measure the two sums against one another and to complete the equation. One is abstracted from friendship, aloof from the rich qualitative diversity of give and take that is friendship's virtue. As Theodor Adorno puts it: "The practical orders of life, while purporting to benefit man, serve in a profit economy to stunt human qualities, and the further they spread, the more they sever everything tender, for tenderness between people is nothing other than the awareness of the possibility of relations without purpose."[9] Franklin's virtue avoids all personal territories where quantitative calculation does not apply.

Contemplating Franklin's comments on the perfectability of the self through the Project of Arriving at Moral Perfection, D. H. Lawrence responded: "The soul of man is a dark forest. The Hercynian Wood that scared the Romans so, and out of which came the white-skinned hordes of the next civilization . . . The *wholeness* of a man is his soul. Not merely that nice comfortable bit which Benjamin marks out."[10] Lawrence is still the best reader of the *Autobiography*, though his mantic tone may disguise the acuity of his observations. The abrupt dismissals of Lawrence's critique which abound in the work of Franklin's apologists generally write it off as a kind of crude and cranky primitivism that grows from a resentment of the clarity and equanimity of Franklin's thought. However, the gist of Lawrence's critique is not that Franklin attains to clarity – the "nice comfortable bit" – but that Franklin's clarity disavows any essential relation with the dense complexity of the person in which it originates by making that complexity into the object of its calculations. Franklin's clarity is "comfortable" because it never admits the tension of contradiction between itself and the remainder of the whole. Lawrence's argument with Franklin is not over the issue of self-overcoming per se, but over Franklin's representation of self-overcoming as an available, facile, and remunerative personal option that presents no substantial threat to the intensity of particular affection – and so renders both transcendence and affection bland. As such, Lawrence's critique of Franklin is an attempt to reveal the suppression at the heart of Franklin's clarity. For Lawrence, the transition from the personal particular to the superpersonal universal cannot be taken for granted: the sense of contradiction between the two must be

---

[9] Theodor Adorno, *Minima Moralia: Reflections from Damaged Life* (London: New Left Books, 1974), pp. 40–1.

[10] D. H. Lawrence, *Studies in Classic American Literature* (New York: Viking Press, 1961), p. 10.

kept alive so that the human may be perceived as a mobile vitality between the two poles.

Franklin does not deny the existence of a "private Franklin," but he
excludes it from self, the speaking I; it does not enter either the resolve
or the timbre of the narrative voice in order to alter, qualify, complicate,
deepen, or question it. Intrusions of the other man are errata, mere mistakes, the clumsy slips of a compositor that need only be identified to be
corrected, rather than signs of a suppressed secrecy that would blight the
mono-tonous equanimity of the text. As Poor Richard was the reductive
compendium of the world's wisdom, supremely indifferent to the complex thought and feeling excluded from his balanced, self-sustaining periods; as the Catholic woman was her frugality; so Franklin the algebraist
of desire has reduced his own plurality to a number of variables in an
equation and identified self with he who calculates the equation, without
expression of regret, sacrifice, or protest from the represented party.

Franklin mentions four errata that he committed during the "dangerous time of Youth." He broke from his brother too willfully. He broke
into the money entrusted to him for Samuel Vernon in order to help
Collins afford his drinking and gambling. He expressed freethinking
opinions about religion. And he dallied with low women instead of actively pursuing marriage with his homely Penelope, Deborah Read.
When his brother's abuses have proved too taxing, he leaves:

> It was not fair in me to take this Advantage, and this I therefore reckon
> one of the first Errata of my Life: But the Unfairness of it weigh'd little
> with me, when under the Impressions of Resentment, for the Blows
> his Passion too often urg'd him to bestow upon me. Tho' he was not
> an ill-natur'd Man: Perhaps I was too saucy and provoking. (A:0)

He confesses resentment and first connects the label of "erratum" with a
moment when circumstances provoked him to a visibly particular reaction: and it is unclear whether it is a mistake because of the dubious
morality of his departure or because he was unconsidering enough to
show a particular and therefore potentially objectionable face, first by
being provoking and then by being resentful. Since he proceeds to defend
his flight to Philadelphia, the latter interpretation is more likely: his manner made him offensive in his brother's eye, and the manner of his departure might make him offensive in the eyes of others. The mistake seems
to lie in the too conspicuous manner of conducting himself, not in the
break itself, which is vindicated by the footnote on resistance to arbitrary
power. In his pride he did not calculate the effect on his brother and in
his resentment he did not calculate the effect on his reputation. The first
erratum sets the tone for those that follow: the flaw lies in the manner of
execution rather than in the deep desire it reveals, so it is truly an erratum, a relatively nonsignifying slip of the hand that is easily remedied.

Unlike the Freudian slip or Mather's stammer, the Franklinian erratum does not signify an obstinate counter-reason that might interfere in the self's design. The errata are mistakes.

The second erratum occurs when his gentler brother John entrusts him with thirty-five pounds owed to Samuel Vernon. The sum is not immediately called for, Collins learns of its existence and persuades Franklin to lend it to him so that he may drink and game: "The Breaking into this Money of Vernon's was one of the first great Errata of my Life" (A:86). After the affair in the rowboat, Collins predictably absconds: "He left me then, promising to remit me the first Money he should receive in order to discharge the Debt. But I never heard of him after" (A:86). Franklin's error is secondhand: Collins wants the money for pleasure, but Franklin allows friendship to overtake calculation. His abuse is less heinous than Collins's, but it is still a breach of calculation that threatens to brand him. Nonetheless, the abuse is expiated, and Franklin emerges unmarked:

> Mr. Vernon about this time put me in mind of the Debt I ow'd him: but did not press me. I wrote him an ingenuous Letter of Acknowledgements, crav'd his Forbearance a little longer which he allow'd me, and as soon as I was able I paid the Principal with interest and many Thanks. So that *Erratum* was in some degree corrected. (A:121–2)

Ingenuousness (or ingeniousness?), thanks, and interest on the principal: these extras repay Franklin's ethical debt, his misuse of funds, and demonstrate that there is economy even in ethics.

The introduction of economy into ethics also plays a role in the account of the third erratum, the writing and printing of his *Dissertation on Liberty and Necessity,* a controversial because freethinking pamphlet: "It occasion'd my being more seriously consider'd by Mr. Palmer, as a young man of some Ingenuity, tho' he seriously expostulated with me upon the Principles of my Pamphlet which to him appear'd abominable. My printing this Pamphlet was another Erratum" (A:96). The mistake is not the freethinking, but letting it be known, which irritates Palmer's piety and so obstructs his admiration for Franklin's ingenuity. Later remarks suggest that the error was not so much in the particular opinions as it was in his unashamed publication of them, an admission that should make his readers suspicious of all of his later pieties, including the letters to Samuel Mather and the Puritan posturing of the first pages of Part One:

> In short I soon became a thorough Deist. My Arguments perverted some others, particularly Collins and Ralph: but each of them having afterwards wrong'd me greatly without the least Compunction and recollecting Keith's Conduct towards me, (who was another Freethinker) and my own towards Vernon and Miss Read which at Times gave me great Trouble, I began to suspect that this Doctrine tho' it might be true, was not very useful. (A:114)

The absolutes of earlier religion, though they acknowledge the authority of a heteronomous power, have the advantage of universality – they demand a consistent application in all circumstances. Freethinking, however, inspires pliable rules, and thus fails to combat vehemently the particular impulses of the immediate moment. The kind of vigilant abstention from particular impulse that is the end of Franklin's "virtue," therefore, may be impeded by a lackadaisical deism that does not strongly challenge the impulses that originate in the hedonistic parts of consciousness. So he discards his *talk* of deism – but not his belief in its truth – in favor of the more rigorous mandates of a revealed morality: he does this because revealed morality is *ingenious* – though philosophically false, perhaps absurd, it does possess the rhetorical force to challenge the impulses of the moment. So it is useful, but useful for maintaining the universality of self, not the universality of piety.

As in the episodes of his departure from his brother and his breaking into Vernon's money, therefore, the erratum of printing the pamphlet has more to do with an injudicious and insufficiently calculating manner of self-presentation than it does with that self-presentation itself. In each case, the erratum is deplored less for its gist, its dense moral core, than for its shortsighted frustration of the cause it was supposed to advance. In each case, Franklin expends without consideration of return. These are examples of waste, not sin. The compositor's hand slips because he has glanced up from the job to eye some attraction passing the window, and the text is marred by an erratum, which can nonetheless be corrected completely because it has no secret substrate, no positive content. Remorse is irrelevant in such a situation, though a reflective, pragmatic, preventative appraisal would be useful: in each case, the task is to do what can be done to recoup the loss, and then to move on to new business which will render the waste negligible. The distance between what would have been the contemporary emotions – defiance, thrill, excitement, egoism, shame, remorse – and the narrator's treatment of them – sums, expenditures, repayments, requital, reinvestment – goes unmediated.

This detachment is most apparent in Franklin's candid treatment of his own lust. Biographers will argue over actual successful seductions, but it is clear that Franklin remained at least verbally bawdy into his seventies, an exuberance about which he complained in his letter to Whately. In the *Autobiography*, however, the candid treatment of philandering admits only that it went on until Franklin married, at which point desire came to be considered a precious resource to be invested wisely: "Rarely use Venery but for Health or Offspring" (*A*:150). Franklin here takes the economic model of desire that guided Mather's thought, but the failure to observe economy in sex is a mistake rather than a sin, an example of waste rather than of the exotic aberrations Mather envisioned, because there is no emotive involvement of self in the uncalculating desire and so no intense mixture of fascination and repulsion. For Mather, self was all of the immanent personal impulses, and the *I* was deeply implicated in the whole consciousness, to its chagrin; but for Franklin, self is a resolution detached from the whole consciousness, so, though the *I* may be pestered by the other impulses, it is not implicated or essentially affected. Consequently, whereas Mather recoiled from the prospect of his son's bastard with horror, Franklin acknowledged his bastard son and raised him, perhaps because not to do so would be to waste an asset.

Franklin's libidinal economy, therefore, represents the modernization of the calculation that Weber contends was implicit in Calvinism:

> The sexual asceticism of Puritanism differs only in degree, not in fundamental principle, from that of monasticism; and on account of the Puritan conception of marriage, its practical influence is more far-reaching than that of the latter. For sexual intercourse is permitted, even within marriage, only as the means willed by God for the increase of His glory according to the commandment "Be fruitful and multiply."[11]

Weber correctly identifies calculation as a central concern in Puritan sexual dogma. But such calculation is a heteronomous law superior to the Puritan self, which has an independent affective vitality. The purity of unclouded investment is an ideal but finally unreachable end. By secularizing the mandate, by appropriating it as the calculating self, and by silencing dissonance, Franklin becomes the calculation that was only an impossible end for Mather.

With these revisions, Puritan libidinal economy becomes the command to use venery as Franklin develops it in his only half-humorous *Advice to a Young Man on the Choice of a Mistress,* in the speech of Polly Baker, and in his meditations on the future population of America. Eros is at worst an erratum that does not cut deeply into the purity of self, and at best it is an exploitable resource. Poor Richard says that "A Ship Under Sail and a big-bellied Woman are the handsomest things that can be seen common," an enthusiastic anticipation of invested capital returning to port that echoes Titania in *A Midsummer Night's Dream:*

> His mother was a vot'ress of my order:
> And, in the spiced Indian air, by night,
> Full often hath she gossip'd by my side,
> And sat with me on Neptune's yellow sands,
> Marking the embark'd traders on the flood,
> When we have laugh'd to see the sails conceive
> And grow big-bellied with the wanton wind;

[11] Max Weber, *The Protestant Ethic and the Spirit of Capitalism* (New York: Scribner, 1958), p. 158.

Which she, with pretty and swimming gait
Following, – her womb then rich with my young squire, –
Would imitate, and sail upon the land,
To fetch me trifles, and return again,
As from a voyage, rich with merchandise. (II.i:123–34)

The similarity of the figures does not belie the difference of tone: Titania's memory of delicious abundance and the rich figuration it provokes is different in kind from Poor Richard's assimilation of pregnancy to the category of prudent investment. Poor Richard's remark recalls Franklin's wish, expressed in *The Nature and Necessity of a Paper Currency*, that Americans would be bold enough to "venture their Money at Sea." Having overcome uncalculating eros, he comes to see sperm as funds to be invested. As he called money prolific in the remark on the breeding-sow in the "Advice to a Young Tradesman," so he treats pregnancy as the burgeoning of biological capital.

With this libidinal economism in mind Franklin presents Deborah Read as an intrinsic part of his plan from the first, though this foresight seems unlikely. Describing his first entrance into Philadelphia, he writes: "Thus I went up Market Street as far as Fourth Street, passing by the door of Mr. Read, my future Wife's Father, when she standing at the Door saw me, and thought I made as I certainly did a most awkward ridiculous Appearance" (*A:76*). In this initial brief presentation of his wife (who, like his mother, never plays an extended part in the account of his life), Franklin comments not on her exceptionality but rather on her membership in the class of established citizens who will someday discard their judgment of Franklin based on the accident of his appearance in favor of acclaim for his independent character. In this reminiscence – a legend of greatness in embryo that ranks with Weems's account of Washington and the cherry tree – Franklin adumbrates a feeling of plan or destiny meant to suggest that the germ of marital economism was in him from the first; the effect is to reduce the subsequent philanderings to relative insignificance, to errata that do not express anything essential about him.

Franklin's path to Ithaca, though, will not be direct; unlike Winthrop, Jr., he will not resist the local vices that infect most "Young Gentlemen *Travellers.*" In England, for example, Franklin begins to sample the pleasures of the place:

> I was pretty diligent; but spent with Ralph a good deal of my earnings in going to Plays and other Places of Amusement. We had together consum'd all my Pistoles, and now just rubb'd on from hand to mouth. He seem'd quite to forget his Wife and Child, and I by degrees my Engagement with Miss Read, to whom I never wrote more than one Letter, and that was to let her know I was not likely soon to return. This was another of the great Errata of my Life, which I should wish to correct if I were to live it over again. (*A:96*)

It is of course difficult to discern the kind and extent of Franklin's affection. However, in the passage quoted above, there seems to be little sense of guilt or remorse over his having neglected her. Rather, the failure to write to her, together with Ralph's forgetting of his family, is classed with the wasted pistoles. In both cases, there is a forgettable failure to calculate the proper allocation of an asset – sperm or money. His neglect of his future wife is an erratum, a mistake without substantial emotional significance, like the printing of the deist pamphlet that is regretted in the next paragraph.

Ralph takes a mistress, then leaves for the country to earn money. Franklin is instructed to look after her, an instruction he observes over-zealously: "I grew fond of her Company, and being at this time under no Religious Restraints, and presuming on my Importance to her, I attempted Familiarities, (another Erratum) which she repuls'd with a proper Resentment, and acquainted him with my Behaviour" (A:99). There is no embarrassment here: again, Franklin is speaking of himself as he would speak of another, because the failure is a failure of calculation; he assumed that since she made herself available to Ralph she was generally available to any who expended time on her, and this presumption rendered him particular in Ralph's eyes.

Ralph then breaks from Franklin, rather than the other way, as in the episode with Collins. But Franklin's philandering does not stop here. Recounting his decision to avoid the kind of freethinking he voiced in the deist pamphlet, he writes:

> And this Persuasion, with the kind hand of Providence, or some guardian Angel, or accidental favourable Circumstances and Situations, or all together, preserved me (thro' this dangerous Time of Youth and the hazardous Situations I was sometimes in among Strangers, remote from the Eye and Advice of my Father) without any *wilful* gross Immorality or Injustice that might have been expected from my want of Religion. (A:115)

The posturing references to providence and paternity, so attentive to the *topoi* employed in Winthrop, Sr.'s letter to his son, should not obscure the two major assertions: Franklin's philanderings were not willful, that is, they were mere errata without significant personal significance; and the remarkable thing is not that they occurred, but that they occurred so *seldom*, and so serve to contrast him with the greater prodigality of others in the same situation. The editors note an expunged clause that followed this gesture at sanctimony: ". . . some foolish Intrigues with low Women excepted, which from the Expence were rather more prejudicial to me than to them" (A:115n). The expunged clause, apparently, posed too great a threat to the pretense of piety in the sentence to which it was once joined. However, its central assertion, that the intrigues were characterized by the foolishness of failing to heed expense, fits perfectly with the earlier assertions that the mistakes were not willful and that they were most remarkable for their infrequency. Franklin's eros is conceded but stripped of powerful content, of its voice or power to represent itself as a participant in self. Failing to calculate the expenditure of money, failing to calculate the expenditure of words in deistic argument (something he is careful not to do in the passage above), and failing to calculate the effect of scattered seed are closely bound in Franklin's thought, in which a pure and perfect economism never butts against any eloquent opponent.

Eventually, he returns to his Deborah Read: "she prov'd a good and faithful Helpmate, assisted me much by attending the Shop, we throve together, and have ever endeavour'd to make each other happy. Thus I corrected that great Erratum as well as I could" (A:129). Was the erratum the abuse of her affection, or the failure to calculate the proper investment of his time and seed? The remarks on the shop and on her being a helpmate imply the latter, a suspicion seconded by the fact that when Franklin wrote this he was again in England and again failing to write to her – perhaps saving the time available for writing for the composition of a wiser investment, the *Autobiography*, which would contribute to the shaping of many sons. Once Franklin has claimed to have overcome uncalculating libido, and once he has recounted the various fiscal and legal negotiations that culminated in an efficient marriage, he drops Deborah Read from the narrative, with one brief reappearance:

> But mark how Luxury will enter Families, and make a Progress in spite of Principle. Being call'd one Morning to Breakfast, I found it in a China Bowl with a Spoon of Silver. They had been bought for me without my Knowledge by my Wife, and had cost her the enormous Sum of three and twenty Shillings, for which she had no other Excuse or Apology to make, but that she thought *her* Husband deserv'd a Silver Spoon and China bowl as well as any of his Neighbours. This was the first Appearance of Plate and China in our House, which afterwards in a Course of Years as our Wealth encreas'd augmented gradually to several Hundred Pounds in Value. (A:145)

As with Mather, the feminine is present to Franklin as an infection of the house's discipline: unlike Mather, he reacts with bemused resignation rather than horror; this is waste, not monstrosity, and the wife's complaint lacks even a deformed vitality. Discipline has no profound opponents.

The errata described in Part One thus prepare for the wholly negational virtues outlined in Part Two because they present Franklin subjecting himself to scrutiny in the same manner in which he scrutinizes Collins or Ralph. The recollection of the errata sets out the two key characteristics of how the self is to relate to the rest of consciousness –

avoidance, and the calculation that culminates in the charts that record his increasingly infrequent slips. The greatest fear of such a self is the captivity of particularity, the blight of being definable or specific: "In the mean time, that hard-to-be-govern'd Passion of Youth, had hurried me frequently into Intrigues with low Women that fell in my Way, which were attended with some Expence and Great Inconvenience, besides a continual Risque to my Health by a Distemper which of all Things I dreaded, tho' by my great good Luck I escaped it" (*A:*128). Though expense and inconvenience are to be regretted, the thought of the distemper calls forth a confession of strong emotion – dread – because the unremovable darkness of the distemper alive and at play within him would streak and mar the purity of his innocence. Franklin is innocent, not because he has not encountered depravity but because he maintains a purity that denies the power and coherence of anything that would seriously challenge his self-preservation. This innocence treats all symptoms of a consciousness or society more diverse than its plan will admit as corrigible mistakes without substantial critical content, an innocence that meets the world and still maintains itself by a constant reductive exercise of will against the threat of qualitative plurality. To such innocence, the particularity of life can appear only as blight or incarceration. Air that is enclosed in a circumscribed space nourishes infection and engenders unpleasant dreams (*W,* II:171–6). The windows must remain open – as they were in a room in an inn that Franklin shared with John Adams, though Adams objected – so that the air may remain mobile. Character, too, fouls or fails if it settles, a shilling or a pistole murdered. "Guests and fish smell after three days." Better to get out of a falling house altogether.

10

A PRIVATE FRANKLIN

No science has yet explored the inferno in which were forged the de
formations that later emerge as cheerfulness, openness, sociability, successful adaptation to the inevitable, [and] an equable, practical frame of
mind.

Theodore Adorno, Minima Moralia

These final and most sublime incarnations of the father cannot be overcome "symbolically," by emancipation: there is no freedom from administration and its laws because they appear as the ultimate guarantors
of liberty. The revolt against them would be the supreme crime again –
this time not against the despot-animal who forbids gratification but
against the wise order which secures the goods and services for the
progressive satisfaction of human needs. Rebellion now appears as the
crime against the whole of human society and therefore as beyond reward and beyond redemption.

Herbert Marcuse, Eros and Civilization

In texts such as the biographies of Winthrop, Jr., and Phips, or *The Christian Philosopher*, Mather's self finds its voice, obliquely and provisionally,
but detectably. As a result, we hear the din of contest, though the pro-
tagonist in this contest is always decided in advance. In Franklin's texts,
however, there is only the single and sane voice. With, perhaps, one exception.

In 1726 Franklin leaves England, shedding the *erratic* man who broke
into Vernon's money, printed the freethinking pamphlet, and pushed
himself on Ralph's mistress. The various low intrigues are behind him,
and his practical Penelope and his Ithaca are ahead. He has found a reputable patron, Thomas Denham, who has acknowledged Franklin's ingenuity and promised to set Franklin up in business upon return. Franklin seems to have been quite conscious of the significance of this voyage
even at the time, because he diverts himself on board ship by writing the

Plan for a Life, an adequate rough draft to which he adheres in the first edition – the life as it will be lived – and which he completes in the second edition – the *Autobiography*. He has escaped from dependence on arbitrary power and he has overcome the temptations of noncalculation. He is made.

But there is a "fatal reverse," an undeserved affliction issuing from an inscrutable source that, unlike Denham, seems not to smile on the new-made Franklin. After a short time in business together, during which Denham "consell'd me as a Father, having a sincere Regard for me," the patron falls sick and dies after a long illness, and Franklin contracts a pleurisy which is nearly fatal: "I suffered a good deal, gave up the Point in my own mind, and was rather disappointed when I found my Self recovering; regretting in some degree that I must now some time or other have all that disagreable Work to do over again" (*A:*107). The first half of this sentence, to the left of the semicolon, is a startling remark. He seems disappointed at the recovery of "my Self," the blank, calculating entity he has just invented in the Plan for a Life. Behind this disappointment, there may be weariness, or even dread, because he has been returned to the beginning when just in sight of the end, as in certain dreams: Denham left him only a small legacy and so his death "left me once more to the wide World" (*A:*107), rather than sheltered in a benign father's esteem for his ingenuity; he has to return to Keimer's shop. But this remark is quickly dispersed on the right of the semicolon, where that recovering Self, which is the fledgling voice of the *Autobiography*, takes over again, enlisting humor to divert the reader from the astonishing outcropping of another voice, the one that lies to the left of the semicolon: this second voice dissolves the astonishment by announcing that he was disappointed to recover only because he would have to suffer the approach to death again. Even this phrase is surprisingly confessional – retaining some of the weariness and dread of the first half of the sentence. Franklin calls dying a "disagreable Work," an irksome expense of otherwise productive time that should have to be undergone only once. But the choice of the word *work* is incongruous: if work is the expenditure of energy and will in converting less to more order, then it would be more appropriate to call recovery work. But Franklin calls *dying* work, a deliberate, intentional struggle against a "disagreable" and obstinate inertia – "my Self" and its dogged tendency to recover. Although it is only an ephemeron, the word *work* preserves the disappointment at recovery from the left side of the semicolon, and disturbs the economically minded humor that asserts that all that is regretted here is having to die again. This sentence shows a rare carelessness on Franklin's part, a carelessness that lets two voices speak. The first voice, the muffled objection to self, survives the humor, and contorts it, thus living past the second voice's attempt to stifle it. The joke does not dissipate its predecessor: it falls flat,

and is too obvious in its intent. The semicolon, attempting to homoge-
nize the two voices, prevaricates: the surpassed man speaks from his depth,
willing to perish if both go together, thus briefly refusing the discipline
that has just been designed while at sea and that returns to its ascendancy
immediately afterward. This first voice may belong to an injured homeostasis deeper than self, one that regards self as injury or pain, rather than
as relief from injury and pain. A homeostasis anticipated, perhaps, in the
elemental aversion to disturbance that Franklin called the sole motive of
life in his *Dissertation on Liberty and Necessity, Pleasure and Pain:* "Now
during the Course of Life we are ourselves continually removing successive Uneasinesses as they arise, and the *last* we suffer is remov'd by the
sweet Sleep of Death" (*P,* 1:65). Death repairs in a single stroke:

> But suppose we pass the greatest part of Life in Pain and Sorrow, sup-
> pose we die by Torments and *think no more* . . . the *Pain,* tho' exquisite,
> is not so to the *last* Moments of Life, the Senses are soon benumm'd,
> and render'd incapable of transmitting it so sharply to the Soul as at
> first; She perceives it cannot hold long, and 'tis an *exquisite Pleasure* to
> behold the immediate Approaches of Rest. This makes an Equivalent
> tho' Annihilation should follow: For the Quantity of *Pleasure* and *Pain*
> is not to be measur'd by its Duration, any more than the Quantity of
> Matter by its Extension; and as one cubic Inch may be made to contain,
> by Condensation, as much Matter as would fill ten thousand cubic Feet,
> being more expanded, so one single moment of *Pleasure* may outweigh
> and compensate an Age of *Pain.* (*P,* 1:68)

The hypothetical private Franklin speaks once and is silent: the death
wish is an *aporia* or gap in the otherwise prevailing unity of narrative
voice, and so it is a sort of gravestone for another self, one that might
prefer intense erratic involvement oblivious to the bleak reason that incessantly subjects all involvements to the calculation of investment and
likely return. This other self might allow itself pleasure in music, "ele-
gantly redundant sound that is unaccountable as part of the working day,"
or in poetry, which Kenneth Burke describes as "the sheer exercise of
'symbolicity' (or 'symbolic action') for its own sake, purely for the love
of the art."[1] Lewis Thomas and Burke are heirs to Kant's contention in
Critique of Judgment that art is "purposiveness without purpose," an exercise of capacity that takes its character as celebration and astonishment
from the fact that it is not in conspicuous service to a practical end. Though,
as Frank Lentricchia has demonstrated, this definition of art is susceptible
to trivializing misconstructions,[2] it nevertheless is one of the possible
challenges to Franklinian calculation.

[1] Kenneth Burke, *Language as Symbolic Action* (Berkeley: University of California Press, 1966), p. 29.
[2] Frank Lentricchia, *After the New Criticism* (Chicago: University of Chicago
Press, 1980), pp. 39–40.

In a bagatelle written for Madame de Brillon in 1779, Franklin remembers having murdered some small change on just such an obstinate eudaemonism:

> When I was a child of seven years old, my friends, on a holiday, filled my pockets with coppers. I went directly to a shop where they sold toys for children; and, being charmed with the sound of a *whistle,* that I met by the way in the hands of another boy, I voluntarily offered and gave all my money for one. I then came home, and went whistling all over the house, much pleased with my whistle, but disturbing all the family. My brothers, and sisters, and cousins, understanding the bargain I had made, told me that I had given four times as much as it was worth; put me in mind what good things I might have bought with the rest of the money; and laughed at me so much for my folly, that I cried with vexation; and the reflection gave me more chagrin than the *whistle* gave me pleasure. (*W,* II:181)

As always, Franklin is being charming and politely ironic with Madame de Brillon. But this observance of their common métier should not dispel the seriousness of this memory snatched from beneath sixty-six years. The failures of calculation are several: not only does he fail to consider frugality when he heads directly for the shop, he never gets to the shop because he is lured by a temptation on the way; and this failure to contemplate the wisest use of the money is as usual paralleled by a failure to contemplate the wisest presentation of character, since his performances disturb the family, subject him to ridicule, and provoke shame. He has spent self as well as money, rather than investing them.

He learns his lesson, and this is the significance of the anecdote. In the *Autobiography,* Franklin's first memory is of his eighth year when he was "put to Grammar School" and showed readiness in learning to read. The story of the whistle, therefore, is the earliest recorded moment of Franklin's life, and it is more revealing than the story of his success in grammar school: the mentioning of his readiness in learning to read is intended to show that his ingenuity was already in place at the age of eight, but the story of the whistle dramatizes the origin or first foundation of ingenuity, its triumphant secession from uncalculating involvement. Franklin responds to the chastising voice of calculation by making it his own, incorporating it so completely that the chastised voice is silenced: "This however was afterwards of use to me, the impression continuing on my mind; so that often, when I was tempted to buy some unnecessary thing, I said to myself, *Don't give too much for the whistle;* and I saved my money" (*W,* II:181). The imposition of calculation onto enjoyment in the episode of the whistle makes it *the first moment of the self,* and, as in Cotton Mather's diary account of the stutter, the self is shown to begin in an imposition of law onto consciousness, in the emergence of a determined and unmodulating voice that surveys, regulates, and attempts to silence the rest of the consciousness in which it originates. In Mather's case, the authority of the imposed law is quite clearly associated with the super-personal prestige of the dynasty as it was incarnated in the will of his father, and the imposed law was consequently opposed to the whole of consciousness, including sexual desire, the desire for independent crea-tivity, and the desire for personal boundlessness, all of which were classed together as the self's proclivity to innovative aberration. In Franklin's case, on the other hand, the law is learned from brothers, sisters, and cousins, but not imposed by them. Franklin's father plays no part in the memory, a conspicuous absence that underscores the true tenor of the anecdote: though he learns from others, the act of imposing law on con-sciousness is internal to self and not an obedient or filiopious acquies-cence. In Mather's account of the stutter, the father is the arbiter of rec-titude and the whole of consciousness is disciplined; in Franklin's account of the whistle, the detached calculating self is the newborn arbiter of rectitude, and the rest of consciousness is disciplined.

Franklin did not rid his life of music. There would be no need to do so once the impulse to the sort of immersion revealed in the episode of the whistle was curbed and directed. So long as calculation was not aban-doned, music could remain among the self's extrinsic, nondefining in-terests. He objected to poetry's complex sound, for example, only when it was carried to the impractical extreme to which Ralph took it. In a letter written to his brother Peter sometime before 1765, Franklin praises some ballads that his brother had written. He laments the modern way of singing, which counts inarticulation a virtue, in which the listener "will not understand three words in ten" (P, 11:541): "The fine singer in the present mode, stifles all the hard consonants, and polishes away all the rougher parts of words that serve to distinguish them one from an-other" (P, 11:542). Peter's ballads do not succumb to this:

> You, in the spirit of some ancient legislators, would influence the man-ners of your country by the united powers of poetry and music. By what I can learn of their songs, the music was simple, conformed itself to the usual pronunciation of words, as to measure, cadence or empha-sis, &c. never disguised or confounded the language by making a long syllable short or a short one long when sung; their singing was only a more pleasing, because a melodious manner of speaking; it was capable of all the graces of prose oratory, while it added the pleasures of har-mony. (P. 11:539–40)

Consequently, Peter's ballads are "well adapted for your purpose of dis-countenancing expensive foppery, and encouraging industry and frugal-ity" (P, 11:539). As Mather had required that the figural elements of the sermon be dominated and directed by the argument – sauce, rather than food – Franklin finds music tolerable once the pure noncalculation of joy in making sound has been subdued to the requirements of correct pronunciation and bourgeois edification. If the joy of patterned voice, in other words, can be demonstrated to be a good investment of self, it is to be valued. Rather than purging himself of the interest in music he describes in the account of the whistle, he economizes it, marshals it, treats it as an investment of self that does not express or define self in the eyes of others.

The best emblem of the economization of music is his armonica (see figure). Many musicians had experimented with the music that might be made by ringing glasses filled with measured amounts of water or blown to precisely different sizes. Franklin saw no need to alter or develop the quality of the music so produced, but he saw that its production might be streamlined to minimize labor and accident. He surmised that the glasses might be "disposed in a more convenient form, and brought together in a narrower compass, so as to admit of a greater number of tones, and all within reach of hand to a person sitting before the instrument" (P, 10:127). More product, less labor: this is the guiding thought behind the development of the armonica, which would make the activity of playing it a sounder investment, particularly, perhaps, if it were played in accompaniment to edifying ballads such as his brother's. Different-sized glasses were lined up with a rotating axle that ran through what would have been their stems. This line of glasses would be put in a box and attached, as in a sewing machine, to a pedal that would rotate the axle. Pedaling with his foot, the musician would make the glasses ring by touching them. The amount of time and energy spent moving from glass to glass was thereby reduced, the number of possible notes was expanded, more than one glass could be rung at a time, and the notes rung on any one glass would be more homogeneous.

The invention of the armonica exhibits the self that triumphed over the enjoyment of the whistle rather than the consciousness that enjoyed the whistle: Franklin made the glasses and their music feasible by dedicating his ingenious frugality to the streamlining of an activity that does not in itself define, express or constrain that free ingenuity. After the invention of the armonica, the new music became feasible enough to attract real interest from, among others, Mesmer, Mozart, and Marie Antoinette, and Franklin's reputation was consequently enhanced. The child's opposition between music and parsimonious calculation is overcome in the act of inventing the armonica. Unfortunately, the armonica later fell from favor. It was rumored that the constant contact of the pads of the fingers with the vibrating glasses jarred the nerves and eventually aggravated a kind of musicians' insanity – patiently eliciting, perhaps, a part of the self that is entirely alien to rational economy, a kind of mental distemper that would brand the armonica-player with his occupation,

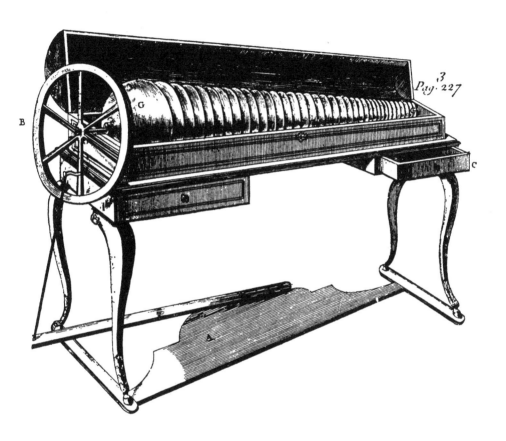

Franklin's glass armonica. Illustration from Jacques Barbeu Dubourg, *Oeuvres de M. Franklin, Docteur ès Loix* (Paris, 1773), II, facing p. 185; reproduced in Leonard W. Labaree, ed., *The Papers of Benjamin Franklin*, (New Haven, Conn.: Yale University Press, 1966), vol. 10, p. 121. Reproduced here by permission of Yale University Press and Yale University Library.

constraining his boundless selfhood. This effect would not happen with the old way of ringing glasses lined up on a table.

In Franklin's lifetime, however, there were no such rumors about the armonica, and it must have seemed, with its superb economization of musical production, to be a marvelously ingenious proof of the compatibility between a calculating, reasonable ingenuity and an interest that did not succeed in defining and therefore overwhelming ingenuity. A victory, perhaps, over the boy Ben's vexation with his brothers' and sisters' and cousins' ridicule. That part of Franklin "charmed with the sound of the *whistle*" has been subdued and rationalized, its cooperation with the prevailing self *taken for granted;* perhaps, however, it expresses itself once more when, emerging from the pleurisy in 1726, it *confesses* to having been "disappointed when I found my Self recovering."

That year, which was the last full year of Cotton Mather's life, represents a crucial juncture in Franklin's life because it contained his exit from England and errata, his return to Deborah Read and the economy of desire, the composition of the Plan for a Life, and the pleurisy. As Dr. P.-J. Cabanis, a member of Madame Helvétius's circle, contends:

> No period in his life is more decisive for the happiness of the rest. One cannot dwell too much on the dangers which encompass him, even in a generally prudent and reasonable system of conduct; and nothing is more instructive than that which shows clearly the road to follow in order not to go astray . . . He was conscious of his errors and resolved to make amends for them. Therefore, he leaves London and returns to Philadelphia. From this moment one can date the philosophy of life from which he never afterwards departed; from this moment he stops groping like a young man. He sees clearly the purpose and the way and never turns aside from it for a single moment.[3]

At the commencement of the antihedonistic rationalism of the self is the episode of the whistle; at the commencement of that self's concrete life-plan is the pleurisy and the remark on recovery.

In the *Autobiography,* Franklin remarks that the Plan for a Life was "Perhaps the most important Part" of the journal he kept during that voyage back with Denham. The equivocal "perhaps" is noteworthy, since the "Journal of a Voyage" is the most intriguing and mysterious of Franklin's writings. The Plan itself no longer exists, but the topic of rational discipline comes up in the sixth entry. Touring the fort at Gosport, Franklin is told "strange stories of the severity of one Gibson, who was governor of this place in the Queen's time, to his soldiers." There is a "miserable dungeon by the town gate, which they call *Johnny Gibson's Hole,* where for trifling misdemeanors he used to confine his soldiers till they were almost starved to death." Franklin concedes that such harsh authority is needed when the soldiers are incorrigibly unruly:

> 'Tis a common maxim, that without severe discipline it is impossible to govern the licentious rabble of soldiery. I own indeed that if a commander finds he has not those qualities in him that will make him beloved by his people, he ought by all means to make use of such methods as will make them fear him, since one or the other (or both) is abso-

[3] Quoted in Bruce Ingham Granger, *Benjamin Franklin: An American Man of Letters* (Norman: University of Oklahoma Press, 1975), p. 224.

lutely necessary; but Alexander and Caesar, those renowned generals, received more faithful service, and performed greater actions by means of the love their soldiers bore them, than they could possibly have done, if instead of being beloved and respected they had been hated and feared by those they despised. (*P*, 1:74)

Good government is a pure expression of the nature of its subjects, who love it; it need not constrain or confine a rebellious opponent.

But the world that Franklin observes in the "Journal of a Voyage" does not conform perfectly to his intelligence in the manner in which Alexander's and Caesar's soldiers conform to their generals' wills. Franklin's discoveries of the rational natures of things are relatively few, and he is often mystified, perplexed, or balked by a strange world that withholds itself. After touring Freshwater Church, Franklin and his companions decide to return to Yarmouth, but the boy who works the ferry refuses to get out of bed. They spot a boat, and Franklin goes to get it:

> I stripped all to my shirt to get the boat, it being fastened to a stake, but missing the causeway, which was under water, I got up to my middle in mud. At last I came to the stake; but, to my great disappointment, found she was locked and chained. I endeavored to draw the staple with one of the tholepins, but in vain; I tried to pull up the stake, but to no purpose; so that, after an hour's fatigue and trouble in the wet and mud, I was forced to return without the boat.

When the expenditure of energy is not yielding the return, the problem is perhaps that industry is not being aided by ingenuity. One of the company recalls having a horseshoe in his pocket, and Franklin uses it to pull out the staple:

> Now we rejoiced and all got in, and, when I had dressed myself, we put off. But the worst of all our troubles was to come yet; for, it being high water and the tide all over the banks, though it was moonlight we could not discern the channel of the creek; but, rowing heedlessly straight forward, when we were got about halfway over, we found ourselves aground on a mud bank; and, striving to row her off by putting our oars in the mud, we broke one and there stuck fast, not having four inches water. We were now in the utmost perplexity, not knowing what in the world to do; we could not tell whether the tide was rising or falling; but at length we plainly perceived it was ebb, and we could feel no deeper water within the reach of our oar.

The expense of energy and ingenuity together does not avail on this mud plain, and Franklin contemplates the likely result: "It was hard to lie in an open boat all night exposed to the wind and weather; but it was worse to think how foolish we should look in the morning, when the owner of the boat should catch us in that condition, where we must be exposed to the view of all the town" (*P*, 1:80). Rather than face that, two of the company jump out, thus lightening the boat, and, on their knees, drag it through the mud to deeper water.

On board ship during the ocean crossing, Franklin comments in the abstract that man is by his nature a sociable being, but his experience teaches the contrary. The passengers grow cross:

> I rise in the morning and read for an hour or two, perhaps, and then reading grows tiresome. Want of exercise occasions want of appetite, so that eating and drinking afford but little pleasure. I tire myself with playing at draughts, then I go to cards; nay, there is no play so trifling or childish, but we fly to it for entertainment. A contrary wind, I know not how, puts us all out of good humor; we grow sullen, silent, and reserved, and fret at each other upon every little occasion. (*P*, 1:86)

This ferocity is repeated outside the ship: "This afternoon we took four large dolphins, three with a hook and line, and the fourth we struck with a fizgig. The bait was a candle with two feathers stuck in it, one on each side, in imitation of a flying fish, which are the common prey of the dolphins." But this ingenious device is less significant than the dolphins' uncommon prey: "They appeared extremely eager and hungry, and snapped up the hook as soon as ever it touched the water. When we came to open them we found in the belly of one a small dolphin, half-digested. Certainly they were half famished, or naturally very savage, to devour those of their own species" (*P*, 1:88). As the voyage progresses, Franklin observes birds, crabs, weeds, and other phenomena, but his experiments yield few concrete results, and rational apprehension is infrequent. The self is mired or lost in this world, which is self-concealing, holding its secret away from the mind, presenting only confusion and consternation:

> The water, which we thought was changed, is now as blue as the sky; so that, unless at that time we were running over some unknown shoal, our eyes strangely deceived us. All our reckonings have been out these several days; though the captain says it is his opinion we are yet a hundred leagues from land; for my part I know not what to think of it; we have run all this day at a great rate, and now night is come on we have no soundings. Sure the American continent is not all sunk under water since we left it. (*P*, 1:97)

On the Isle of Wight, two days after the visit to Johnny Gibson's Hole, the day after getting stuck in the mud, the company visits Carisbrooke Castle where, as Franklin notes, Charles I sought refuge (and was subsequently incarcerated) during the interlude between his defeat at Naseby and his execution. Charles, maladept at conciliation and sacrifice to a new regimentation of the world, is mentioned only briefly, so that Franklin can move to a physical description of the castle. According to Franklin, it is in fact two castles rather than one:

It is divided into the lower and upper castle, the lower enclosing the upper which is of a round form, and stands upon a promontory to which you must ascend by near a hundred steps; this upper castle was designed for a retreat in case the lower castle should be won, and is the least ruinous of any part except the stairs before mentioned, which are so broken and decayed that I was almost afraid to come down again when I was up, they being but narrow and no rails to hold by. (*P*, 1:77)

Like the erratic self that is on the verge of being given up, the lower castle may be more easily won by marauding forces, more easily breached. The upper castle, the "coop," is safer, and, once up, one is reluctant to go down again. Its other advantage is that it permits a large survey, as does money, of the immense subordinate surrounding diversity: "From the battlements of this upper castle (which they call the coop) you have a fine prospect of the greatest part of the island [the Isle of Wight], of the sea on one side, of Cowes road at a distance, and of Newport as it were just below you" (*P*, 1:77).

The sight of Newport recalls the fact that for Franklin the sense of elevation requires a constant negating contrast with an accompanying sense of depth, of the road not taken, as in the *Dissertation on Liberty and Necessity* written some months earlier: "The *highest Pleasure* is only Consciousness of Freedom from the *deepest Pain*" (*P*, 1:66). "*Freedom from Uneasiness* is the End of all our Actions." (*P*, 1:65). So the description of the coop's prominence is immediately supplemented by a longer account of the castle's wells:

There is a well in the middle of the coop, which they called the bottom-less well, because of its great depth; but it is now half filled up with stones and rubbish, and is covered with two or three loose planks; yet a stone, as we tried, is near a quarter of a minute in falling before you hear it strike. But the well that supplies the inhabitants at present with water is in the lower castle, and is thirty fathoms deep. They draw their water with a great wheel, and with a bucket that holds near a barrel. It makes a great sound if you speak in it, and echoed the flute we played over it very sweetly. (*P*, 1:77–8)

These wells are not actually bottomless, but practically so, filled with useless litter in the case of the coop's well, and with needed water in the other. They are *aporiae* or deeps in the lighted world: they are voiceless, but part of Franklin's voice or music returns in echo, that part made mysterious by what remains below.

INDEX

Mather's and Franklin's opinions and theories concerning individual topics are listed under the topics, rather than under their names.

For EU product safety concerns, contact us at Calle de José Abascal, 56–1°,
28003 Madrid, Spain or eugpsr@cambridge.org.

www.ingramcontent.com/pod-product-compliance
Ingram Content Group UK Ltd.
Pitfield, Milton Keynes, MK11 3LW, UK
UKHW042151130625
459647UK00011B/1283